CHARLES RENNIE MACKINTOSH

Charles Rennie Mackintosh

EDITED BY WENDY KAPLAN

GLASGOW MUSEUMS

ABBEVILLE PRESS   PUBLISHERS
New York   London   Paris

Front cover: *Order-Desk Chair*, 1904. See plate 168.
Back cover: *A House for an Art Lover Competition Entry: Perspective of the
Reception and Music Room*, 1901. See plate 162.
Spine: *Clock*, 1917. See plate 248.
Endpapers (hardcover only): *Design for Stencilled Mural Decoration for
the Lounge Hall* (detail), 1916. See plate 179.
Frontispiece: Detail of *Doors*, 1903. For the Salon de Luxe, Willow Tea Rooms,
Glasgow. Pine, painted white, with leaded-glass panels and metal handles, 77 x 27 in.
(195.5 x 68.5 cm), each leaf. Morgan Grenfell Property Asset Management Ltd

Editor, Abbeville Press: Nancy Grubb
Designer: Joel Avirom
Production Editor: Abigail Asher
Production Manager: Lou Bilka

This volume was published to accompany an exhibition by Glasgow Museums,
Glasgow School of Art, and the Hunterian Museum and Art Gallery,
University of Glasgow.

EXHIBITION SCHEDULE
Glasgow Museums, McLellan Galleries, May 25–September 30, 1996
The Metropolitan Museum of Art, New York, November 19, 1996–February 16, 1997
The Art Institute of Chicago, March 29–June 22, 1997
Los Angeles County Museum of Art, August 3–October 12, 1997

The Charles Rennie Mackintosh book and exhibition are funded by the City of
Glasgow District Council and The Whyte & Mackay Group.

EDITOR'S NOTE
Dimensions are given height x width x depth. Unless otherwise indicated, the
support for drawings and watercolours is cream-coloured paper. The British practice
of labelling the bottom floor of a building as the ground floor and the floor above
it as the first floor has been followed throughout.

First edition
2   4   6   8   10   9   7   5   3   1

Library of Congress Cataloging-in-Publication Data
Charles Rennie Mackintosh / edited by Wendy Kaplan.
p.   cm.
Includes bibliographical references and index.
ISBN 1-55859-791-3 (cloth)
ISBN 0-7892-0080-5 (paper)
1. Mackintosh, Charles Rennie, 1868–1928—Criticism and
interpretation. 2. Arts and crafts movement—Scotland. I. Mackintosh,
Charles Rennie, 1868–1928. II. Kaplan, Wendy.
N6797.M23C47   1996
709'.2—dc20   95-47759

CONTENTS

I. Mackintosh in Context

II. Architecture

III. Art and Design

IV. Conclusion

Directors' Foreword

Charles Rennie Mackintosh was arguably the greatest architect and designer Scotland has produced. This exhibition presents the full riches of his diverse output from buildings and interiors to graphics, metalwork, glass, and textiles. These are set against the story of his life and in the context of the latest scholarship. The creative collaboration with his wife, Margaret Macdonald, which produced some of the most atmospheric and beautiful interiors of his career, is given particular attention.

Appropriately, the exhibition opens in the centenary year of the competition for the Glasgow School of Art. Mackintosh was educated at the Glasgow School of Art and he created for it his masterwork, which remains at the heart of its campus, still fully in use for its original purpose. The exhibition is the first—and long-overdue—authoritative retrospective in Mackintosh's native city, and the first comprehensive introduction of his work to an American audience.

Wonderful objects have been borrowed from private and public collections around the world. The greater part of the exhibition draws on Glasgow's outstanding Mackintosh collections: that of the University of Glasgow, owner of the extensive Mackintosh Estate and the remarkable interiors from Mackintosh's home, The Mackintosh House; the Glasgow School of Art, which houses an impressive collection of furniture, designs, and watercolours; and Glasgow Museums' important holdings from Mackintosh's tea rooms and work by Glasgow Style designers.

Models and films have been specially commissioned to convey the extraordinary qualities of Mackintosh's buildings and interiors. We have restored items specially for the exhibition. Particularly significant is the Ingram Street tea rooms, of which the Ladies' Luncheon Room, returned to its original white and silver finish, will be one of the show's chief attractions.

The exhibition will tour from the McLellan Galleries, Glasgow, to The Metropolitan Museum of Art, New York; The Art Institute of Chicago; and Los Angeles County Museum of Art. We would like to thank our colleagues there who have made this elaborate and ambitious project possible.

Julian Spalding
Director
Glasgow Museums

Professor Malcolm D. McLeod
Director
Hunterian Museum
and Art Gallery
University of Glasgow

Professor Dugald Cameron
Director
Glasgow School of Art

Studio-drawing room from the Mackintoshes' home at 78 South-park Avenue, Glasgow. The room has been reconstructed as part of The Mackintosh House, Hunterian Art Gallery, University of Glasgow, using fitments from the original house and furnished with the Mackintoshes' own furniture.

Sponsor's Statement

The work of Charles Rennie Mackintosh commands worldwide acclaim, and as producer of another indigenous product with international appeal—Scotch whisky—the Whyte & Mackay Group is delighted to support the world's largest-ever Mackintosh exhibition.

The exhibition provides a magnificent tribute to Glasgow's most famous designer and architect, utilising the combined and extensive expertise of Glasgow Museums, the Hunterian Art Gallery, and Glasgow School of Art.

As an established sponsor of the visual arts in Scotland, we are proud to be associated with this ambitious project. We are confident that visitors will be fascinated by the opportunity to view Charles Rennie Mackintosh's out-standing contribution to architecture and design, a unique style that has become a recognisable symbol of Glasgow's cultural heritage.

Ken Hitchcock
Chairman and Chief Executive
Whyte & Mackay Group

Acknowledgements

Glasgow Museums is fortunate to have had so many dedicated and enthusiastic supporters to create this book and the exhibition.

The Hunterian Art Gallery and Glasgow School of Art have been wonderful partners, and together we have enlisted the generous assistance of colleagues in museums and libraries across the world. In particular, gratitude must go to our colleagues in the three tour venues, at The Metropolitan Museum of Art, New York; The Art Institute of Chicago; and Los Angeles County Museum of Art. We wish to thank them and also the many private lenders who have contributed works from their own collections.

Grateful thanks are due to the scholars who wrote the essays for this volume. Their critiques of each others' drafts contributed to the collaborative nature of the project and helped ensure both accuracy and spirited debate. Special acknowledgement must be extended to Alan Crawford and Pamela Robertson, who commented extensively on the essays, generously sharing their expertise about Mackintosh. Thanks also go to Wendy Kaplan, Curator of the Wolfsonian Foundation, Miami Beach, Florida, who expertly planned, managed, and edited *Charles Rennie Mackintosh*. Nancy Grubb, Executive Editor at Abbeville Press, helped to make the production of the book an enjoyable and rewarding task.

Scholarship and flair have been brought to the project by its curators Pamela Robertson, Curator of the Mackintosh Collection at the Hunterian Art Gallery, University of Glasgow, and J. Stewart Johnson, Consultant for Design and Architecture at The Metropolitan Museum of Art, New York. The project coordinator was Daniel Robbins, Curator of British Art and Design at Glasgow Museums, and advice has been given by Roger Billcliffe as curatorial consultant. The entire project has been led by Stefan van Raay, Senior Curator of Art at Glasgow Museums, supported by a professional and experienced team from Glasgow City Council's museums department. We are extremely grateful to Mr. and Mrs. Donald Taffner for their generous support of the models of Glasgow School of Art commissioned for the exhibition from Brian Gallagher of B. G. Models Ltd.

The success of the exhibition and its publication owes a great deal to the special efforts of Daniel Robbins, project coordinator, and Alison Brown, administrative officer for the Mackintosh exhibition. They attended to the countless details of exhibition planning, including coordinating loans and the checklist, overseeing the restoration of the Ingram Street tea rooms by conservator Andrew Stone, and obtaining all the photographs in this volume. Their organisational skills and commitment to the project were invaluable assets.

None of this would have been possible without the generous financial support of the Whyte & Mackay Group and the truly dedicated staff of Glasgow Museums. Thank you.

List of Lenders

Art et Curiosité Inc. (Christopher Payne)
Asenbaum Collection
The British Museum
Charles Rennie Mackintosh Society, Glasgow
City of Aberdeen Art Gallery and Museums
Congregation of Ruchill Parish Church, Glasgow
The Danish Museum of Decorative Art, Copenhagen
The Detroit Institute of Arts
Dumbarton District Libraries, Dumbartonshire, Scotland
Glasgow Museums
Glasgow School of Art
William Hardie Ltd
Hunterian Art Gallery, University of Glasgow
Kenneth Lawson Esq., Banffshire
MAK-Austrian Museum for Applied Arts, Vienna
The Metropolitan Museum of Art, New York
Morgan Grenfell Property Asset Management Ltd
Musée d'Orsay, Paris
Museum für Kunst und Gewerbe, Hamburg, Germany
National Galleries of Scotland, Edinburgh

National Gallery of Canada, Ottawa
The National Library of Ireland, Dublin
The National Trust for Scotland, The Hill House,
    Helensburgh
Andrew McIntosh Patrick
Ernst Ploil, Vienna
Private collection; courtesy The Fine Art Society, plc
Royal Ontario Museum, Toronto
Sheffield City Art Galleries, Sheffield, England
George Smith
Strathclyde Regional Archives, Glasgow
Donald and Eleanor Taffner
Tate Gallery, London
Victoria and Albert Museum, London
Virginia Museum of Fine Arts, Richmond

The organisers would also like to thank all the private lenders who have so generously made their collections available to this exhibition.

Introduction

■■
WENDY KAPLAN

Unlike many design reformers at the turn of the century, Charles Rennie Mackintosh was neither a peripatetic lecturer, voluminous correspondent, nor prolific pamphleteer. He proselytised only through his work, leaving his legacy more open to interpretation than that of most of his architectural contemporaries.

Throughout the century, critics and historians have invented the Mackintosh they needed. As early as 1902 Hermann Muthesius introduced, in the Munich magazine *Dekorative Kunst*, the myth that would until very recently prevail: Mackintosh and his wife, Margaret Macdonald, were ridiculed and rejected by English critics at the 1896 Arts and Crafts Exhibition Society show but embraced and even idolised when their work was displayed at the 1900 Vienna Secession. In the 1930s the historian Nikolaus Pevsner gave Mackintosh and his links with Vienna an important place in the development of Modernism. Mackintosh's first biographer, Thomas Howarth, amplified this view in 1952 with his account of Mackintosh's continuing acceptance abroad but rejection at home, leading to his exile from Glasgow and, eventually, to an impoverished and obscure death. A staunch champion of Modernism, Howarth insisted that Mackintosh's work be seen as a harbinger of it and discounted the many elements that would not support his assertion.

This monolithic view of Mackintosh has been challenged in recent years, and with the publication of *Charles Rennie Mackintosh* one hopes that its death knell will be sounded. This volume presents a more multifaceted Mackintosh, whose passion for decoration, color, discontinuity, and sensuality in design does not negate his white abstractions so loved by Modernists. Rather, the full recognition of all these qualities produces a more complex and mysterious portrait than the old myth—a story much richer and more full of contradiction.

Past writings have often viewed Mackintosh as an isolated genius whose work sprang sui generis out of Glasgow's unreceptive soil. The first section of essays in this volume, "Mackintosh in Context," serves as an antidote to this position, firmly placing him in the nexus of his native city, which supplied the progressive, prosperous climate and appreciative patrons he needed to flourish. Glasgow School of Art in particular provided a supportive atmosphere, as well as the impetus for the artistic circle around and alongside Mackintosh that resulted in the Glasgow Style. His fruitful collaboration with three artists he met at Glasgow School of Art—Margaret Macdonald, her sister Frances, and Herbert McNair, who with Mackintosh became known as the Four—presents an even more specialised contextual focus. Margaret Macdonald became Mackintosh's wife in 1900, the year they first embarked upon a series of stunningly inventive interiors, most notably for exhibition displays, tea rooms, and their own residences. Margaret Macdonald's role in these interiors and in other aspects of work generally considered to be by her husband's hand alone has become one of the most provocative issues in Mackintosh studies.

Just as scholarship of the 1930s, '40s, and '50s was subject to the prejudices and proclivities of the time, so too is scholarship of the 1990s. Now that unbridled enthusiasm for Modernism has waned, these highly decorated, symbolic interiors are no longer dismissed as "inferior" Mackintosh but instead command the enthusiastic approbation of contemporary scholars, often inspiring heady speculation regarding their psychosexual meaning. And with conventional "patriarchal" history increasingly disparaged, Margaret Macdonald's role as Mackintosh's collaborator and most important influence has become championed by feminists.

The collaborative work of the Four deserves careful scrutiny, as does the nature of the Mackintoshes' partnership in many of the interiors and their furnishings. However, such adjustments run the risk of overcorrection, and the last part of Janice Helland's essay provides an example. Here Helland posits that some of Mackintosh's Walberswick flower drawings were probably collaborative efforts. Since the majority of these are signed both "CRM" and "MMM," this would seem a reasonable assumption, but leading Mackintosh scholars deny this view and have stated their case with compelling evidence. First, the signatures are in Mackintosh's hand; he often recorded those present while he was sketching by putting his companions' initials on the work. Second, apart from one lost watercolour, known only by its listing in an exhibition catalogue, no evidence exists to support the notion that Margaret Macdonald ever painted directly from nature, whereas her husband drew botanically correct flowers beginning in the 1880s and continuing through the rest of his life. Much of the new thinking about Margaret Macdonald's role is a healthy corrective to the unjust anonymity suffered by women artists. Furthermore, the new work on the Mackintoshes' collaboration and that of the Four goes a long way towards dispelling the myth that Mackintosh worked alone, isolated by his genius.

Had Mackintosh, however, been only the sum of the influences upon him, he would not merit this book. While part of the second section, "Architecture," continues to counterbalance the myth of isolation, the essays about Glasgow School of Art (his greatest public building) and The Hill House (his domestic masterpiece) focus on his originality, uncompromising intelligence, and the creativity with which he transformed traditional references. New attention is also given to the architecture of the later, London years, after his unique qualities were no longer in demand. Although Mackintosh never had more than a few (albeit fiercely loyal) patrons, his work must have appealed to a broad audience for a time: his tea rooms were popular; a letter by Margaret Macdonald discusses Mackintosh imitators throughout Glasgow; and commissions came in steadily for many years. But shortly after the turn of the century, architectural taste turned away from the "Free Style," with its emphasis on individuality and the vernacular, to the classical. Mackintosh seemed unable to make this shift and lacked interest in the kind of structure that was to characterise twentieth-century urban life—the high-rise, commercial, steel-framed building.

Hermann Muthesius credited Mackintosh as the only British architect who fully realised the goal of *Gesamtkunstwerk*—a completely unified work of art. In addition to being a designer of buildings and their contents—from large case pieces and built-in settles to wall stencils, lighting fixtures, and flatware—Mackintosh was a highly accomplished graphic designer and painter. This volume's "Art and Design" section offers fresh interpretations of Mackintosh's interiors and furnishings (to which his wife contributed in varying degrees but very considerably in the early years of the century) and his development as a painter. During the London years (between 1915 and 1923), Mackintosh was also a textile designer, an area of activity not covered here since this work has been fully documented by Roger Billcliffe's book on the subject (see the bibliography).

One purpose of *Charles Rennie Mackintosh* and the exhibition it accompanies is to correct commonly held misconceptions about him. As suggested earlier, conventional histories have maintained that Mackintosh played a central role in the formation of European Modernism. They have claimed ubiquitous accolades for the displays in Vienna and Turin, widespread coverage of his work in art periodicals, and profound influence on an entire generation of forward-looking architects, particularly Josef Hoffmann. This volume does not include an essay on Mackintosh's influence in Europe because while the text was in preparation serious questions were raised about the accuracy of the established account.[1] Reviews of the Vienna exhibit were by no means entirely laudatory (one described the Viennese installation as "hellish"); and, whether extolled or condemned, the Mackintoshes' work received less press attention than that of several other British architects and designers. Only a handful of articles have been traced in period European journals, many by a single contributor—Mackintosh's ardent supporter Muthesius. Finally, there is evidence that Viennese architects and designers like Hoffmann exerted more influence on Mackintosh than the other way round, though Hoffmann certainly admired Mackintosh; and only isolated examples of designs or buildings in Europe directly inspired by Mackintosh have been located so far.

This leaves the topic in a state of flux. The old account is discredited, but no new and more thoroughly researched account has been put in its place. The subject certainly calls for further research, since Mackintosh's appreciation by the progressive design cognoscenti (e.g., Hoffmann, Koloman Moser, Fritz Wärndorfer, and, of course, the prolific, powerful Muthesius) is well documented, and since he did receive some commissions in Germany and Vienna. Many period accounts attest to his celebrity, but their statements have yet to be tested fully by a comprehensive examination of visual and documentary records. Concerning his reputation in England during his lifetime, evidence points to general indifference rather than outright rejection.

All this makes Mackintosh's more recent history, and indeed, apotheosis, even more fascinating. The volume's conclusion elaborates with a many-tiered analysis of his reputation since his death in 1928. His scholarly renown, first characterised by a highly selective reading of his work, has been followed by almost a plethora of revisionist accounts; his popular image has been shaped both by careful reproductions and by rampant commercial exploitation. This volume does not seek to replace the old orthodoxies about Mackintosh with new ones. Rather, it provides a much-needed forum for stimulating new scholarship and evenhanded assessments that allow many different Mackintoshes to emerge.

1. These conventional histories are questioned in Alan Crawford, *Charles Rennie Mackintosh* (London: Thames and Hudson, 1995), pp. 91–95, 130–34.

■■ OVERLEAF
1. Charles Rennie Mackintosh photographed by James Craig Annan, 1893.

Chronology

■■

ALAN CRAWFORD

1868

June 7—Charles Rennie Mackintosh is born at 70 Parson Street, Glasgow, the son of Margaret Rennie McIntosh and William McIntosh, a clerk in the police force (plate 2).

1874

The McIntosh family moves to 2 Firpark Terrace, Dennistoun, Glasgow.

1875

Mackintosh attends Reid's Public School (presumably until 1877).

1877

Attends Allan Glen's Institution, a private school for the children of tradesmen and artisans, which specialises in vocational training.

2. William McIntosh in Highland dress, with the world-champion Glasgow police tug-of-war team of which he was captain, 1889.

1883

September—begins classes at Glasgow School of Art, attending either in the early morning or in the evening. Enrolls as a student each year until 1894, winning many prizes in local examinations and competitions; submits work to the National Competition organised by the Department of Science and Art at South Kensington in London.

1884

Begins a five-year pupilage with John Hutchison, architect, of Glasgow.[1] (Little evidence of his work for Hutchison still exists.)

1885

Francis Newbery is appointed headmaster of Glasgow School of Art; in 1889 he founds the Glasgow School of Art Club, whose annual exhibitions help to promote the work of talented students, past and present, including Mackintosh.

December 9—Mackintosh's mother dies.

1886–87

Mackintosh sketches old buildings in Glasgow, Rowallan Castle, Ayrshire, and elsewhere.

1889

Joins the firm of Honeyman and Keppie, architects, as a draughtsman, probably in the first half of this year (plate 3).

July—sketches at Elgin, Morayshire.

1890

Summer—a pair of semidetached houses is constructed at 120–22 (now 140–42) Balgrayhill Road, Glasgow—Mackintosh's first design to be executed; they are built for his uncle, William Hamilton.

3. The staff at Honeyman and Keppie. Mackintosh is standing at the right, and Herbert McNair is standing next to him, 1890.

September—wins the competition for the Alexander Thomson Travelling Studentship with a design for a public hall (see plate 77) and chooses to go on a tour of Italy. About this time, his competition design for a science and art museum (see plate 78) fails to win the British Institution Scholarship.

Sketches at Largs, Ayrshire.

1891

February 10—presents lecture, "Scotch Baronial Architecture," to the Glasgow Architectural Association.

March 21—leaves on his scholarship tour of Italy, reaching Naples on April 5. The places he visits, studying and sketching, include Sicily, Rome, Orvieto, Siena, Florence (plate 4), Pisa, Ravenna, Ferrara, Venice, Padua, Verona, Cremona, Brescia, Bergamo, Como, and Pavia. He begins his journey home in July.

Toward the end of the year—enters the Royal Institute of British Architects' Soane Medallion competition with a design for a chapter house. Honeyman and Keppie's entry in the limited competition for the Glasgow Art Galleries (see plate 81), to which Mackintosh contributes, may belong to this time, or to early 1892. Both are unsuccessful.

1892

Early in the year—the McIntosh family moves to 2 Regent Park Square; between October 1892 and October 1893 they move again, to Holmwood, at 82 Langside Avenue, then return to Regent Park Square, no. 27, between October 1895 and May 1896.[2]

July—Mackintosh's design for a chapter house wins a gold medal in the National Competition.

Probably middle of the year—interiors are designed at Craigie Hall, Rowan Road, Glasgow, and at the Glasgow Art Club, 187–91 Bath Street, both of which seem to show Mackintosh's hand in the treatment of scrolling foliage and other details.

September 6—presents a lecture, "A Tour in Italy," to the Glasgow Architectural Association.

November 19—designs his earliest recorded graphic work, an invitation to a meeting of the Glasgow School of Art Club on this date.

Late in the year—enters a design for a railway terminus in the Soane Medallion competition and is again unsuccessful.

His earliest-known symbolic watercolour, *The Harvest Moon* (see plate 203), is dated 1892; "Elizabethan Architecture" lecture and his untitled lecture on architecture may belong to this year.

1893

February—presents a lecture, "Architecture," aligning himself with the progressive elements in contemporary British architecture.

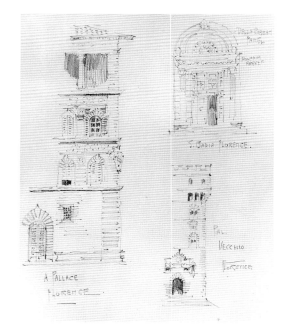

4. Charles Rennie Mackintosh. *Sketchbook: Drawings of Architecture in Scotland and Italy*, c. 1890–91. Pencil, $5^{1}/_{16}$ x $5^{1}/_{8}$ in. (12.8 x 13.0 cm). The National Library of Ireland, Dublin.
Mackintosh's sketches are of the Palazzo Vecchio, the Palazzo Guadagni, and probably the Badia Fiorentina, all in Florence.

Probably sometime this year—changes the spelling of his name from McIntosh to Mackintosh, for unknown reasons (his father had earlier done the same). Presumably, much of 1893 is spent on his design of additions to the premises of the *Glasgow Herald* (see plate 201)—the first substantial building by Honeyman and Keppie whose design can confidently be attributed to Mackintosh. Work on that site begins in February 1894 and ends in the summer of 1895.[3]

Around this time Mackintosh's interests expand beyond architecture into the fine and decorative arts. With Herbert McNair, a fellow draughtsman at Honeyman and Keppie, he gets to know a group of middle-class women art students at Glasgow School of Art who call themselves "the Immortals." There is a romantic attachment between Mackintosh and one of the Immortals, Jessie Keppie, sister of his employer, John Keppie. As artists, Mackintosh and McNair establish a particularly close relationship with the sisters Margaret and Frances Macdonald, forming a smaller group usually referred to as the Four.[4] These contacts are of great importance in developing Mackintosh's wider interests in art.

Steps along this path that belong to 1893 are: the first number of "The Magazine," a periodical produced in one handmade copy by the Immortals; Frances Macdonald's brooding watercolour, *Ill Omen* (Hunterian Art Gallery, University of Glasgow); studio photographs of Mackintosh in artistic dress rather than that of a professional man (plate 1); and a suite of furniture for his friend David Gauld, which may have been the first furniture designed by Mackintosh, apart from fittings in interiors for Honeyman and Keppie.

1894

April—the April number of "The Magazine" contains three symbolic watercolours by Mackintosh; one of them, *Cabbages in an Orchard* (see plate 206), is accompanied by a satiric-symbolic commentary.

May–July—probably works on designs for the Anatomical School, Queen Margaret College, Glasgow (see plate 84). Construction begins in September and ends in November 1895.

September—goes on the first of about fourteen sketching tours in England, this time to the northern Cotswolds.

November—two symbolic watercolours by Mackintosh appear in "The Magazine." Work by Margaret and Frances Macdonald, exhibited with the Glasgow School of Art Club, is described in the local press as "clever" but also "ghoullike," "hideous," and "weird."[5] The epithet "the Spook School" dates from this time or shortly after.

1895

First half of the year—Martyrs' Public School, 11 Parson Street, a commission from the Glasgow School Board, is on the drawing board at Honeyman and Keppie (see plate 85). Construction begins towards the end of 1895 and ends sometime in 1898.

January—paints two elaborately titled symbolic watercolours, *The Tree of Personal Effort The Sun of Indifference* (see plate 207) and *The Tree of Influence—The Tree of Importance—The Sun of Cowardice* (Glasgow School of Art). These do not include figures of the sort that are central to the Macdonald sisters' work; instead, they are made up of simplified organic forms similar to those Mackintosh would later use as details on buildings and furniture.

February—the annual exhibition of the Glasgow Institute of the Fine Arts is announced by a poster by Mackintosh in the style of Aubrey Beardsley.

June—sketches in Hampshire, Dorset, and Somerset, England.

1896

Early in the year—a competition is proposed for the design of a new building for Glasgow School of Art on a new site, at 167 Renfrew Street; the competition is limited to eight (later twelve) architectural firms, including Honeyman and Keppie.

June—the conditions of the School of Art competition are published. The deadline is October 1.

October—Mackintosh and the Macdonald sisters exhibit watercolours, furniture, and metalwork with the Arts and Crafts Exhibition Society in London. The reviews of this exhibition do not bear out the received account, that the work of Mackintosh and the Macdonalds "evoked a storm of protest from public and critics alike."[6] Most reviews do not mention them; a few give measured approval.[7]

Designs schemes for stencil decorations on three floors of Kate Cranston's newly built tea rooms at 91–93 Buchanan Street, Glasgow (see plate 45). The furnishing and decoration of the interiors is chiefly by George Walton and is carried out between December 1896 and June 1897; Mackintosh's schemes are probably executed early in 1897. (The building still stands, but the interiors were destroyed, probably about 1918, after Cranston sold the property.)

Sketches in Norfolk, England.

1897

First half of the year—designs Queen's Cross Church, 870 Garscube Road, Glasgow (see plate 89). The plans are approved in June; building work begins in August and ends in September 1899.

January—Honeyman and Keppie are declared winners of the School of Art competition. The design is by Mackintosh; John Keppie is responsible for the erection of the building (see plate 100).

July—the *Studio* publishes an article on Mackintosh and the Macdonald sisters by its former editor, Gleeson White.[8] This probably makes Mackintosh known to progressive architects and designers in Europe, where the *Studio* was widely read.

August–September—sketches in Norfolk and Suffolk, England.

October—plans for the School of Art building are approved by the Dean of Guild Court (the local office responsible for assuring the safety of new buildings). Construction begins in November.

1898

May—a competition is announced for the design of buildings for an International Exhibition in Glasgow, planned for 1901. Mackintosh designs a scheme, which does not win.

Second half of the year and possibly also early 1899—designs furniture (see plate 160) for Miss Cranston's tea rooms at 114 Argyle Street, which are enlarged and redecorated between June 1898 and April 1899.[9] (The building still stands, but Cranston sold the property in 1918 and almost no trace of the tea-room interiors now remains.) The design of the Ruchill Street Free Church Halls probably also belongs to this period.

August—sketches in Devon, England.

November—the Munich art magazine *Dekorative Kunst* publishes the first substantial German-language article about Mackintosh and other Glasgow designers.[10]

Mackintosh's first two comprehensive domestic interiors to be executed probably belong to 1898: a bedroom (see plate 46) at Westdel, 2 Queen's Place, Glasgow, for the publisher and bookseller Robert Maclehose, and a dining room at Nymphenburgerstrasse 86, Munich, for Hugo Bruckmann, editor of *Dekorative Kunst.* The Westdel bedroom is particularly important, for it is probably the first of his white domestic interiors with furniture designed as an integral part of the decorative scheme. (Of these two interiors, only part of the fitted furniture at Westdel is known to survive in situ.)

1899

Most likely not involved in any major new design during this year, being preoccupied with detailing the interior of the School of Art.

May–July—Mackintosh, the Macdonalds, and McNair exhibit with the newly formed and antiacademic International Society of Sculptors, Painters and Gravers in London.

June 14—Frances Macdonald and Herbert McNair marry at the Episcopal Church, Dumbarton. They move to Liverpool, where McNair will teach at University College (later the University of Liverpool).

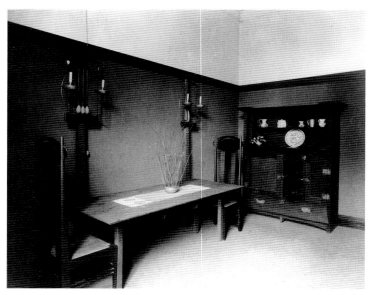

5. The dining room, 120 Mains Street, Glasgow. Photographed by T. and R. Annan Ltd., c. 1900.

December 20—formal opening of Glasgow School of Art.

1900

First half of the year—this period is full of new schemes, including two important interiors. One is the flat at 120 Mains Street, Glasgow, in which Mackintosh and Margaret Macdonald will live after they marry (plate 5); it is said to have been completed by March 1900.[11] The other is the Ladies' Luncheon Room and related rooms at Miss Cranston's Ingram Street tea rooms, which are completed in November. (Mackintosh was to work again at Ingram Street in 1907, 1909–10, 1911, and 1911–12. The tea rooms continued in use until 1950, when they were bought by Glasgow Corporation to save them from destruction. The interiors were removed in 1971 and have been partially reconstructed by Glasgow Museums; see plate 183.)

May—designs for the printing office of the *Daily Record* go to the Dean of Guild for approval; the first stage of this building (see plate 93) is erected between June 1900 and May 1902, the second between November 1903 and May 1904.

August—completes designs for Windyhill (see plate 92), his first detached middle-class house, for William Davidson; the building is completed late in 1901.

August 22—Mackintosh and Margaret Macdonald (plate 6) marry, at the Episcopal Church, Dumbarton.

November—the Mackintoshes and McNairs exhibit with the Vienna Secession; the Mackintoshes go to Vienna to install their work. Progressive Viennese critics react strongly to the

6. Margaret Macdonald, photographed by Thomas Craig Annan in the drawing room at 120 Mains Street, c. 1900.

intense atmosphere and symbolic imagery of their exhibit (see plate 63), writing about "hobgoblins" and "torture chambers," much as Glaswegian critics had talked of "the Spook School" in 1894–95.[12] Mackintosh's encounter with progressive design in Vienna provides him with inspiration for many years to come.

1900–1901

Designs Das Haus eines Kunst-Freundes (A House for an Art Lover) in a competition sponsored by the Darmstadt, Germany, publisher Alexander Koch. The entry is incomplete and so cannot be considered for the prize; but in 1902 Koch publishes the designs in a lavish portfolio (see plate 162), which must have contributed to Mackintosh's reputation in Europe.

1901

Becomes a partner in Honeyman, Keppie and Mackintosh.

June–July—sketches on Holy Island, Northumberland, England, with Margaret Macdonald and others.

September—a two-stage competition for the Anglican cathedral in Liverpool is announced; the deadline is later extended to June 30, 1902. Mackintosh's entry (see plate 97) does not get past the first stage.

Late in the year he is also working on the drawing-room interior and other fittings at 14 Kingsborough Gardens, Glasgow.

1902

Early in the year—the publisher Walter Blackie asks Mackintosh to design a detached family house for him in Helens-

burgh, a town northwest of Glasgow that was favoured by Glaswegian businessmen as a place of residence. The earliest surviving drawings date to March 1902; building work begins quite soon—the roof is on by January 1903, and The Hill House (see plate 118) is completed early in 1904.

At about the same time Mackintosh designs a music room at Carl-Ludwigstrasse 45, Vienna, for Fritz Wärndorfer, supporter of the Secession and later of the Wiener Werkstätte. It is substantially complete by the end of the year; a frieze of gesso panels by Margaret Macdonald is not installed until 1907–8. (The house was sold in 1916 and the interiors either dispersed or destroyed; but the gesso panels survive in the MAK-Austrian Museum for Applied Arts in Vienna.)

March—*Dekorative Kunst* publishes a long article on the Mackintoshes by Hermann Muthesius, the most sensitive and substantial contemporary account of their work. The illustrations include two speculative designs for small studio houses, one in the country and the other in town.[13]

April—the Mackintoshes travel to Turin for the *International Exhibition of Modern Decorative Art*. Mackintosh designs the overall installation for the Scottish section, which includes a room setting by the Mackintoshes, the Rose Boudoir (see plate 67).

July—sketches on Holy Island.

December 22—the exhibition *Architecture and Design of the New Style*, at which Mackintosh exhibits a room setting, opens on the Petrovka in Moscow.

1903

February—drawings for alterations to 217 Sauchiehall Street, Glasgow, to create Miss Cranston's Willow Tea Rooms (plate 7), go to the Dean of Guild for approval. Building begins in March; the tea rooms open on October 29. (The Willow Tea Rooms went out of use in the 1920s; however, they have been partly reconstructed for use as a shop, and their exclusive Salon de Luxe has been reopened as a tea room.)

May—suffering from eyestrain and overwork, Mackintosh takes a trip to the Orkney Islands.

June—the Glasgow School Board appoints Mackintosh to design Scotland Street School (see plate 72). Designs are submitted in October; construction begins in December and ends in August 1906.

December 1903 or January 1904—exhibits a bedroom at an exhibition organised by the Dresdener Werkstätten für Handwerkskunst in Dresden, Germany.

7. The Mackintosh hoarding in front of 217 Sauchiehall Street, Glasgow, during the rebuilding of the facade of the Willow Tea Rooms, 1903. From *Dekorative Kunst* (April 1905): 257.

1904

Designs the decoration and furnishing of the hall, dining room, drawing room (see plate 173), and two bedrooms at Hous'hill, Nitshill, Glasgow, for Kate Cranston and her husband, John Cochrane. Judged by the number of new designs, this is Mackintosh's largest domestic commission. Work probably begins in the spring of 1904; it is completed in the spring of 1905. (The Hous'hill furniture was sold at auction in 1933 and the house was later demolished.)

Spring or summer—sketches in the Scilly Islands, England.

1905

March—*Deutsche Kunst und Dekoration* publishes an article about The Hill House.[14] At about this time Mackintosh shows a sober and rectilinear dining room in an exhibition sponsored by the Berlin furniture manufacturer A. S. Ball.

April—*Dekorative Kunst* publishes an article about the Willow Tea Rooms.[15]

August—sketches in Norfolk, England.

November—sketches in Sussex, England.

Late in the year—begins work on Auchinibert, a house at Killearn, Stirlingshire, for F. J. Shand. Construction is completed in 1908. At about the same time designs the Dutch Kitchen (see plate 195) for the basement of Miss Cranston's Argyle Street tea rooms, which is probably completed towards the end of 1906.

1906

Mackintosh completes his interior of the boardroom at Glasgow School of Art this year.

March 30—buys 6 Florentine Terrace, Glasgow, a mid-nineteenth-century terrace house (plate 8); between April and September the Mackintoshes alter and redecorate it for their own occupation. The address later changes to 78 Southpark Avenue.

August—sketches on Holy Island.

November—Dean of Guild approval is granted for Mackintosh's designs for Balgray Cottage, Cloak, Kilmacolm. He adds to this building in 1908 and 1913, when it becomes known as Mossyde.

1907

February 1—Honeyman, Keppie and Mackintosh are appointed architects for the extensions to Glasgow School of Art (see plate 117). Most of the drawings are completed by June and approved by the Dean of Guild on November 14; building work starts almost immediately.

Mackintosh works on the Oak Room (see plate 196) for Miss Cranston's Ingram Street premises at the same time as, or shortly after, the School of Art extensions.

1908

May have devoted much of 1908 to supervising the building of the School of Art extensions. The only other work of this year is the new entrance to the Lady Artists' Club, 5 Blythswood Square, Glasgow.

February 10—his father dies.

June—Mackintosh sketches at Cintra, Portugal.

1909

Designs interiors and furniture for the ladies' rest room and the Oval Room at Miss Cranston's Ingram Street tea rooms;

8. 6 Florentine Terrace, Hillhead, Glasgow—the house the Mackintoshes bought in 1906. Photographed in 1963.

the work, though not large, seems to have lasted throughout the year and into the early part of 1910.

June—sketches in Sussex.

Summer—designs the card room and some other work at Hous'hill; execution of the work is probably spread out over the rest of the year.

December 15—formal opening of the extensions, Glasgow School of Art.

1910

Mackintosh designs some furniture for Glasgow School of Art during this year, but the bulk of work connected with the extensions is over. Apart from that work, Mackintosh has completed only two detached houses and six interiors in the past five years, and he reaches a point where he has almost no new work coming in. No new buildings or interiors belong to this year, and little furniture. The financial records of Honeyman, Keppie and Mackintosh suggest that his partner John Keppie experiences a similar loss of work; but it is accompanied in Mackintosh's case by depression and heavy drinking.

April–May—sketches in Kent, England.

1911

April—designs interiors for the White Cockade Tea Rooms at Glasgow's Scottish National Exhibition; they are probably executed in May and June.

Summer–autumn—designs the Chinese Room (see plate 197) at the Ingram Street tea rooms.

Late in the year—designs the Cloister Room (see plate 198) at the Ingram Street tea rooms; this is probably executed during the first half of 1912.

1912

March 11—transfers ownership of 6 Florentine Terrace to Margaret Macdonald.

April—designs a hairdressing salon at 80 Union Street, Glasgow.

1913

Early in the year—at about this time works (or tries to work) on two competitions for buildings in Glasgow: a College of Domestic Science in Woodlands, and a Teachers' Training College in Jordanhill. Perhaps as a result of depression or heavy drinking, he fails to produce the work for the training college in time, and it is agreed that his partnership in the firm should end. He sets up on his own but fails to find any work.

June (or earlier)—designs covers for Blackie's series of books called Rambles among Our Industries.

July—sketches on Holy Island.

October (or earlier)—designs covers for Blackie's series Rambler Travel Books.

1914

June—Mackintosh's partnership in Honeyman, Keppie and Mackintosh is formally dissolved.

Mid-July—the Mackintoshes go on holiday to Walberswick, Suffolk, England (plate 9). Three weeks later World War I breaks out. So that Mackintosh can rest, they decide to stay on in Walberswick and rent out 6 Florentine Terrace for a year.

1915

Early May—having connections with Germany and Austria, Mackintosh is suspected by local people of being a spy; his house is searched, and letters from Germany and Austria are found.

June 14—Mackintosh is ordered to leave Norfolk, Suffolk, and Cambridgeshire.

July–August—Mackintosh is in London and in touch with Patrick Geddes, who is running a summer-school course entitled "The War: Its Social Tasks and Problems." Various Mackintosh designs, including the two elevations for buildings in an arcaded street (see plate 140), may date from this period.

Autumn—the Mackintoshes settle in Chelsea, then well established as an artists' quarter of London, where they live for the next eight years. They each have a studio and live in lodgings nearby. Mackintosh is at 2 Hans Studios, 43A Glebe Place (plate 10), from at least the middle of 1916; Macdonald is at 2 Cedar Studios, 45 Glebe Place, but it is not clear from when.

9. The estuary at Walberswick, Suffolk. Photographed by Francis Frith in 1919.

10. 2 Hans Studios, 43A Glebe Place, Chelsea.

At about this time Mackintosh begins to paint still-life compositions of flowers, in watercolour; at least ten of these survive, along with a similar number of decorative flower paintings; what appears to be the earliest of these is exhibited in 1916.

Late in the year—about this time Mackintosh is asked by W. J. Bassett-Lowke to design alterations and interior decorations for 78 Derngate, Northampton, England (see plate 144). The structural alterations are approved by the local authority on July 4, 1916; much of the work seems to have been completed in time for Bassett-Lowke's marriage in March 1917. (The house and most of Mackintosh's fittings survive, but without any of his furniture or decorations.)

1915–23

The Mackintoshes increase their small income by making designs for printed textiles. They seem to have produced several hundred of these (most by Mackintosh), which they sold to various manufacturers; William Foxton and Sefton's are the names recorded. It is not known how many of these designs were actually produced, and few manufactured examples survive. They are not easy to date, but the earliest may belong to 1915. Both Mackintosh's textile designs and his watercolours show the influence of avant-garde movements in the arts from about 1910 onwards, particularly that of the Fauves and of Post-Impressionism; the textiles also show the influence of Viennese design.

During these years Mackintosh exhibits work at the International Society of Sculptors, Painters and Gravers in London (1916, 1917), the *British Arts and Crafts Exhibition* in Detroit (1920), the second and third International Water Color Exhibitions in Chicago (1922, 1923), and the Goupil Gallery in London (1923).

1916

October—the Mackintoshes exhibit a collaborative work—a painted panel and candlesticks entitled *The Voices of the Wood*—with the Arts and Crafts Exhibition Society in London.

December—the Dean of Guild approves designs for the Dug-Out (see plate 199), a basement tea room attached to the Willow Tea Rooms at 217 Sauchiehall Street, Glasgow. Construction begins in February 1917 and is completed in August. (The Dug-Out does not survive.)

1917–19

Mackintosh has only a little new work, which comes mostly from Bassett-Lowke. Designs alterations and interiors for Candida Cottage, Roade, near Northampton, for Bassett-Lowke himself (1918–19); a dining room in Northampton for F. M. Jones (Bassett-Lowke's brother-in-law) (1919); and the redecoration and refurnishing of the guest bedroom at 78 Derngate (second half of 1919; see plate 181). Otherwise there is only alterations work at Little Hedgecourt (see plate 146), near East Grinstead, Sussex, England, for the photographer E. O. Hoppé.

This scarcity of work is not for want of trying. On August 15, 1919, Mackintosh writes to Davidson, "I have a lot of schemes on hand for various people, but all for the future."[16]

1920

January—Mackintosh is asked to design a studio house for the painter Harold Squire at 49 Glebe Place, Chelsea. Building work begins in July and is probably finished in 1921.

February—asked to design a studio house for Arthur Cadogan Blunt (another painter) at 48 Glebe Place and studios for the sculptor Francis Derwent Wood at 50 Glebe Place. Mackintosh works on these during the year, but his designs (see plate 153) are not built.

March—asked to design a block of studios and studio flats for the Arts League of Service (see plate 149), on the site of Cheyne House in Upper Cheyne Row, Chelsea. This is not built.

June—asked to design a theatre in Chelsea for the avant-garde dancer Margaret Morris, also not built (see plate 155).

July 2–29—the Mackintoshes go on vacation at Worth Matravers, Dorset, England. Two important watercolour landscapes—*The Village, Worth Matravers* and *The Downs, Worth Matravers* (both now at Glasgow School of Art)—survive from this holiday.

Probably December—designs a second block of studios for the Arts League of Service, at 48 Glebe Place (see plates 137 and 148), but like that in Upper Cheyne Row, this design goes unrealised. A set of portrait photographs of Mackintosh, taken by E. O. Hoppé, dates from about this time (plate 11).

1921–23

Little evidence of Mackintosh's life survives from this period apart from stray events: Frances Macdonald McNair

11. Mackintosh photographed by his friend E. O. Hoppé, c. 1920.

dies on December 12, 1921; Mackintosh designs bindings for the novels of G. A. Henty for Walter Blackie in 1922; and he exhibits Chelsea studio designs at the Royal Institute of British Architects in December 1922. At some point in 1923 the Mackintoshes take a long holiday in the south of France.

1923–27

The Mackintoshes seem to have stayed on in France in 1923. Such evidence as we have for these years, mainly dated paintings and letters, shows them in different parts of the Roussillon, the southernmost Mediterranean district of France. During this period Mackintosh paints a series of watercolours, of which forty-one survive. They include flower studies and four deliberately naive views of cargo boats, but the majority are landscapes—views of hillsides, rocks, and clustered buildings. Like the two watercolours of July 1920, they are preoccupied with landscape as layers and planes, but in the south of France, Mackintosh is also concerned with pure and brilliant colour.

Mackintosh exhibits still lifes and landscapes at the fourth, fifth, and sixth International Water Color Exhibitions in Chicago (1924, 1925, and 1926) and at the *British Artists Exhibition* in Paris (1927).

1924

January—at Amélie-les-Bains.

April—perhaps at Collioure, an artists' colony favoured by Henri Matisse and others.

1925

February—at Ille-sur-Têt.

July—at Mont Louis.

December 28—at the Hôtel du Commerce, Port Vendres (plate 12), a small working port three kilometres southeast of Collioure. If the Mackintoshes had a settled base in the south of France, it was probably Port Vendres.

1927

May–June—Macdonald is in London for medical treatment. The letters that Mackintosh writes to her during these weeks are almost the only substantial evidence we have, during the course of his life, of his everyday habits, thoughts, and feelings.

Autumn—Mackintosh becomes seriously ill from cancer of the tongue and is taken back to London for hospital treatment.

1928

When Mackintosh comes out of hospital, Macdonald and he rent rooms in Willow Road, Hampstead (a suburb of London), and later move to Porchester Square, Paddington.

Autumn—Mackintosh goes into a nursing home.

December 10—Mackintosh dies.

1928–32

Macdonald lives an unsettled life, staying mainly in hotels in England and France.

1932

December—Macdonald returns to Chelsea, where she dies on January 7, 1933.

12. Postcard of a cargo ship in the harbour at Port Vendres, with the Hôtel du Commerce in the background, c. 1911.

NOTES

The dates given in this chronology for the execution of buildings in Glasgow are, for the most part, based on the Dean of Guild Court's "Reports on Buildings" in the Strathclyde Regional Archives, Mitchell Library, Glasgow City Libraries. Unless otherwise indicated, all locations are in Scotland.

1. Thomas Howarth, *Charles Rennie Mackintosh and the Modern Movement*, 3d ed. (London: Routledge and Kegan Paul, 1990), pp. 3–4. When he was applying to become a fellow of the Royal Institute of British Architects in September 1906, Mackintosh stated that his apprenticeship with Hutchison started in 1883 and his position with Honeyman and Keppie in 1888, but the registers at Glasgow School of Art suggest that he may have misremembered. His occupation in 1883 is not recorded in the registers, but his father's is, as if Charles were not yet in employment; from 1884 to 1888 his occupation is given as "apprentice architect" (reflecting his employment by Hutchison), and from 1888 to 1892 as "architectural draughtsman."

2. Mackintosh was still at 2 Firpark Terrace in late December 1892. See Pamela Robertson, ed., *Charles Rennie Mackintosh: The Architectural Papers* (Wendlebury, England: White Cockade Publishing, 1990), pp. 233–34. Other dates are based on *Post Office Glasgow Directories* and voters' rolls in the Mitchell Library.

3. Various writers—including Thomas Howarth (*Mackintosh*, pp. 61–62)—have wanted to narrow down Mackintosh's share in this design. However, on May 11, 1898, Mackintosh wrote to Hermann Muthesius, "The building in Mitchell Street was designed by me." (A copy of this letter is in the Hunterian Art Gallery, University of Glasgow.)

4. Howarth (*Mackintosh*, p. 25) states that they were "at once christened *The Four*." The earliest documented use of this name, however, appears to have occurred after Mackintosh's death.

5. Responses to their work included: "Clever": *Glasgow Evening News*, November 10, 1894, pp. 1–2; "weird": *Bailie* (Glasgow), November 14, 1894, p. 11; "ghoul-like" and "hideous": *Quiz* (Glasgow), November 15, 1894, p. 13.

6. Howarth, *Mackintosh*, pp. 38–39.

7. Janice Helland, "The Critics and the Arts and Crafts: The Instance of Margaret Macdonald and Charles Rennie Mackintosh," *Art History* 17 (summer 1994): 209–27.

8. Gleeson White, "Some Glasgow Designers and Their Work," part 1, *Studio* 11 (July 1897): 86–100.

9. The principal evidence for this dating is in the Dean of Guild's "Reports on Buildings," but see also Howarth, *Mackintosh*, p. 124, citing the records of Francis Smith, who made the furniture.

10. "Die schottischen Künstler: Margaret Macdonald, Frances Macdonald, Chas. R. Mackintosh, T. Morris und J. Herbert McNair," *Dekorative Kunst* (November 1898): 48–49, with illustrations on pp. 69–76.

11. Howarth (*Mackintosh*, p. 46) says that the completed Mains Street rooms were photographed in March 1900. However, some slight doubt is cast on this by Mackintosh's letter to Hermann Muthesius of July 12, 1900, in which it sounds as though work was still in progress: "I have also been very busy at the work in my own house which I am getting ready." (A copy of this letter is in the Hunterian Art Gallery, University of Glasgow.)

12. For "hobgoblins," see Eduard Sekler, "Mackintosh and Vienna," in *The Anti-Rationalists*, ed. Nikolaus Pevsner and J. M. Richards (London: Architectural Press, 1973), p. 136; "torture chamber": *Neues Wiener Tagblatt*, November 15, 1900. For a selection of negative quotations from reviews, see Werner J. Schweiger, *Wiener Werkstaette: Design in Vienna, 1903–1932* (London: Thames and Hudson, 1984), pp. 246–47 n. 72. Schweiger's evidence, which may be partial, is at odds with the received account that in Vienna, Mackintosh "received unstinted praise, and his work was widely acclaimed by artists and public alike." (Howarth, *Mackintosh*, p. 154.)

13. Hermann Muthesius, "Die Glasgower Kunstbewegung: Charles R. Mackintosh und Margaret Macdonald-Mackintosh," *Dekorative Kunst* (March 1902): 193–221.

14. Fernando Agnoletti, "The Hill-House Helensburgh," *Deutsche Kunst und Dekoration* (March 1905): 337–68.

15. [Fernando Agnoletti], "Ein Mackintosh-Teehaus in Glasgow," *Dekorative Kunst* (April 1905): 257–75.

16. Letter in the Hunterian Art Gallery, University of Glasgow.

Cast of Characters

WENMAN JOSEPH BASSETT-LOWKE (1877–1953)
A manufacturer of engineering models and model railway engines, and a keen Modernist, for whom Mackintosh designed alterations and interior decoration at 78 Derngate, Northampton, England.

WALTER BLACKIE (1860–1953)
A member of the long-established Glasgow publishing firm of Blackie and Son. Mackintosh designed The Hill House, Helensburgh, for him.

KATE CRANSTON (1849–1934)
A Glasgow restaurateur who employed Mackintosh to design several of "Miss Cranston's" famous tea rooms. Though married, she retained her maiden name for business purposes.

WILLIAM DAVIDSON (1861–1945)
A Glasgow provisions merchant and patron of contemporary art, who was Mackintosh's client at Windyhill, Kilmacolm. He was a lifelong champion of Mackintosh's reputation.

THE FOUR
The name given to Frances Macdonald, Margaret Macdonald, Herbert McNair, and Charles Rennie Mackintosh, in reference to their work together during the mid-1890s. It was probably not used until after Mackintosh's death.

PATRICK GEDDES (1854–1932)
An Edinburgh-based intellectual with a special interest in the development of cities, and a friend and admirer of Mackintosh.

JOHN HONEYMAN (1831–1914)
A distinguished late Victorian architect in Glasgow and the senior partner in the firm of Honeyman and Keppie, in which Mackintosh spent most of his professional career.

JOHN KEPPIE (1862–1945)
An architect, and partner in Honeyman and Keppie from 1889. In the early 1890s he collaborated with Mackintosh on a number of buildings; after Mackintosh became a partner in 1901, they worked more independently.

FRANCES MACDONALD (1873–1921)
A painter and decorative artist. In 1899 she married Herbert McNair and began using the name "Frances McNair"; for simplicity she is cited throughout the text of this book as "Frances Macdonald."

MARGARET MACDONALD (1864–1933)
A painter and decorative artist, like her younger sister Frances. After marrying Charles Rennie Mackintosh in 1900 she generally signed herself "Margaret Macdonald Mackintosh," but for simplicity "Margaret Macdonald" is used throughout the text of this book.

JAMES HERBERT MCNAIR (1868–1955)
An architect and decorative artist. His name is often spelled "MacNair," but since he used this form for only a few years around 1900, he is cited as "Herbert McNair" in the text here; he rarely used "James."

13. Francis Newbery (1853–1946). *Charles Rennie Mackintosh,* 1914. Oil on canvas, 43¹/₂ x 24³/₁₆ in. (110.5 x 61.4 cm). Scottish National Portrait Gallery, Edinburgh.

ANNA MUTHESIUS (1870–1961)
A pioneer of progressive and artistic dress. She was married to Hermann Muthesius, and they were both good friends of Mackintosh and Margaret Macdonald.

HERMANN MUTHESIUS (1861–1927)
A German architect employed by the Prussian Board of Trade between 1896 and 1903 to report on British technical and cultural activities, and later a leading advocate of standardisation in design. He publicised Mackintosh's work in Germany.

FRANCIS HERBERT NEWBERY (1855–1946)
A painter and teacher. As headmaster of Glasgow School of Art he did much to encourage the young Mackintosh.

JESSIE NEWBERY (1864–1948)
A decorative artist. She was one of the principal exponents of Glasgow Style embroidery, both in her own work and in her teaching at Glasgow School of Art. In 1889 she married Francis Newbery, and she and her husband were close friends of Mackintosh and Margaret Macdonald.

JAMES SALMON JR. (1873–1924)
A Glasgow architect whose houses and offices designed around 1900 were adventurous in style and sometimes also in construction. He was a friend of Mackintosh.

GEORGE WALTON (1867–1933)
A designer and interior decorator in Glasgow during the 1890s. His interiors were early examples of the Glasgow Style and set the scene for the early interiors by Mackintosh and Margaret Macdonald.

FRITZ WÄRNDORFER (1867–1939)
A Viennese businessman and patron of the arts. He was a keen supporter of the Secession movement, and Mackintosh designed a music room for his house in Vienna in 1902.

I

MACKINTOSH IN CONTEXT

Mackintosh and the City

■■

JULIET KINCHIN

It is curious to note how most of the great triumphs of art have been won in cities, and in cities, too, whose life was oftentimes of the busiest and most complex description. . . . A civic life would seem to knock fire out of men, like the sparks evolved from the contact of flint and steel.[1]

Francis Newbery, 1897

The image of the gigantic, grimy Glasgow has long served as a foil for discussion of Mackintosh as a Romantic genius. It was the city in which he spent his formative years and the most productive part of his career as a professional designer and architect. Before he was even born, Glasgow had already been demonised in the popular imagination as some sort of "Dantean Hell" by authors like Thomas Carlyle, who likened it to "a murky simmering Tophet, of copperas fumes, cotton-fuzz, gin riot, wrath and toil, created by a Demon, governed by a Demon."[2] In a similarly rhetorical vein, Desmond Chapman-Huston, writing in 1910, evoked the urban context of the Mackintoshes' home in Southpark Avenue: "It is far away in that mist-encircled, grim city of the north which is filled with echoes of the terrible screech of the utilitarian, and haunted by the hideous eyes of thousands who make their God of gold. Vulgar ideals, and the triumph of the obvious, are characteristic of the lives of the greater proportion of its population; and yet, in the midst of so much that is incongruous and debasing, we find a little white home, full of quaint and beautiful things, with a big white studio."[3]

The construction of Mackintosh as both a Romantic and a Modernist hero has been achieved at the expense of Glasgow. Crudely summarised, the scenario is as follows. We observe the isolated, tragically misunderstood genius pitched in incessant struggle against "the enemy"[4]—the personification of a monstrous and philistine city seething with greed, filth, corruption, and human abasement. Against the odds, Mackintosh's art triumphs, but his spirit is broken in the process; it is his native city that ignores, represses, and ultimately rejects our hero, driving him to drink, depression, and finally emigration. In this view the city embodies a set of oppressive limitations to be transcended and, at last, abandoned.

14. Sir David Muirhead Bone (1876–1953). *A Shipyard Scene from a Big Crane*, 1917. Lithograph, 18³⁄₁₆ x 14 in. (46.0 x 35.5 cm). Hunterian Art Gallery, University of Glasgow.

The Modernist interpretation of Mackintosh has tended to suppress the relation of his artistic practice to everyday life and to a specific place. His architecture and design are seen to float free somehow of factors such as the distinctive institutional, commercial, and industrial formations of the city, market forces, the local skill base, the social structuring of space, and the specific nature of the Glasgow bourgeoisie. In this view it does not seem relevant that the basic context of a Scottish city was different in detail from its English counterparts, and that geographically, racially, socially, and spiritually Glasgow differed from Scotland's other three cities, despite their shared national history.

These were not issues that Mackintosh or most art critics of the period wanted to talk about. Many, however, were touched on by the maverick Patrick Geddes. This Scottish polymath and social theorist had many friends in Glasgow, among them the Mackintoshes and Newberys. Geddes's vision of the inherent "life force" of cities and of the need to reconcile technological, social, and aesthetic facets of urban living provides a touchstone for this essay. Although admiring the reaction of Carlyle, John Ruskin, and William Morris against the brutalising force of industrial cities, Geddes differed from them in accepting urbanisation and urbanism as both necessary and potentially life enhancing. In this respect his ideas fed off an optimistic, idealising strain evident in Scottish intellectual history since the eighteenth century. Enlightenment thinkers had generally viewed the city as the principal manifestation of progress and civilisation. In the words of David Hume, "Industry, knowledge and humanity, are linked together, by an indissoluble chain" in an economically dynamic city.[5]

Like Hume before him, Geddes felt that "a great new age of cities is preparing,"[6] and while recognising his own limitations as an artist or designer, he worked closely with others to realise his vision of the urban environment. Rather than offering a blueprint for the city of the future, Geddes constantly stressed the need for design to evoke "the social personality" of the community, its regional character, and its unique civic spirit, which had to arise from within. Cities and people were to evolve together.[7] The starting point for the creative renewal of social life was an historical awareness of place, peeling back the layers to make contact with the most ancient traces of settlement. Looking to Germany, Geddes observed, "In the heart of her great modern industrial and commercial centres the antique spirit of her great free cities of the Middle Ages, which had never died away, is again beating with a new life."[8] Significantly, it was to the imposing spiritual presence of Glasgow's medieval cathedral that Mackintosh turned as a student architect in 1890 (plate 15).[9] It was all too easy to forget that Glasgow had been a major medieval city and centre of learning and then, in the eighteenth century, an elegant and vibrant mercantile centre.

Through the discussion of five interrelated themes this essay seeks to demonstrate that Mackintosh's creativity tapped into Glasgow's "life force"

and that the city shaped his design work in complex, sometimes contradictory ways. It can be argued that the tangible form of his architecture and design expressed a distinctive civic consciousness and a sense of cosmopolitan regional identity, while also reflecting the many conflicts and tensions that living in Glasgow entailed. On the one hand, Mackintosh's stylistic assurance and theatrical panache seem in tune with the buoyancy of the city's economy,

15. Charles Rennie Mackintosh. *Glasgow Cathedral*, 1890. Pencil and watercolour, 15 1/2 x 11 3/16 in. (39.3 x 28.4 cm). Hunterian Art Gallery, University of Glasgow.

its internationalism, and its climate of thrusting, competitive individualism. On the other, his work's excessive tension and exaggeration point to an ideology under threat and to the disruptive potential of the prevailing social, economic, and technological forces. Similar creative tensions characterised other great manufacturing centres where the "New Art" (also known as Art Nouveau and National Romanticism) flourished—cities like Turin, Italy; Nancy, France; Chicago; and Brussels. This was the friction implied in Francis Newbery's metaphor of flint on steel.

All great Western cities in the nineteenth century were experiencing change at an unprecedented level, but in Glasgow it was felt in a peculiarly acute way. The urban atmosphere of intensified psychical and visual stimulation could be alternately depressing, threatening, or exhilarating. The impact on the visual and intellectual culture of the city was profound, and Mackintosh was in the thick of it. His work involved incessant interaction with friends, colleagues, officials, clients, retailers, manufacturers, builders, engineers, and artisans. Daily he would negotiate routes through the streets and spaces of the city and its hinterland, observing the incessant change of the city around him.

Glasgow's spectacular growth entailed the constant renewal and extension of the built environment, along with the creation of a physical infrastructure to facilitate the expansion of the city's industrial capitalism. Except for the absence from his oeuvre of urban housing, industrial building, and industrial design, Mackintosh's output (both planned and executed) gives a fair indication of the opportunities Glasgow afforded for someone in his position and of the skills on which he could draw. He produced a steady stream of designs for furniture, metalwork, textiles, and stained glass; schemes for a railway station, concert hall, museum, and shopping arcade; exhibition design, villas, domestic interiors, schools, tea rooms, department stores, offices, and churches. The task he set himself was to clothe "in grace and beauty the new forms and conditions that modern developments of life—social, commercial and religious—insist upon."[10] Place, Work, and Folk—these were the ingredients identified by Geddes as the stuff of "civic life," ingredients that did indeed spark fire from Mackintosh.

INTERNATIONALISM

It is not only the immediate size of the area and the number of persons which . . . has made the metropolis the locale of freedom. It is rather in transcending this visible expanse that any given city becomes the seat of cosmopolitanism. The horizon of the city expands in a manner comparable to the way in which wealth develops. . . . For every thread spinning out of the city ever new threads grow as if by themselves.[11]

Georg Simmel, 1902

To be Scottish was to be European, and to be a middle-class Glaswegian in this period of intensive global capitalism was to participate automatically in a cosmopolitan and imperial culture. The internationalism arising from Glasgow's trade and industry was amplified by cultural reverberations from ancient political alliances with Scandinavia and Europe. As one of the richest cities in the world and as the centre for an immense network of trade and manufacture, Glasgow operated in an international rather than a narrowly Scottish or British context. Against this backdrop it is hardly surprising that Glaswegian artists, designers, and architects did not seem to have the inbuilt resistance to Continental or foreign influence that blinkered many of their English contemporaries. Trying to fathom the influences in George Walton's work for Kate Cranston at Buchanan Street, the English architect Edwin Lutyens exclaimed, "There is tradition of every country and I believe planet! of the universe—yet 'tis all one."[12] Conversely, it was in Europe that Mackintosh's reputation was strongest. While on a town-planning tour of Germany, Geddes remarked: "It is still something of a surprise to the wandering Scot to find 'Mackintosh' almost as accepted a descriptive term in architecture—and this not only in Germany, but from Belgium to Hungary—as in costume in Great Britain. We see his influence in city after city."[13]

Through an advantageous coastal location Glasgow commanded a vast international market, and mental horizons were constantly expanded by the two-way traffic of artefacts and people through the city. The steady stream of colossal ships and locomotives that poured out of the yards along the River Clyde provided a tangible metaphor of the rail and sea network that bound Glasgow into the bigger world picture. The North British Locomotive Company was reputed to be the largest such firm in the world (plate 16), and by

16. North British Locomotive Co., Glasgow. *Catalogue Cover,* 1908. Chromolithograph, 8½ x 11 in. (21.6 x 28.0 cm). From *Pamphlet Descriptive of an Express Passenger Locomotive and Tender Built by North British Locomotive Company, Glasgow, for the Egyptian State Railways,* published for the Franco-British Exhibition, London, 1908. Glasgow Museums.

17. *Advertisement for Brownlee's.* From Alan Woodward, ed., *Scotland's Industrial Souvenir* (Glasgow, c. 1905). Glasgow Museums.

1900 up to half the world's new shipping tonnage (including luxury liners) was "Clyde-built." Glasgow's moving palaces helped to disseminate the reputation of the city's firms both for engineering expertise and for well-made, stylish furnishings all over the world.

A phenomenal range of industrial skills and products, from cast-iron temples for India to carpets for Australia, were being exported from Glasgow at the beginning of the century (plate 18). There was no sense of having to filter either the city's trade or its artistic standards through London. As the Brownlee's advertisement so graphically illustrates (plate 17), connections in the international arena were made direct. (In this particular enterprise timber was being imported and joinery despatched.[14])

The new "scientifically" organised factories that were being built along the Clyde were geared to production levels far exceeding local demand. By 1882, for example, Wylie and Lochhead was churning out a thousand miles of wallpaper every fortnight. Many such firms had branches abroad backed up by a network of agents and buyers throughout Europe, the British Empire, and the Americas. The publishing business run by Mackintosh's client Walter Blackie had branches in England, the United States, India, and Australia, and Blackie himself had been trained partly in Canada. Increasing a share in world markets required aggressive canvassing for sales and staying abreast of political change as well as technological developments abroad.

It was in the economic interest of Glasgow companies, small and large, to participate in the many international exhibitions of the period. On home territory the ethos of voracious imperial expansion was demonstrated in a series of hugely popular and financially successful international exhibitions, in 1888, 1901, and 1911, which showed Glasgow to the world and the world to Glasgow.[15] As a young apprentice architect in 1888, Mackintosh would have been caught up in the spectacle of James Sellars's exotic "Baghdad by the Kelvin" and the sudden influx of visitors and foreign imports to the city. The 1901 exhibition was the largest ever held in Britain (plates 19 and 26). Well over eleven million visitors attended, which was more than double the number at London's Great Exhibition in 1851. Although his designs for the main buildings in 1901 were rejected in favour of James Miller's exotic wedding-cake extravaganza, Mackintosh was involved in various smaller displays. In terms of progressive design the star of the show was undoubtedly the highly coloured Russian Village designed by Fedor Shekhtel (plate 20), who approached Mackintosh to exhibit in Moscow the following year.[16] Such were the cultural spin-offs of a massive investment reflecting the strength of the trading connections between Scotland and Russia.

In the well-established tradition of "the Enterprising Scot" many Glaswegians sought work abroad, whether driven by ambition, evangelism, or economic necessity.[17] A by-product of this diaspora was the swelling of the city

18. *Advertisement for Macfarlane's.* From Alan Woodward, ed., *Scotland's Industrial Souvenir* (Glasgow, c. 1905). Glasgow Museums.

19. General view of Glasgow International Exhibition, 1901, showing Main Exhibition Hall, designed by James Miller (1860–1947). From the official souvenir album.

20. The Russian Village, designed by Fedor Shekhtel (1859–1926), at the Glasgow International Exhibition, 1901. From the official souvenir album.

museum's ethnographic and archaeological collections. An engineering professor teaching in Tokyo, for example, arranged an extensive Glasgow-Japan cultural exchange in 1878.[18] In addition to emigration, independent foreign travel for business, education, or leisure was commonplace within the middle classes. For Mackintosh's friends and associates it was a routine matter to study, work, or take a holiday abroad. On a student scholarship Mackintosh himself could afford an Italian trip in 1891. Later he would oversee exhibitions of his work in Vienna (1900) and Turin (1902), and he was in regular contact with an international coterie by means of letter and telegraph. Before the outbreak of World War I he and Margaret Macdonald had apparently contemplated moving to Vienna, although they finally settled in the south of France. Friends, clients, and admirers from far afield also sought the couple out in Glasgow. By contrast, in the provincial backwater of Walberswick on the east coast of England, Mackintosh's foreign mail was enough to arouse suspicion. Admittedly, war was in progress at the time, but in Glasgow such contacts would hardly have led to his being accused of spying.

Fine and decorative arts from overseas were retailed in Glasgow with entrepreneurial flair. The city was famed for its numerous department stores that developed from the 1830s (plate 21). Alongside these large emporia existed a small network of sophisticated dealers and decorators who had been fostering a cosmopolitan appreciation of Continental and oriental artworks among the city's cognoscenti.[19] Vincent van Gogh's portrait of the dealer Alexander Reid, his only British sitter, provides an eloquent testament to the strength of Glaswegian connections with contemporary artists abroad.[20] From the 1870s, French art of the Barbizon school and Dutch painting from the Hague had figured prominently in collections being formed by wealthy individuals. Such tastes were also encouraged by the opportunity to see and purchase foreign paintings through the Glasgow Institute of the Fine Arts (established 1861), which from the outset encouraged overseas artists to submit work.

Influence from this traffic in European and oriental art was evident in the work of local artists, whose work was often promoted and sold through the same dealer networks. Although the artists' reputation was made largely by exhibitions in London and Germany, the support of local dealers and patrons was vital to the survival of a distinctive "Glasgow school." (Alexander Reid even went so far as to underwrite a trip to Japan by two local artists, George Henry and Edward Atkinson Hornel, in 1893–94.) Reflecting in 1897 on the rise to prominence of the Glasgow school of painters in the 1880s and early 1890s, Newbery commented, "The enterprise of the Fine Art dealer in Glasgow in bringing these pictures to the city was of paramount use and importance, and the young minds could not see without carrying away impressions."[21] Designers, too, were inspired by the exposure to avant-garde tendencies in late-nineteenth-century European art. Musing on the famous George

21. *Advertisement for Pettigrew and Stephens*, Sauchiehall Street, 1901. From the *Glasgow Post-Office Directory*, 1900–1901.

Walton–Mackintosh tea-room interiors, Lutyens could observe, "Whistler is worshipped and Degas tolerated, Rodin . . . admired for the love of oddity."[22]

Over many centuries Glasgow's architecture had developed a strongly European flavour. This tradition was bolstered by links with the Ecole des Beaux-Arts in Paris, where a large proportion of the British students between 1850 and 1890 came from Glasgow. Marked similarities to Canadian and North American cities were also far from coincidental. In addition to trade connections, the pattern of extensive emigration from the west of Scotland over several generations created extended family networks. Leading Glaswegian architects and engineers frequently looked to American models.[23] And with its grid layout, Glasgow qualified as a metropolis in the American or Continental sense. This was in marked contrast to London, which Hermann Muthesius considered "an immense village," unplanned and haphazard.

The mystical symbolism, linear severity, and molten qualities of Continental Art Nouveau evidently appealed to Mackintosh and many of his contemporaries. The Four in particular had no compunction about distorting the "natural" qualities of wood and developed a highly charged Symbolist iconography in their work. Surveying British art schools, the *Studio* magazine picked up on the fact that Glasgow was unusual, if not unique, in employing foreign teaching staff (such as Maurice Greiffenhagen, Eugène Bourdon, and the Belgian Symbolist Jean Delville).[24] One can see why H. F. Jennings talked in 1902 of a "Scotto-Continental 'New Art.'"[25] In constructing reference points for Mackintosh and his Glasgow contemporaries, this seems a more meaningful framework than a "British avant-garde," which lumps them together with the leading lights of the English Arts and Crafts movement, such as M. H. Baillie Scott and C.F.A. Voysey. Although the Scottish and the English designers shared the same desire to break with historical revivalism and at times made use of similar stylistic devices, their cultural backgrounds were very different—a divide recognised at the time. In fact, Scotland was, and is, a very different country from England. Distinctive social structures and institutions survived the union with England in 1707: Scotland still has a different educational system, a different body of law, a different established church, and a different banking system. The society that bred William Morris and his English followers was very different from the one in which Mackintosh operated.

Mackintosh evidently knew and respected his English architecture. He kept in touch with critical debates in the South, and there was a steady flow of eminent English visitors to the city—including C. R. Ashbee, Walter Crane, William Morris, and Voysey—many of whom designed for Glasgow firms and lectured at Glasgow School of Art. From the viewpoint of Glasgow, however, England was in many senses just another component of Europe. Francis Newbery, himself an Englishman, was struck by the open response of his students to all outsiders. "To have been born in Glasgow was neither considered of special merit nor a particular recommendation, nor was the welcome anything the colder because a man, other than a Scotch man, was working in Glasgow, as the result of accident or migration."[26]

COMMERCE AND CULTURE —THE MUNICIPAL VISION

The 1901 International Exhibition demonstrated the assurance and pragmatic dynamism of a municipal vision that united industry, art, and science. At this point Glasgow's economic and cultural progress seemed unstoppable. Physically, the city spread ever outwards, and boroughs at its periphery were enveloped; in the 1891 revision of the municipal boundaries Glasgow had officially mopped up an additional half-million citizens. To keep this colossal organism under control required a highly developed municipal machinery. (Compared to other British cities in this period Glasgow employed a higher than average number of controlling agents such as municipal officials, prison officers, and constables. One of them was Mackintosh's father, a policeman.) These mechanisms of administrative control developed into a world model of "municipal socialism."

This notion of the city-state filled a vacuum in the mental life of the bourgeoisie created by the lack of an aristocracy. One result was that the identity and form of the Glaswegian middle classes were fundamentally bound up with the concept of the city. The industrial and mercantile elite, who exerted political control, literally built their ideology into the city's infrastructure and institutions through a vigorous programme of improving the water supply, sanitation, housing, health, arts provision, and education. On October 24, 1902, the *Times* (London) noted that Glasgow was "more responsible than any other town or city in the UK for the spread of the various forms of municipal progress which have been developed in the new municipalisation."

The tremendous civic pride in such achievements was parallelled by an aggressive display, in public and private, of individual wealth and cultural prowess, following the precedent set by the city's mercantile elite in the eighteenth century. Competitiveness and materialism characterised public acts of philanthropy or involvement in the arts as well as business affairs. The bourgeois ideal in Glasgow contained no perceived conflict between commerce and culture, nor between promoting self-interests and what they saw as the greater good of the community. Like the great merchant princes of the Italian city-states in the Renaissance, Glasgow's elite aimed to excel politically, economically, *and* culturally.

The commissioning of design and craft in both the workplace and the home operated at a largely individual level. Choices in both spheres were generally made on the basis of personal recommendations by family, friends, and associates. Competitive tendering and committee-based decisions did not become the norm until well into the twentieth century. Although a gendered hierarchy prevailed in terms of who bought what, similar networks of design patronage spanned public and private life. This continuity was strengthened by

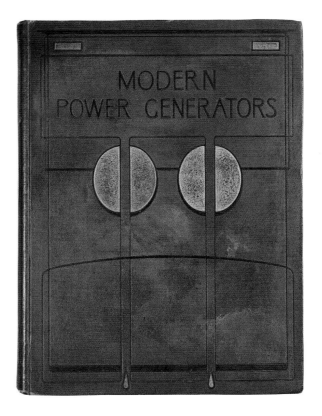

22. Talwin Morris (1865–1911). *Book Cover: "Modern Power Generators,"* 1908. One of two volumes published by the Gresham Publishing Co., a branch of Blackie's. Cloth binding, 13 1/2 x 9 3/4 in. (34.2 x 24.8 cm). Robert Gibbs.

the importance of business-related entertaining at home, which was more pronounced in Glasgow than in a city, like Edinburgh, that was dominated by the professions. Consistency of image and status projected across both spheres was therefore important, as the tastes of Walter Blackie and Kate Cranston illustrate (compare plate 22 with 118 and plate 192 with 173).

Although united by a strong class consciousness and identification with the city, the middle classes in Glasgow were a large and increasingly stratified group, ranging from a spectacularly wealthy elite to a mass of foremen, clerical workers, and shopkeepers and their families. No single style could have satisfied such diverse consumers and incomes, and the highly specialised nature of the city's architectural profession and furnishing industry ensured a wide range of stylistic options from which to choose (compare plates 23 and 47). An increasing variety of retail outlets, both large and small, developed in the vibrant commercial district around Buchanan Street. Colossal furnishing stores coexisted with the numerous craft studios and small firms of artist-decorators that proliferated during the 1890s, stimulated by developments at the School of Art (see plates 43 and 44). A city the size of Glasgow was large enough to absorb, indeed welcome, an occasional loner like Mackintosh, who was able to sustain a reasonable livelihood from the sheer variety of design work on offer. In a revealing letter to Anna Muthesius in 1903, Margaret Macdonald wrote, "We both wish that we could go & live somewhere in the south of England, but the bread-and-butter being here, we cannot."[27]

Relatively few individual patrons employed Mackintosh directly. Nevertheless, the schools and tea rooms he designed were public spaces in which his style exerted an appeal across the full spectrum of the middle classes and to both men and women. This support ultimately outweighed any element of local dissent. Glasgow's "artistic" tea rooms, a peculiarly localised phenomenon (see Alan Crawford, "The Tea Rooms: Art and Domesticity," in this volume), were closely identified with the tenor of life in the city: "It is not the accent of the people, nor the painted houses, nor yet the absence of Highland policemen that makes the Glasgow man in London feel that he is in a foreign town and far from home," remarked "J. H. Muir" in 1901. "It is a simpler matter. The lack of tea shops."[28]

These spaces were renowned for being "homely," and it is significant that so many of them were established and run by women. Most public interiors—such as banks, churches, municipal chambers—were commissioned by groups of men, but Glasgow's tea rooms brought women's artistic patronage and influence out of the domestic realm into the public arena. Kate Cranston was without a doubt Mackintosh's most generous and consistent patron. Her chain of tea rooms was one of the pleasures of the city, where thousands of ordinary people had access to a vision of urban chic, fantasy, and modernity.

Both those who used Mackintosh buildings and those who commissioned work from him clearly felt that his style matched their values and priorities. Even though his work challenged certain codes and conventions, it remained

23. Specimen drawing room, on view at Wylie and Lochhead's showrooms, Buchanan Street, Glasgow, c. 1900. From *Illustrations of Furniture and Interior Decorations* (Glasgow: Wylie and Lochhead Ltd., Manufacturers of Artistic Furniture, Upholsterers and Decorators, 1903), p. 44.

fundamentally connected with bourgeois values and identity in the city. So to what elements of the middle-class mind-set in Glasgow did his aesthetic appeal? What aspects of class consciousness, urban experience, and areas of discrimination did Mackintosh and his associates from the School of Art exploit?

Citizens were proud of Glasgow's economic and cultural apparatus, which functioned independently from national and upper-class power structures. In this respect Mackintosh was certainly in tune with commercial attitudes. No one could accuse him of replicating London or Edinburgh fashions, or of aping aristocratic tastes. On the contrary, he struggled to free himself from the orthodoxies of an architectural establishment that he described as "so smeared and blurred with stupidity—so invaded and dominated by the spirit of dulness [sic]."[29] Without the deadening hand of national institutions—a royal academy, national galleries, museums, and libraries—imposing their cultural authority on artistic activity in the city, it was easier for artists and designers to find their own level in the marketplace. Although not to everyone's taste, Mackintosh's distinctive style clearly appealed to clients of independent, cosmopolitan, and civic-minded outlook, like Cranston and Blackie. His aesthetic assurance matched their commercial competence and confidence. As Newbery observed: "Produced in a city in Scotland, the art of Glasgow is less influenced by metropolitan considerations than is the work of many of the English and provincial towns and cities, and it carries certain local and national imprints which are most interesting in these days of centralisation."[30]

More generally speaking, the popularity of a progressive Glasgow Style (see Daniel Robbins's essay in this volume), from roughly 1890 to 1915, coincided with a prosperous plateau in the city's entrepreneurial culture. With occupations and incomes largely dependent on external market forces, a dynamic, assertive, and competitive spirit was to the fore. In Glasgow's business community people often had to trust their instincts and go out on a limb. For them, the daring qualities of Mackintosh's work must have struck a chord, even if they did not want to live with it all the time (see, for example, plate 160). Conversely, in the period of retrenchment following the First World War (owing to the loss of export markets to competitors like Germany and America and to the delay in adopting new materials and technologies), the progressive image and self-conscious distortions or exaggerations of Mackintosh's work no longer captured the dominant ethos of the city.

The Glasgow bourgeoisie were a precarious, volatile group lacking the old indicators of land and family connections. Their position amidst such a great density of diverse people without shared backgrounds or class made visual indicators of status and difference assume particular importance. This emphasis on individualism and on material culture as a physical expression of economic achievement had been a facet of Glasgow's culture since the Enlightenment. The city's economic prosperity was rooted in control of property, capital, and labour, which in turn lent themselves to dramatic objectification in expenditure on fashionable goods and material possessions.

The idea that Glasgow taste was somewhat vulgar and ostentatious was apparent as early as 1809, when it was remarked that the new rich had "plunged into unlimited extravagance, and made fashion their model in everything—their house, their furniture, their dress, their taste, their opinions."[31] Competitive furnishing of Glasgow houses continued unabated, as noted in 1858: "The sense of vision would seem to be consulted in the decoration of the homes of people at the expense of all other senses, and in this there is growing rivalship . . . in a thriving population where the genius of trade and manufacture was continually creating material wealth."[32] Nearly fifty years later Edwin Lutyens picked up on the same qualities of overstatement and theatricality in his description of a visit to the newly opened Buchanan Street tea rooms in 1897 (see plate 187). He recounted how James Guthrie had taken him "to a Miss Somebody's who is really a Mrs. Somebody else. She has started a large Restaurant, all very elaborately simple on very new school High Art Lines. The result is gorgeous! and a wee bit vulgar! . . . It is all quite good, all just a little outré, a thing we must avoid and shall too."[33] Although appreciative, Lutyens clearly felt more at ease with the qualities of restraint, gentility, and unassuming "good taste" that were widely perceived as characteristic of English design. Hermann Muthesius commented on this essential cultural difference with the observation that the Englishman had no urge to impress; "he even avoids attracting attention to his house by means of extravagant design or architectonic extravagance, just as he would be loth [sic] to appear personally eccentric by wearing a fantastic suit."[34]

The same general drift is apparent in H. F. Jennings's oft-quoted rant against the "Scotto-Continental 'New Art,'" in which he talked of "extravagance bordering on insanity" and "lunatical topsy turvydom."[35] This critical language of instability as applied to Mackintosh's design resonated throughout other areas of bourgeois experience. Glasgow's unrestrained free-market economy was characterised by large-scale capital investment and financial fluctuation. Fortunes were rapidly made and lost (a recurrent theme of the Glasgow novel), and the degree of risk was dramatically illustrated by the notorious bank crash of 1878, in which thousands were ruined. Because of the integrated nature of the economy, any snags in the wider trade cycle had a widespread effect. The note of anxiety this introduced to the general optimism was a unifying element in the middle-class Glaswegian outlook. Mackintosh succeeded in giving physical form to the sense of risk and drama implicit in Glasgow's boom-bust economy.

That economy was interdependent and intensively skill-based. Its backbone—ships, locomotives, heavy engineering, and textile production—connected to numerous smaller ancillary trades. Although operating on a colossal scale, such industries relied upon skilled, labour-intensive specialisation rather

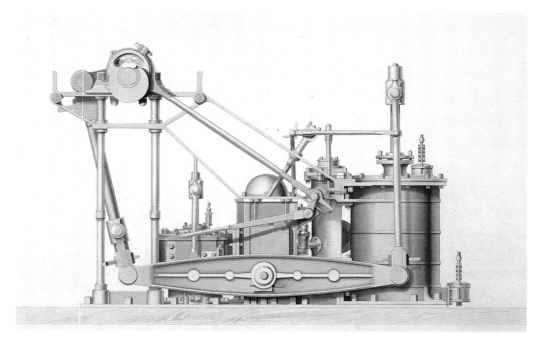

24. Robert Napier and Sons, Glasgow. *Drawing of a Napier Side-Lever Marine Engine for the Paddle Steamer Admiral*, 1840s. Ink and watercolour, 15¾ x 19¹¹/₁₆ in. (40.0 x 50.0 cm). Glasgow Museums.

than standardised mass production. Of particular relevance to Mackintosh was the abundance of people with prototyping skills and the ability to translate drawings quickly into three-dimensional forms. Furthermore, the outfitting of countless ships and trains had ensured the development of a skilled and specialised furnishing industry. Each vessel was a one-off triumph of art, craft, and industry combined. The close-fitting, odd-shaped compartments that had to balance within the hull and withstand movement at sea required high standards of naval engineering and carpentry. Although Mackintosh had little or no involvement with the city's major industries, his practise was locked into the skill base they had created, and the commercial and industrial profile of the city meant that his audience was sensitive to the importance of design.

Design and craft skills were at a premium in Glasgow, applied both to building and enhancing "the City Beautiful" and to supporting a diverse range of industries. In addition to the huge numbers actively involved in meeting this demand, there were a great many people whose livelihoods depended on their ability to discriminate efficiently in matters of design. Styling had selling power, and good design could ensure that artefacts functioned economically and withstood intensive long-term use. The many types of design activity that flourished in the city shared an emphasis on drawing skills and the conceptual development of three-dimensional forms on paper. Mackintosh himself was not a particularly meticulous draughtsman by the standards demonstrated in the exquisite Napier drawing (plate 24). He saw himself very much as an artist but was nevertheless part of a wider community of designers who were daily to be seen clutching drawing materials on the trams and subway, whether bound for work or for classes at the School of Art and the Technical College.

The delicate linear forms and colour washes that characterised technical drawing in the heavy industries were qualities paralleled in the graphic style of the Four and their contemporaries (plate 25). Such echoes reflected close links in the training available for architecture, the fine and decorative arts, engineering, and industrial design. Glasgow had a distinguished and diversified tradition in design education, dating back to the establishment of the Foulis Academy in 1755, which (unlike the Royal Academy in London) placed greater emphasis on design than fine art from the outset. Also preceding developments in England was the establishment of Glasgow's Mechanical Technical Institute in the early nineteenth century. By Mackintosh's time, however, the main educational providers were Glasgow School of Art and Glasgow and West of Scotland Technical College. The latter was more technically oriented than the School of Art, but the two institutions did collaborate on the teaching of common subjects like architecture and furniture design, encouraging the development of a shared sensibility. E. A. Taylor, who had connections with both institutions, was an example of someone who made the transition from working as a draughtsman in a Clyde shipyard to designing furniture, stained glass, and interiors (plate 25 and see plate 48).

25. E. A. Taylor (1874–1951). *Design for a Display Cabinet*, c. 1900. Pencil and watercolour, 7⅝ x 5¹⁵/₁₆ in. (19.5 x 15.0 cm). Glasgow Museums.

26. General view of the Machinery Hall, Glasgow International Exhibition, 1901. From the official souvenir album.

27. George Walton (1867–1933). *Coatstand*, c. 1897. For Miss Cranston's tea rooms, Buchanan Street, Glasgow. Ebonised wood, 72 x 16⅛ x 14⅛ in. (183.0 x 41.0 x 36.0 cm). Glasgow Museums.

As the international exhibitions so powerfully demonstrated, pride in the city's unrivalled feats of engineering (plate 26) was common to all classes. To most Glaswegians the Forth Railway Bridge (completed in 1890) was a marvel and a thing of beauty; to William Morris it was "the supremest specimen of all ugliness."[36] Large-scale industrial items—ships, cranes, and locomotives— were all part of the cityscape and the spectacle of urban living. The river seethed with water-borne traffic, and almost every day newly assembled locomotives would roll through the city to the docks for export. The starkly dramatic, gaunt silhouettes of the cranes (plate 14), which still dominate the Clydeside, would have been imprinted, albeit subliminally, on the imagination of designers like George Walton and their clients (plates 27). Arguably, the value attached to technological progress and industrial skills was expressed metaphorically in the aggressively modern, sleek, and stylised forms of Mackintosh's furniture. Although his choice of materials and construction methods was not technologically innovative, on a visual or more abstract level he alluded to the smooth finish associated with industrial forms, and certain detailing evokes the formal language of engineering (plate 28). Mackintosh did not express his intensified subjectivity through what David Pye has termed "the workmanship of risk," nor did he leave a "handprint" to authenticate his creativity.[37]

The skill and the precision of the engineer were fundamental to the perception of craft in Glasgow, in contrast to the Morrisian craft ideal, which focussed on vernacular and manual traditions. In general, Glaswegians took a rather dim view of the quaint idiosyncracies of handicraft. When 160 Russian carpenters were shipped to Glasgow to construct a village at the 1901 International Exhibition (plate 20), it was not so much their exotic clothes and prodigious vodka intake that amazed the locals as their haphazard working methods. To men familiar with sophisticated machinery and used to working from detailed specifications, all the Russians' axe wielding while smoking and drinking must have seemed unbelievably crude.

Glasgow's industrial wealth was founded on the manipulation of metal rather than wood, and the fabric of the city was characterised by stone, not timber or brick. The surrounding area contained rich resources of iron and coal, whereas the already limited wood stocks in the west of Scotland had been depleted by the rural iron industry in the early nineteenth century. (On his late-eighteenth-century tour through the Western Islands, Dr. Johnson had made various scathing remarks about the dearth of trees, and when his walking stick went missing he was convinced it had been stolen. "Consider, Sir, the value of such a piece of timber here."[38]) A heightened perception of the qualities associated with metal—a material that could be bent, punctured, welded, and moulded with great precision—pervades Glasgow Style furniture and interiors: their streamlined, fluid forms are

28. Charles Rennie Mackintosh. Detail of door jamb, Martyrs' Public School, Glasgow.

29. Charles Rennie Mackintosh. *Writing Desk*, 1901. For Michael Diack. Oak, stained dark, with leaded-glass-and-metal panels and silvered-brass fittings, 47⅝ x 48¾ x 15¾ in. (121.8 x 124.0 x 40.0 cm). George Smith.

offset by knots of tangled decorative detail and by the use of punched motifs and decorative riveting. In particular, the sculptural quality and neutral finishes of furniture by the Four negated the nature of the wood being used (plate 29).

Georg Simmel, an academic in Berlin at the time, was fascinated by the impact of urban living on the mental life of the individual. "Punctuality, calculability, exactness are forced upon life by the complexity and extension of metropolitan existence," he remarked in 1902. "The same factors which have coalesced into the exactness and minute precision of the form of life have coalesced into a structure of the highest impersonality; on the other hand, they have promoted a highly personal subjectivity."[39] Mackintosh's work seems to express both these tendencies in visual, sensual terms. It is difficult, if not impossible, to prove a causal connection between such abstract concepts and style, particularly as such connections would often have been made indirectly and subconsciously. Nevertheless, the suggestion seems reasonable that an artist as sensitive as Mackintosh absorbed, synthesised, and on some level translated into physical form the experiences of urban living and working in Glasgow.

"A Murky Simmering Tophet"

Underlying the bourgeois optimism about continued progress and economic expansion was increasing disquiet at the appalling social consequences of rapid urbanisation. By 1900 Glasgow was one of the most intensely urban environments in the world, with more people living near the heart of their city than in any comparable metropolis. With few planning, environmental, or fiscal constraints, the city's prodigious, unbridled growth had created staggering extremes of wealth and poverty. The American novelist Nathaniel Hawthorne, visiting Glasgow in 1857, was alternately amazed and appalled by the spectacle of the city. His account vividly captures the shocking social and visual dislocations, as well as the evidence of simultaneous growth and decay:

> My wife and I walked out, and saw something of the newer portion of the city; and really I am inclined to think it the stateliest city I ever beheld. The Exchange, the other public buildings and the shops, especially in Buchanan-street, are very magnificent; the latter, especially excelling those of London. . . . Later in the forenoon, we again walked out and went along Argyle-street, and through the Trongate and the Saltmarket. The two latter were formerly the principal business streets, and, with the High-street, the abode of the rich merchants and other great people of the town. The High-street, and still more the Saltmarket, now swarm with the lower orders, to a degree which I never witnessed elsewhere; so that it is difficult to make one's way among the sallow and unclean crowd, and not at all pleasant to breathe in the noisomeness of the atmosphere. The children seem to go unwashed from birth, and perhaps they go on gathering a thicker and thicker coating of dirt until their dying days.[40]

Admittedly, Hawthorne's visit preceded the municipal clean-up programme initiated in the 1860s, but the congestion and deprivation remained a constant even thereafter. This was the darker side of industrial expansion captured in Thomas Annan's haunting photographs of the slums (plate 30). At the bottom of the social scale, wages were low compared to the national average and seasonally erratic. In 1887 Glasgow still had the highest death rate in the

U.K., the highest number of persons per room, and the highest proportion of the population occupying one-apartment homes.[41] This new magnitude of human abasement created tense, easily inflamed relations with labour and an unprecedented rise in crime, pollution, prostitution, and disease. Life-threatening epidemics recurred throughout Mackintosh's time in Glasgow, and the essential fragility of the municipal vision became particularly apparent in 1901, when outbreaks of smallpox and even the bubonic plague threatened to undermine the massive public-relations exercise of the city's great International Exhibition. The spectre of the lower classes—the apparent source of homicidal violence, disease, and moral depravity—loomed large in the middle-class consciousness.

A siege mentality was intensified by the unusually cramped and high-density pattern of building in Glasgow, which meant that different social classes were forced to live cheek-by-jowl. The city's labour force and slums were centrally, inescapably located in the functional heart of the city, which made it difficult to regulate class interaction. This physical proximity of the underclass heightened middle-class anxieties but also bolstered their sense of group identity; their relations with other social groups were perhaps the most significant element in the formation of middle-class values.

In search of greater amenity, the middle classes steadily shifted their homes to developments to the west and south of the centre. Mackintosh's own gradual migration from one end of the city to the other followed this general pattern. Following their marriage in 1900, he and Margaret Macdonald settled in Mains Street near the city centre, where the drizzling greyness, the filth, and the smog all took their toll. Writing to Anna Muthesius in 1903, Macdonald confided: "We in Glasgow have been having a terrible winter. It has been most depressing. For two months we have had the gas lighted nearly the whole of the day—the fog has been so thick and black it is just like night. Day after day—it becomes most depressing & it is so very bad for one's eyes, trying to work always by gaslight. We have been trying to find some place we might go and live, so that we should be out of it next winter."[42] In 1906 they moved to the more salubrious heights of Hillhead in the West End, an area buffered by the university, Kelvingrove Park, and the new Glasgow Art Gallery and Museum, though even here the thudding heartbeat of the city's Clydeside industry could be heard.[43]

Design was a tool with which to combat, psychologically and socially, the forces of fragmentation and alienation that threatened to pull society apart. Art, architecture, and design (in a variety of styles) could be manipulated to reimpose meaning and coherence on the fluid conditions of city life, while also masking its unpalatable aspects. To suppress the level of anxiety and bolster a fragile sense of self, the middle classes invested heavily in objectification of their identity. Mackintosh's designs were not to everyone's taste, but they presented one type of aesthetic solution to the pressures described

30. Close No. 101 High Street, Glasgow. Photographed by Thomas Annan, c. 1868–71.

above. He offered clients a self-contained environment, a visually coherent package that sent out strong messages of individuality and control. References to history, nature, and reality were processed and transformed through his artistic temperament. At the same time the sense of control was achieved by means of reconciling rather than eliminating the many dialectically opposed tendencies in his style: horizontal/vertical, practical/spiritual, serenity/unease, masculine/feminine. All such oppositions were melded within a delicate, holistic balance.

On one level, the white interiors created by Mackintosh and Macdonald can be read as a manifestation of an intensified middle-class obsession with health and self-preservation in Glasgow. Viewed in relation to Mary Douglas's classic definition of dirt as "matter out of place," these interiors made a statement about "matter" being effectively controlled and threatened boundaries being redrawn.[44] The advent of modern environmental controls has made it difficult to re-create the starkness of the contrast between the blackened, smoggy reality of the streets and the Mackintoshes' drawing room in South-park Avenue, described by one visitor in 1905 as "amazingly white and clean-looking. Walls, ceiling and furniture have all the virginal beauty of white satin."[45] To preserve such an oasis of light and calm in a grimy, sooty city was an uphill struggle. Nevertheless the constant physical battle against dirt not only helped keep disease at bay but also provided a material analogy for spiritual and sensual values. Social anthropologists like Douglas have pointed to the correlation between the growth of urban, industrialised societies and an increased sense of "interiority" as well as a heightened awareness of the human body.[46]

Not only the actual filth of the city but also social outsiders (another form of "matter out of place") were kept at arm's length by means of style and taste. Whether confronted by the austerity and airy repose of the Mackintoshes' house or the cushioned opulence of more traditionally historicist interiors (see plates 161 and 23), outsiders were made to feel uncomfortable. Both styles of environment were equally overpowering. Both were exclusive in that they demanded of visitors a knowledge of stylistic conventions (shared with the inhabitants) and a knowledge of whether these conventions were being adhered to, suppressed, or subverted. In the Mackintoshes' interior the uncomfortable forms, impractical colours, and self-conscious use of cheap materials represented an indulgence of more-spiritual values that was possible only in the absence of material need (an example of what Michael Baxandall has termed "selective inhibition" in display).[47] Design helped to choreograph human behaviour, and its impact could produce physiological symptoms, as suggested in the following account of entering an "artistic" household in Glasgow. It was written by the novelist Catherine Carswell, a former student at the University of Glasgow, who would have been familiar with Mackintosh's work:

Even to herself Joanna did not admit how nervous she became in the Lovatts' house. But from the moment the front door closed between her and the street, there was always a tightening of all her nerves. As she passed through the square entrance hall, so unlike any other known to her, with its black-tiled floor, bright blue carpet, and white walls hung with black-framed etchings, her very muscles would stiffen a little with the involuntary effort which these decorations seemed to demand. In the same way the rooms, though they were neither so large as the rooms at Collesie Street, nor nearly so rich as Aunt Georgina's, imposed a peculiar restraint . . .—these were evidences of a world in which Joanna did not yet move easily, a world where the small talk, like the material furnishings, had its own shibboleths of seeming freedom and simplicity.[48]

The "seeming simplicity" of Mackintosh's and Macdonald's interiors was elaborately constructed, and at a price. Although there was no flaunting of expenditure in terms of the materials and labour involved in the production of the furnishings, the overall effect was incredibly labour intensive to maintain. Like other middle-class households, the Mackintoshes were dependent on domestic servants to sustain their environment. Hermann Muthesius clearly saw the impracticality of their style and recognized that most people could not live this way, or would not want to. Even their most enthusiastic supporters found the Mackintoshes' aesthetic hard to accommodate in its entirety for their own homes, which is hardly surprising given the emphasis in the discourse surrounding domesticity on the projection of each owner's individuality and taste.

Glasgow's "New Art" was certainly more difficult to relate to in the context of intimate, one-on-one encounters in the home than in the relative anonymity of public spaces like the tea rooms. The physical proximity to throngs of strangers in the public areas of the city heightened a sense of mental distance and freedom in the individual. This mental freedom was the essence of a truly metropolitan social life, and it was a freedom that Mackintosh's creations enhanced. On many different levels he provided both a critique of and an escape from Carlyle's "murky simmering Tophet."

CITY AND COUNTRY

By 1901 approximately 40 percent of Scotland's population was concentrated in the Clyde Valley. Not surprisingly, the intellectual and cultural power of Glasgow transcended the physical boundaries of the city. The tentacles of its communications network reached into a huge hinterland spread along the Clyde and north into the western Highlands and Islands. Towns in which Mackintosh carried out work—like Kilmacolm, Bowling, and Helensburgh— could easily be commuted to by train or steamer. With family and friends he frequently followed the mass exodus going "doon the watter" in summer.[49]

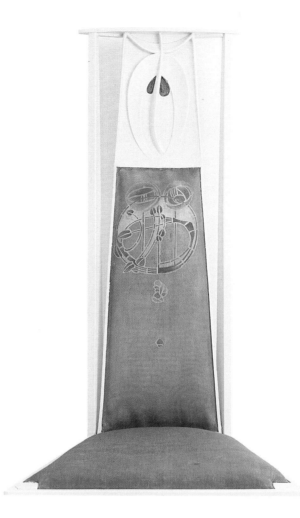

31. Charles Rennie Mackintosh. Detail of stencilled back from *High-Backed Chair*, 1902. Colour wash stencilled on linen. Hunterian Art Gallery, University of Glasgow. See plate 166.

Such ties to the land were emotionally reinforced by the extended family links of those who had migrated to the city. Mackintosh was a case in point, being linked on his father's side to Paisley (and Ireland) and through his mother's family to the town of Ayr on the west coast. All these connections with the Scottish land—economic, emotional, and recreational—formed a significant element of urban thinking.

In some respects, however, the axis with the countryside was fraught with ambivalence. As already noted, Glasgow's population was in constant flux, and most inhabitants were only one or two generations removed from rustic surroundings. Migration from the Highlands in particular fed the expansion of the industrial sector, and the natural drift of the rural population to the city had been intensified by the agricultural depression in Scotland and the Highland Clearances.[50] For many, the move to the city meant freedom from preexisting identities, a new start. As one can see from the local press, country cousins were a standard source of amusement in Glasgow. The upwardly mobile were keen to make evident their sense of difference and their firm identification with the bourgeois ethos of the city. Even while in the country, in their heads they were living in the city. This was the antithesis of cultural attitudes south of the border. As Hermann Muthesius observed, "In England one does not 'live' in the city, one merely stays there."[51] The last thing most Glaswegians wanted was to mobilise associations of rural living through the houses, clothes, and other possessions they chose. References to the country and to vernacular traditions were important but needed to be filtered through urban perception. In this sense the New Art would have struck a chord, in that it presented nature processed for the urban palate, with all folksiness and rough edges removed (plate 31).

For cities of Glasgow's scale and complexity Geddes coined the term *conurbation* to convey the idea of a city that embraced an entire region. It expressed a new, synoptic view of the city, which brought together the previously polarised and distinct concepts of town and country. In a conurbation these elements formed a single organism that, to remain healthy, had to coexist in interdependent balance. The provision of public parks (more than in any other British city) encouraged nature to penetrate right into Glasgow, providing a necessary "lung" and recreational space for its inhabitants. On a clear day the hills to the north, snowcapped in winter, were visible from Glasgow, testifying to the closeness of this life-giving relationship. Since 1856 a municipal water supply, so vital to health and well-being, had been piped in directly from Loch Katrine in the Trossachs.

Organicism, synthesis, and balance—features central to the concept of conurbation—were principles that also informed the Glasgow Style. Mackintosh's designs echoed Geddes's views in microcosm, blending the urban and the "natural." They expressed a psychological identification with the city while also drawing on a wide range of organic imagery and symbolism. The regenerative, sensual power of nature offered an antidote both to the drab and deadening world of work and to the tired historicism of mainstream taste. For Mackintosh, entering good Modern architecture was "like an escape into the mountain air from the stagnant vapours of a morass."[52] The conventionalised abstraction of natural forms was an important feature of the design curriculum at Glasgow School of Art, which followed the South Kensington model. Students were also encouraged to "Go to Nature" directly, drawing plant life in the school and sketching outdoors (see plate 211).[53] Some, like Jessie M. King and E. A. Taylor, would spend the summer on the Isle of Arran, a popular artists' haunt. In such designers' work (see plate 47), distinctive colours were distilled from the magnificent scenery around Glasgow—the heathery purples, misty greys, muted pinks and greens—but used to express mystical harmonies rather than to portray the countryside as a place where a rural population lived and worked. This urban view of nature was in marked contrast to the cottagey celebration of rural life and vernacular skills embraced by many members of the English Arts and Crafts movement. To Morris and his followers, the establishment of craft communities in idyllic English villages like Chipping Campden offered a retreat from the corruption of the city.

Rural life in Scotland was a rather different matter. Glasgow was within easy reach of sublime expanses of nature, but these had little to do with pretty villages, bosky dells, and window boxes. Both the climate and the whole pattern of agriculture were unlike those in England. This was an era of agricultural depression, continued Clearances, land-reform agitation, and mass emigrations. Vast tracts in the west of Scotland in the late nineteenth century were characterised by large estates running sheep and deer, sparsely interspersed with crofting communities. The crofting system was not just small-scale farming but a unique way of life that had been threatened by the brutal dispossessions and forced emigrations of the Clearances (plate 32). Many of those evicted Highlanders who were not packed onto ships bound for Canada, America, or Australia converged on Glasgow. The "Crofting Wars"—bitter confrontations between the dispossessed and the landowners, which came to a head in the 1880s and prompted military intervention—were given prominent news coverage in Scotland. The bitterness and trauma of this episode in Scottish history, and the general severity of the nineteenth-century agricultural depression, were not easily forgotten. All this made it difficult in the context of Glasgow to adopt a romanticised rural life into city homes. The "Kailyard" strand of Scottish fiction tended to emphasise the hardship and even misery of life on the land, while demonstrating the purity of spirit and moral fibre of those who struggled to get by.[54] The cabbage patch in Kailyard fiction and in paintings by the Glasgow school stands in sharp contrast to the sweetly pretty hollyhocks that surround the cottage doors in paintings such as Helen Allingham's evocative images of the English village.

The evocation of cosy cottage interiors was also inappropriate in terms of most Glasgow housing. Unlike English city dwellers, the majority of Glaswegians, of all classes, were literally separated from the land by virtue of living in tenemented dwellings. (Mackintosh himself was born in a third-floor home.) This pattern was the European norm, whereas England's terraced and semidetached housing was the exception, as Hermann Muthesius was quick to point out.[55]

32. Little North Uist evictions, 1895.

Despite the strong strain of Arts and Crafts ideology in the teaching at Glasgow School of Art, its graduates and teachers made few attempts to flee city life for good. For the most part, Glasgow-trained designers like Mackintosh continued to live and work in the city, even though repelled by its squalid aspects. The Scottish Guild of Handicraft was an interesting but isolated and short-lived attempt to emulate C. R. Ashbee's enterprise in Scotland. As a cooperative it offered an alternative lifestyle and model of production, while also challenging the political status quo through its members' involvement with the new Independent Labour Party in Scotland. Mackintosh shunned such affiliations, and in keeping with the markedly "individualistic art training" he had received at Glasgow School of Art,[56] he exhorted his fellow art workers to look inwards and get on with doing their own thing. "You must be Independent, Independent, Independent—don't talk so much but do more—go your own way and let your

neighbour go his. . . . Shake off all the props—the props tradition and authority give you—and go alone—crawl—stumble—stagger—but go alone."[57]

THE SPIRITUAL CITY

Protestantism, with all its complex Scottish ramifications, was such an integral part of Glasgow's culture and history as to be inescapable, even for those not preoccupied with religion. The figure of John Knox, crowning the Necropolis next to the medieval cathedral, was as important a feature of the Glasgow skyline as the cranes looming over the Clyde. The spectacular Necropolis, established in 1836, expressed the visual and metaphorical dominance of the Church of Scotland and its adherents—Glasgow's Great and Good—who inhabited this city of the dead. This was a sight that was framed by the view from the tenement in which Mackintosh grew up (plate 33).

33. View from the Glasgow Necropolis, looking down towards the tenement where Mackintosh grew up. Photographed by Edwin Smith, 1954.

Although Glasgow also had a large Catholic community, it was largely composed of recent immigrant Irish or Highland workers who lacked the wealth and political clout necessary to impinge on the world of the New Art. The association of Celtic culture with Ireland, and hence Catholicism, was therefore socially problematic, which could explain why the Celtic revival, with its range of suitably sinuous forms, was not more evident in Glasgow designs, but remained centred on Edinburgh, where the Celtic connection was not so socially problematic.[58]

The artistic expression of something as vague as "religious temperament" is obviously difficult to analyse, but tags such as "puritan" and "spiritual" were used both by the designers themselves and by contemporary observers. Hermann Muthesius remarked on the peculiarly Scottish "blend of the puritan and romantic,"[59] and Mackintosh himself spoke of the need to respond to the "religious pressures of modern life," to express "the etherial, indefinable side of art."[60] George Logan, an active member of the Salvation Army, also described his decorative-art work in spiritual terms and incorporated angels, cherubs, and fairies in his designs at every available opportunity.[61] His friend Jessie M. King, a minister's daughter, believed that she was in touch with the "little people."[62]

In common with other European centres in the late nineteenth century, Glasgow had an active Spiritualist Church and Theosophical Society, which interested many artists and designers.[63] One senses a tangle of associations linked to the ornament and forms of the Glasgow Style, ranging from faint subconscious allusion to the full-blown symbolism that earned the early work of the Four its nickname, "the Spook School." (Recent studies have begun to unravel a range of potential readings of this personal and mystical symbolism.[64]) The drooping plant forms and emaciated figures are half-dead; the willowy, waistless female figures evoke an inspirational rather than a maternal, life-bearing role of women; and the soaring, attenuated verticals, the muted secondary colours, and the airy tones all reinforce the ethereal, other-worldly aspects of the style. Physical comfort and material well-being come low on the list of the Four's priorities.

In his book *The Evolution of Sex* (1889) Patrick Geddes presented companionable love and cooperation as the highest manifestations of the evolutionary process. The principle of "equal but different," of gendered opposites integrated to form a unity of impression, was also central to Theosophical thought. W. B. Yeats, a committed Theosophist, felt that society was entering one of those rare periods characterised by unity of spiritual and material existence and by the interpenetration of the sexes, which would find expression in a bisexual art that had the perfection of each partner without voiding the identity of the other.[65] He could almost have been talking about the interiors of 78 Southpark Avenue, in which the Mackintoshes created a circuitous journey of the imagination, aestheticising the daily round of activities within their home in a series of visual and tactile experiences representing different facets of a spiritual transformation. The inhabitants would move between the dark nether regions of the "masculine" preserve (the ground-floor hall and dining room) and the heightened spirituality and lightness of the "feminine" rooms above. Physically and metaphorically, they would ascend through the house into increasingly intimate spaces, ever more removed from the outer world. There is the sense of a steady casting off of vulgar sensation and the debris of the phenomenological world, starting with the symbolic divesting of outer garments in the transitional space of the hallway, and culminating in the unclothed intimacy of the white bedroom above.[66] Ultimately even this extreme expression of interiority can be seen as a response to the city, a withdrawal fostered by the intensity of social change and the pressures of urban life.

The appreciation, commissioning, design, and production of objects are all shaped by the culture in which people live, and only by first exploring the city of Glasgow can one appreciate the genesis and the truly innovative aspects of Mackintosh's style. Images, associations, accumulated memories—the very culture of a city—were being constantly interpreted and recycled around him and through his work. The problems of tracking and conclusively defining these elements are formidable, but nonetheless little doubt can remain that Mackintosh and his audience responded to shared patterns of meaning, patterns that resonated through their sensory, emotional, and aesthetic experience.

NOTES

1. Introduction to David Martin, *The Glasgow School of Painting* (London: George Bell and Son, 1897), p. xiv.

2. Carlyle, in James Pagan, *Sketches of the History of Glasgow* (Glasgow: Stuart, 1847), p. 105.

3. Desmond Mountjoy [Desmond Chapman-Huston], *A Creel of Peat: Stray Papers* (London: Adelphi Press, 1910), p. 5.

4. "It is gratifying to defy a powerful enemy, and that is why Mackintosh is happy to work in Glasgow." ("Ein Mackintosh-Teehaus in Glasgow," *Dekorative Kunst* [April 1905]: 258.)

5. David Hume, "On Refinement in the Arts," in Hume, *Essays Moral, Political and Literary* (1741–42; Oxford: Oxford University Press, 1963), p. 278.

6. Patrick Geddes, *Cities in Evolution* (1915; London: Ernest Benn, 1968), p. 277.

7. Ibid., chaps. 17–18, passim (pp. 363, 392).

8. Ibid., p. 175.

9. There was a tremendous upsurge of interest in the cathedral during the late nineteenth century, stimulated in part by Walter Scott's Romantic description of it in his novel *Rob Roy* (1818). One of the leading figures in the campaign to conserve the cathedral was John Honeyman, with whom Mackintosh was working from 1889. In 1888 Mackintosh sketched the cathedral chapter house, and his design for a chapter house was awarded a gold medal in the South Kensington competition of 1892.

10. Charles Rennie Mackintosh, "Seemliness (1902)," in Pamela Robertson, ed., *Charles Rennie Mackintosh: The Architectural Papers* (Wendlebury, England: White Cockade Publishing, 1990), p. 222.

11. Georg Simmel, "Die Grosstadte und das Geistesleben," in Simmel, *Die Grosstadte: Vortrage und Aufsatze zur Stadteaustellung* (Dresden, Germany, 1902); extract reprinted in *Art in Theory, 1900–1990*, ed. Charles Harrison and Paul Wood (Oxford: Blackwell Publishers, 1992), p. 133.

12. Edwin Lutyens to Emily Lutyens, June 1, 1898, *The Letters of Edwin Lutyens to His Wife Lady Emily*, ed. Clayre Percy and Jane Ridley (London: Collins, 1985), p. 57.

13. Geddes, *Cities in Evolution*, p. 186.

14. For centuries timber had been imported to Glasgow from Scandinavia, the Baltic, and North America. Brownlee's, started in 1849, was the largest and most suc-cessful of the city's timber merchants. They profited from the early application of the available technology—planing machines, circular and band saws—and they went on to establish a hugely successful chain of timber merchants in the United States.

15. For a fuller account of these events, see Perilla Kinchin and Juliet Kinchin, *Glasgow's Great Exhibitions: 1888, 1901, 1911, 1938, 1988* (Wendlebury, England: White Cockade Publishing, 1988).

16. See Catherine Cooke, "Fedor Osipovich Shekhtel," *AA Files* (Architectural Association School of Architecture), no. 5 (January 1984): 4–8.

17. See Jenni Calder, ed., *The Enterprising Scot: Scottish Adventure and Achievement* (Edinburgh: Royal Museum of Scotland, 1986).

18. See Antonia Lovelace, *Art for Industry: The Glasgow-Japan Exchange of 1878* (Glasgow: Glasgow Museums, 1991); and Olive Checkland, *Britain's Encounter with Meiji Japan, 1868–1912* (Edinburgh: Macmillan, 1989).

19. For a general survey of industrialist collectors and dealers, see Elizabeth Cumming, "Industry and Art," in *Glasgow 1900: Art and Design* (Amsterdam: Van Gogh Museum, 1992), pp. 9–14; also Frances Fowle, "The Hague School and the Scots: A Taste for Dutch Pictures," *Apollo* 134 (August 1991): 108–11.

20. See Ronald Pickvance, *A Man of Influence: Alexander Reid, 1854–1928* (Edinburgh: Scottish Arts Council, 1968).

21. Newbery, in Martin, *Glasgow School of Painting*, p. xxii.

22. Edwin to Emily, June 1, 1898, *Letters of Edwin Lutyens to His Wife*, p. 57.

23. John James Burnet, for example, worked with McKim, Mead and White; Donald Matheson made a study tour of the States in 1903 to research the remodelling of Glasgow's Central Station.

24. *Studio Yearbook of Decorative Art* 30 (1904):111.

25. H. F. Jennings, *Our Homes and How to Beautify Them* (London: Harrison and Sons, 1902), p. 61.

26. Newbery, in Martin, *Glasgow School of Painting*, p. xxi.

27. Margaret Macdonald to Anna Muthesius, 1903, private collection.

28. "James Hamilton Muir," in *Glasgow in 1901* (Glasgow and Edinburgh, 1901), p. 176.

29. Mackintosh, "Seemliness (1902)," p. 222.

30. "Some Work by the Students of the Glasgow School of Art," *Studio* 19 (May 1900): 233.

31. L. Smith, *Northern Sketches or Characteristics of Glasgow* (Glasgow, 1809), p. 153.

32. *Illustrated Railway Guide Edinburgh-Glasgow* (Glasgow, 1858), p. 328.

33. Edwin to Emily, June 17, 1897, *Letters of Edwin Lutyens to His Wife*, p. 50.

34. Hermann Muthesius, *The English House*, 3 vols., trans. Janet Seligman and ed., with an introduction by, Dennis Sharp (London: Crosby Lockwood Staples, 1979), p. 10. Originally published as *Das englische Haus* (Berlin: Wasmuth, 1904, 1905).

35. Jennings, *Our Homes and How to Beautify Them*, p. 61.

36. "There never will be an architecture in iron, every improvement in machinery being uglier and uglier, until they reach the supremest specimen of all ugliness—the Forth Bridge." (William Morris, 1889; in Thomas Mackay, *The Life of Sir John Fowler, Engineer, Bart.. K.C.M.G., etc.* [London, 1900], chap. 11, "The Forth Bridge.")

37. For a fuller discussion of the "workmanship of risk," see David Pye, *The Nature and Art of Workmanship* (Cambridge: Cambridge University Press, 1968), pp. 4–9.

38. *Johnson's Journey to the Western Islands of Scotland and Boswell's Journal of a Tour to the Hebrides with Samuel Johnson, LL.D*, ed. R. W. Chapman (1785; London: Oxford University Press, 1924), p. 375.

39. Simmel, "Die Grosstadte und das Geistesleben," pp. 131–32.

40. *The English Notebooks of Nathaniel Hawthorne*, ed. Randall Stewart, General Series, no. 13 (1941; New York and London: Modern Language Association of America, 1962), p. 512.

41. J. B. Russell, "The House in Relation to Public Health," *Transactions of the Insurance and Actuarial Society of Glasgow*, 2d ser., no. 5 (1887): 11.

42. Margaret Macdonald to Anna Muthesius, 1903, private collection.

43. See Catherine Carswell, *Open the Door!* (London: Chatto and Windus, 1920), p. 87: "From here she overlooked the whole park. . . . It was a little world to itself, shut in and stuporose. But beyond it to the south . . . Joanna could see where the real world began. Nay she could hear, coming from the Clyde across all that distance yet as if it were the beating of her own heart, the dull steady pounding of the yards."

44. See Mary Douglas, *Purity and Danger: An Analysis of the Concepts of Purity and

Taboo (London: Routledge and Kegan Paul, 1966).

45. E. Kalas, "The Art of Glasgow" (1905); reprinted in the Mackintosh memorial exhibition catalogue (Glasgow: McLellan Galleries, 1933), p. 3.

46. This theme is taken up by David Brett in his book *C. R. Mackintosh: The Poetics of Workmanship* (London: Reaktion Books, 1992), chap. 4. In Carswell's novel *Open the Door!* Joanna (a student at Glasgow School of Art) is described as "a fugitive from the realities immediately surrounding her town existence, and her intenser life was lived in her flights" (p. 31); "In town Joanna led almost wholly a dream life. The indoor life" (p. 38).

47. Michael Baxandall, *Painting and Experience in Fifteenth-Century Italy* (Oxford: Oxford University Press, 1972).

48. Carswell, *Open the Door!* p. 164.

49. Rare photographs in Glasgow School of Art show the self-titled "Immortals," an art-school group of which Mackintosh and the Macdonalds were part, larking around in parts of Ayrshire, where John Keppie had various houses (see plate 54). Likewise, the Macdonalds' parents took over Dunglass Castle in Bowling from Blackie's chief designer, Talwin Morris.

50. "Clearances" refers to a widespread policy in the Highlands of Scotland during the early to late nineteenth century whereby landlords forcibly evicted tenant crofters from the land to replace them with more profitable sheep. This systematic destruction of a traditional form of land tenure and agriculture led to mass emigration.

51. Muthesius, *English House,* p. 7. As John Cockburn put it in his novel *The Tenement* (Edinburgh, 1925), p. xv: "Despite its size and pretensions, Glasgow cannot escape the fact that its citizens, if not lately, then in the beginning, were drawn from rustic surroundings."

52. Mackintosh, "Seemliness (1902)," p. 222.

53. Ruskin's exhortation "Go to Nature" was reiterated by many Arts and Crafts designers such as Voysey.

54. *Kailyard,* which can be translated as either "cabbage patch" or "kitchen garden," is a pejorative term applied to a genre of Scottish fiction popularised in the late nineteenth century through the novels of J. M. Barrie and Ian Maclaren (whose novel *Behind the Bonnie Briar Bush* is the original source of the term).

55. Muthesius, *English House,* pp. 8–9, 144.

56. J. Taylor, "The Glasgow School of Art," in *Arts and Crafts: A Review of Work Executed by Students in the Leading Art Schools of Great Britain and Ireland,* ed. C. Holme (London: Studio Publications, 1916), pp. 124–25.

57. Mackintosh, "Seemliness (1902)," p. 223.

58. Mackintosh cannot have failed to be aware of strained Catholic-Protestant relations. The Catholic "Celtic" football club was established in 1887, and the regular Saturday afternoon matches against the Protestant "Rangers" provided a ritual enactment of hostility between the factions that each team represented. The simmering violence erupted at the 1909 Scottish Cup Final in Glasgow, when supporters from both sides invaded the pitch, set pay boxes on fire, broke gaslights, and threw stones at the police and firemen.

59. Hermann Muthesius, "Die Glasgower Kunstbewegung: Charles R. Mackintosh und Margaret Macdonald-Mackintosh," *Dekorative Kunst* (March 1902): 193–221.

60. Mackintosh, "Seemliness (1902)," p. 223.

61. George Logan, "A Colour Symphony," *Studio* 36 (November 1905): 118.

62. For a fuller account of her work, see Colin White, *The Fairy Tale World of Jessie M. King* (Edinburgh: Canongate, 1989); and Jude Burkhauser, ed., *"Glasgow Girls": Women in Art and Design, 1880–1920* (Edinburgh: Canongate, 1990).

63. Maurice Maeterlinck was particularly influential in this respect. Also, Jean Delville (the Belgian Symbolist artist who taught at Glasgow School of Art from about 1901 to 1907) was deeply interested in Theosophy, as demonstrated in his book *The New Mission of Art.* According to Clifford Bax, who wrote the introduction to the English translation of 1910, many of Delville's Glasgow pupils followed him when he returned to Brussels. The Theosophical Society in Glasgow had five branches during the 1890s.

64. See Janice Helland, "The 'New Woman' in *Fin-de-Siècle* Art: Frances and Margaret Macdonald" (Ph.D. diss., University of Victoria, Canada, 1991); Burkhauser, ed., *"Glasgow Girls"*; Brett, *C. R. Mackintosh*; and Timothy Neat, *Part Seen, Part Imagined: Meaning and Symbolism in the Work of Charles Rennie Mackintosh and Margaret Macdonald* (Edinburgh: Canongate, 1994).

65. See W. B. Yeats, *A Vision* (London: MacMillan, 1937); and Jan Gordon, "Decadent Spaces: Notes for a Phenomenology of the Fin de Siècle," in Ian Fletcher, ed., *Decadence and the 1890s* (London: Edward Arnold, 1979).

66. See Juliet Kinchin, "The Gendered Interior: Essays in Nineteenth-Century Taste," in *The Gendered Object,* ed. Pat Kirkham (Manchester, England: Manchester University Press, 1996), forthcoming.

Glasgow School of Art and the Glasgow Style

■■

DANIEL ROBBINS

One of the characteristics of this end of the nineteenth century is a speciality for rough and ready classification, and it is even applied—or rather misapplied—to things artistic. A favourite instance of this is to take the whole of those virile workers whose natal genesis happened north of the Tweed and bunch them up as "the Glasgow School." Lavery and Guthrie the painters; George Walton, the decorative designer; Craig Annan, the photographer; D. Y. Cameron, the etcher; the Misses Macdonald, metal; and Oscar Paterson and Harry Thomson, the glass workers.

W. J. Warren, *Amateur Photographer,*
August 11, 1899.[1]

W. J. Warren would be dismayed that almost a century later his "virile workers" continue to be subject to this unfortunate tendency. The intervening years have seen some modifications. An evaluation now of progressive art and design in turn-of-the-century Glasgow would categorise the "Glasgow Style" as a subheading that distinguishes the city's designers from the Glasgow school of painters who had flourished a decade before. Almost inevitably, the name of Charles Rennie Mackintosh would be placed firmly at the head of this subcategory. In fact, the Glasgow Style is increasingly defined by the extent to which an object, a graphic, or an interior comes close to Mackintosh's own output. The more it looks like Mackintosh, the more authentically in the Glasgow Style it seems to be. The perception has been created that during this period no designer or decorative artist emerged from Glasgow School of Art without directly or indirectly coming under his influence. As the notion of a unified Mackintosh-centred movement has grown, a sense of the environment that helped shape it has diminished. The Glasgow Style has become removed from the context of a city and a School of Art that were bursting with a rich variety of design activity.

Surveying the school's submissions to the national competition, held under the South Kensington system,[2] gives an immediate sense of how limited a role the Glasgow Style played in relation to the school's total output. Prior to 1901, when the school's funding was transferred to the Scottish Education

34. Margaret Macdonald (1864–1933). *Invitation Card for a Glasgow School of Art Club "At Home,"* 1893. Line block, 5¼ x 6⅛ in. (13.1 x 15.6 cm). Hunterian Art Gallery, University of Glasgow.

35. Joseph M. Sadler (Glasgow School of Art student, dates unknown). *Design for Axminster Carpet,* 1896–97. From *An Illustrated Record of National Gold, Silver and Bronze Medal Designs, Model Drawings etc.,* edited and compiled by John Fisher (London: Chapman and Hall, 1899), p. 9.

Department, success in this annual competition was crucial to the school's prospects, for the number of awards gained by an institution directly influenced the size of the government grant it received the following year. The 1890s witnessed a dramatic increase in the number of prizes awarded to Glasgow School of Art. Just 21 were given at the beginning of the decade; by 1898 this figure had risen to 121, the first of three consecutive years when the school won the highest number of awards in Britain.[3] Yet this preeminence was not won through the efforts of Glasgow Style designers; in fact, their names are barely represented amongst the winners of the almost six hundred major awards given to the school during the decade. The motifs and idiosyncracies of the new style may have become common currency within the school by the end of the century, but the judges' reports do not reflect this. The very few illustrations that survive of prize-winning work from this period also indicate that for most of the students passing through the school and returning to employment in the city, the Glasgow Style was of limited significance and only peripheral to their concerns (plate 35).

Exploring the relationship between the Glasgow Style and Glasgow School of Art reveals that the style was a more limited and fleeting phenomenon than its association with Mackintosh has led us to believe. And it also makes clear that even though Mackintosh was central to the creation of the striking and original visual language that distinguished the Glasgow Style, he did so only in close association with the other members of the group that has become known as the Four: his friend Herbert McNair and the Macdonald sisters, Frances and Margaret. Mackintosh had only an incidental involvement in the emergence of the Glasgow Style, whereas circumstances within Glasgow School of Art during the 1890s were crucial to the style's formation and development. The school's headmaster from 1885 to 1917, Francis Newbery (plate 36), was instrumental in creating these circumstances and, subsequently, in consolidating and perpetuating the Glasgow Style.

The emergence of the style coincided with the growing prominence of Glasgow School of Art as one of the leading institutions for art instruction in Britain. It was a position achieved, to a significant degree, through Newbery's efforts. His qualities have been well documented: his energy, ambition, and determination; his commitment to design teaching; and above all his enthusiastic encouragement of individuality were key to creating a sympathetic and stimulating environment.[4] By 1901, in an article reporting the school's recent achievements, the *Glasgow Herald* noted the advances that had been made in the sixteen years since Newbery's appointment. The government grant and the school's expenditure on salaries had both almost doubled.[5] The teaching staff had increased from just eight full-time staff in 1885 to forty-seven part- and full-time staff in 1900—sixteen of whom were teaching in the decorative arts.[6]

This exciting period in the school's history culminated in the completion of the first phase of Mackintosh's new building and the school's release from the watchful eye of South Kensington. From this point forward, as was acknowledged in 1899 by Thomas Armstrong (the recently retired director for art at South Kensington), the school was trying "to eat [its] cake and have it."[7] Accompanying this growing independence must have been a heightened sense of the school's identity as an institution, which in turn would have provided fertile ground for the development of a visual language that could stimulate a sense of individuality within a common vocabulary.

THE GLASGOW SCHOOL OF ART CLUB

One of Newbery's earliest initiatives provided the platform on which just such a language could emerge. The Glasgow School of Art Club was established in 1889, with membership confined to past and present students (plate 34). Monthly competitions, with prizes awarded by Newbery, ran throughout the school year, but the annual exhibition held each autumn became the focus of the club's activities. The annual exhibition contained work completed during the summer vacation, which complemented the students' curriculum-led work. Individuality was particularly encouraged.

36. Francis Newbery, headmaster of Glasgow School of Art, 1885–1917. Photographed c. 1885.

By 1900 these exhibitions were receiving national press attention, and the reviews in publications such as the *Studio* provide a revealing picture of the emerging style. Between 1889 and 1893 the shows passed without particular comment, a situation that changed the following year with the first presentation of work by the Four. Exactly which works were shown is unknown, but the local press was struck by the extraordinary "nightmare" quality characterised by the works' peculiar distortion of human form (see plate 57).[8] The 1894 prizes were awarded by the Glasgow painter Alexander Roche, who wondered quite where these "graveyard" works were proceeding. His comments provoked a strong response from Newbery: "Mr. Newbery adverting to the remarks of Mr. Roche said that he had rather encouraged what Mr. Roche so vigorously condemned" and continued that "as to the style of design condemned . . . it might lead to the graveyard, but he believed it would lead to somewhere else in the first place."[9] It led, in fact, to a number of students finding inspiration in the strange linearity, the stylised organic motifs, and the seductive, ethereal quality evident in the earliest work of the Four, and ultimately it led to the development of a recognisable Glasgow Style vocabulary.

Nature was its principal source. Birds in flight, insects, and particularly butterflies were common. Flowers and especially the rose (the motif most associated with the style) were also found in the work produced at the school. The use of a distinctive palette—particularly of purples, greens, and pinks—was most evident within the needlework department at the School of Art. Above all, the Glasgow Style was characterised by the linear stylisation of these essentially unremarkable motifs. The excessive curvaceousness of Continental Art Nouveau was avoided in favour of a tighter, sparer, and more controlled linearity. Newbery's wife, Jessie Newbery, who taught needlework at the school, acknowledged this in describing her enthusiasm for "the opposition of straight lines to curved; of horizontal to vertical."[10] In the most effective Glasgow Style work, these elements came together with highly original results. As W. Fred stated in 1902: "The atmosphere of the works is severe, clear, serious, rigid; the choice of materials as well as motifs is a bit puritanical. In addition . . . there is a strange thinness of lines that almost dissolve into a chain of dots."[11]

The uncompromising stylisation of human form that stimulated such a strong response in 1894 was not taken up as a common theme at the school, remaining a concern of the Four alone. The human form does figure in later Glasgow Style work, but it was treated in a less stylised, less angular manner and not combined with plant forms to ambiguous effect (plates 39 and 40). One chief obstacle to popular appreciation was thereby avoided. As was noted by an anonymous reviewer in 1901, "The quite peculiar combination" of human and plant forms was characteristic of the Four's work, and "this use of the human figure is especially the central source of criticism for many people of these works."[12] When the figure was absent, the press generally welcomed the work of the Four and their contemporaries.

At the Art Club show of 1896 it was reported that "finger plates and the cabinet & tea caddie by H. M'Nair were much admired."[13] The exhibition was praised for its "freshness" and "originality," with the contributions of the female members in embroidery and hammer work particularly noted.[14] An illustration of work from the 1898 exhibition shows that a common language had been established (plate 37). Reviewing the opening of the Art Club exhibition in 1900, the *Evening Times* (Glasgow) stated that "the work exhibited showed marked progress, particularly in the arts and crafts department, in which Newbery, believing that the commonest articles of everyday use should be artistically made, has always encouraged students to interest themselves. The work done in this department is, of course, principally done by women students, who are devoting themselves to it more seriously and with more gratifying results than ever before."[15]

In 1901 the designer and critic Lewis F. Day acknowledged that "Glasgow had broken fresh ground, that the local school had long been making daring attacks upon traditions which the world at large was still content to accept. Certain of its adherents had taken us more or less captive by the strength of

37. A selection of work from the Glasgow School of Art Club exhibition, 1898. Clockwise from top left: *Line Illustration*, Jessie M. King; *Tea Cosy*, designed by Jessie Newbery and executed by Edith Rowat; *Line Illustration*, Jessie M. King; *Mirror Frame* in glass mosaic, B. McElwee; *Inlaid Mirror Frame*, Alice McCulloch; *Sofa-Cushion Cover*, designed by Jessie Newbery and executed by Bella Rowat; *Inlaid Mirror Frame*, Alice McCulloch; *Mirror Frame* in repoussé lead by De Courcy Lewthwaite Dewar; and at centre, *Brass Repoussé Plate*, Margaret T. Wilson. From the *Scots Pictorial*, November 26, 1898, pp. 302–3.

38. Students at Glasgow School of Art, c. 1894–95, including Margaret Macdonald (centre, front row) and Frances Macdonald (extreme right, front row). Francis Newbery is sitting behind her. The photograph may have been taken in one of the technical studios at the school.

their colour and astonished us by the weirdness of their design."[16] In the same year the chairman of the school's governors, Sir Francis Powell, reported that the school's design work "had created for itself a similar, he might almost say a superior position to that which was known in artistic circles as the Glasgow School of Painters."[17] A "Glasgow Style," stemming from the experiments of the Four, was clearly gaining ground throughout the 1890s. However, this was not just the result of individual creativity but was in part a consequence of developments at the school during the early 1890s.

THE TEACHING OF DESIGN

The provision of an adequate technical education suited to the needs of Glasgow's manufacturers had been a concern for the school's governors for some time prior to Newbery's arrival. In 1885, the year of his appointment, a new position was created for a special master who would be responsible for "the teaching of 'Design' as applied to the varied local manufacturers."[18] After protracted lobbying of the town council, funding was made available, and the technical studios opened in 1893, offering courses in glass staining, pottery, repoussé, metal working, stone carving, and bookbinding (plate 38).

Making the instruction relevant to the city's needs was a continual preoccupation for Newbery. However, surprisingly little was done to consolidate the relationship between the studios and the local manufacturers through joint initiatives, job placements, or competitions. Only a limited number of links with industry were forged. Newbery was able to report that some posters designed at the school had been taken up commercially and that there had been an increased demand for book cover designs.[19] Yet even as late as 1909, the professor of design was still being asked by Newbery to produce a report on how the studio courses could be made more "in touch with manufacturers."[20] Although this connection remained ill-defined, the opening of the technical studios had one very immediate and significant result. For the first time in the history of the school, a quantity of handcrafted decorative-art objects was being produced by the students. Here was a whole new currency in which ideas could be exchanged, developed, and exhibited. Once the technical studios were open, it was inevitable that the decorative arts would become more prominent and a new kind of work appear.

The courses offered were not in themselves particularly innovative. The teaching staff that Newbery selected and consulted was influenced by his familiarity with the South Kensington system and his strong enthusiasm for the English Arts and Crafts movement. He actively cultivated connections with the Arts and Crafts leaders during the years immediately following his appointment. A series of lectures brought some of the movement's most inspiring figures to Glasgow in the late 1880s. Walter Crane and William Morris (Newbery considered the latter a friend) each addressed an annual reunion of past and present students of the school. At the third annual reunion, in 1889, Morris gave a talk entitled "The Arts and Crafts," affirming that "the pleasure of creating something which without their individuality would never have existed was the greatest pleasure the world afforded."[21]

The timing of these visits during a period when the school was moving towards the opening of its technical art studios is significant. So too was the display of the "major part" of the second Arts and Crafts Exhibition Society show in the Glasgow Corporation Galleries in 1890. Transferred from the New Galleries, Regent Street, London, the exhibition included works by many of the leading Arts and Crafts members. It proved to be "of special interest and value to designers, decorators and persons connected with art industries in general, and to the students in the School of Art, by whom it was largely taken advantage of."[22]

The subsequent staffing of the technical studios and design courses reinforced such links. Most significantly, in 1908 the school was almost successful in appointing as professor of design one of the major figures of the English Arts and Crafts movement, the designer and architect C.F.A. Voysey. A commitment to his London practice ruled him out of contention, and instead the school appointed another Englishman, the decorative painter W.E.F. Britten.[23] Of the four heads of the design department appointed by Newbery, only the first, John Guthrie, was from Glasgow. For the instruction of enamelling, Newbery despatched one of his former students, De Courcy Lewthwaite Dewar, to the Central School of Arts and Crafts in London, and in 1905, unhappy with the instruction being offered in the school, Newbery led a delegation to Birmingham, London, and finally to C. R. Ashbee at Chipping Campden in the Cotswolds to discover what was being produced and how it was being taught.[24]

The Glasgow Style, therefore, was not formed in isolation and not through local forces alone. The direction of Newbery's thinking and the structures he put in place made the advent of something broadly like it almost certain. Yet Newbery could not have foreseen that the opening of the technical studios would coincide with the Four's finding their collective voice and that consequently the studios would so rapidly develop their own visual identity. This grafting of an unconventional decorative treatment onto an imported Arts and Crafts tradition defines the Glasgow Style within Glasgow School of Art.

The new emphasis on making objects did not immediately replace drawing as the central component of art training. Instead, the initial interaction of these two was a significant factor in the formation of the Glasgow Style. The Macdonald sisters were amongst the first students to have access to the technical studios after they opened. Both were full-time students and so had greater opportunity for regular contact with their colleagues in the studios than did either Mackintosh or McNair. It was Margaret and Frances who were the first to translate the early "Spook School" graphic work into the decorative arts (plate 39). The type of objects they were producing in the mid-1890s—beaten-metal candlesticks, sconces, and mirrors—became standard productions of the Glasgow Style around 1900. Nevertheless, their relative unfamiliarity with materials and processes and the very newness of the technical courses meant that for the Macdonalds and their contemporaries, drawing—the physical act of working through designs on paper—remained the dominant modus operandi within the school.

"Glasgow," it was noted in 1890 in a comparison with other major British cities, "was peculiar in its variety of manufacturers, and hence, a difficulty arose in adapting the school to so many diverse branches."[25] Yet these difficulties did not extend to drawing and designing, which remained constant requirements, regardless of their application. Inherent in the process of drawing is a heightened sense of line and composition. It is not surprising, therefore, that the Glasgow Style was most concerned with applied decoration, with the working out of a linear pattern on the surface of a material—whether an embroidered textile, a design beaten out of metal, an enamelled plaque on the side of a casket, or a tooled-leather book cover (plates 40 and 41). The result was to give coherence to the work of the studios but to place emphatically decorative concerns ahead of formal considerations. For instance, even though ceramic decoration was being taught from 1896, the school did not acquire its own kilns until 1911.[26]

The emphasis on drawing may also partly explain why, from the late 1890s, the most representative Glasgow Style work was produced in the needlework department. There were also several other reasons why this department flourished. Under the leadership first of Jessie Newbery and then of Ann Macbeth, it had greater continuity than any of the other departments

39. Frances Macdonald (1873–1921). *Mirror: "Honesty,"* c. 1896. Beaten tin on a wood frame, 28¾ x 29 in. (73.0 x 73.6 cm). Glasgow Museums.

■■ OPPOSITE, TOP
40. Marion Wilson (1869–1956).
Triptych, c. 1905. Beaten tin, centre
panel: 23¼ x 23¾ in. (59.0 x 60.2
cm), side panels: 23¼ x 10⅝ in. (59.0
x 27.0 cm), each. Glasgow Museums.
■■ OPPOSITE, BOTTOM
41. Unknown designer. *Book Cover*,
c. 1900. Tooled leather, 11½ x 5½ in.
(29.4 x 14.1 cm). Brian McKelvie.

in the school and succeeded in establishing an independent identity and reputation. The innovative teaching methods pioneered by the department continued to be influential in needlework education well into the new century.[27]

More relevant here, embroidery is the activity that has the most intimate connection with drawing. Picking out a line with needle and thread (plate 43) is in essence the same process as drawing it in pen and ink. It is possible to establish a needlework design with pencil and colour on paper (plate 42); in fact, both Jessie Newbery and Ann Macbeth often designed embroidered panels that they did not actually execute. This concentration on surface pattern was appropriate within the needlework department, but when applied throughout the technical studios it proved unresponsive to different materials, preventing an approach that took their diverse characteristics into account. Ultimately, this transfer of a graphic sensibility into decorative-art production limited the scope of the Glasgow Style, but in the short term it prompted a common linear quality in the work of the studios. What the Four contributed were certain key stylisations that gave the Glasgow Style its signature vocabulary.

Although Francis Newbery could not have predicted that the work in his studios would immediately take on this uncompromising appearance, his contribution was that he allowed the style to flourish and became its greatest champion. With the expansion of the technical studios towards the end of the 1890s, new teaching posts were established. Newbery deliberately consolidated the emerging style through a series of appointments. The illustrator and

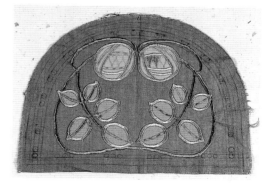

■■ ABOVE, LEFT
42. Jessie Newbery. *Design for a Pulpit Fall: "Be Ye Doers of the Word and Not Hearers Only,"* c. 1900. Pencil and watercolour, 13¹³⁄₁₆ x 19¾ in. (35.5 x 50.1 cm). Glasgow School of Art.
■■ ABOVE
43. Jessie Newbery (1864–1948). *Tea Cosy* (unfinished), c. 1900. Linen with silk thread appliqué embroidery, 11½ x 16 in. (29.4 x 40.8 cm). Glasgow Museums.
The pencil outline for the design is visible on the fabric.

graphic artist Jessie M. King was appointed to the book-decoration classes in 1899. Helen Muir Wood taught enamelling and block-cutting classes for a short period from 1900 and was succeeded by De Courcy Lewthwaite Dewar. In the same session, Dorothy Carleton Smyth began courses in sgraffito and gesso, and Macbeth, who was to remain on the teaching staff until 1920, was appointed Jessie Newbery's assistant in the needlework department. Finally, Agnes Harvey began teaching metalwork design in 1903.[28]

With the exception of Jessie Newbery, this group had all attended the school during the 1890s. They represent a single generation of students-turned-teachers who would have been coming through the school when the work of the Four was at its most potent and fast gaining attention. Their own appointments, coming such a short time later, put them in an ideal position to perpetuate the same style that had informed their student work, adding to the sense of cohesion in the output of the studios. Because the courses they taught were either brand new or still very fresh, each department was evolving from the same recent starting point, rather than inheriting long-established traditions or independent identities. This lack of an inhibiting past, together with Newbery's enthusiastic encouragement, was a powerful factor in consolidating the new style, as was the opportunity for members of this group to work in several media. Besides needlework, Jessie Newbery taught enamelling and mosaic decoration; Macbeth, bookbinding and metalwork; and Smyth, metalwork and mosaics.

PROMOTING THE GLASGOW STYLE

In the years immediately after 1900, with this group in position and both teachers and students working within Mackintosh's inspiring new school building, the Glasgow Style reached its height. The decorative artist and teacher Robert Anning Bell was immediately struck by what he saw in the studios. In 1903 he submitted a report on Glasgow School of Art in which he recognised "the very interesting development known as the Glasgow style" and continued by noting how "agreeable it is to find a development so local and so definite as that which has in recent years expressed itself in Glasgow. That it is disliked by some distinguished artists is quite probable; that it has some regrettable mannerisms is quite true, but none the less here is a distinct local style built around the personality of a few distinguished men and women."[29] The style clearly had established a presence.

By this date Anning Bell did not even need to go to Glasgow to see work in the Glasgow Style. Newbery was busily taking it beyond the city, promoting the style and his school through a series of exhibitions at home and abroad. Displays at international expositions presented an opportunity to raise the school's profile and to put it in competition with progressive schools from all over the Continent and beyond. Between 1895 and 1905 work was sent from Glasgow to Liège, Venice, London, Paris, Turin, Cork, Budapest, and St. Louis, amongst others. Such participation proved rewarding. At Liège, the school's submission received high praise, and a gold medal was awarded at Paris in 1900. Additional awards came at Budapest. At the Exposition Universelle in Paris of 1900 and the *Women's Work Exhibition* at Earl's Court, London, of the same year; at the Glasgow International Exhibition of 1901; and at the Cork International Exhibition and Turin *International Exhibition of Modern Decorative Art,* both of 1902, the Glasgow contributions came primarily from the same small group who taught at the school. Work by Jessie Newbery, Dorothy Carleton Smyth, Jessie M. King, De Courcy Lewthwaite Dewar, Ann Macbeth, Agnes Harvey, and Helen Muir Wood was included in three or more of these five exhibitions. Their contributions constituted a significant part of the total number of works shown, climaxing at Glasgow in 1901, where they accounted for almost half of the forty-seven works submitted.[30]

Newbery had a flair for exhibition design and theatrical displays. Aware that the presentation of a coherent body of work would help give the school a distinct identity, he shaped the submissions to these exhibitions by emphasising the new style rather than providing a representative sampling of the school's total output. What was perceived as the Glasgow Style at the beginning of the century and what we continue to see as the source of its international reputation comprised a very similar type of work produced by a small group of individuals during a limited period around the turn of the century. However, even Newbery could do little to sustain the style very far into the new century. A second report on the school compiled by Anning Bell, in 1911, makes a striking contrast to his comments of 1903. Although acknowledging the work being produced by the needlework department to be "by far the best" in the school, he complained that "a style of design suitable to Embroidery seems to have crept in everywhere" and concluded that in the pottery, lettering, and metalwork classes, amongst others, there should be "less work done of the nature of bric-a-brac and more which aimed at association with architecture."[31]

By 1911 it had been almost two decades since the first works by the Four had appeared. The uncompromising personal expression that had originally made them so compelling could not be sustained by a wider group. Except in the needlework department, the further the style got from its original expression, the less distinctive it became. Once the new language had been developed and applied to various media, the question of what happens next inevitably emerged. None of the group who taught in the school at the turn of the century was able to supply an answer, and the work produced in the school's technical studios became increasingly formulaic. (One exception was the large body of work produced by Jessie M. King, who owed the least to the Four; it reveals a personal vision that was developed independently and purposefully.)

The question of individuality is a central paradox of the Glasgow Style. Contemporary reviews repeatedly described the work of those involved as "individual," yet it was an individuality contained within a quite limited environment. The historian Theodore Zeldin has noted that "small groups often limit the individuality of their participants and diminish their capacity to venture outside."[32] The Glasgow Style designers had few reasons to venture outside the school. Being almost exclusively from the middle classes, they had little economic need to market their skills in the commercial world beyond. Their work was therefore produced primarily for the school. By as early as about 1905, little aesthetic development seems to have been taking place in the style. This lack of meaningful evolution stands in marked contrast to the progress evident in Mackintosh's own work during this period.

THE ARTISTIC INTERIOR

In 1911 Mackintosh was working on his last major Glasgow commission: two interiors—the Chinese Room (see plate 197) and the Cloister Room (see plate 198)—at Miss Cranston's Ingram Street tea rooms. From about 1904 the organic quality that had characterised his white interiors of around 1900 was increasingly being replaced by more geometric concerns. The rapid development of his work makes it difficult to compare it with the hand-produced decorative-art objects made at the school during the late 1890s and early 1900s.[33] Indeed, it is questionable that Mackintosh had any sense of commitment to what was happening at the school. He never taught there, and his direct influence on the students was therefore limited. Nor did he ever contribute to the formation of a coherent design philosophy in the pages of a journal, newsletter, or magazine. There is no indication that Mackintosh ever sought a teaching post at the school or did anything to encourage the emergence of the Glasgow Style; and, in fact, the notion of a school operating under his leadership does not sit happily with Mackintosh's passionate commitment to individuality.

Janice Helland has noted that at the time when the Macdonald sisters were pioneering their first production of decorative-art objects, Mackintosh was preoccupied with furthering his architectural career.[34] His own decorative-art production was almost entirely linked to specific interior commissions. The school and the work of the Glasgow Style designers within it was less important to him than his own work and the wider architectural world in which he was trying to establish himself. His contribution in this larger context was chiefly in developing the interior as a *Gesamtkunstwerk*—a total work of art. The concept of the unified artistic interior was not, however, a Glaswegian invention. Its appearance in the city reflected developments taking place on the Continent and in the work of English Arts and Crafts architects such as C.F.A. Voysey and M. H. Baillie Scott. Examples of work from both sources were reproduced in the design press during the later 1890s.

In Glasgow, the concept did not appear within the School of Art in tandem with decorative-art production. The strict division of design work by gender excluded women from architectural training and practice. Despite some close personal alliances with the designers involved[35] and despite a shared decorative vocabulary, the predominantly female group identified earlier had only

limited involvement in creating the room as a work of art. A course devoted to interior decoration was not established at the school until 1900, after the first unified interiors had already appeared in Glasgow. In this sense, the school was responding to a new awareness of interior decoration and design in the city rather than setting the agenda. Mackintosh, in his professional work, had done much to make this necessary.

The completion of two tea-room interiors, at Buchanan Street and Argyle Street, gave the Glasgow public their first real brush with the artistic interior in the new style. Nothing quite like them had been seen[1] in the city before, and their impact was recognised by Hermann Muthesius in 1902: "Still today they are the most worthwhile sights in Glasgow. Designed partly by Mackintosh and partly by Walton, they portrayed not just the best of interior design in Scotland, but in the whole of Britain."[36] George Walton had set up his firm of "Ecclesiastical and House Decorators" in 1888. Coming from a family of painters, he brought a refined sense of colour, surface, and texture to the work of his firm (plate 44). Although initially limited to paper hanging

44. George Walton (1867–1933). *Eros*, 1898. Marble, slate, metal, glass, and mother-of-pearl, 49¼ x 72¹/₁₆ in. (125.0 x 183.0 cm). Hunterian Art Gallery, University of Glasgow.

At least three versions of this highly decorative panel were made; this example probably came from Miss Cranston's tea rooms, Argyle Street, Glasgow.

and painting, George Walton and Co. produced increasingly unified interiors through the 1890s.[37]

Having greater experience than Mackintosh, Walton took the dominant role in the tea-room commissions. At Buchanan Street he was entirely responsible for the decoration and furnishing of four interiors, while Mackintosh's contribution was limited to wall decorations in the stairwell and in two other rooms furnished by Walton. Mackintosh's uncompromising murals hardly contributed to the unity of the whole, making little effort to conform to Walton's more conventional furnishings (plate 45). At Argyle Street, Mackintosh designed uncharacteristically solid furniture, which again did not sit happily with Walton's more florid interior decorations. If these collaborative interiors fell short of stylistic unity, they nevertheless brought the concept of the interior as a work of art into the public domain, and the interiors designed by Walton alone demonstrated what could be achieved by allowing a single individual control over every aspect of the design. In this, the Buchanan Street and Argyle Street interiors were a foretaste of the tea rooms designed entirely by Mackintosh at Ingram Street (see plate 183) and at the Willow Tea Rooms (see plate 192), both completed after Walton departed for London in 1897.[38]

By 1900 Mackintosh had also completed his first domestic interior commissions—starting with a bedroom at Westdel, Glasgow, for the publisher Robert Maclehose in 1898. One of his beautifully executed designs for the scheme was exhibited at the Glasgow Institute of the Fine Arts exhibition in 1899. The interior was shown in three elevations, with each element considered in relation to the whole to create a single effect (plate 46). From this first integrated white room stemmed other, increasingly sophisticated interiors, including those at the Mackintoshes' own Mains Street flat and climaxing in their submission to the *International Exhibition of Modern Decorative Art* at Turin in 1902 (see plate 67) and their music salon for Fritz Wärndorfer in Vienna in the same year. These schemes achieved a seamless unity of decorative art and interior design.

Just as the early work produced by the Four had triggered creative responses at the School of Art, so the concept of the interior as a work of art enjoyed a brief popularity with certain sections of Glasgow's design community. Indeed, in 1904 Margaret Macdonald wrote to Hermann Muthesius about the proliferation of "Mackintosh tea rooms, Mackintosh shops Mackintosh furniture &c" that had appeared in the city.[39] However, rather than reporting this in triumph, the tone of her letter conveys the same sense of ambivalence, almost bemusement, that characterised Mackintosh's relationship to the emerging Glasgow Style within the School of Art.

The new emphasis on interior design was reflected in the increased number of schemes submitted to the annual Glasgow Institute of the Fine Arts exhibitions. Both Mackintosh and Walton had been occasionally exhibiting

45. Charles Rennie Mackintosh. Stencil decorations in the ladies' tea room, Miss Cranston's tea rooms, Buchanan Street, Glasgow. Photographed by T. and R. Annan Ltd., 1897.

46. Charles Rennie Mackintosh. *A Bedroom: South Wall Elevation,* c. 1898. For Westdel, Glasgow. Pencil and watercolour, 9¼ x 17 in. (23.6 x 43.1 cm). Hunterian Art Gallery, University of Glasgow.

since the early 1890s. Mackintosh showed some early architectural work and watercolours, while Walton submitted stained-glass designs, furniture, and photographs of some of his completed interiors. However, Mackintosh's Westdel scheme was the first interior in the new style to be presented as a consciously artistic set of watercolours. A number of similar presentations followed. In 1904 the designer John Ednie exhibited a scheme for a banqueting hall and a "coloured decorative sketch of a fireplace in the new art manner" that were "both prettily presented as drawings, and show fanciful yet restrained design."[40] The fanciful interior reached its peak in the work of Ednie's colleague George Logan. His design for a music room (plate 47) breaks down boundaries between the natural world and interior design to create a dreamlike, fairy-tale environment.

This exhibition of designs as works of art in themselves was one example of the increasing status of the interior. A more commercial response came from the established Glasgow furnishing firm of Wylie and Lochhead. At the Glasgow International Exhibition of 1901, the company commissioned a large pavilion containing three interiors, each entirely decorated and furnished by a different designer. The bedroom was contributed by Ednie, the library by Logan, and the drawing room by E. A. Taylor (plate 48). None of these designers (all of whom were employed by Wylie and Lochhead) is known to have achieved or even attempted a complete interior prior to this

47. George Logan (1866–1939). *Design for a Music Room*, c. 1905. Pencil, ink, and watercolour on canvas, 20½ x 24 in. (52.0 x 61.0 cm). Glasgow Museums.

exhibition. The decision to exhibit complete room settings was not one that would have been taken by them alone; they were commissioned to create them so that Wylie and Lochhead would be seen to be at the forefront of progressive design.

The form that the interiors took suggests a familiarity with Walton's and Mackintosh's work and also with the decorative art being produced at the School of Art. The *Art Journal* reported, "Praiseworthy pains have been taken to make each separate room complete in all the details of its design."[41] In Taylor's interior the furniture was stained purple and the walls were covered with green silk whose tone "grew stronger" in the colouring of the carpet. The furniture was precisely arranged and despite its "tendency to the straight-up" was considered "distinctly graceful."[42] The inclusion of motifs then popular in Glasgow (butterflies in Taylor's drawing room, roses in Logan's library), the spare arrangement of furniture, and the use of bold colour connect these interiors to the Glasgow Style.

The Wylie and Lochhead rooms were showpieces presenting an ideal in which visual coherence was placed above practical concerns. For example, the elaborately inlaid hexagonal table (plate 49) designed by Logan for the library occupied a specific position within a rose motif woven into the carpet, but its awkward low stretchers made it impractical and easily damaged. Wylie and Lochhead's customers were not required to take "all or nothing" of what was

being offered, for adopting such a rigid position would have been commercially disastrous for the firm. (Much of Mackintosh's own failure to establish a broad client base can be explained by his insistence on that kind of total commitment.) In the promotional material accompanying their exhibition, the firm eagerly explained that these interiors could be adapted to the client's requirements—just one of many possible styles in which the expanding middle classes could decorate their homes.

Despite Wylie and Lochhead's determined sales pitch, the concept of the interior as a work of art translated into few commissions. The continued existence of a number of Mackintosh's interior schemes (see, for example, plate

176) provides a very immediate sense of the qualities of the Glasgow Style interior, but no comparable scheme by his Wylie and Lochhead contemporaries has survived. This is not simply a question of inadequate conservation. The Wylie and Lochhead interiors illustrated in the design press around 1900 show that only modified versions of their exhibition interiors were ever commissioned. The opportunity to create a full interior scheme unhindered by any existing fixtures in a room or by the client's possessions seems never to have materialised. Ironically, one of the company's most significant post-1901 Glasgow Style domestic commissions was not in Glasgow but in a house in suburban Birmingham.[43]

Perhaps the scarcity of this type of commission, combined with Wylie and Lochhead's desire to keep looking forward to the next style, hastened the departure of their Glasgow Style designers. Taylor left the firm in 1906 and moved away from Glasgow two years later. Ednie also left in 1906, to become a freelance designer and architect. Logan remained as chief designer throughout his working life, but as his pattern book illustrates, he moved with equal ease across a range of styles.[44] Certainly at Glasgow School of Art, the interior decoration courses rapidly lost their momentum. In his 1911 report Anning Bell noted that the stencilling and stained-glass studios seemed to have "lost attraction" and appeared to be "disused."[45]

The fact that the Glasgow Style interior failed to have any real impact outside the exhibition hall underlines the limitations of the style and again connects it with the work of the decorative-arts studios at Glasgow School of Art. What could be artfully expressed in two dimensions or in the artificial circumstances of a temporary exhibition was harder to achieve in the context of someone's living space. Mackintosh alone developed a small but sufficiently sympathetic client base to support—for a brief period—his creation of interiors that really were inhabitable works of art and that incorporated a variety of decorative arts. The success of those specific interiors has so hidden the shortcomings of the broader Glasgow Style that it has assumed a significance well beyond its limitations.

There was, nevertheless, one occasion that resulted in an unique presentation of the Glasgow Style. At the *International Exhibition of Modern Decorative Art* at Turin in 1902, Mackintosh played a central role in the single most significant presentation of the Glasgow Style on the Continent. The timing of that event was crucial; five years earlier or later, the Scottish section could not have achieved the same impact. As always, Newbery played a key role. At the invitation of the Italian organisers he took charge of the Scottish section and devoted his energies to mustering an unique display of the Glasgow designers.

Turin marked the only occasion when the Wylie and Lochhead designers showed work alongside the group from the school. The designed interior was well represented: Mackintosh and Margaret Macdonald created a room setting,

the Rose Boudoir (see plate 67); the McNairs also contributed an interior, a Lady's Writing Room. But Newbery also engaged Mackintosh to design the displays, and it was the latter's skillful presentation of the decorative-art material produced by his contemporaries that made the Scottish section so effective. Furniture designed by Taylor and Ednie was shown against Mackintosh's walls, and smaller objects were placed inside his display cases (plate 50).[46] At Turin, Mackintosh not only created a sympathetic setting for the presentation of the Glasgow Style but also must have convincingly suggested that the Glasgow Style was a coherent movement involving a wide variety of individuals with a common sense of purpose. In a metaphorical way, Mackintosh continues to play that role today.

NOTES

1. W. J. Warren, "Mr. George Walton, Designer and Decorator," *Amateur Photographer*, August 11, 1899, pp. 110–12.

2. In 1853 a Science Division was added to the newly formed Department of Practical Art, and the Government Department of Science and Art came into being. Administered by the Board of Trade and eventually based in South Kensington, London, the department was responsible for operating a national curriculum for art instruction.

3. Figures compiled from the annual reports of Glasgow School of Art, Glasgow School of Art Library.

4. I am grateful to George Rawson, librarian at Glasgow School of Art, for sharing his extensive research on Newbery and for all his help in the preparation of this essay. See also Jude Burkhauser, "Fra Newbery, Jessie Newbery, and the Glasgow School of Art," in Burkhauser, ed., *"Glasgow Girls": Women in Art and Design, 1880–1920* (Edinburgh: Canongate, 1990).

5. Undated press clipping, Glasgow School of Art Library.

6. Information regarding the increase in staff numbers was compiled from the annual reports of Glasgow School of Art, Glasgow School of Art Library.

7. Thomas Armstrong, address to the 56th Annual Meeting and Distribution of Prizes at Glasgow School of Art, in the *Annual Report of the Glasgow School of Art*, 1899, pp. 10–18.

8. Unidentified review in Francis Newbery's scrapbook of press clippings, Mitchell Library, Glasgow City Libraries.

9. "Glasgow School of Art Club," *Daily Mail* (London), November 9, 1894.

10. Jessie Newbery, in Gleeson White, "Some Glasgow Designers and Their Work—Jessie Newbery," *Studio* 12 (October 1897): 48.

11. W. Fred, "Die Turiner Ausstellung: Die Sektion Schottland," *Dekorative Kunst* (August 1902): 400–406. I am grateful to Alan Crawford for allowing me to quote from his translation of this article.

12. "Die VII. Ausstellung der Wiener 'Secession,'" *Dekorative Kunst* (February 1901): 171–89.

13. Unidentified press clipping, Newbery scrapbook, Mitchell Library.

14. Ibid.

15. "Glasgow School of Art Club, Annual at Home," *Evening Times* (Glasgow), November 10, 1900.

16. Lewis F. Day, "Decorative and Industrial Art at the Glasgow Exhibition, First Notice," *Art Journal* (1901): 215–16.

17. Powell, in *Glasgow Herald,* undated press clipping, Glasgow School of Art Library.

18. Unidentified press clipping, Glasgow School of Art Library.

19. The use of posters designed at the school is recorded in *Annual Report of the Glasgow School of Art,* 1895, p. 7; and of the book covers in *Annual Report of the Glasgow School of Art,* 1897, p. 9.

20. Minutes of the School Committee, May 5, 1909, Glasgow School of Art Governors' Minutes, Glasgow School of Art Library.

21. "Mr. William Morris on 'Arts and Crafts,'" unidentified press clipping, Newbery scrapbook, Mitchell Library.

22. *Kelvingrove Museum and Corporation Galleries of Art, Glasgow, Report of the Year 1890,* p. 4.

23. Minutes of Sub-Committee on Design, May 22, 1908, Glasgow School of Art Governors' Minutes, Glasgow School of Art Library.

24. *Report of Deputation Appointed to Visit English Arts and Crafts Schools, Guilds of Handicraft and Decorative Artists,* February 1905, Glasgow School of Art Library.

25. *Glasgow Herald,* January 29, 1890.

26. *Annual Report of the Glasgow School of Art,* 1911, p. 5.

27. See Liz Arthur, "Jessie Newbery (1864–1948)," in Burkhauser, ed., *"Glasgow Girls."*

28. These appointments are recorded in the annual reports of Glasgow School of Art.

29. Robert Anning Bell, "Report on the Glasgow School of Art," March 26, 1903, typewritten manuscript in the Glasgow School of Art Library.

30. The school's submissions to these exhibitions are recorded in the archives of Glasgow School of Art. The Paris submission is contained in "Glasgow School of Art Correspondence, 1897–1904," p. 209. The *Women's Work Exhibition* at Earl's Court is ibid., p. 242. Details of the Cork submission are drawn together in archive reference 7:061.4. Extensive correspondence relating to the contribution to Turin is bound together as "International Exhibition of Modern Decorative Arts, Turin 1902, Documents 1–4."

31. Anning Bell's report is recorded in Minutes of Sub-Committee on Design, March 13, 1911, Glasgow School of Art Governors' Minutes, Glasgow School of Art Library.

32. Theodore Zeldin, *A Brief History of Humanity* (London: Sinclair Stevenson, 1994), p. 37.

33. See William Eadie, *Movements of Modernity: The Case of Glasgow and Art Nouveau* (London: Routledge and Kegan Paul, 1990), pp. 105–7.

34. Janice Helland, "The Critics and the Arts and Crafts: The Instance of Margaret Macdonald and Charles Rennie Mackintosh," *Art History* 17 (summer 1994): 209–27.

35. For instance, in 1908 Jessie M. King married E. A. Taylor, who had been a Wylie and Lochhead designer until 1906.

36. Hermann Muthesius, "Die Kodak-Laden George Walton," *Dekorative Kunst* (March 1902): 202. I am grateful to Wendy Fairclough for translating this article.

37. For the early years of Walton's career, see Karen Moon, *George Walton: Designer and Architect* (Wendlebury, England: White Cockade Publishing, 1993), pp. 23–40.

38. Walton moved to London in the summer of 1897, although his workshops and retail premises remained in Glasgow.

39. Macdonald to Hermann Muthesius, Christmas 1904, Hunterian Art Gallery, University of Glasgow.

40. *Glasgow Herald,* May 14, 1904, book of press clippings, Art Gallery and Museum Library, Kelvingrove, Glasgow.

41. Lewis F. Day, "Decorative and Industrial Art at the Glasgow Exhibition, Second Notice," *Art Journal* (1901): 242.

42. Ibid., p. 241.

43. This commission—at 32 Radnor Road, Birmingham—is discussed in Juliet Kinchin, "The Wylie and Lochhead Style," *Journal of the Decorative Art Society* 9 (1985): 4–16.

44. George Logan's pattern book containing several hundred designs for furniture is in the collections of Glasgow Museums, registration number E1981–86.

45. Anning Bell, report, March 13, 1911.

46. Mackintosh's contribution to the Turin exhibition is discussed in Pamela Robertson and Juliet Kinchin, "The Scottish Section," in Rossana Bossaglia, Ezio Godoli, and Marco Rosci, eds., *Torino 1902: Le arti decorative internazionali del nuovo secolo* (Turin: Fabbri Editori, 1994).

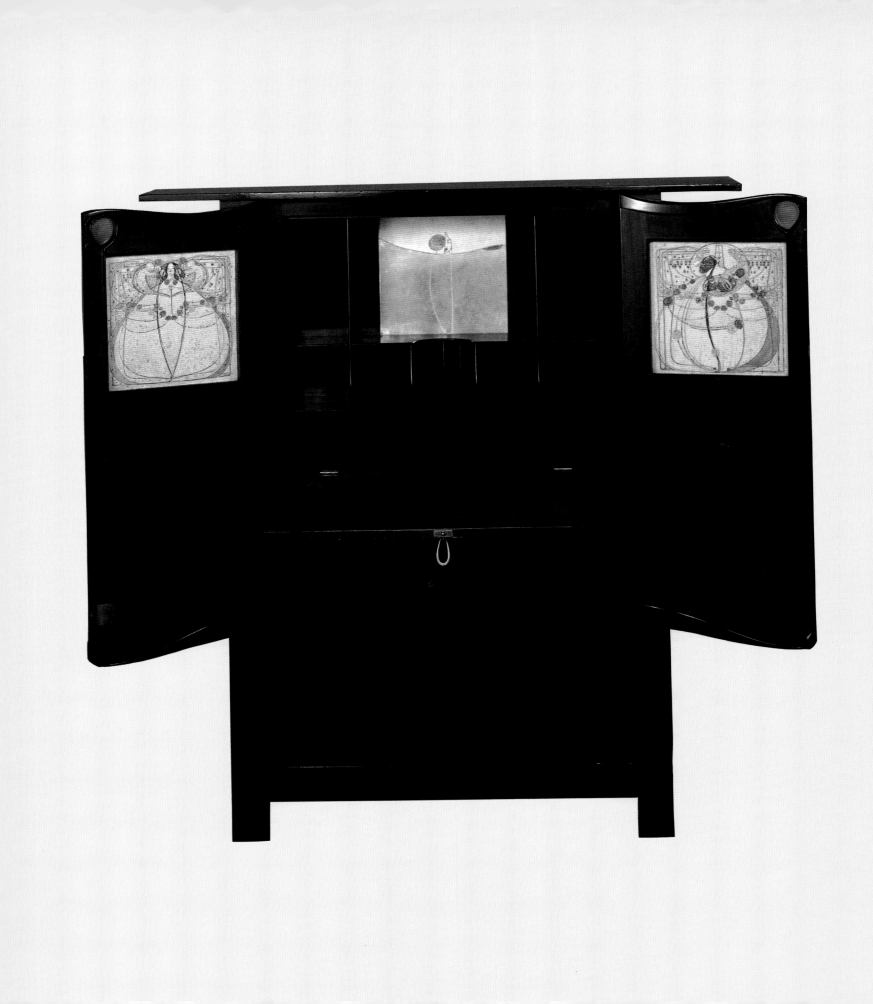

Collaboration among the Four

■■

JANICE HELLAND

Most writing about the Four—Margaret Macdonald, Frances Macdonald, Herbert McNair, and Charles Rennie Mackintosh—has focussed upon Mackintosh as the so-called leader of the group. The goal of this essay is to expand traditional concepts of the "collective" and the "individual" by considering the less individual aspects of Mackintosh and thus opening up a discussion of his work in relation to others'.[1] Three kinds of collaboration by the Four will be discussed here: first, shared authorship; second, shared production with individual authorship retained over the component parts; and finally, exclusive authorship, in which the work itself suggests collaborative production but a single maker has been credited.

We must understand that the Mackintosh in existence now is not the Mackintosh who walked the streets of Glasgow but the Mackintosh who has been made for us by the people who have written about him. The constructed Mackintosh has become an individual genius, a man who struggled and created on his own, usually against adversity; he has become a "hero" of the twentieth century. Within this story, neither his collaborators nor his patrons nor the public users of the architecture play a significant role.

Even though most design and architectural projects require cooperative production, most critical and art-historical discourse glorifies one maker over another. Writers about Mackintosh have consistently played down the collaborative elements of his work in favour of designating the architect-designer a "prophet of pure perfection."[2] For example, a cabinet designed by Charles Rennie Mackintosh with panels designed and made by Margaret Macdonald becomes "Mackintosh furniture."[3]

The collaborative process suggests a cooperative production that decentres the elite, individual artist. In 1897 the Glaswegian decorative artists

51. Charles Rennie Mackintosh and Margaret Macdonald Mackintosh. *Writing Cabinet,* 1902. For the Rose Boudoir, *International Exhibition of Modern Decorative Art,* Turin. Ebonised wood, with glass insets; painted-gesso-and-metal panels by Margaret Macdonald Mackintosh, 58¼ x 48¹³⁄₁₆ x 11¹³⁄₁₆ in. (148.0 x 124.0 x 30.0 cm). MAK-Austrian Museum for Applied Arts, Vienna.

Edward Charles Carr and J. Tytler Stewart explained this process in the journal the *Artist:* "We always work together; always consult together before any work is begun; satisfy ourselves as to who is best fit to undertake such and such portions of it; one sometimes designs, sometimes the other; likewise with the actual workmanship." They insisted that "before all" they agreed jointly "upon the lines to be followed" and then, as the work progressed, each benefitted "by the other's correction and criticism." In this way, "all work done is really the work of both, and to assist matters the work of each, in almost any direction, is particularly equal with that of the other."[4] One might assume that collaborative work by members of the Four began in much the same way, with the sharing of ideas that would eventually manifest themselves in a finished product.

Frances Macdonald and Margaret Macdonald had studied at Glasgow School of Art between 1890 and 1894; the Hope Street studio that they opened in 1895 was conveniently near the studio of a colleague from the school, Herbert McNair. Neither McNair nor the sisters, all of whom had independent incomes, were concerned about supporting themselves with their studio work, and consequently in addition to their commercial projects, all three of the artists made and exhibited one-of-a-kind objects and watercolours.

The three artist-designers had intrigued a Glaswegian audience as early as 1894, when their unusual drawings were hung in the Institute of the Fine Arts along with work by other students from Glasgow School of Art, including Charles Rennie Mackintosh. The conservative weekly *Quiz* told its readers that "the 'ghoul-like' designs of the Misses Macdonald . . . were simply hideous, and the less said about them the better."[5] The *Evening News* (Glasgow) recognised the work of a number of the students as "quite remarkable" and pronounced many of the pictures "fearfully, wonderfully and weirdly 'new.'"[6] The critic for the *Bailie* criticised the "weird designs, the impossible forms, lurid colour and symbolism."[7] These comments have often been cited as examples of Glasgow's hostility towards new art, but they did focus public attention on the artists and on Glasgow School of Art. Francis Newbery, head of the school, took full advantage of the publicity and moved one of the offensive works to the entrance of the institute "as an inducement to step inside and see the 'graveyard.'"[8] This notorious exhibition may well have been the first time that all four artists exhibited together. However, it is highly unlikely that this was their first meeting; they all attended the School of Art, were active in the Glasgow School of Art Club, and had probably known each other for at least two or three years.

SHARED AUTHORSHIP

In January 1895, within weeks of the student exhibition, Frances and Margaret Macdonald made their mark in Glasgow as commercial designers with their collaboratively produced *Drooko* poster (plate 52). The elegantly severe poster, commissioned by a local umbrella manufacturer to advertise his wares, prompted critics to proclaim the Macdonald sisters "the only 'new' poster designers who have yet arisen in Glasgow."[9] The "weird picture drawn by the Misses Macdonald for Mr. Joseph Wright" was exhibited, along with a number of other posters, in the vestibule of the institute.[10] A local critic insisted that the *Drooko* poster provoked "serious qualms of conscience to the nocturnal reveller."[11] Like "the 'new school' posters advertising the opening of the Fine Art Institute," the *Drooko* poster attracted "considerable attention which is the first essential of a good poster," but opinion differed as to whether posters

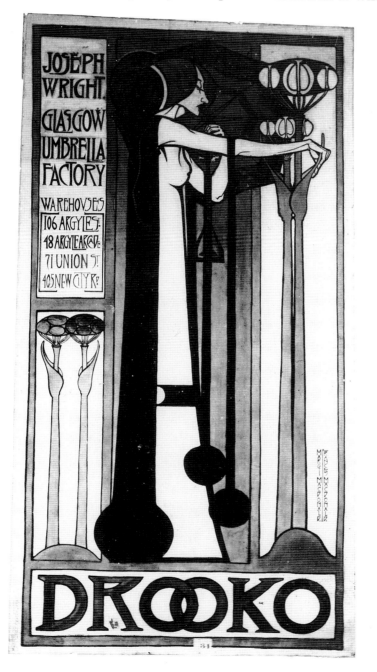

52. Frances Macdonald (1873–1921) and Margaret Macdonald (1864–1933). *Poster for Drooko. Joseph Wright, Glasgow Umbrella Factory,* 1895. From *Dekorative Kunst,* no. 2 (1899): 74.

were "Art or not."[12] A second poster also attracted the attention of the Glaswegian public: the Institute of the Fine Arts poster (plate 53) made by the sisters and McNair. The poster was parodied in the pose that Frances Macdonald struck when she and her friends were photographed during a holiday near Dunure (plate 54).[13]

The Macdonalds' *Drooko* poster and the McNair-Macdonald Institute of the Fine Arts poster exemplify the first kind of collaborative project—shared authorship. In shared authorship the hands of the individual makers cannot be distinguished, and the product is viewed and marketed as collective; the makers acknowledge having pooled their labour, and the viewer understands the work as having been made by more than one person. The Macdonald sisters and McNair also designed and executed the *Mirror: "Vanity"* (plate 55) and a screen, *The Birth and Death of the Winds* (plate 56). Thus, even though the prototype for the designs might be located in Frances Macdonald's *A Pond* (plate 57)—a drawing she made for an 1894 issue of the Glasgow School of Art student journal, "The Magazine"—the completed works must be attributed to all three artists.

Like the collaborative posters, the mirror and the screen first appeared before the public in 1895, this time at an arts-and-crafts exhibition organised by Newbery.[14] Mackintosh was linked with his three friends in reviews of the exhibition. "The furniture designs are also excellent, the work of Messrs McNair and McIntosh [*sic*] and the Messrs [*sic*] Macdonald being of course the most remarkable." Together, the work of these artists was acknowledged as characteristic of their style, and "clever."[15] However, even though Mackintosh was identified with the other three artists, he did not participate in their joint

:: OPPOSITE

53. Frances Macdonald, Margaret Macdonald, and James Herbert McNair (1868–1955). *Poster for The Glasgow Institute of the Fine Arts,* c. 1895. Lithograph printed in four sections, 92¹⁵/₁₆ x 40⅞ in. (236 x 102.0 cm). Glasgow Museums.

:: BELOW

54. The Glasgow Four with their friends at Dunure, c. 1895. Top: Frances Macdonald; centre, left to right: Margaret Macdonald, Katherine Cameron, Janet Aitken, Agnes Raeburn, Jessie Keppie, John Keppie; foreground, left to right: Herbert McNair, Charles Rennie Mackintosh.

ventures. Quite likely his work at Honeyman and Keppie kept him busy preparing architectural drawings, whereas the Macdonalds and McNair were free to work out of their studios on projects of their own choosing.

SHARED PRODUCTION

Mackintosh contributed much more frequently to the second kind of collaborative project, which can be termed "shared production"—that is, the overall product has been made by more than one person, with individual authorship retained over the component parts. Among the Four this kind of working together was the most characteristic and distinctive.

The most interesting example of shared production by the Macdonalds is a group of pictures representing the four seasons: Margaret's *Summer* and *Winter* (plate 58) and Frances's *Spring* and *Autumn* (plate 59). Each piece is unique, but the group elaborates upon one theme, and the formats and styles of the four pieces are similar. The four seasons are meant to be viewed together and can be read as a set, yet each unit could be exhibited by itself. *Summer* and *Spring* were, in fact, hung in the second exhibition (1899) of London's newest and most

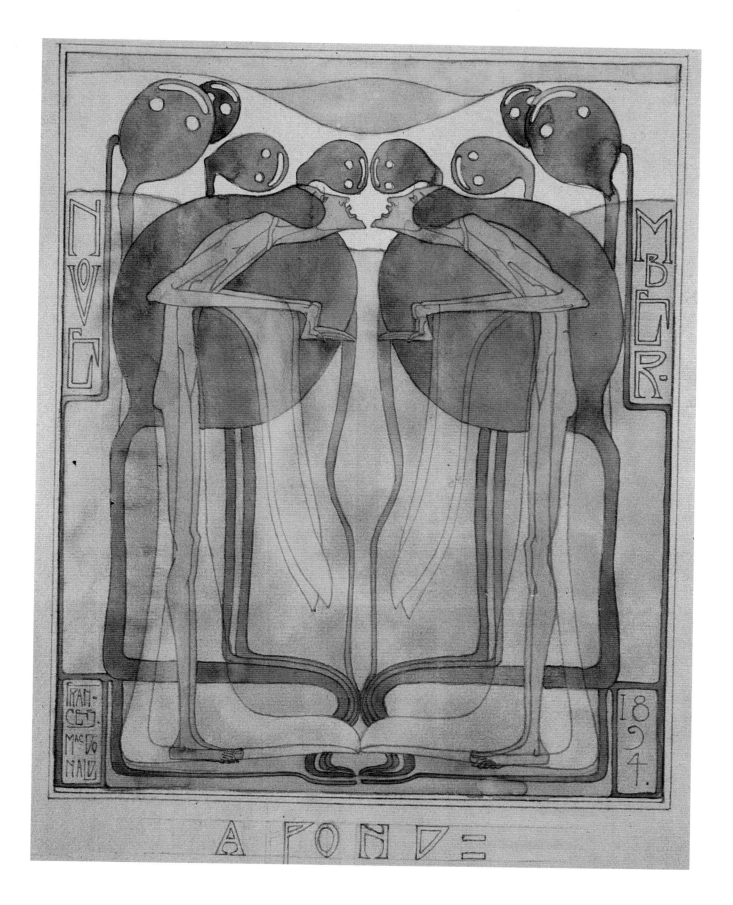

"vital" venue,[16] the International Society of Sculptors, Painters and Gravers, under the presidency of the controversial James McNeill Whistler. In 1899 the organisers proposed to show viewers and critics that arts and crafts could be exhibited "in a gallery with painting and sculpture,"[17] thus providing the Macdonald sisters an ideal venue for work that combined the delicacy of gouache with the severity of beaten lead. All the members of the Four put work into this exhibition, but the paired pictures by the sisters were the only collaborative works; Mackintosh contributed a watercolour drawing, *The Black Thorn*, and McNair sent two watercolours, *Hope and Love* and *The Lovers* (current locations all unknown). The critic for the *Evening News* commended a number of drawings by the same "quartette" that had been "responsible for such extraordinary poster work on the Glasgow hoardings," while insisting that their exhibits at the society's show represented "a vast improvement" on the earlier work: the "desire to startle . . . had passed away."[18]

Therefore, by 1899 (the year Frances Macdonald and Herbert McNair married), the four artists, though not yet called the Four, were perceived as a "quartette." The following year Margaret Macdonald married Charles Rennie Mackintosh, and at this point they began working together on collaborative projects. Much of their work together, as well as most of the collaborative work made by Frances and Herbert, is "shared production," though it has been treated differently than the shared production manifested in the Macdonalds' seasons pictures. Although we know that each sister was responsible for two of the four pictures, we do not know which artist conceived the overall design, and art historians have not been concerned with making any such attribution.

This situation changes when one is dealing with work produced jointly by Margaret Macdonald and Charles Rennie Mackintosh. For example, the 1902 ebonised desk illustrated in plate 51 is viewed by the public and by critics as being "by Mackintosh," even though its metal, glass, and gesso panels are by Macdonald; it is unknown whether the panels were made for Mackintosh's desk body or vice versa. Thus, even though authorship in this instance seems clear, it is in fact blurred at the level of production as well as of reception. Similarly, in September 1901, *Dekorative Kunst* illustrated a cabinet with a silver panel (plate 60) as having been made by Charles Rennie Mackintosh; the silver panel made by Macdonald was illustrated independently in that journal the following March and credited to her.[19] Unlike the seasons pictures, which could be shown either separately or together, the cabinet and the silver panel constitute one piece, a unit made by two artists who contributed separate parts. This unit must be understood as a whole; the parts belong together in the same way that a frame belongs around a picture.

That the desk was labelled a "Mackintosh" by *Dekorative Kunst* (and would be labelled the same way by many art historians today) has to do with the way art is written about and assigned to a hierarchy, rather than with the way any particular piece was produced. For example, as early as 1889 a review of the second show of the Arts and Crafts Exhibition Society of London insisted that "excrescences and eccentricities" were as out of place in furniture design as they were in architectural design. Furniture design was "a kind of minor and lighter form of architecture, equally dependent on constructive soundness of design and execution, and governed by much the same principles as architectural design."[20] Accordingly, the critics focused most of their attention on the fine-arts exhibits or on the furniture; they devoted little space to discussion of crafts.[21]

■■ OPPOSITE, LEFT
58. Margaret Macdonald. *Winter*, 1898. Pencil, watercolour, and gouache on vellum with beaten-lead frame, image: 18⅝ x 7⅞ in. (47.2 x 19.6 cm); frame: 27⁹⁄₁₆ x 14⅛ in. (70.0 x 36.0 cm). Glasgow Museums.

■■ OPPOSITE, RIGHT
59. Frances Macdonald. *Autumn*, 1898. Pencil and gouache on vellum with beaten-lead frame, image: 17¹⁵⁄₁₆ x 5¹³⁄₁₆ in. (45.4 x 14.7 cm); frame: 27⁹⁄₁₆ x 14⅛ in. (70.0 x 36.0 cm). Glasgow Museums.

60. Margaret Macdonald Mackintosh and Charles Rennie Mackintosh. *Cabinet,* 1900. From *Dekorative Kunst* (September 1901): 174.

Little has changed since then; Margaret Macdonald's silver panel is still considered "craft," as well as small and "feminine." Furniture is still more likely to be written about as architecture or as fine art is written about, especially if the designer of the furniture is known first and foremost as an architect. This is clearly demonstrated by Nikolaus Pevsner's discussion of Mackintosh in *The Sources of Modern Architecture and Design,* in which Mackintosh is treated first as an architect and then as a designer: "Mackintosh's furniture has the same sureness and originality as his architecture."[22] Pevsner insists on the "masculine" quality of Mackintosh's work and on the architect's resistance to more "feminine" elements of design:

The radicalism of ornamental abstraction and the lyrical softness of the colours also contradict each other, and it is the tension between the sensuousness and the structural elements that makes Mackintosh's decoration unique. . . . The hard verticals and horizontals [of Mackintosh's chairs] must have been an attraction to Mackintosh in themselves, an aesthetic counterpoint to his tense curves, and a safeguard that the frail blooms and feminine hues do not cloy.[23]

A second form of shared production, in addition to the making of component parts of a unit like furniture or a suite of pictures, occurred in the designing of rooms: the Scottish Room[24] at the eighth Vienna Secession exhibition (1900), the rooms at the *International Exhibition of Modern Decorative Art* in Turin (1902), and the interiors that the artists made for themselves.

At the Vienna Secession the four artists were publicised for the first time as working together: "There is a Scotch interior by Mr. and Mrs. Mackintosh, who have been assisted by Mr. and Mrs. McNair." The review in the *Artist* discussed the room as a whole, commenting upon its "curious Japanese style," its "half-mystical, half-religious subjects," and its attempt at originality, which reached "the very limits of possibility."[25] More than anything else, the Vienna exhibition represented the debut of the Mackintoshes as a vital force in decorative art on the Continent.[26] It signalled the end of collaboration between the two women while simultaneously indicating new and different directions for their work. For example, Margaret Macdonald exhibited *The May Queen* (plate 61)—a gesso panel made for the Ingram Street tea rooms—and two metal panels for a smoking cabinet designed by Mackintosh.

These narrow panels (plate 62) repeat a shape Macdonald used frequently, one seen to best advantage in the fabric hanging also included in the Scottish Room at the Vienna Secession (plate 63). In the smoking cabinet her panels beautifully complement the long, narrow doors. The eyelike motifs on the hanging have been repeated, side by side, at the top of the panel she called *Day*. The long, slender bodies of the two women in the design are narrowed to enhance the graceful pattern of the silver panel. In this instance, the women's faces look up as if towards the sun. In the second panel, *Night*, Macdonald introduced a curved line running down the length of the body of the central figure, thus turning what could have been rigid repetition into elegant asymmetrical design. The overall effect of the cabinet and its panels is one of lightness rather than weightiness, height rather than breadth, and drama rather than routine. If elements of the room are to be isolated for discussion—for example, the hangings or the panels—we must always remember that they form part of a unit, with all the components contributing to the room's meaning.

Similarly, Margaret Macdonald's rhythmic, symmetrical panel *The May Queen* had been designed to hang opposite Mackintosh's panel *The Wassail*, in the Ingram Street tea rooms.[27] Roger Billcliffe has noted that Mackintosh over-

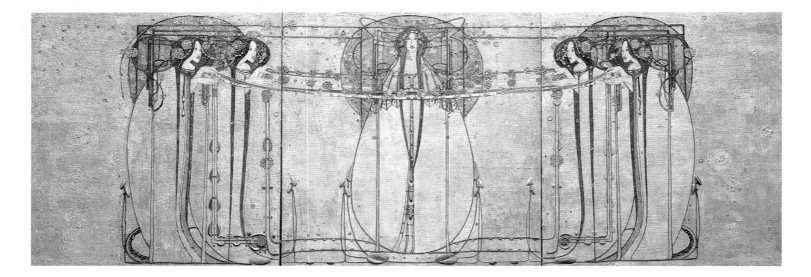

■■ OPPOSITE, TOP

61. Margaret Macdonald Mackintosh (1864–1933). *The May Queen*, 1900. For the Ladies' Luncheon Room, Miss Cranston's tea rooms, Ingram Street, Glasgow. Three panels of oil-painted gesso on hessian and scrim, set with twine, glass beads, thread, mother-of-pearl, and tin leaf, each panel: 62½ x 60 in. (158.8 x 152.4 cm), total length: 15 ft. (4.57 m). Glasgow Museums.

■■ OPPOSITE, BOTTOM LEFT

62. Charles Rennie Mackintosh and Margaret Macdonald Mackintosh. *Smoking Cabinet*, 1900. From *Dekorative Kunst* (September 1901): 172.

■■ OPPOSITE, BOTTOM RIGHT

63. Detail of the Scottish Room, Vienna Secession exhibition, 1900. Top: Margaret Macdonald Mackintosh, *The May Queen*, painted gesso panels designed for the Ingram Street tea rooms; far right: Margaret Macdonald Mackintosh, fabric panel; far left: Frances and Margaret Macdonald, silver clock. From *Dekorative Kunst* (September 1901): 175.

■■ ABOVE

64. Margaret Macdonald Mackintosh (1864–1933). *The White Rose and the Red Rose*, 1902. For the Rose Boudoir, *International Exhibition of Modern Decorative Art*, Turin. Painted gesso on hessian, set with string, glass beads, and shell, 39 x 39¹⁵/₁₆ in. (99.0 x 101.5 cm). Hunterian Art Gallery, University of Glasgow.

came the spatial awkwardness of the Ingram Street tea rooms "by introducing a mezzanine level" as well as "by visually lowering the height of the rest of the room by placing at a high level two long gesso panels, each about five feet deep."[28] The gesso panels, each of which depicts a celebration associated with a changing of the seasons, "faced each other across the room and complemented the individual patches of colour in the white panelling and woodwork." The overall effect of the "expanses of white enamel," the use of coloured glass, and the contrast of light and dark made by the dark furniture and the light panels created an unique atmosphere for a Glasgow tea room. It was this room that inspired Mackintosh and Macdonald in the design for the Scottish Room at the Vienna Secession.

The next important international venue to include rooms (or parts of rooms delineated by screens) designed by the Four was the *International Exhibition of Modern Decorative Art*, which opened in Turin in the spring of 1902. As in Vienna, the Scottish decorators were noted as having contributed the "most quaint and curious" part of the exhibition.[29] There was, however, some confusion as to who they were and with whom they had collaborated. The

65. Detail of the Scottish section, *International Exhibition of Modern Decorative Art*, Turin, 1902. Frances McNair, *Legend of the Snowdrop* (painted panel); James Herbert McNair, *The Legend of the Birds* (painted panel); Frances McNair, appliquéd tablecloth; James Herbert McNair, writing desk with metal panels and chair; Frances McNair, *The Frog Prince* (watercolour and gold paint on vellum). From *Dekorative Kunst* (August 1902): 401.

Italian critic Alfredo Melani insisted that he had "for several years been acquainted with the products of Margaret and Francis [*sic*] Macdonald" and with the work of Mackintosh and Jessie Newbery. He continued with accolades for the rooms and the decorative work made by "Mr. and Mrs. Macdonald," singling out the work of "Mrs. Macdonald" (plate 64) as being of "particular interest." The author's confusion was later corrected when he congratulated the Mackintoshes "(erroneously spoken of . . . as Mr. and Mrs. Macdonald)" for their contribution to the exhibition. It did not help the McNairs' reputation on the Continent to have had *Dekorative Kunst* reproduce two photographs of their section of the show, giving credit to "Charles R. Mackintosh and Margaret Macdonald-Mackintosh."[30]

Although both couples contributed significantly to the exhibition, only the Mackintoshes were able to travel to the Continent to assist with the installation of the exhibits and to meet with other artists and decorators; both the

McNairs were teaching in Liverpool and had family responsibilities.[31] The McNairs' work at Turin reflected their commitment to their new life together and to their recently born child. Most of what they sent was from their own home at 54 Oxford Street in Liverpool: a dark settle designed by McNair with an embroidered curtain by Macdonald, a desk with beaten-metal panels, a table and chairs, and a "baby's crawling rug on which the young mind creeps through art to a quaint knowledge of Natural History."[32] Frances Macdonald's watercolour *The Frog Prince* was hung in this exhibition as it had been in Vienna, this time near to McNair's elegant dark wood desk (plate 65). Two panels made earlier for Vienna hung on either side of a small, fragile-looking table, near two low-backed chairs. The furniture represented the private space of the home, thus highlighting the work of the McNairs as directed towards teaching, private life, the production of watercolours, and the designing of their own personal space. The *Studio* suggested that, although the McNair-Macdonald part of the room shared many characteristics with the Mackintosh-Macdonald part, there was "in everything a personal note." In addition, the anonymous author of the *Studio* article about the Scottish section at Turin used a description of the settle by the McNairs (plate 66) to delineate masculine and feminine realms of production: "The dainty craft of these fittings proclaim the woman's hand, while the sturdy structure of the chair itself attests to the work of the man."[33]

The Mackintosh-Macdonald contribution to the Turin exhibition, the Rose Boudoir (plate 67), also suggested intimacy, but the work in their area spoke much more loudly of commission than did the McNair-Macdonald section. In addition to Mackintosh's growing success as an architect, his visibility as a designer had increased significantly with the opening of Miss

ABOVE, LEFT
66. Detail of the Scottish section, Turin. James Herbert McNair, settle with leaded glass; Frances McNair, embroidered curtain and embroidered cushion; Frances McNair, appliquéd carpet. From *Dekorative Kunst* (August 1902): 403.
ABOVE, RIGHT
67. Detail of the Scottish section, Turin. Charles Rennie Mackintosh and Margaret Macdonald Mackintosh, the Rose Boudoir, 1902. From *Deutsche Kunst und Dekoration* (September 1902): 587.

Cranston's tea rooms in Buchanan Street in 1897. Here the public first saw Mackintosh's decorative stencils adorning the walls of rooms designed by George Walton.[34] When Cranston decided to expand her growing business to Argyle Street, "Mackintosh was given the lion's share of the commission—the design of all the furniture—while Walton was responsible for the wall decorations and the general layout of the spaces."[35] By 1900, when Mackintosh assumed sole responsibility for Cranston's Ingram Street tea rooms, Macdonald was working with him on the interior, much of which would be seen in Vienna and Turin.

Like the McNairs, Mackintosh and Macdonald did not draw a neat distinction between their public and their private interiors; they used the same colours, shapes, and rhythms to make a space for the tea-drinking public of Glasgow as they used for the interior of their own home. The Rose Boudoir at Turin was related to their pristine white environment at 120 Mains Street (1900), while at the same time referring back to Glasgow's public space of the tea room—specifically the Argyle Street and the Ingram Street tea rooms.

Their work for the exhibition in Turin and the flat they made for themselves created an effect of intimacy and harmony as well as of strength and unity. All three rooms in Turin—one in white, silver, and rose; a second in white and grey gold; and the third in "golden purple and white"—exemplified the "feeling of quiet repose, of coolness and of freshness" characteristic of their work at this time.[36] The bedroom in the Mains Street flat (plate 68) combined the elegance of a slightly curved line used decoratively on the bedstead and on the doors of the armoires with the serenity of white and pale grey, making an atmosphere of calm, quiet, and containment. The sitting room, now beautifully re-created at the Hunterian Art Gallery in Glasgow,[37] shares these qualities. When the German art historian Richard Muther wrote about the Scottish part of the Vienna Secession, he focussed on the repetition of elongated shapes: tall, thin candles, chairs, and cupboards as well as pictures of slim, elliptic figures drawn with stringlike lines or tall, lofty obelisk forms. He commented on the armless female figures and the "unique style" that recalled a line of columns or Gothic pillars, and then he described Margaret Macdonald in the same terms as he did her work, as looking like a Gothic pillar, her coat resembling the fluting on a column, her hat the capital.[38] Some German critics associated the Scots with the eighteenth-century romantic but rational Johann Wolfgang von Goethe[39]; Muther implicated the less refined, more sensuous philosophy of Friedrich Wilhelm Nietzsche in the work and insisted upon the unity between the artists and the art.[40] Their spaces—whether domestic, exhibited, or commissioned—were made for aesthetic pleasure and, as such, spoke directly to the senses.

In Turin the ebonised-wood desk designed by Mackintosh with panels of painted gesso and silver by Macdonald (plate 51) embodied the strength of their collaborative efforts. The wood complemented the panels, and neither over-

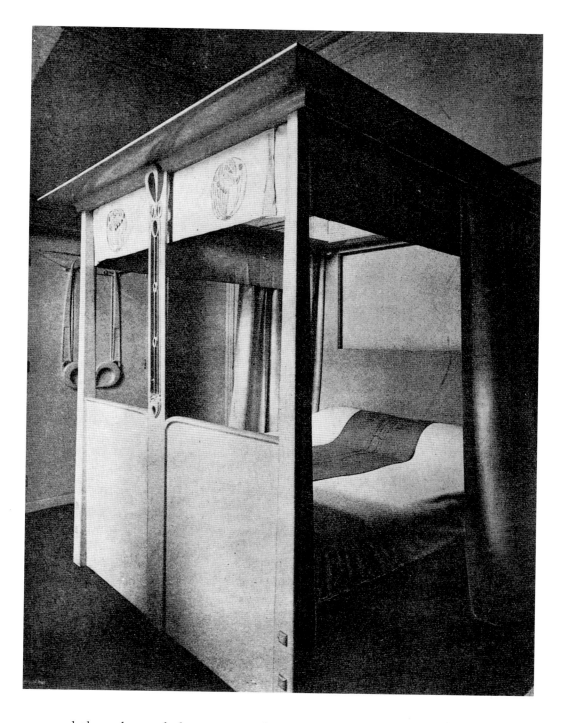

powered the other; a balance was achieved between the verticals of the desk and the curvilinear designs on the inside panels. Each individual piece in this section of the exhibition, as well as the Scottish display as a whole, achieved an effect much like that of the Mackintosh-Macdonald desk: they all embodied a dignity and thoughtfulness that, according to the *Studio*, won for them a "place among those with whom decorative art is at once the highest and the truest expression of man's worship of the beautiful."[41]

68. Charles Rennie Mackintosh and Margaret Macdonald Mackintosh. Bedroom at 120 Mains Street, Glasgow, 1900. From *Modern British Domestic Architecture: Special Number of "The Studio"* (1901): 112.

The conflation of public with private continued as Mackintosh and Macdonald worked together on the Willow Tea Rooms (plate 69), which opened on Sauchiehall Street in the autumn of 1903. By 1903 Glasgow was accustomed to tea rooms, particularly those of Kate Cranston, but nevertheless the "Sauchiehall Street house" marked "an unique departure." Among the rooms, wrote an *Evening News* reporter, the "dainty and elegant" Salon de Luxe was the "most charming." The "wide curved windows" had leaded casements and bronze fittings; "two groups of crystal lights" hung from the vaulted ceiling; the woodwork was white enamel, and "the lower walls silver silk and the upper decorated with panels of mosaic glass in purple, white and silver."[42] The tea house took its name from the "Willow Tree" plaster frieze on the white, silver, and rose ground floor as well as from the street where it was located (Sauchiehall means "alley of the willow"). Macdonald designed "a panel in coloured plaster" to hang opposite the polished-steel fireplace in the vaulted upstairs room, the Salon de Luxe. According to Billcliffe, this large panel, *O Ye, All Ye That Walk in Willowwood* (plate 70), was her "most individual contribution" to the tea rooms, "although her influence can be felt in all the different elements of the room."[43]

As with many of Macdonald's other works, *Willowwood* is best experienced within the collaborative setting for which it was designed. Removed from this context, it might appear too frivolously decorative for the late-twentieth-century viewer. In its setting it becomes a gem in an area meant to be jewel-like in order to turn what might have been a dour environment of temperance and tea into a sumptuous haven for quiet conversation. Cranston intended "that her Tea Rooms should offer an alternative to the bars and drinking clubs which were a blight on Scottish life," providing an atmosphere in which men and women might drink coffee or tea, write letters, read books, or converse without encountering drunkenness.[44]

Given this intention, it is appropriate that Macdonald's *Willowwood* harmonised the intimate and the sensuous with the extravagant. The three female figures bring the serenity of the boudoir into the tea room. The curvilinear line is played out on a raised surface encrusted with beads; the rose motif suggests a private garden. This response to the challenge of making the straightlaced world of the anti-alcohol tea rooms inviting to the sophisticate has succeeded. Far from imposing temperance upon an unwilling participant, this unique interior seduces the visitor with its charms. To isolate the gesso panel from its environment (that is, from its collaborative project) is to remove its power and its purpose.

The contribution of all four artists to the Vienna and Turin exhibitions, and the contribution of Margaret Macdonald and Mackintosh to Cranston's tea rooms, represents "shared production"; even though Mackintosh has been highlighted as the significant contributor, the projects all were collaborative. How the projects are perceived depends to a large extent on how individualism and collectivism are valued.

69. Detail of the Salon de Luxe, Willow Tea Rooms, showing Margaret Macdonald Mackintosh's gesso panel *O Ye, All Ye That Walk in Willowwood*. Photographed by T. and R. Annan Ltd., 1903.

Exclusive Authorship

The tendency to search for a genius-creator has been most clearly reflected in the response to the watercolour pictures of flowers signed with the initials "CRM MMM": Charles Rennie Mackintosh and Margaret Macdonald Mackintosh. The signing of the pictures in this way turns the connoisseur's drive to assign attribution into a task similar to solving a complex puzzle; elaborate stylistic analyses and a search for sources in the oeuvre of the artist are means often used to solve such a puzzle, and these tend to continue the myth of the individual genius-creator.

Many of these double-signed drawings were produced at Walberswick, England. The Mackintoshes vacationed there with the Newberys in 1914, and when the war broke out, they decided to remain in the quiet seacoast village. The time spent there was a transition between their Glasgow years and their move to London—between leaving families and friends in Scotland and beginning a different life with different directions. The village offered the two artists an atmosphere of repose within an artists' community. An 1897 article in the *Artist* called Walberswick a "picturesque and paintable little place," a neighbourhood that was "as absolutely primitive as anything could be," and where one could find the "quietest quiet."[45] The tranquillity, along with the potential for like-minded companionship, must have attracted the Mackintoshes, who had visited the Newberys there on more than one occasion. A young Scottish artist later described her Walberswick vacations (also with the Newberys) as "long weeks of hot sunshine, sandy lanes, hedges powdered white with dust; and cottage gardens a riot of vegetable-marrows, sunflowers, Madonna-lilies, opium-poppies and larkspur."[46]

This environment nurtured the production of a series of watercolour drawings signed CRM MMM, and in 1939, when *Country Life* reproduced one of the drawings, *Gorse, Walberswick* (plate 71), it was attributed to both C. R. Mackintosh and Margaret Macdonald Mackintosh.[47] The drawing was owned by Randolph Schwabe, Slade Professor of Fine Arts at the University of London, a friend and neighbour of the Mackintoshes in Chelsea. After Macdonald's death in 1933, Schwabe had done "what he could to sort out the drawings, paintings and designs, separating with certainty in all but a few cases the work of Toshie from Margaret's."[48] Given the artists' history of collabo-

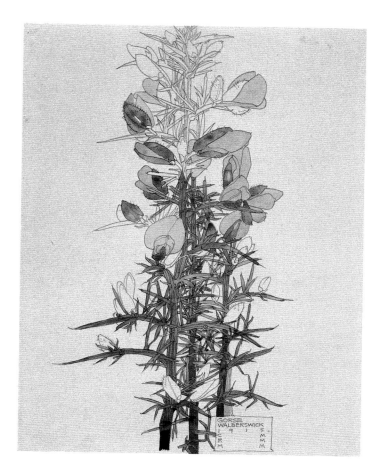

ration and Schwabe's intimate knowledge of their work, at least some of the jointly signed watercolours were probably also jointly made.

According to Billcliffe these pictures "were intended for a book of flower studies to be published in Germany," but the outbreak of World War I "prevented publication of the book."[49] Perhaps, as Billcliffe suggests, the initials inform us of "the people who were with him [Mackintosh] when he made the drawing."[50] Perhaps because so much of Mackintosh's work was done with his wife, he wanted her included in these as well. Or perhaps the couple did indeed make the pictures together. As Pamela Robertson insisted in her catalogue essay for *Mackintosh Flower Drawings*, "Mackintosh is meticulous about titling, signing and dating."[51] The flower studies were certainly a departure for Mackintosh from his previous work. So, too, they might have been for Macdonald, who did exhibit an untraced floral work entitled *Geraniums* in the 1893 exhibition of the Royal Scottish Society of Painters in Water-Colours.

Years before these flower pictures were made, Gleeson White, in his frequently quoted *Studio* article about the work of the Macdonald sisters, announced "with some relief" that the Macdonalds were "quite willing to have their work jointly attributed—for actuated by the same spirit, it would be

▪▪ OPPOSITE
70. Margaret Macdonald Mackintosh. *O Ye, All Ye That Walk in Willow-wood*, 1903. For the Salon de Luxe, Willow Tea Rooms, Glasgow. Painted gesso on hessian, set with glass beads, 64¾ x 23 in. (164.5 x 58.4 cm). Private collection.
▪▪ ABOVE
71. Charles Rennie Mackintosh. *Gorse, Walberswick*, 1915. Pencil and watercolour, 10¹¹/₁₆ x 8¼ in. (27.2 x 21.0 cm). Trustees of The British Museum, London.

difficult, if not impossible, for an outsider to distinguish the hand of each on the evidence of the finished work alone."[52] However, this way of working undermines attribution, an important practice that plays a large role in museums and galleries, in the art market, and most significantly, in the ideology that underlies traditional conceptions and definitions of modern art making. While attribution of a work to either of the sisters would not alter its commercial or critical value, this would not be true of work made with their male partners, and most particularly with Mackintosh, by far the best known and most highly valued of the four. Collaboration disturbs art-historical and critical discourse, particularly if the hand of one collaborator is worth more, either ideologically or economically, than the hand of the other.

Hence the flower pictures signed "CRM MMM" have been debated and pronounced to be "by Mackintosh." Because an individual model of art making is much more familiar and acceptable than a collaborative model of art making, and because we have come to value the individual genius, we are virtually unable to set aside concerns with clear attribution and accept how unclear the conditions of artistic production can be. Four voices speak for the Glasgow Four: we might endeavor to accept the variation as well as the unity of those four voices.

NOTES

I am grateful to Brian Foss for his helpful advice and comments. The research for this essay was funded by the Social Sciences and Humanities Research Council of Canada.

1. Keith Moxey has elaborated on this concept, suggesting that the author or the artist "is a creation of the interpretations to which his or her work has been subjected in the course of time." (Keith Moxey, *The Practice of Theory, Poststructuralism, Cultural Politics, and Art History* [Ithaca, N.Y.: Cornell University Press, 1994], p. 58.)

2. Martin Filler, "Mackintosh, Prophet of Pure Perfection," *House and Garden*, March 1983.

3. Alan Crawford suggests (see his essay "The Mackintosh Phenomenon" in this volume) that Hermann Muthesius wrote about the work of Mackintosh *and* Macdonald, thus affirming the inclusion of the decorative. (Hermann Muthesius, "Die Glasgower Kunstbewegung: Charles R. Mackintosh und Margaret Macdonald-Mackintosh," *Dekorative Kunst* [March 1902]: 216–17.) In fact, Muthesius highlighted Mackintosh. For example, when he discussed "Mackintosh's" ornamental work with its "very personal meaning . . . especially evident in the female figures on p. 219 to 221," the pieces he referred to were designed and made by Macdonald. He later singled out the pieces on "p. 220 and 221" as "produced by Mrs. Macdonald-Mackintosh." Muthesius understood Macdonald's "sensitive linear pieces" as contrasting with Mackintosh's "bold, architectural forms." But, according to Muthesius, this "opposition signifies completion. The male and the female elements are joined together. There is the danger that Mackintosh's well-defined forms could disappear beneath the sentimental and superficial decorative panels or wall designs, and female grace could destroy male valour. These ornamental pieces serve as a warning sign against such decoration: it should be sparse but at the same time well expressed and effective." This kind of "inclusion of the other" merely enhanced already established gender stereotypes; it did not and does not open up a space for partnership. (I thank Michelle Veitch for her assistance with German translations.)

4. Carr and Stewart, in "Some Industrial Art in Glasgow: And the Fugitive Thoughts It Suggests," *Artist* (London) (February 1897): 76.

5. *Quiz* (Glasgow), November 15, 1894, p. 13.

6. *Evening News* (Glasgow), November 9, 1894, p. 2, and November 13, 1894, p. 4.

7. *Bailie* (Glasgow), November 14, 1894, p. 11.

8. Unidentified clipping, Francis Newbery's "Clipping Book," Glasgow School of Art Library, p. 47.

9. *Evening News* (Glasgow), January 24, 1895, p. 2.

10. *Evening News* (Glasgow), February 9, 1895, p. 2.

11. *Evening News* (Glasgow), February 4, 1895, p. 2.

12. *Evening News* (Glasgow), January 28, 1895, p. 2.

13. The friends spent weekends with John Keppie and his sister Jessie in two bungalows on the coast of the Firth of Clyde near Dunure, about three miles north of Culzean Castle. Six photographs taken from that time show the friends featured in what George Rawson calls "a series of 'artistically posed' comic images." (George Rawson, "Mackintosh, Jessie Keppie and 'The Immortals': Some New Material," *Charles Rennie Mackintosh Society Newsletter* 62 [summer 1993]: 4.)

14. *Evening News* (Glasgow), April 12, 1895, p. 6.

15. *Evening News* (Glasgow), April 6, 1895, p. 5.

16. *Glasgow Herald*, May 9, 1899, p. 6. E. A. Walton, Bessie MacNicol, Francis Newbery, and Edward Hornel were among the other Glaswegians represented in this exhibition.

17. *Architectural Review* (May 1899): 311–12.

18. *Evening News* (Glasgow), May 22, 1899, p. 4.

19. "Die VIII. Ausstellung der Weiner 'Secession,'" *Dekorative Kunst* (September 1901): 174. The same cabinet was reproduced in *Deutsche Kunst und Dekoration* (September 1902): 578, and attributed to "Charles Rennie Mackintosh, Glasgow." The attribution of the panel to Macdonald appeared in Muthesius, "Die Glasgower Kunstbewegung," p. 220.

20. *Builder* (London), October 12, 1889, p. 253.

21. For a discussion of the contribution of Mackintosh and Macdonald to the Arts and Crafts Exhibition Society shows in London, see Janice Helland, "The Critics and the Arts and Crafts: The Instance of Margaret Macdonald and Charles Rennie Mackintosh," *Art History* 17 (summer 1994): 209–27.

22. Nikolaus Pevsner, *The Sources of Modern Architecture and Design* (London: Thames and Hudson, 1968), p. 138.

23. Ibid.

24. *Saal X*, assigned to the Four, was called the Scottish Room ("das 'schottische Zimmer'") even though, as Alan Crawford suggests, it may not have been a completely separate room. ("Ausstellung der Weiner 'Secession,'" p. 176.)

25. W. Fred, "8th Exhibition of the Secession," *Artist* (New York) 30 (March 1901): 87.

26. Further research needs to be done on how the Scots were received in Vienna, but certainly they were "seen": *Neue Freie Presses* reported that over twenty-four thousand people visited the exhibition. Quoted in Eduard Sekler, "Mackintosh and Vienna," *Architectural Review* 144 (December 1968): 455.

27. Roger Billcliffe and Peter Vergo, "Charles Rennie Mackintosh and the Austrian Art Revival," *Burlington Magazine* 119 (November 1977): 739–46.

28. Roger Billcliffe, "Mackintosh and Cranston—A Pioneering Partnership," *Arts in Virginia* 26, no. 12 (1986): 19.

29. Alfredo Melani, "The First International Exhibition of Modern Decorative Art at Turin, II," *Journal of Decorative Art and the British Decorator* (July 1902): 195.

30. "Die Turiner Ausstellung," *Dekorative Kunst* (August 1902): 401, 403.

31. McNair replaced Robert Anning Bell as lecturer on art at the University of Liverpool in 1898. (*Glasgow Herald*, June 28, 1898, p. 6.) Macdonald began teaching at the university, though not on salary, after 1900–1901. Sylvan McNair was born June 18, 1900; he was their only child.

32. "The International Exhibition of Modern Decorative Art at Turin—the Scottish Section," *Studio* 26 (July 1902): 96.

33. Ibid.

34. When Mackintosh exhibited the designs for the wall stencils in 1898, a Glasgow critic insisted that the drawings, which represented the human figure as "pure convention," were "in revolt from accepted canons of taste." (*Glasgow Herald*, April 2, 1898, p. 4.)

35. Billcliffe, "Mackintosh and Cranston," p. 16. On the other hand, Perilla Kinchin insists that "the lion's share of the work remained to the trusted Walton." (Perilla Kinchin, *Tea and Taste: The Glasgow Tea Rooms, 1875–1975* [Wendlebury, England: White Cockade Publishing, 1991], p. 92.)

36. "Scottish Section," p. 94. The "delegate for Scotland, appointed by the Turin Committee" was Francis Newbery; the architect was Mackintosh.

37. The Hunterian reconstruction is of the Mackintoshes' second home, 78 Southpark Avenue (1906), but much of the furniture and the colour scheme remained the same as in the flat at 120 Mains Street.

38. Richard Muther, *Studien und Kritiken* (Vienna: Wien-Verlag, 1900), p. 89.

39. Hermann Muthesius thought the Scots brought to mind Goethe. (Muthesius, "Die Glasgower Kunstbewegung," p. 204.)

40. Muther, *Studien und Kritiken*, p. 90.

41. "Scottish Section," pp. 94, 103.

42. *Evening News* (Glasgow), October 29, 1903, p. 7.

43. Billcliffe, "Mackintosh and Cranston," p. 22.

44. Ibid., p. 15.

45. *Artist* (London) (November 1897): 558.

46. Cecile Walton, "More Lives Than One," unpublished memoir, 1951, p. 246.

47. *Country Life*, April 15, 1939, unpaginated.

48. Randolph Schwabe to William Davidson, March 12, 1933, Hunterian Art Gallery, University of Glasgow. Schwabe owned at least eleven of the double-signed watercolours.

49. Roger Billcliffe, *Mackintosh Watercolours*, 2d ed. (London: John Murray, 1987), p. 16.

50. Ibid., p. 14.

51. Pamela Robertson, *Mackintosh Flower Drawings* (Glasgow: Hunterian Art Gallery, University of Glasgow, 1988), p. 7.

52. Gleeson White, "Some Glasgow Designers and Their Work," part 1, *Studio* 11 (July 1897): 90.

II

Architecture

The Glasgow Years

■■
DAVID WALKER

Late Victorian Glasgow was a good place for a young architect to start his career. Its buildings might be velvety black with soot, but Glasgow's institutions, business houses, and developers probably spent more money on architecture than any other British provincial city. An architect could prosper there, just as successfully as in London. Clients were no more afraid of innovation in building than in the industrial processes and engineering that made the city rich. And above all, it was a city open to influences. Though they shared the same professional journals as their British colleagues, the ablest Glasgow architects looked as much to Europe and America as to London.

These were Glasgow traditions. In the 1840s and 1850s Charles Wilson had followed the German architects Leo von Klenze and Friedrich von Gärtner, and Alexander Thomson had followed Karl Friedrich Schinkel rather than Charles Barry or other London luminaries. From 1855 onwards John Baird and James Thomson, and the engineer Robert McConnell, had been the first in Britain to experiment with iron facades for commercial buildings. And in the southern suburbs Alexander Thomson's brilliantly original neo-Greek Holmwood, Cathcart (1857), and his double villa in Mansionhouse Road, Langside (1856), had shown how unafraid the prosperous Glasgow middle class was of houses far removed from London fashions. As the century progressed, Glasgow's links with Paris and the United States grew even stronger; and so, it should be said, did its links with London. For it was openness that characterised Glasgow's late Victorian architecture, not separatism.

This was a different climate from that of Mackintosh's Arts and Crafts contemporaries in England—most of them pupils of George Frederick

72. Charles Rennie Mackintosh. The Scotland Street front of Scotland Street School, Glasgow, 1903–6.

Bodley, George Devey, Ernest George, Richard Norman Shaw, and Philip Webb. The practices of masters and pupils were steeped in the English rural building traditions of the fifteenth, sixteenth, and seventeenth centuries. Mackintosh was to draw on these traditions himself, but he grew up in a less insular architectural world. Ultimately, the international crosscurrents in Glasgow's architectural profession, together with his own inquiring and experimental cast of mind, made his architecture much more complex and imaginative than that of the English Arts and Crafts men. The aim of this essay is to chart these crosscurrents in relation to Mackintosh's early work and to outline the development of his mature style.

GLASGOW ARCHITECTURE, 1870s–80s

In 1884 Mackintosh was apprenticed to John Hutchison, an undistinguished architect whose best-known building is the former Wylie Hill department store at 20–24 Buchanan Street (1888–89). It is unremarkable apart from the smaller details, for which Mackintosh may have been responsible.[1] But when, on the completion of his articles in 1889, Mackintosh joined Honeyman and Keppie, he became part of a leading practice in Glasgow. He was already a brilliant draughtsman, and he found scope for his own talents at Honeyman and Keppie. At the same time the practice introduced him to an existing situation; it immersed him in the currents of progressive architectural taste as they had developed in Glasgow in the 1870s and 1880s. Of these, three seem particularly important: the influence of the Aesthetic movement, coming from England; the refinement and revival of Scottish traditions both academic and vernacular, which could now be called, for want of a better term, the New Academic movement; and the influence of the French Beaux-Arts tradition.

John Honeyman was fifty-eight when Mackintosh joined the practice. His architecture reflected his time in William Burn's office in London in 1853–54: Early English and Early Decorated churches with graceful spires; scholarly neo-Greek and High Renaissance public and commercial buildings; and Tudor, Renaissance, and Baronial houses. Only his iron facade for F. and J. Smith's warehouse on Gordon Street (1872) and his observatory at Paisley had been innovative. His architecture hardly changed in thirty-five years, apart from the sudden change in his domestic work from the conventional Victorian Baronial of Roundelwood, Crieff (1883), to the wholly convincing tower-house form of Skipness, Kintyre (1884), built in true late-sixteenth-century style (plate 73). This can be attributed to the influence of his friend David MacGibbon, whose great survey of Scottish domestic architecture (with Thomas Ross) was published as *The Castellated and Domestic Architecture of Scotland* in 1887–92. Mackintosh would also feel the influence of MacGibbon and Ross.[2]

Honeyman's practice had ranked fourth in Glasgow in terms of volume of work. But the mid-1880s were disastrous for him financially, and in 1889 he went into partnership with John Keppie, a much younger man who was at that

73. John Honeyman (1831–1914). Skipness, Kintyre, Argyll, 1884. The new house under construction within the forecourt of the old.

time an assistant in the distinguished firm of Douglas and Sellars. Keppie had been James Sellars's favourite pupil, but Sellars died in 1888. Campbell Douglas, with characteristic generosity, allowed Keppie to take a setting-up commission with him when he left to join Honeyman, and within a very few years several of Douglas's best clients had followed. From Honeyman's point of view, this was a kind of reverse takeover of the senior partner's practice by the younger; what was left of his practice after eight years of decline became, in effect, a continuation of James Sellars's. Honeyman was the elder statesman of this new practice, with the practical experience to reassure clients; Keppie ran the business side, and at first did much of the designing. This arrangement left Honeyman time to concentrate on ecclesiastical and restoration work, which interested him most. Within a few years the practice ranked fourth in Glasgow again. The newness of this partnership presented opportunities to the young Mackintosh. At Honeyman and Keppie, unlike so many hard-driven Scottish practices, a young man without connections could flourish and be encouraged to think and design for himself. A better architectural education was to be had at John James Burnet's, but none of the leading draughtsmen there were allowed to get beyond interpreting the master's sketch designs.[3]

It is unlikely that Honeyman influenced Mackintosh architecturally, beyond transmitting a firm belief in purity and in particular a fastidious avoidance of the eclectic northern European Early Renaissance styles that had become as much the stock-in-trade of second-rate practitioners in Glasgow as they were in London. But Honeyman should not be overlooked. He commanded the respect of the younger men, as a council member of the Royal Institute of British Architects from 1876 to 1884 and as a friend of leading architects such as MacVicar Anderson, Charles Barry Jr., Richard Norman Shaw, and J. J. Stevenson. Despite failing eyesight he drew and photographed with enthusiasm; he was also a prominent antiquary and an indefatigable polemicist on a wide variety of subjects, from taxation to town planning. When Mackintosh began to lecture on architecture in the early 1890s, Honeyman probably gave him encouragement and the free run of his library.

The first exponent of the Aesthetic movement in Scotland was the Glasgow architect William Leiper, who in his London years had been on the fringes of the circle around William Burges and E. W. Godwin. The interiors of two large houses by Leiper—the Scots Baronial Colearn at Auchterarder (1869) and the François Premier Cairndhu at Helensburgh (1872)—were decorated in an Anglo-Japanese style typical of the Aesthetic movement in London. His half-timbered and tile-hung houses of the 1870s and 1880s show that he was thoroughly familiar with the work of Shaw and had perhaps even seen something by George Devey. But Leiper's practice was essentially a domestic one outside the city and had only limited impact. Mackintosh would have been aware of him as one of the more progressive designers in Glasgow, but they had nothing in common beyond an interest in the Japanese.[4]

The central figure in Glasgow during the 1870s and much of the 1880s was arguably Campbell Douglas, whose work belonged to the New Academic movement. New Academic buildings could be early Italian Renaissance, François Premier, neo-Jacobean (both English and Scottish), or even a kind of early or late Georgian in style; but they were always elegant and refined in their details, which were never mechanically repeated. Their inspiration came initially from the Continent, in ways that are not yet clear, but there were also debts to England, and New Academic buildings were at times indistinguishable from those of the Aesthetic movement and the "Queen Anne" style—that eminently practical, seventeenth-century brick style, which transformed the better class of English domestic architecture during the very late 1860s and early 1870s. Douglas was in partnership with J. J. Stevenson (later a leading exponent of "Queen Anne" in London) in the 1860s and with James Sellars from 1872 until Sellars's death in 1888. Close and influential links remained between Douglas and Stevenson. The latter's office provided a ready welcome to promising assistants who sought London experience, and it was a stepping stone to other Aesthetic movement practices. In this way it had a profound influence on architectural development in Scotland from the late 1870s onwards.[5]

During the early and mid-1870s Douglas and Sellars still thought the future lay in a simplified version of Alexander Thomson's Schinkel-based neo-Greek idiom, updated by some modern French Beaux-Arts and Aesthetic movement touches in the details, as at St. Andrew's Halls (1873–77) and Kelvinside Academy (1877), both in Glasgow. But in 1877, for the New Club in West George Street, Glasgow, they suddenly opted for a lavish "Modern French" design, a belated product of Sellars's visit to Paris in 1872. Its ornate Aesthetic movement interiors, of a refined Free Renaissance variety (plate 74), were the precursors of the more elaborate interior work done in the early

THE NEW CLUB : SKETCH OF ENTRANCE HALL

1890s by John Keppie in association with Mackintosh, at the offices of the Fairfield Shipbuilding Yard and Engine Works, at Craigie Hall, and at the Glasgow Art Club. Two years later, on Douglas and Sellars's building for the Glasgow Herald at 65 Buchanan Street, elaborate Franco-Netherlandish gabled attics of the sort then fashionable in London were combined with Corinthian columns in a monumental giant order that had no counterpart in London work.[6]

The other influential New Academic was the Edinburgh architect Robert Rowand Anderson. He sought inspiration farther afield than his Scottish contemporaries, and his work had a marked influence on that of his Glasgow

74. James Sellars (1843–1888). The New Club, 144–46 West George Street, Glasgow. *Perspective of the Entrance Hall*, c. 1878. Pencil, 10¹³⁄₁₆ x 8¾ in. (27.5 x 22.2 cm). Crown Copyright: Royal Commission on the Ancient and Historical Monuments of Scotland.

counterparts during the early 1880s. In 1875 he won the limited competition for Edinburgh University's new Medical School and Graduation Hall with a northern Italian (mainly Venetian) Early Renaissance design—the product of a study tour of contemporary university medical buildings that had taken him as far afield as Leipzig. In scholarship and sophistication it merited comparison with such buildings as McKim, Mead and White's Madison Square Garden, New York, of a few years later. By contrast, Anderson's Glasgow Central Station (1877–86) synthesised the Italian Early Renaissance of the Medical School with northern European Early Renaissance window surrounds and tall gables, the latter to accommodate the required height of seven storeys (plate 75). Its bay design was to form the basis of Honeyman and Keppie's more severely Italianate design for the Manchester Technical Schools a decade later.[7]

In the 1880s, at the Normand Hall, Dysart (1883), and at St. Cuthbert's Church, Colinton (1887), Anderson adopted features from mid-seventeenth-century Scottish public buildings, particularly the Old College of Glasgow, whose threatened demolition aroused strong feelings in the 1870s. Anderson's choice proved influential. Others who followed suit included his pupil Sydney Mitchell at Well Court, Edinburgh (1884); James Sellars with robust early-eighteenth-century Scottish forms at the Coupar Institute, Cathcart (1887); and Honeyman and Keppie at the Canal Boatmen's Institute, Port Dundas (1893), and at Queen Margaret College, Glasgow (1894).[8]

Anderson's work in the 1880s was partly shaped by the experience of his principal assistant, George Washington Browne, who had been an assistant at Douglas and Sellars, then worked for Stevenson and for William Eden Nesfield in London.[9] Browne's return to Scotland gave the two leading practices in Edinburgh and Glasgow their first inkling of Nesfield's work. The vernacular simplicity of Nesfield's Plas Dinam, Montgomery (1872), and the formal grandeur of the Stuart-style palace of Kinmel, Denbigh (1871), must have been a revelation.[10] Echoes of Kinmel can be found in some of Anderson's public buildings well into the following century, and at Nile Grove, Edinburgh, Anderson and Browne designed a "Queen Anne" art suburb equivalent to Bedford Park outside London.

Otherwise, Scottish architects remained remote from the most progressive domestic work south of the border. Of the leading Arts and Crafts practitioners, only Shaw published much, and the mainstream of the English rediscovery of the vernacular and of the beauty of traditional materials remained hidden from view in Scotland. None of the buildings by Devey, Webb, or Nesfield, for example, were easily seen. Mackintosh might just have glimpsed the white-walled simplicity of Devey's Macharioch (1872) in Kintyre,[11] but he probably knew nothing of Webb's even more austerely vernacular Arisaig (1863) in Lochaber. The Scots did not become aware of the Arts and Crafts movement until the 1890s, when its influence was more widely spread.[12]

The 1870s and 1880s saw one of the more surprising developments in British architectural history—the steady stream of students from well-off Glasgow families who sought a more sophisticated education at the Ecole des Beaux-Arts in Paris rather than in London. Few British students had attended the Ecole before, and none had been Scottish. In the autumn of 1874 John James Burnet, the seventeen-year-old son of the prosperous architect John Burnet Sr., joined the atelier of Jean-Louis Pascal; he enrolled in the Ecole in 1875. (In the Beaux-Arts system, the atelier was the place for work and tutorials, the Ecole for lectures and examinations.) Burnet returned home in 1877 and won the competition for the Glasgow Institute of the Fine Arts building in May 1878 with a design intended to blend "the severe and refined Greek . . . with the full flowing lines of the Renaissance in order to get a full share of

75. Robert Rowand Anderson (1834–1921). Central Station and Hotel, Gordon and Hope Streets, Glasgow, 1877–86.

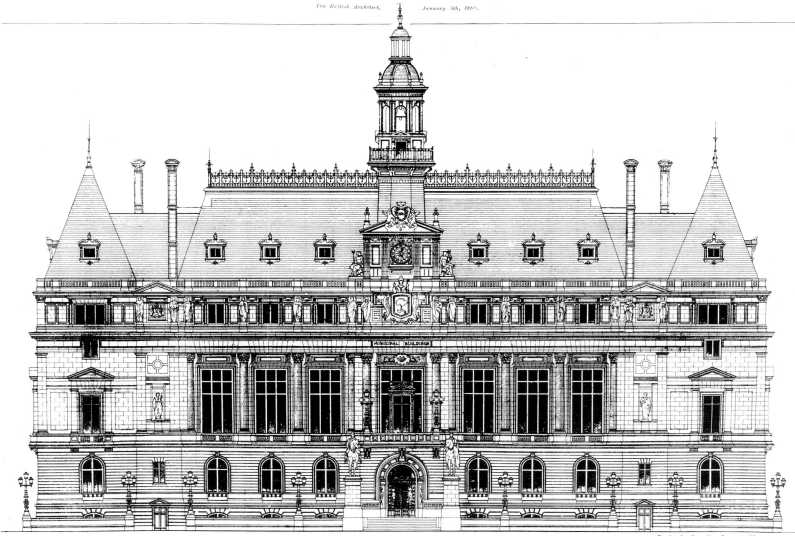

GLASGOW MUNICIPAL BUILDINGS.

ELEVATION to GEORGE SQUARE

Design by Jno. Jas. Burnet, Glasgow.

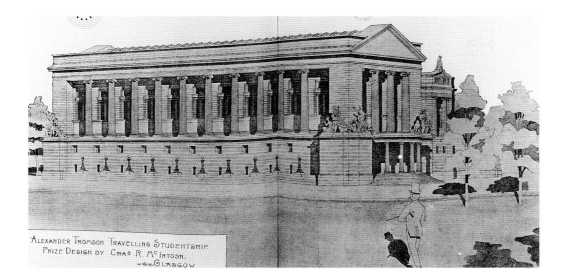

breadth and dignity." His was not among the winning entries in the competitions of 1880 and 1881–82 for the Glasgow Municipal Buildings, but his Beaux-Arts designs (plate 76) created something of a sensation.[13]

In the meantime, two other apprentices from Burnet's office, John Archibald Campbell and Alexander Nisbet Paterson, had made their way to Pascal's atelier, while an unrelated architect, Robert Douglas Sandilands, had joined the atelier of Julien Guadet. By 1885 Douglas and Sellars had begun to feel their position as the leading practice in Glasgow under threat, and Keppie was encouraged to attend the Ecole. No record of him survives there, but he spent eighteen months at Pascal's in 1885–86. On his return he assisted Sellars with his successful Moorish competition entry for the Glasgow International Exhibition of 1888, a design that anticipated aspects of Mackintosh's work of the 1890s. Sellars's principal entrance featured a Japanese-inspired motif of twin beams clasping an upright, which Mackintosh was to use first at Martyrs' Public School and most prominently on the staircase in the School of Art. The general outline and some rooftop details of Sellars's Main Building were repeated in Mackintosh's competition entry for Glasgow's International Exhibition of 1901. Keppie seems to have been the common factor.[14]

Mackintosh experienced the Beaux-Arts approach indirectly—through Keppie and through Burnet's teaching at the School of Art. It is not easy to gauge just what he took from it. His first biographer, Thomas Howarth, recorded that Mackintosh particularly admired Sellars and Burnet, and their influence is marked in his two successful student competition designs of 1890. The Alexander Thomson Travelling Studentship design (plate 77) was pure Sellars Grecian, with sculptural groups and lamp standards similar to those of Sellars's St. Andrew's Hall. Mackintosh's design for a science and art museum, which won a silver medal in the National Competition at South Kensington (plate 78), took inspiration from Burnet's Beaux-Arts designs for the Municipal

▪▪ OPPOSITE
76. John James Burnet (1857–1938). Glasgow Municipal Buildings, George Square. *Competition Entry: The George Square Elevation*, 1880. From the *British Architect*, January 5, 1883.
▪▪ ABOVE
77. Charles Rennie Mackintosh. *Design for a Public Hall*, 1890. From the *British Architect*, November 28, 1890, p. 402.

78. Charles Rennie Mackintosh. *A Science and Art Museum: Front Elevation*, 1890. Ink and watercolour, 18¹⁄₈ x 34⁵⁄₈ in. (46.0 x 88.0 cm). Hunterian Art Gallery, University of Glasgow.

This student design was awarded a silver medal in the National Competition of the Department of Science and Art, South Kensington, 1890.

Buildings of eight years earlier and from those by Sellars, which (since Sellars kept himself up-to-date) also have a Beaux-Arts character.[15] Mackintosh's writings contain no hint of the ideas of Guadet, the Ecole's leading theorist, who had codified Beaux-Arts training into "that basis of logic which can only be acquired from studying the classics," but Mackintosh's two papers on architecture do contain paraphrases of the Beaux-Arts beliefs that external effects must reflect internal realities and that everything had to be controlled by absolutes founded in logic; thus, they conform to a unified view of theory and practice.[16]

Furthermore, Mackintosh may have emulated Burnet's perfectionism. The working methods of Burnet's office reflected the practical requirements of Beaux-Arts logic: every aspect of the design was studied again and again until Burnet was sure that the best possible result had been achieved. Mackintosh probably experienced this perfectionism at first hand, since Burnet was a visiting teacher at Glasgow School of Art. Although few of Mackintosh's preliminary studies have survived, there can be little doubt that his own working practices must have been very similar to achieve the profoundly studied and imaginative details that he did. That intensity of design effort differed from the more relaxed approach of the English Arts and Crafts architects.

Burnet's domestic work, which Mackintosh would have known from the exhibitions of the Royal Scottish Academy and the Glasgow Institute of the Fine Arts, contained stylistic elements of the Aesthetic movement and of the

Arts and Crafts. Burnet's liking for big roofs swept low down anticipated Voysey's houses of the early 1890s, and at Corrienessan, Loch Ard (1887), this theme was developed further with an American-style verandah porch—in all but material this was a Shingle Style house. There is an echo of Burnet, perhaps, in Mackintosh's very early house, Redclyffe, Springburn (1890), where the central roof sweeps low between the broad canted bays. But these houses and Mackintosh's later masterpieces are fundamentally different. Although Corrienessan was, when built, one of the most advanced houses in Britain, its design was developed from contemporary architecture, not from firsthand observation of traditional building.[17] Mackintosh may have admired Burnet, but he differed from him on some basic principles of design.

MACKINTOSH: EARLY WORKS

In the spring and early summer of 1891 Mackintosh went on a sketching tour of Italy, as a result of having won the Thomson Travelling Studentship. This experience widened his horizons and enhanced his standing in the office of Honeyman and Keppie. It was becoming clear that Keppie was not really a designer, however brilliant a draughtsman and watercolourist he may have been. Like Campbell Douglas, he seems to have been content to forget the normal relationship of employer and employed, and desiring to win competitions and secure new business, he allowed Mackintosh to do most of the design and presentation work. The magnificent Early Renaissance–style woodwork that the firm installed in Craigie Hall, Bellahouston, in 1892–93, and the similar chimneypieces and doorpieces in their extensions to the Glasgow Art Club in Bath Street of the same date are examples of this phase of collaboration. At Craigie Hall, Mackintosh developed the details from his Italian sketchbooks, and the published drawing of the Art Club work is his, with characteristic lettering and metalwork details.[18]

In the work of these years, Keppie and Mackintosh drew not only on the Glasgow traditions already analysed but also on Mackintosh's experiences in Italy and on the best contemporary English work. On his return from Italy, for instance, Mackintosh would have seen the published drawings in the limited competition for London's new South Kensington Museum (now the Victoria and Albert).[19] The designs of the two leading competitors, Aston Webb and John Belcher (plates 79 and 80), had a profound effect on contemporary British architecture and on Mackintosh in particular, as is made clear by a series of competition entries in the next few years. Honeyman and Keppie's entry in the second stage of the competition for the Glasgow Art Galleries (plate 81) echoes Webb's design in the corner pavilions and the fenestration of the centrepiece. Many other details are directly related to Mackintosh's Italian sketchbooks: the internal details of the central hall were taken from Pavia, Verona, and elsewhere, and the apsidal feature on the end elevation came from Como Cathedral.[20]

79. Aston Webb (1849–1930). South Kensington Museum (now the Victoria and Albert Museum), London. *Perspective of the Winning Competition Design* (though not as built), 1891. Ink on linen-backed paper, 25¼ x 47⁷⁄₁₆ in. (64.0 x 120.5 cm). The British Architectural Library, Royal Institute of British Architects, London.

80. John Belcher (1841–1913). South Kensington Museum, London. *Competition Entry: Exhibition Road Elevation*, 1891. From the *Architect*, October 16, 1891 (Architectural Illustration Society, 2d series, plate 422).

   The building on the left is the former Science Schools (1867–71).

81. Charles Rennie Mackintosh. Draughtsman: probably Alexander McGibbon (1861–1938). The Glasgow Art Galleries, Kelvingrove. *Competition Entry: Perspective from the Northeast*, 1892. From the *British Architect*, August 26, 1892.

DESIGN FOR THE COMPLETION OF THE SOUTH KENSINGTON MUSEUM (Motto : Prince Albert.)
ELEVATION TO EXHIBITION ROAD

GLASGOW ART GALLERIES, FINAL COMPETITION.
DESIGN BY
MESSRS HONEYMAN & KEPPIE, GLASGOW.

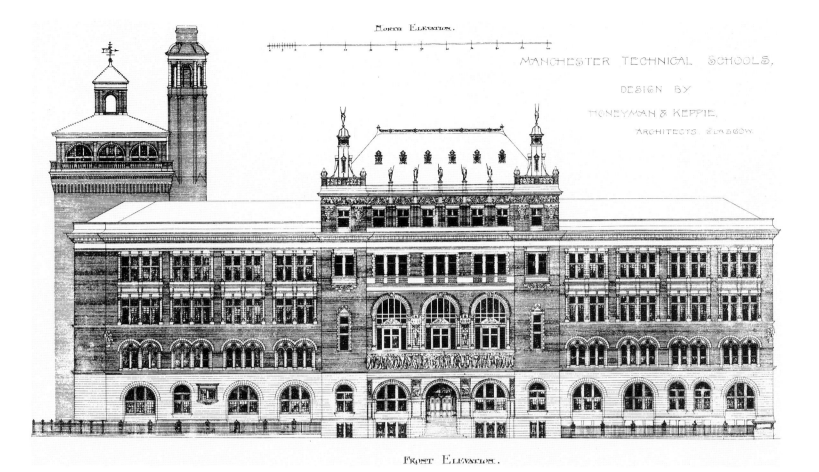

NORTH ELEVATION.

MANCHESTER TECHNICAL SCHOOLS,

DESIGN BY

HONEYMAN & KEPPIE,

ARCHITECTS. GLASGOW.

FRONT ELEVATION.

501. *Design for Royal Insurance Buildings, Buchanan Street, Glasgow*, JOHN HONEYMAN, A.R.S.A., AND KEPPIE, Architects.

In 1892 the *British Architect* praised Honeyman and Keppie's competition design for the Manchester Municipal Technical Schools, suggesting that the assessor should have given his reasons for not placing it among the first three. Their symmetrical composition (plate 82) combined the fenestration of Anderson's Central Station with Art Nouveau turret features that can only have been by Mackintosh. It featured a big, square machicolated tower with a tall octagonal turret, half reminiscent of Italy and half adapted from the pavilions of Webb's South Kensington design.[21] Reverberations of that competition can also be sensed in Honeyman and Keppie's competition design for the Royal Insurance building in Buchanan Street, of 1894 (plate 83), with its semi-octagonal pilastered angle rising up into an aediculed dome only slightly simplified from the subsidiary cupolas of Belcher's South Kensington design.[22] We can see early stirrings of Mackintosh's unorthodox originality in this Royal Insurance design. Unusual and imaginative elements that were to be significant for the future are the concave, bowed-back cornices over the pediments of the doorpiece and the first-floor windows (perhaps derived from Belcher's building for the Institute of Chartered Accountants in London); the curving parapets of the projecting end bays; and the omission of any crowning cornice. All were to be features of Glasgow School of Art's east elevation (plate 88).

The pilastered octagonal angle-tower reappeared in the large extension that Honeyman and Keppie built for the printing works of the *Glasgow Herald* (1893–95), to Mackintosh's design (see plate 201).[23] It was particularly well considered in relation to the narrowness of Mitchell Street, where a conventional tower would have been two-thirds hidden. It is stepped out near the top; then comes a deep stage of unprecedented design, curving upwards, its angles masked by elongated shields; this acts as a cantilever for the top stage. Within the parapet is a cap-house with a broad-eaved, depressed-ogee roof. This deeply shadowed and distinctly profiled crowning feature seems to have been enlarged from the similar but smaller turret at James MacLaren's high school (1889) in Stirling, which Mackintosh must have known. MacLaren's turret in turn was probably developed from the towerlets of J. D. Sedding's Holy Trinity Church, Sloane Street, London.[24]

The main elevation of the Glasgow Herald printing works is even more interesting. The oblong windows are forward-looking for their date, and on the second and third floors they have recessed and canted glazing—an idea probably borrowed from Halsey Ricardo, one of the most original of contemporary London architects, who had used the motif on a small office building in Great George Street, Westminster, in 1888.[25] The two uppermost floors, rising above a plain-parapetted cantilevered balcony, seem to reflect Mackintosh's interest in the Baroque style developed by Burnet and his partner John Archibald Campbell in the late 1880s, with strongly profiled sixteenth- and seventeenth-century Scottish details. But there was no example of Burnet and Campbell's work in this mode in Glasgow itself in 1893, and it is possible that Mackintosh developed the treatment independently. It may even be that Mackintosh's work encouraged Burnet to develop his own ideas further: the depressed-ogee heads of the top floor and the sinuous keystones breaking up into the equally sinuous pediments with concave cornices were far bolder details than anything by Burnet at that date, and in a general way these two upper floors probably gave a powerful boost to the adoption of seventeenth-century Scots Baroque for urban buildings of the 1890s.

The Anatomical School for Queen Margaret College of 1894–95 (plate 84)[26]—now entombed in later extensions for the British Broadcasting Corporation—belongs to the same aesthetic family as the top floors of the Glasgow Herald building. The main part has the same depressed-ogee architraves in simplified form, linked by a semioctagonal stair tower to the higher museum wing. This has a plain gable rising from within a plain parapet, a feature that could have been developed from early Scots tower-houses such as Liberton but also has marked affinities with MacLaren's farmhouse at Glenlyon (plate 90).[27] The overall composition strongly hints at that of The Hill House some seven years later. The stair tower rises into a very Scottish termination, modelled on the cupola of the seventeenth-century tollbooth at Dysart, which had been a Sellars motif and here was probably suggested by Keppie. Both the widely

■■ OPPOSITE, TOP
82. Charles Rennie Mackintosh. Municipal Technical Schools, London and Oxford Roads, Manchester. *Competition Entry: Front Elevation*, 1892. From the *British Architect*, November 4, 1892.
■■ OPPOSITE, BOTTOM
83. Charles Rennie Mackintosh. Draughtsman: probably Alexander McGibbon. Royal Insurance building, 106–12 Buchanan Street, Glasgow. *Competition Entry: Perspective*, 1894. From *Academy Architecture*, 1895, p. 56.

UNIVERSITY of GLASGOW MEDICAL QUEEN MARGARET COLLEGE DERRITT JOHN HONEYMAN AND KEPPIE ARCHITECTS

THE SCHL BOARD OF GLASGOW MARTYRS PUBLIC SCHOOL JOHN HONEYMAN & KEPPIE ARCHTS

84. Charles Rennie Mackintosh. *Anatomical School, Queen Margaret College, University of Glasgow: Perspective from the Southwest,* c. 1895. Ink, 19⁹⁄₁₆ x 31¹¹⁄₁₆ in. (50.0 x 80.5 cm). William Hardie Ltd.

■■ RIGHT, BOTTOM
85. Charles Rennie Mackintosh. *Martyrs' Public School: Perspective from the Northeast,* 1896. Ink, 24¹⁄₈ x 36⁷⁄₈ in. (61.3 x 92.5 cm). Hunterian Art Gallery, University of Glasgow.

spaced balusters and the projection of the roof through an arch in the parapet are markedly Burnet features, the latter appearing at his remodelling of Nunholme (1886), a large villa on Glasgow's Dowanhill,[28] and at University Gardens (1887).

Martyrs' Public School (1895–98) has a standard Board School plan, with a galleried central hall and segregated entrances and stairs at each end (plate 85). The design is relatively conventional, apart from the twinned beams at the roof trusses, inspired by Japan or by Sellars, which show that Mackintosh's mature style, already evident in his furniture, was beginning to appear in his architectural woodwork. Mackintosh's early indebtedness to Burnet is still evident. The doorpieces have Burnet's characteristic broad architrave, though the stretched console brackets have an originality far beyond anything Burnet would then have contemplated. And the concave sides of the quasi-balcony of the north frontage, already seen on the Glasgow Herald building, derive from Burnet's Athenaeum Theatre (1891), a narrow-frontage elevator building that must surely have impressed Mackintosh, even if he made no other direct use of it. On the flank elevations, the combination of a semicircular-headed window with a cutting of the parapet line and a plain-parapeted flanking turret is significant, for it was to recur on the central entrance of Glasgow School of Art. The short section of deep, close-bracketed eaves was similarly to reappear there in dramatically extended form.[29]

MACKINTOSH: THE LECTURES

The first phase of Mackintosh's architecture, when he was working in collaboration with Keppie, came to an end in the mid-1890s. We have seen how much he was influenced by his contemporaries but also how distinctive his work was becoming. Before embarking on his mature work, we should pause to consider the development of the ideas and images that made up his progressivism during this period.

Between 1891 and 1893 Mackintosh gave four lectures on architecture.[30] "Elizabethan Architecture," delivered in 1892, was obviously drawn from rather obsolete sources in Honeyman's library and contains few suggestions of his work to come, apart from the possibility that such houses as Longleat set a useful precedent for the large and regularly spaced gridded windows of Glasgow School of Art. But "Scotch Baronial Architecture," given to the Glasgow Architectural Association in February 1891, and Mackintosh's lectures on contemporary architecture tell us a great deal about his thinking.

The Baronial lecture was almost wholly taken from MacGibbon and Ross's *Castellated and Domestic Architecture of Scotland.* This reliance on one source has shocked some later commentators as amounting to plagiarism, but the historical development of Scottish domestic architecture had never been adequately explained before, and this was the only text that Mackintosh could have used. MacGibbon and Ross drew attention not only to the great turreted piles of the nobility and gentry but also to the simple masses of smaller mercantile houses covered with the rough lime-based plaster known in Scotland as "harling." They transformed the perception of what Scottish architecture should be from the Victorian proportions and mechanical masonry of a house like Anderson's Allermuir (1879–84) at Colinton to the low, traditional proportions and harling of his pupil Robert Lorimer's Grange at North Berwick, or Stronachullin Lodge, Ardrishaig,[31] both of 1893–94, and ultimately to Mackintosh's own Windyhill and The Hill House. Mackintosh's interest in the simple vernacular forms of sixteenth- and seventeenth-century building was evident early in his career, notably in his sketch of the rear elevation of Provand's Lordship, Glasgow, made in May 1889. His sketching tours, from 1894 onwards, among the often unstudied and unillustrated vernacular architecture of English towns and villages, were an extension of that interest, with identifiable results in Glasgow School of Art and in his major houses.

Mackintosh's first lecture on contemporary architecture, probably delivered in 1892 to an unknown literary society, is of great interest if not always very articulate. The principles it propounded were drawn from John Ruskin, from George Baldwin Brown (professor of fine art at Edinburgh University), and ultimately from A.W.N. Pugin. Mackintosh rejected as absurd make-believe not only the temple-based public architecture of the Thomson-Sellars-Honeyman school but also the entire spectrum of Renaissance styles then in vogue. And, despite the then-fashionable philosophy of integrated eclecticism implied in Mackintosh's own design for the Glasgow Art Galleries, he went so far as to say that one style must be weakened by the introduction of another, supporting his argument with a passage from Sir Joshua Reynolds's *Discourses on Art*. Mackintosh may or may not have been aware of the simple, unaffected functionalism of vernacular Gothic, which William Morris and his circle had discovered in Ruskin's *Stones of Venice* (1851–53)—particularly in the central chapter, "The Nature of Gothic," which Morris reprinted as a separate volume. Although Mackintosh surprisingly did not quote it, paragraph 38, which clearly refers to English domestic Gothic rather than that of the more formally composed Venetian palaces, set out the Arts and Crafts approach to architectural design:

> Gothic is not only the best, but the *only rational* architecture . . . And it is one of the chief virtues of the Gothic builders that they never suffered ideas of outside symmetries and consistency to interfere with the real use and value of what they did. If they wanted a window they opened one; a room, they added one; a buttress they built one; utterly regardless of any established conventionalities of external appearance knowing (as indeed it always happened) that such daring interruptions of the formal plan would rather give additional interest to its symmetry than injure it.[32]

Ruskin's message, and ultimately that of Mackintosh's paper, was of a Puginian truthfulness to the necessities of building and of a preference for national rather than cosmopolitan characteristics.

The second lecture contains less original thought than the first, but it tells us more. As Robert Macleod was the first to point out, it was largely quoted from *Architecture, Mysticism and Myth* (1891) by W. R. Lethaby, a former assistant of Richard Norman Shaw and the focus of an influential Arts and Crafts circle in London.[33] Reading Lethaby probably suggested fresh

86. James MacLaren (1853–1890). 10–12 Palace Court, Bayswater, London, 1889–90. From the *Architect*, July 22, 1892 (Architectural Illustration Society, 2d series, plate 407).

thoughts to Mackintosh: that "all great and living architecture has been the direct expression of the needs and beliefs of man at the time of its creation" (which prompted Mackintosh to search for the first principles of architecture in simple traditional buildings on both sides of the border); and that "to get architecture the architect must be one of a body of artists possessing an intimate knowledge of the crafts."

With Gerald Horsley and Mervyn Macartney, Lethaby was one of the organisers of the Architectural Illustration Society, which sponsored some six hundred plates in the *Architect* between 1886 and 1892, with a view to improving architecture and its illustration. In his second lecture on architecture, Mackintosh identified six heroes of contemporary architecture—Belcher, J. F. Bentley, G. F. Bodley, J. D. Sedding, Shaw, and Leonard Stokes; of these, five were well represented in the society's plates, together with retrospectives of the work of Devey and Nesfield. Although Philip Webb was conspicuously absent, the plates still provided a fairly comprehensive survey of all that was best in contemporary English architecture, with a bias towards vernacular-based work.

Virtually all of Mackintosh's heroes were, in varying degrees, pioneers of the free Tudor, which, as John Summerson observed, was to become "the most profoundly characteristic and most distinctly unifying architecture in Britain round 1900."[34] That was as true of Scotland, to which the style was not native, as it was of England. With borrowings from Sedding and his pupil Henry Wilson, this style appeared in Mackintosh's competition design for a railway terminus (1892); his sketch design for a church of about the same date; the Conservative Club at Helensburgh (1894–95); Queen's Cross Church, Glasgow (plate 89); and ultimately, in a more vernacular form, in the house called Auchinibert in Killearn (1905–8).[35] Among the society's plates, some were of even greater importance for Mackintosh's development—those that showed the work of James MacLaren and that of his successors William Dunn and Robert Watson.

MacLaren, who had been an assistant with Douglas and Sellars, was part of the extraordinarily gifted circle in that office and transferred to J. J. Stevenson in London. In 1887 he won a competition for the extension of Stirling High School; we have already seen how the remarkable tower in his design, rising round-angled from a telescopic base, influenced Mackintosh. Then, with even more significance for Mackintosh, came the double house that MacLaren built at 10–12 Palace Court (plate 86) in 1889–90 for the two daughters of Sir Donald Currie.[36] The overall composition, with banded brick and stone at the top floor and tall chimneystacks, derived from Shaw; the clever asymmetrical balance of the slim vertical of the canted bay and its associated wrought-iron balcony came from Stevenson and Anderson.[37] But the deep sculptured frieze of stylised foliage, very similar in feeling to those by Louis Sullivan, was American in inspiration, as were the nonperiod details of the doorpieces, the nearest counterparts to which are found in the more original American brownstone buildings.

For Currie, MacLaren also designed the town hall at Aberfeldy, Perthshire (1889), with rough hammer-dressed arches inspired by H. H. Richardson. On Currie's nearby Glenlyon estate MacLaren and his successors Dunn and Watson built a remarkable series of Dorset- and Scottish-inspired vernacular buildings,[38] which were to have a profound influence on British domestic architecture in the 1890s generally (plates 90 and 91). MacLaren died in 1890, aged thirty-seven, just as he was on the point of achieving a nonperiod idiom that was still well within the English and Scottish architectural traditions. Mackintosh must have learned a lot from him, even if he was highly selective in the motifs he adopted, characteristically developing them far beyond anything that MacLaren had ever imagined.

MACKINTOSH: MATURE WORKS

Mackintosh's design for Glasgow School of Art was originally prepared for a limited competition, between March and October 1896.[39] It was extraordinarily severe, but its severity can be understood in light of the competition brief. The governors imposed strict financial restraints—details such as those at Martyrs' Public School simply could not be afforded—and the specifications for the studio windows ensured that Mackintosh, and the other competitors, set them out regularly on the north (the front) elevation. Another important circumstance that may have encouraged acceptance of so severe a design was the publication in 1895 of the winning design for the Passmore Edwards Settlement in London, by A. Dunbar Smith and Cecil Brewer (plate 87).[40] Smith and

87. A. Dunbar Smith (1866–1933) and Cecil Brewer (1871–1918). Passmore Edwards Settlement (now Mary Ward Centre), Tavistock Place, London, 1895–98. From *Neubauten in London* (Berlin: Wasmuth, 1900), plate 23.

Brewer eliminated all period detail in favour of plain brick walls, a simple and massive stone porch (the hoodmould of which has the same low curve as on Mackintosh's Royal Insurance building), and railings set in a swinging dwarf parapet of concave curves, swept up at the entrances. Mackintosh adapted these railings for Glasgow School of Art, transforming them with his own highly original metalwork details. Like MacLaren's Palace Court, the Passmore Edwards Settlement must have seemed to fulfill Mackintosh's hopes for a truly modern architecture; and the publicity it attracted may have encouraged the directors of the Department of Science and Art at South Kensington to approve a nonacademic design for Glasgow.

The main elements of the facade of Glasgow School of Art (see plates 100 and 104) were largely Mackintosh's own. The architraved doorpiece was developed from that at Martyrs' Public School, as was the composition above, and the canted bay to the left is easily related to Mackintosh's sketches of vernacular houses in Lyme Regis, England, made in 1895. Only the central window, together with the railed balcony that unites it with the canted bay, seem to have been adapted from MacLaren's double house in Palace Court, the window being refined and developed with a concave cornice-transom on the Belcher model.

The east elevation, in which the MacLaren window makes a second appearance, is similarly one of the most original designs of the age (plate 88). The absence of strings and the recessed, elongated bows with linked sills probably derived ultimately from the severe monumentality of such Shaw houses as 42 Netherhall Gardens, London (one of the plates by the Architectural Illustration Society),[41] and from the elongated windows of Swan House in Chelsea, though the bows have a more immediate source in the Campbeltown Club House by H. E. Clifford, a Glasgow contemporary of Mackintosh's, which was exhibited at the Glasgow Institute of the Fine Arts in 1896.[42] But the sheer height of unadorned masonry on the school's east elevation was without parallel. The northern half, which originally had no openings at all, rises to an almost featureless parapet broken only by a tapered octagonal turret and a set-back, curvilinear gablet.

The specifications for the studios required that the return wall be blank at this point, but Mackintosh's treatment is still remarkable; any other architect would have felt obliged to relieve the blankness with niches or an inscription panel. As originally designed, the west elevation was to have had rather similar qualities, with asymmetrical gables, large arched windows, and a two-storeyed oriel to the library carried up through a blind storey to the parapet. Throughout the design, whatever the borrowings, Mackintosh experimented with each element to see what more might be got out of it, until it was his own. On the east elevation, for instance, each element of the oriel at Maybole Castle, which Mackintosh had sketched in 1895, was restudied and restyled in his own idiom, taking on a new identity as the base of the turret.

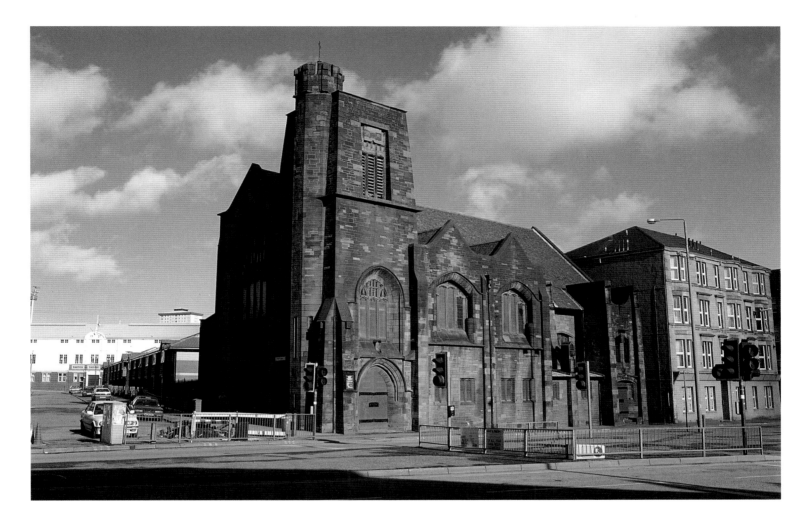

The School of Art was Mackintosh's most radically original building of the 1890s. Queen's Cross Church (plate 89), on the other hand, which he designed in 1897, shows his continued indebtedness to progressive English work; the free Gothic practiced by Henry Wilson and Leonard Stokes still held his interest. Queen's Cross Church was a cleverly planned building with a tower flanking the chancel and linked to a double transept, a Honeyman device to concentrate the congregation near the pulpit; the wide-arched ceiling with steel tie beams followed the model of Shaw's Harrow Mission Church at Shepherd's Bush, London. The boldly tapered topless design of Mackintosh's tower was long ago identified as deriving from his sketch of the church at Merriott in Somerset,[43] though it also occurs in Henry Hare's exactly contemporary design for Westminster College, Cambridge.[44] The other details are closer to Stokes or even to Smith and Brewer—the transept windows are in some ways like the doorpiece at their Passmore Edwards Settlement.

Mackintosh's domestic work, which began in earnest with Windyhill (1900–1901), at Kilmacolm, was profoundly influenced by his sketching tours. In 1894 he sketched simple, traditional buildings in Gloucestershire and

▪▪ OPPOSITE
88. Charles Rennie Mackintosh. The east front of Glasgow School of Art, 1896–99.
▪▪ ABOVE
89. Charles Rennie Mackintosh. Queen's Cross Church, 870 Garscube Road, Glasgow, 1897–99.

Worcestershire, and in 1895 he was in Dorset and Somerset. As a result he took up harling and traditional split-boulder rubble instead of the staple material of Victorian building in Scotland, stugged snecked rubble—that is, irregular courses of squared and stipple-tooled stones, levelled with small stones called *checks*. The first portent of Mackintosh's vernacular taste was his remodelling of the plain Georgian inn at Lennoxtown, Stirlingshire, in 1895, with oblong windows of English casements and a striking inn sign adapted from that of the Rising Sun at Wareham in Dorset, sketched earlier in the same year.[45] Additional study tours were made to East Anglia in 1896 and 1897 and Devon in 1898. These, together with his studies of Scottish domestic architecture of the seventeenth and early eighteenth centuries, provided the basic ideas for his two major houses, Windyhill and The Hill House, Helensburgh (see plate 118).

We do not know whether Mackintosh turned with renewed interest to the Architectural Illustration Society's plates of the houses and hotel at Glenlyon (plates 90 and 91) by MacLaren and by Dunn and Watson, then nine years in the past, but they have a number of features in common with Windyhill and The Hill House, which suggests that Mackintosh may have known them. The southwest front of Windyhill (plate 92) has the same traditional treatment of the eaves and the same unadorned openings punched into the harling as Glenlyon House and the Fortingal Hotel. All of these houses have the wholly convincing, traditional proportions of solid and void that eluded nearly all other contemporary Scottish architects. The monolithic treatment of the porch of the hotel is essentially the same as that of the main doorpiece at The Hill

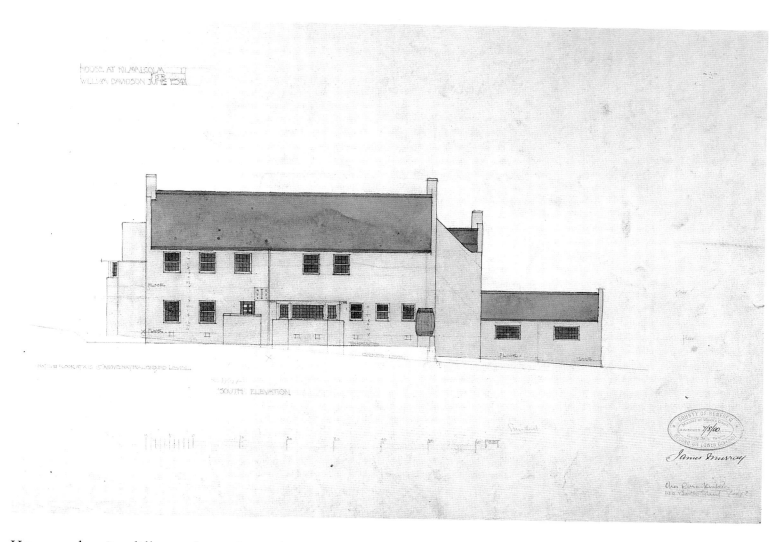

92. Charles Rennie Mackintosh. Windyhill, Kilmacolm. *Southwest Elevation,* 1900. Pencil and watercolour, 15 3/16 x 22 1/16 in. (38.6 x 56.0 cm). Hunterian Art Gallery, University of Glasgow.

House and quite different from the archaeologically correct moulded doorpieces adopted at most of the better Scottish houses of this date. Moreover, MacLaren's farmhouse has not merely the robust cubic qualities of The Hill House but also a very similar set-back gable treatment and strongly battered chimneys. Only the treatment of the eaves at The Hill House is English—deeply shadowed to shelter the bow on the garden front—providing a strong contrast with the severely topless parapet of the projecting wing.[46]

There is a profound understanding of the true nature of the vernacular in Windyhill and The Hill House. To a limited degree, they were anticipated by Robert Lorimer's work. His Colinton cottages of 1893 onwards drew their inspiration from MacLaren's cottages in Glenlyon, albeit with tile roofs rather than thatch. The cottagey vernacular scale of Lorimer's work at Colinton, so different from the visibly stone-built and relatively high-ceilinged houses by Lorimer's former master Robert Rowand Anderson, was very new for Scotland.[47] Lorimer made simple harled houses acceptable again to well-off Scottish middle-class clients. Although harling was a centuries-old traditional

DAILY RECORD BUILDINGS

Scottish finish and still acceptable to old gentry, by mid-Victorian times it had come to be regarded as a cover for inferior materials and hence was scorned during a period when visibly solid construction was thought necessary for even the most inexpensive houses. The interiors of Lorimer's harled houses differed significantly from Mackintosh's; Lorimer designed for clients who, like himself, had a taste for good antique or at least historically based furniture. Mackintosh's houses, like Voysey's or Baillie Scott's, were fitted out with contemporary interiors and furnishings conceived as an architectural unity for clients unafraid of the new.

In 1900 Mackintosh designed a second smaller but still sizeable newspaper office, the Daily Record building (plate 93), which did not achieve the prominence it should have done at the time because it was hidden in Renfield Lane. In concept it has much in common with the Glasgow Herald building but takes on a different character from the use of patterned white-glazed brick. Its gently undulating, segmentally arcaded ground floor is reminiscent in detail (particularly in the section of the arch) of Smith and Brewer's entrance detail at the Passmore Edwards Settlement, but was probably worked up independently.

The upper facade of the Daily Record building (plate 94) is of a type then becoming popular in Glasgow for lane elevations, in which oblong windows like those on Chicago office buildings are set back between brick pilasters. Mackintosh's windows differ in still having small-paned timber sashes, as on the Glasgow Herald building, rather than the steel casements usually provided by Henry Hope of Birmingham, which were becoming more common for such locations at the time. At the top it breaks into cantilevered oriels, which may have been suggested by the rear elevation of Burnet's Atlantic Chambers (1899), the whole being crowned by a massive bracketed cornice and simplified seventeenth-century Scots dormers. The simple geometric patterns of the pilasters in green tiles on the front elevation of the Daily Record building are repeated at the back, set into white-glazed brick. These have not received quite the attention they should. They appear to relate to the Lethaby-inspired Tree of Life motifs on the east-gable end of the Passmore Edwards Settlement; however simple, they also anticipate Mackintosh's more severely geometric, Viennese-inspired phase from 1909 onwards.[48]

In 1903–4 Mackintosh designed his last completely new and major work in Glasgow, the Scotland Street School (plates 72 and 95). Like his earlier Martyrs' Public School, it followed a standard arrangement prescribed by the Scotch Education Department—

three storeys of classrooms to the front and rear of spinal corridors, those at the front being sandwiched between staircases and blocks of mezzanine storeys containing cloakrooms and ancillary accommodation. Exactly the same arrangement can be seen in J. H. Langlands and William Gillespie Lamond's excellent Harrison Townsend–inspired schools at Dens Road (1909) and Whinnybrae (1912–13) in Dundee and John Alexander Carfrae's equally skillful if more conservative schools for the Edinburgh Board.[49] The elements that made Mackintosh's Scotland Street School remarkable were the stepping back of the mezzanines and the mullioned semicylindrical stair towers, which were probably derived from MacGibbon and Ross's restoration drawings of the Earl's Palace at Kirkwall. As at the Daily Record building, the refinement of detail that Mackintosh brought to the simple mass of regular functional building that forms its south frontage has not always had the recognition it deserves. As David Brett has shown, the Tree of Life motif, combined with the thistle, reappears here in a much more complex but equally abstract formation of cubes and triangles, indicating that Viennese work had already begun to influence Mackintosh's move away from purely natural forms.[50]

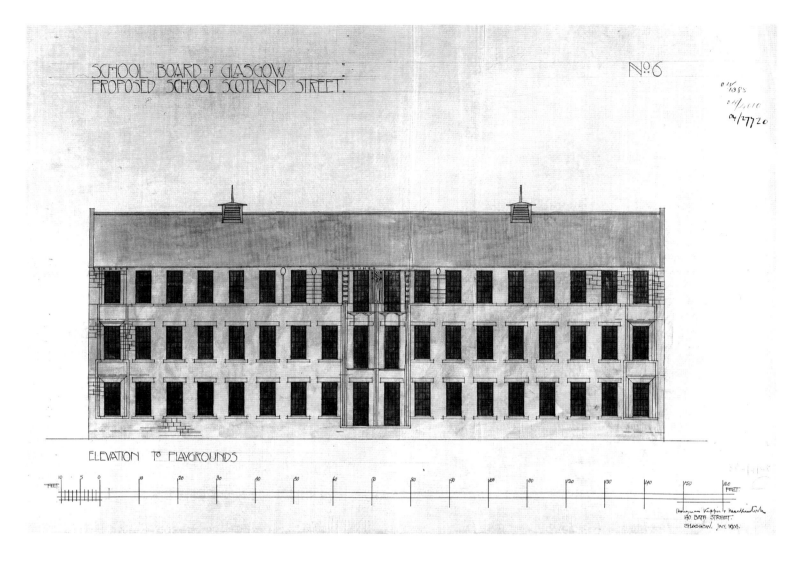

SCHOOL BOARD OF GLASGOW
PROPOSED SCHOOL SCOTLAND STREET.

ELEVATION TO PLAYGROUNDS

95. Charles Rennie Mackintosh. *Scotland Street School: South Elevation*, 1904. Ink and watercolour on linen, 17⁹/₁₆ x 25¹/₁₆ in. (44.6 x 63.7 cm). Strathclyde Regional Archives, Glasgow.

In March 1907 Mackintosh revised the design of the still-unbuilt western third of Glasgow School of Art. One of his changes was to raise the southern half of the Scott Street elevation, containing the library, higher than the other facades, to the height of the set-back attic (see plate 117). The origins of the revised design are difficult to discern. The tall library oriels might just have been a refinement of the canted bays with steel casements on the rear elevation of office blocks by James Salmon and John Archibald Campbell, and the boldly expressionist stepped architrave of the great west door might have an identifiable relationship to Burnet's architraves. The entire southern half of the facade was executed in finely polished ashlar, contrasted with the darker snecked rubble of the upper floors of the northern half so that it stands out like a tower; here Mackintosh demonstrated an unprecedented originality and subtlety in the use of materials. The design has a soaring quality far beyond anything previously achieved in Glasgow or indeed anywhere else in the United Kingdom. The rear elevation of Charles Holden's Central Library in

Bristol (1905–6) and Campbell's Northern Building on Glasgow's St. Vincent Street (1908) are the nearest parallels, but neither has the same magic.[51]

Despite an architectural success that must have been apparent to even the most conservative elements in Glasgow, the building of the School of Art's west wing was not completed without acrimony. In February 1908 there was a serious dispute because Mackintosh revised the doorpiece to a more magnificent design—the governors of the school called it "extravagant."[52] And that was trivial compared with the dispute at Scotland Street, where the School Board's initial concern about the difficulty of cleaning Mackintosh's small-paned classroom windows escalated into a series of busybody complaints, which resulted in the crude insertion of raised sills at the gymnasium windows.[53] These events, and the termination of the firm's engagement at Auchinibert before the house was completed, sorely tried Keppie's patience and made him reluctant to entrust Mackintosh with any clients other than those he had attracted on his own.

Between the completion of the west wing of Glasgow School of Art in 1909 and the final dissolution of the partnership in June 1914, Mackintosh secured no commissions for new building, his only substantial work being the refitting of the Chinese Room and the Cloister Room at the Ingram Street tea rooms in 1911–12.[54] The final breaking point came with the last two of a long series of disappointments in limited competitions, first for the College of Domestic Science in Park Drive, Woodlands, in Glasgow, and then for the Teachers' Training College at Jordanhill in Glasgow. The submission for the latter was a large one—including the main college, a hostel, a demonstration school, and a lodge and gates—and Mackintosh could not complete all of it within the required time. At the last minute a dull but cleverly planned scheme for the demonstration school was provided by an assistant in the firm, A. Graham Henderson, and it was the only element in the submission that found favour with the assessors.[55]

These developments have to be seen against a background of difficulties within the firm over a much longer period. The initial stage of happy cooperation between Keppie and Mackintosh ended abruptly when Mackintosh's engagement to Keppie's sister Jessie was broken off—if engagement it was, and not simply an understanding.[56] It was Mackintosh's special position within the firm as architect of the still-to-be-completed Glasgow School of Art and the steady fee income from the tea rooms he designed for Kate Cranston that made him indispensable and resulted in his becoming a partner on Honeyman's retirement in 1901. From that date onwards, Keppie tended to keep all the commissions from his own clients to himself and his own assistants, with variable results. There were three large commercial buildings on Sauchiehall Street—T. and R. Annan's at no. 518, the rather good nos. 137–41, and the dreadfully bad nos. 309–13, all of 1903–4; and there was a large City Improvement Trust block at 307–33 Hope Street as well as the Savings Bank at Park-

PROPOSED NATIONAL BANK BUILDINGS • GLASGOW. DESIGN B N°5.

BUCHANAN

ST VINCENT STREET ELEVATION

96. Charles Rennie Mackintosh. National Bank of Scotland buildings, St. Vincent and Buchanan Streets, Glasgow. *Competition Entry: Elevations*, 1898. Ink and watercolour, 23¾ x 35⅝ in. (60.5 x 91.4 cm). Hunterian Art Gallery, University of Glasgow.

97. Charles Rennie Mackintosh. *Competition Entry for the Anglican Cathedral, Liverpool: Perspective*, 1902. Ink and watercolour, 24⅜ x 36¼ in. (61.9 x 92.0 cm). Hunterian Art Gallery, University of Glasgow.

head, both of 1908, the latter a reworking of Mackintosh's Royal Insurance competition design of fourteen years earlier.[57] None of these otherwise bears much evidence of Mackintosh's influence.

Apart from Kate Cranston and the Blackies, Mackintosh had few private clients.[58] He had a plan, at one stage, to set up an office in Vienna for half the year, but Keppie did not encourage the idea.[59] Mackintosh was thus left to secure new work through competitions, but in none was he successful. It is a great misfortune that so many of these competition designs have been lost. Only those designs for the National Bank of Scotland at the corner of Buchanan Street and St. Vincent Street of 1898 (plate 96), for the International Exhibition of 1901 (also 1898), and for Liverpool Cathedral (plate 97) survive. The National Bank design is interesting in that it shows that as late as 1898, and perhaps even beyond, Mackintosh was prepared to design in Belcher-inspired Baroque if it would win competitions. And it shows, at least in elevation and detail, that Mackintosh could match Burnet and Campbell at their own game.

RIVAL PRACTICES, GLASGOW, 1895–1914

Left to himself, Keppie was no match for his Glasgow contemporaries. Robert Sandilands, with his Beaux-Arts training in the organisation of really large buildings, tended to win the big public commissions. In 1896 Burnet had vis-

DESIGN Nº2

PERSPECTIVE

Honeyman, Keppie & Mackintosh
140 BATH STREET GLASGOW

98. John James Burnet. Draughtsman: Alexander McGibbon. Waterloo Chambers, 15–23 Waterloo Street, Glasgow. *Perspective*, 1899. From *Academy Architecture*, 1899, p. 115.

ited the United States, where he had cousins; as a result, he and his partner Campbell (who was in independent practice from 1897) had a mastery of large elevator office buildings and department stores, which could be seen in American cities but were almost unknown in Europe. Burnet's Atlantic Chambers (1899); his Waterloo Chambers, also of 1899 (plate 98), with a staircase atrium on the American model; and his McGeoch's Ironmongery Warehouse (see plate 139), with its tall mullioned facade in the manner of Sullivan, were all modern American in concept even if Beaux-Arts in detail. So, too, were Campbell's Britannia Building (1898) and his large block on the corner of Hope Street and West George Street (1902).[60] For clients with more adventurous tastes, there was Henry Edward Clifford, whose carefully crafted neo-Tudor houses commanded the respect of Hermann Muthesius; his commercial buildings included the brilliantly rippling facades of the Bell, Aird and Coghill printing works (1900–1901).[61] And then there was the practice of James Salmon Jr. and John Gaff Gillespie.

Salmon, a former pupil of William Leiper, made his debut with the tall, richly sculptured office block of Mercantile Chambers on Bothwell Street (1897–98). This was followed by the structurally daring, narrow-frontage "Hatrack" at 142–44 St. Vincent Street (1899), a sculpturesque design of Continental and London Art Nouveau inspiration, and by Lion Chambers, 170 Hope Street (1906), an even slimmer reinforced-concrete structure. Mackintosh and Salmon were friends, but Salmon won a larger share of the market

99. James Salmon Jr. (1873–1924).
Nether Knockbuckle, 1907 (left), and
Den o'Gryffe, 1905–7, Kilmacolm.
Photographed by James Salmon,
c. 1912.

among those prepared to build stylistically adventurous houses. Examples are
12 University Gardens, a terrace house with fine interiors strongly influenced
by Mackintosh (1900), and a remarkable series of houses at Kilmacolm, beginning with the stone and half-timbered Rowantreehill (1898) and ending with
the idiosyncratic, harled, and strongly geometrical vernacular of three houses,
Northernhay and Den o' Gryffe (both 1905) and Nether Knockbuckle (1907;
plate 99), these three being variations on the theme of a square pavilion with
splayed angles. These houses are superficially English, some having half-
timbering, and they are akin to Windyhill and The Hill House in their use of
harling, but the later houses differ markedly from Mackintosh's in having hori-
zontally proportioned glazing close to, or flush with, the wall plane. Despite
their rather folksy appearance, the inspiration at Nether Knockbuckle and perhaps also at Den o'Gryffe came from Eastern Europe, a part of the world in
which Salmon had a particular interest. Their interiors were a simplification of
Mackintosh's style, with ingenious light fittings designed by Salmon himself.

The partnership of Salmon and Gillespie ended in much the same way as
that of Keppie and Mackintosh. After a long series of quite imaginative but
unsuccessful designs submitted in competition, the more classically minded
Gillespie won the competition for the Stirling Municipal Buildings in 1907
with a clever evocation of the style of early-sixteenth-century Scottish palaces.
No corresponding success came Salmon's way. In 1913 Gillespie broke the
partnership, retaining the Stirling commission. Salmon's surviving records

indicate that as junior partner he found himself on his own on even worse terms than Mackintosh. A well-connected physician wife enabled him to remain in practice until his early death in 1924.[62]

While Mackintosh's more limited client base undoubtedly played a part, both Mackintosh and Salmon had suffered from being associated with a decorative style for which the mood had passed. Indeed, by the early years of this century all the progressive practices in Glasgow had begun to feel themselves threatened by the lower-key classicism of James Miller.[63] Even Burnet—who lost the Caledonian Railway, his most important client, to Miller—found his individual interpretation of the Baroque was no longer in fashion. However, Burnet's selection as architect for the neo-Greek Edward VII Galleries at the British Museum in London, at the end of 1903, at once reestablished him as a classicist and made him a national figure. A still-extensive client base enabled him to make the transition from the stylish neo-Baroque of Forsyth's Department Store, Edinburgh (1905–6), and General Buildings, Aldwych, London (1909), to the stripped-down classical modern Kodak Building, Kingsway, London (1910–11), and in turn to the severe brick-and-tile modern of the Alhambra Theatre (1910) and Wallace Scott Tailoring Institute (1913), both in Glasgow. Throughout his long career Burnet never hesitated to adapt to the needs of the times, always with an eye to what was happening in the United States. The Beaux-Arts training, with its emphasis on the best solution to the programme set by the client, was far more adaptable than we tend to think.

Mackintosh learned to be an architect in the stimulating and cosmopolitan atmosphere of late Victorian Glasgow, and he continued to find inspiration in the work of his contemporaries, especially Burnet, Smith and Brewer, and MacLaren. But his originality also increased, from the mid-1890s onwards. His greatest architectural work is framed by the two stages of Glasgow School of Art. Although in the years around 1900 he was full of work and creativity, the flow of commissions had begun to dry up well before the second stage of the school was finished. Had his support continued, Mackintosh might well have moved in a direction similar to Burnet's, but only small building works and interiors were left to him in Glasgow.

It cannot have been easy for Mackintosh to become a follower rather than a leader, but he did. He had achieved a European reputation with a decorative art based on natural forms, but now he wholeheartedly adopted the severe, rectilinear style of Josef Hoffmann and other progressive architects and designers in Vienna. Their influence can be seen in the stepped and receding rectilinear forms of the west doorpiece of Glasgow School of Art, in the brilliant interior of the Cloister Room in the Ingram Street tea rooms (1911–12), and in the Bassett-Lowke house in Northampton (1916). All of these show what might have been.

NOTES

1. Thomas Howarth, *Charles Rennie Mackintosh and the Modern Movement*, 3d ed. (London: Routledge and Kegan Paul, 1990), pp. 3–4. Contrary to Howarth's statement that the building was "completely destroyed" by fire in the early 1900s, the facade and basic structure survived.

2. For Honeyman's career, see David Walker, "The Honeymans," *Charles Rennie Mackintosh Society Newsletter* 62 (summer 1993): 7–12; 63 (winter 1993): 5–8; and 64 (spring 1994): 5–8; see also Brian Edwards, "John Honeyman, Victorian Architect and Restorer, and Partner of Charles Rennie Mackintosh," *Charles Rennie Mackintosh Society Newsletter* 36 (February 1984): unpaginated. For MacGibbon and Ross, see David Walker, "The Architecture of MacGibbon and Ross: The Background to the Books," in *Studies in Scottish Antiquity*, ed. David Breeze (Edinburgh: John Donald, 1984), pp. 391–449. Honeyman and MacGibbon had been fellow assistants at William Burn's London office in 1854.

3. For Keppie, see William Buchanan, "The Mackintosh Circle," part 3, "Mackintosh, John and Jessie Keppie," *Charles Rennie Mackintosh Society Newsletter* 32 (midsummer 1982), unpaginated; and David Walker, "Scotland and Paris, 1874–1887," in *Scotland and Europe: Architecture and Design, 1850–1940*, ed. John Frew and David Jones (St. Andrews: St. Andrews Studies in the History of Scottish Architecture and Design, 1991), p. 33.

4. For Leiper, see Simon Green, "William Leiper's Houses in Helensburgh," in *Architectural Heritage*, vol. 3, *The Age of Mackintosh*, ed. John Lowrey (Edinburgh: Architectural Heritage Society of Scotland, 1992), pp. 32–42.

5. For Stevenson, see Mark Girouard, *Sweetness and Light: The "Queen Anne" Movement, 1860–1890* (Oxford: Clarendon Press, 1977), particularly pp. 38–42, 110–19; and Girouard, *The Victorian Country House*, 2d ed. (New Haven, Conn., and London: Yale University Press, 1979), particularly pp. 366–74.

6. For Sellars, see John Keppie, "James Sellars," *Scottish Art Review* 1, no. 7 (1888): 191–93; David Walker, "James Sellars," *Scottish Art Review*, n.s., 11, no. 1 (1967): 16–19, and 11, no. 2 (1967): 21–24; and Walker, "Scotland and Paris," pp. 25–27.

7. For Anderson, see Sam McKinstry, *Rowand Anderson: "The Premier Architect of Scotland"* (Edinburgh: Edinburgh University Press, 1991); and for Central Station, see Colin Johnston and John R. Hume, *Glasgow Stations* (Newton Abbot, England: David and Charles, 1979), pp. 38–49.

8. Well Court attracted attention in W. R. Lethaby's circle in London; see the Architectural Illustration Society's plates 411–13 in *Architect*, July 29, 1892, p. 72. It had previously appeared in *British Architect*, August 23, 1889, p. 128. In *Architectural Review* 144 (November 1968): 355–56, I suggested its influence on Honeyman and Keppie's competition design for the rebuilding of Glasgow's High Street. For Honeyman and Keppie's Canal Boatmen's Institute and Queen Margaret College, see Howarth, *Mackintosh*, pp. 59–65.

9. For Browne, see Deborah Mays, "A Profile of Sir George Washington Browne," in *Age of Mackintosh*, ed. Lowrey, pp. 52–63.

10. For Nesfield, see J. M Brydon, "William Eden Nesfield," in Alastair Service, ed., *Edwardian Architecture and Its Origins* (London: Architectural Press, 1975), pp. 26–38. Kinmel was first published by the Architectural Illustration Society, pls. 384–87, *Architect*, July 17, 1891, p. 38.

11. For Macharioch, see Jill Allibone, *George Devey, Architect, 1820–1886* (Cambridge: Lutterworth Press, 1991), p. 88.

12. For Webb, see Girouard, *Sweetness and Light* and *Victorian Country House*; and George Jack, "An Appreciation of Philip Webb," in Service, ed., *Edwardian Architecture and Its Origins*, pp. 16–25. The best biography is still W. R. Lethaby, *Philip Webb and His Work* (London: Oxford University Press, 1935).

13. For Burnet, see David Walker, "Sir John James Burnet," in Service, ed., *Edwardian Architecture and Its Origins*, pp. 192–215; for Glasgow architects who studied in Paris, see Walker, "Scotland and Paris." For teaching methods at the Ecole des Beaux-Arts, see Richard Chafee, "The Teaching of Architecture at the Ecole des Beaux Arts," in *The Architecture of the Ecole des Beaux Arts*, ed. Arthur Drexler (London: Secker and Warburg, 1977), pp. 61–110.

14. For the Glasgow International Exhibition of 1888, see Perilla Kinchin and Juliet Kinchin, *Glasgow's Great Exhibitions: 1888, 1901, 1911, 1938, 1988* (Wendlebury, England: White Cockade Publishing, 1988), and numerous references in *British Architect* for 1888, particularly the illustration of the principal entrance, in the July 13 issue, p. 33. The lantern over the dome and the subsidiary towers of Mackintosh's Industrial Hall for the 1901 exhibition both have brackets like those on the towers flanking the entrance to Sellars's Main Building for 1888; the twin beams clasping an upright recur on Mackintosh's design for a concert hall for 1901.

15. Howarth, *Mackintosh*, pp. 7–12, 54–55.

16. Pamela Robertson, ed., *Charles Rennie Mackintosh: The Architectural Papers* (Wendlebury, England: White Cockade Publishing, 1990), pp. 152–211.

17. For Burnet's early domestic work, see David Walker, "The Country Houses, Villas and Related Hotel Designs of Sir John Burnet," in *Scottish Country Houses, 1600–1914*, ed. Ian Gow and Alistair Rowan (Edinburgh: Edinburgh University Press, 1995), pp. 298–323; and Walker, "Mackintosh's Scottish Antecedents," in Patrick Nuttgens, ed., *Mackintosh and His Contemporaries in Europe and America* (London: John Murray, 1988), pp. 32–38.

18. Roger Billcliffe, *Charles Rennie Mackintosh: The Complete Furniture, Furniture Drawings and Interior Designs*, 3d ed. (London: John Murray, 1986), pp. 28–30.

19. For the South Kensington designs and competition generally, see John Physick, *The Victoria and Albert Museum: The History of Its Building* (Oxford: Phaidon; London: Christie's, 1982), chap. 11. For Webb's designs, see *Building News*, August 7, 1891, p. 178; September 11, p. 377; and November 20, p. 716. For Belcher's, see *Builder*, November 12, 1892, p. 378.

20. See Robertson, ed., *Architectural Papers*, pp. 65–125; and *British Architect*, July 13, 1888, p. 33; August 31, p. 149; and September 7, p. 177. Michelle Copley, "The Establishment of the Gallery and Museum at Kelvingrove" (M.A. diss., University of St. Andrew's, 1995), shows that Waterhouse's award to Simpson and Allen was not made without dissent on behalf of the final Mackintosh-designed submission.

21. *British Architect*, October 28, 1892, p. 314, and November 4, p. 332.

22. *Academy Architecture*, 1895, p. 56.

23. *Academy Architecture*, 1894, p. 89; see also Michael Donnelly, "Charles Rennie Mackintosh and the Glasgow Herald," *Charles Rennie Mackintosh Society Newsletter* 34 (spring 1983): unpaginated; and *Glasgow Herald*, May 20, 1899.

24. For Stirling High School and MacLaren generally, see Alan Calder, *James MacLaren, 1853–1890: Arts and Crafts Architect* (London: Royal Institute of British Architects, 1990); and Alastair Service, "James MacLaren

and the Godwin Legacy," in Service, ed., *Edwardian Architecture and Its Origins*, pp. 100–18. For Sedding, see J. P. Cooper and H. Wilson, "The Work of John D. Sedding," in Service, ed., *Edwardian Architecture and Its Origins*, pp. 258–79.

25. *British Architect*, May 18, 1888, p. 354; see also Service, ed., *Edwardian Architecture and Its Origins*, p. 84.

26. Howarth, *Mackintosh*, pp. 63–65; *Academy Architecture*, 1895, p. 70; Billcliffe, *Complete Furniture*, pp. 32–33.

27. *Architect*, June 19, 1891, p. 372 (Architectural Illustration Society, 2d ser., pl. 372).

28. *Scottish Country Houses*, ed. Gow and Rowan, p. 309.

29. The most informative account of Martyrs' School is Peter Ballantine, "Martyrs' Public School," *Charles Rennie Mackintosh Society Newsletter* 9 (autumn 1975): unpaginated. See also David Brett, *C. R. Mackintosh: The Poetics of Workmanship* (London: Reaktion Books, 1992), pp. 83–87; and Robert Macleod, *Charles Rennie Mackintosh: Architect and Artist*, 2d ed. (London: Collins, 1983), pp. 44–47.

30. Robertson, ed., *Architectural Papers*, pp. 127–211.

31. For these houses and other related work by Lorimer, see Peter Savage, *Lorimer and the Edinburgh Craft Designers* (Edinburgh: Paul Harris Publishing, 1980); for Allermuir, see McKinstry, *Rowand Anderson*, pp. 86–88.

32. John Ruskin, *The Works of John Ruskin*, 39 vols., ed. E. T. Cook and Alexander Wedderburn (London: George Allen, 1902–12), vol. 10, p. 212.

33. Robert Macleod, *Charles Rennie Mackintosh* (Feltham, England: Country Life, 1968), pp. 33–38. For Lethaby, see Godfrey Rubens, *William Richard Lethaby* (London: Architectural Press, 1986).

34. John Summerson, *The Turn of the Century: Architecture in Britain around 1900* (Glasgow: University of Glasgow Press, 1976), p. 24.

35. For the railway terminus design, Queen's Cross Church, and Auchinibert, see Howarth and other writers; for the Conservative Club at Helensburgh, see Fiona J. Sinclair, "Some Observations on No. 40 Sinclair Street, Helensburgh," *Charles Rennie Mackintosh Society Newsletter* 59 (summer 1992): 5–7.

36. The Palace Court houses were illustrated in *Architect*, July 22, 1892, p. 56 (Architectural Illustration Society, 2d ser., pl. 407).

37. In particular, at Stevenson's 8 Palace Gate, London, and Anderson's Conservative Club, Edinburgh.

38. These appeared in *Architect* in 1891–92, in the second series of plates by the Architectural Illustration Society: June 18, 1891, p. 372, pl. 372 (farmhouse); July 10, 1891, p. 22, pls. 380–83 (cottages and steading); May 20, 1892, p. 333, pl. 390 (hotel); and June 24, 1892, p. 413, pl. 399 (Glenlyon House).

39. The most detailed account of the building is William Buchanan, ed., *Mackintosh's Masterwork: The Glasgow School of Art* (Glasgow: Richard Drew Publishing, 1989); see also James Macaulay, *Charles Rennie Mackintosh: Glasgow School of Art* (London: Phaidon, 1993); and, for an interesting study of particular details, Brett, *Mackintosh*, pp. 75ff.

40. *Building News*, May 17, 1895, p. 688; June 21, 1895, pp. 865–66; August 9, 1895, pp. 189, 209; and, for the completed building, October 19, 1900, pp. 532–33, 539, 557.

41. *Architect*, March 7, 1890, p. 150 (Architectural Illustration Society, 2d ser., pl. 204). For Shaw's work generally, see Andrew Saint, *Richard Norman Shaw* (New Haven, Conn., and London: Yale University Press, 1976).

42. *Academy Architecture and Architectural Review* (1896), vol. 1, p. 83.

43. Howarth, *Mackintosh*, pp. 175–80; Macleod, *Mackintosh: Architect and Artist*, pp. 68–73.

44. *Academy Architecture and Architectural Review* (1897), vol. 1, p. 18.

45. Andrew McLaren Young, *Charles Rennie Mackintosh (1868–1928): Architecture, Design and Painting* (Edinburgh: Edinburgh Festival Society and Scottish Arts Council, 1968), no. 112.

46. For Windyhill and The Hill House, see Howarth, *Mackintosh*, pp. 98–107; and James Macaulay, *Charles Rennie Mackintosh: Hill House* (London: Phaidon, 1994).

47. Savage, *Lorimer*, chap. 3. Mackintosh would have known about these cottages from the Royal Scottish Academy exhibitions.

48. Howarth, *Mackintosh*, pp. 174–75. For a discussion of the Daily Record doorpiece (still of Burnetian derivation) and the Tree of Life motif, see Brett, *Mackintosh*, pp. 81–82, 131–33.

49. David Walker, "Lamond of Dundee," *Architectural Review* 123 (April 1958): 269–72. There is no adequate study of Carfrae's schools for the Edinburgh Board.

50. Brett, *Mackintosh*, pp. 131–33.

51. For Holden, see Nikolaus Pevsner, "Charles Holden's Early Work," in Service, ed., *Edwardian Architecture and Its Origins*, pp. 386–92; and Eitan Karol and Finch Allibone, *Charles Holden, Architect: 1875–1960* (London: Royal Institute of British Architects, 1988). For Campbell, see Andor Gomme and David Walker, *The Architecture of Glasgow*, 2d ed. (London and Glasgow: Lund Humphries in association with John Smith, 1987), p. 206.

52. Buchanan, ed., *Mackintosh's Masterwork*, p. 206.

53. Minutes of the School Board of Glasgow, Strathclyde Regional Archives, Mitchell Library, Glasgow City Libraries.

54. Billcliffe, *Complete Furniture*, pp. 214–16.

55. Personal information from the late Alexander Smellie, who was in the office for the whole period of the partnership, 1901–13. See also the corrected version of events of 1913 in Howarth, *Mackintosh*, p. xxvii (in which, however, the *Builder* reference is given as July 17, 1913, when it should be July 4, 1913, p. 10, for the announcement and July 11, 1913, p. 38, for illustration of the schemes).

56. The evidence for Mackintosh's engagement to Jessie Keppie consists principally of Thomas Howarth's recollections of his meetings with the Keppies in the 1940s and is less precise than one could wish; see Howarth, *Mackintosh*, p. xxvi. The story of the engagement came as a surprise to Alexander Smellie seventy years later; he considered that it could never have been more than an understanding, dependent on Mackintosh's becoming a partner.

57. Office records of Honeyman, Keppie and Mackintosh; for T. and R. Annan's, see *Academy Architecture and Architectural Review* (1904), vol. 1, p. 90; for Parkhead, see Gomme and Walker, *Architecture of Glasgow*, p. 230.

58. Andrew Pinkerton ("Keppie Henderson Archives: An Important Source for Mackintosh Research," *Charles Rennie Mackintosh Society Newsletter* 45 [spring 1987]: 4–6) shows that in 1913 a summary of fee income was prepared for the years 1901–12. Keppie introduced income of £16,303 and Mackintosh only £4,934, less than the £5,467 he drew as a partner. That should, however, be seen against Smellie's comment that the small but steady flow of work from Kate Cranston was sometimes helpful when the office was quiet.

59. Personal information from Alexander Smellie, who recalled disagreement and disappointment on the subject but was unable to fix the date.

60. For Burnet, see Walker, "Sir John James Burnet," pp. 202ff; for Campbell, see Gomme and Walker, *Architecture of*

Glasgow, pp. 210, 289; and A. Stuart Gray, *Edwardian Architecture: A Biographical Dictionary* (London: Duckworth, 1985), p. 133. No adequate study of Campbell's work has been published, although the core of his office archive survives.

61. See Gomme and Walker, *Architecture of Glasgow*, p. 290; Gray, *Edwardian Architecture*, p. 144; and Hermann Muthesius, *The English House*, trans. Janet Seligmann and ed., with an introduction by, Dennis Sharp (London: Crosby Lockwood Staples, 1979),

figs. 264, 270–72, 469, 478, and 481–83. Clifford's smaller houses figured regularly in *Academy Architecture.*

62. For Salmon and Gillespie, see David Walker, "The Partnership of James Salmon and John Gaff Gillespie," in Service, ed., *Edwardian Architecture and Its Origins*, pp. 236–49; Frank A. Walker, "Six Villas by James Salmon," *Architectural History* 25 (1982): 114–19; Patricia A. Cusack, "Lion Chambers: A Glasgow Experiment," *Architectural History* 28 (1985): 198–206; and Ray-

mond O'Donnell, "James Salmon: Architecture from Sculpture," *Charles Rennie Mackintosh Society Newsletter* 42 (winter 1985–86): 5–7, an extract from a larger, unpublished work. Salmon's office records from 1913 onwards and photographs of work built in partnership are now in the National Monuments Record of Scotland.

63. For Miller, see Audrey Sloan with Gordon Murray, *James Miller, 1860–1947* (Edinburgh: Royal Incorporation of Architects in Scotland, 1993).

Glasgow School of Art

■■
MARK GIROUARD

How astonished Mackintosh's Glasgow contemporaries would be if they could return to the School of Art today and see the flocks of reverential pilgrims that come from all over the world to worship at the shrine of the master. But they would be astonished not because their dangerous revolutionary had been canonised by the Establishment, but because a building that had excited so little comment in their own time was being treated as a masterpiece.

The new building of the School of Art was the result of a competition held in 1896. The assessors who chose the winning design consisted of two Glasgow worthies (one of them a former lord provost) and Francis Newbery, the enterprising and energetic head of the School of Art. There is no evidence that he had any difficulty persuading them to choose Mackintosh. Since the school came under the supervision of the Department of Science and Art in South Kensington, London, the designs were also sent to the two directors there; they independently picked out the same set that had been selected in Glasgow. Once chosen, the design had to be approved by the Dean of Guild Court, the planning authority for Glasgow; it may have asked for some comparatively minor alterations, but there is no reason to suppose that it otherwise made difficulties about accepting the design.

The building came into existence to the accompaniment of modest approbation from the Glasgow papers. "The plans . . . are of the most complete description and embrace all recent ideas and improvements." "The practical requirements of the School have dominated the style of the building." "The elevation presents the appearance of a plain business-looking edifice."[1] These comments expressed reactions to the design before building work started, but as the structure rose to the completion of the first stage, the tone of the com-

100. Main entrance on the north front.

ments remained much the same. Glasgow was going to be proud of having "one of the most commodious and best equipped art-schools in the kingdom." "The building appears to be in every way suitable for the requirements of art education."[2] Reports of the opening of the first stage, in December 1899, concentrated on the success of the school and the dresses of the fashionable ladies who were present; the little written about the architecture included nothing that was critical. "The opinions passed by the guests at yesterday's function were varied, but all expressive of admiration." One of the speakers pointed out, "Both in building and furnishings the School is primarily utilitarian." (That report is from the *Evening Times* [Glasgow] of December 21, 1899.) The *Evening Times* was also the one newspaper to go a little further than approbation of the utility, convenience, and cheapness of the new school. "Externally it is, as everyone with an appreciation of artistic simplicity and fine design is bound to confess, a structure which will long remain a monument to the strong originality and artistic conception of Glasgow designers."

At the first annual public meeting of the school's supporters after the opening, Sir T. D. Gibson Carmichael, one of the speakers, "congratulated the School of Art upon its new buildings. . . . He was delighted and he confessed surprised to hear from Mr. Fleming that they were absolutely satisfied with the new premises (laughter). It was the first building he ever heard of where the architects did exactly what they were told (laughter)."[3] The architects, as was reported at the time, were a well-established Glasgow firm, Honeyman and Keppie; Mr. Keppie, representing the firm, had made one of the speeches at the opening.

The years 1897–99 saw the construction of a little less than two-thirds of the school, made up of the centre and the east wing; the west wing was to be built when money was available. Under Newbery the school continued to increase in attendance and reputation to such an extent that not only was the building finished, to a slightly different design, in 1907–9, but in the same period it was also enlarged by an extra storey throughout and by other lesser additions. At this stage the name of Charles Rennie Mackintosh, recently made a partner in Honeyman and Keppie, was first publicised as the designer. There is no doubt that he was equally responsible for the first portion, but (as he wrote to Hermann Muthesius) while it was being built, he was "under a cloud, as it were."[4] By this he meant not that he was in any way disapproved of but that he was officially invisible because he was not a partner; then, as often enough today, it was the partners who took the credit.

When the completed building was opened in December 1909, even less was said in the press about its architecture than in 1899. The school had "imposing new premises," the extensions were "in keeping with the part originally erected," and the building as a whole now presented "a thoroughly business-like aspect."[5] The *Evening Times*, in its series "Prominent Profiles," featured Mackintosh, "whose name comes prominently before his fellow men in connection with the opening of the extension of the Glasgow School of Art."[6] The profile had little to say about the school itself but dwelt at some length on Mackintosh's European reputation. It was in no way controversial, and the accompanying drawing showed no romantic bohemian but a paunchy professional man in a suit, holding a pipe in one hand.

For anyone brought up in the belief that the School of Art was a revolutionary building, that it shocked contemporaries, and that Mackintosh was virtually hounded out of Glasgow because he was too far in advance of his time, the building's quiet reception must seem odd. But the comments, within their limits, were accurate and to the point. The school was, and is, "plain," "business-like," and "primarily utilitarian." It was and is "in every way suitable for the requirements of art education." Its architect, at least for the first stage of the building, had indeed done exactly what he was told.[7]

THE BRIEF

One of the pleasures of visiting the School of Art is the discovery that this great masterpiece is also a thoroughly workmanlike building, sensibly planned, solidly and simply detailed for the knockabout and casual life of an art school, still being used in an unselfconscious way for the purposes for which it was designed, and still successfully resisting the mounting pressure to freeze it as a monument. The school's practical suitability for its purpose was what satisfied opinion at the time; what only a few perceptive critics (like the unknown reporter on the *Evening Times*) recognised was the inventive genius that suffused every detail of the building and made the simplicity imposed by budget and function into a strength rather than something to be put up with. In walking through the school one is constantly delighted by the sense of Mackintosh at work in every detail—ebullient, playful, creative, endlessly able to use very simple elements and put them together in a novel way. Yet the end result is never overpowering; the feel of the school as a sensible workplace predominates.

The school grew happily and—for the first stage, at least—smoothly out of the constraints that controlled it: the client, the money available, the brief, and the site. Much was due to Francis Newbery, who was effectively the client, even though he had to carry his Building Committee with him. Like Kate Cranston of the tea rooms and the Blackies of The Hill House, Newbery appreciated and admired Mackintosh, and he was prepared to tolerate the architect's ways of working and those defects or awkwardnesses of character hinted at, with irritating coyness and imprecision, by those who knew him. Newbery, who had known Mackintosh since the latter's student days, was a friend as well as an admirer and backed him loyally at every stage of his career. Newbery was also a well-known public figure in Glasgow, a showman, revelling in a certain swagger and pomposity of manner and turnout, as Maurice Greiffenhagen's portrait of him, in gleaming top hat, demonstrates. Newbery

101. A pilaster in the boardroom.

was the effective creator of the school, in that he lifted it from a modest local concern sheltered in a corner of the City Art Gallery and Museum to perhaps the biggest and best-known art school in the British Isles, catering to students coming from all over Scotland and, in a modest way, from all over the world, with a cosmopolitan staff in touch with the latest developments in London and on the Continent.

In practical terms Newbery knew just what he wanted and put it in a carefully worded brief: large, well-lit studios, divisible by moveable partitions, running along the north side of the site; square-headed windows rising "to a height above the floor equal to three quarters the depth of the room" and "free from mullions and small panes"; wide corridors with good wall spaces for exhibition purposes; electric lighting and good heating and ventilation; the possibility of a "museum" adjoining the staircase, for the display of the casts of sculpture or ornament considered essential for the art schools of that time.[8] The school also had to provide a setting for Newbery as personality, showman, and fund-raiser and for the parties, exhibitions, and entertainments that he and his wife put on with style, which were attended by all the top people in the city and which helped establish the image of the school as a success and a worthwhile recipient of donations. All this had to be done on a minimum budget, in order to escape any criticism of unnecessary extravagance.

Mackintosh kept close to the practical aspects of the brief, but he was also alive to what was appropriate, in terms of the purpose of the building and its situation. It is not for reasons of stylistic preference or development that there are similarities between the School of Art and his Scotland Street School (see plate 72): they are both educational buildings built on the cheap in unprestigious districts. He had written in or around 1892 about the impossibility of building a "shed or bare ungainly store in some fashionable street or square"[9]; it is arguable that had the school been in modish Blythswood Square it would have looked very different.

In 1898, when Mackintosh designed a main-street frontage in the commercial centre of Glasgow for the National Bank (see plate 96), he produced a free Classic facade decorated with some elaboration.[10] In 1907–9 his new boardroom in the School of Art had classical panelling and pilasters, as was expected of boardrooms, even if Mackintosh did play games with the detailing (plate 101). When he designed a cathedral for Liverpool in 1903 (see plate 97), it was unmistakably a grand and elaborate Gothic building, even if Gothic of a personal and unacademic nature. Without positive evidence it would be rash to suppose that in these cases Mackintosh was abandoning his own preferences in the hope of winning a competition or pleasing a client. It is just as likely that he designed to suit the function of the room or building. He attacked the "imitation of Greek temples" for modern buildings,[11] but one has only to look at his designs to see that that does not mean he was against getting ideas and motifs from old buildings; what was important for him was that the architect should re-create his sources with the imagination of an artist and in a way appropriate to their use.

Mackintosh's sources have been carefully investigated in recent years by David Walker and others. It has become impossible to portray him any longer as an isolated genius. He has taken his place as, on the one hand, a Glaswegian and a Scot, absorbing ideas and motifs from old Scottish buildings of the past and from Glasgow's own flourishing architecture. If one turns from the north front of the School of Art (plate 104) to Alexander Thomson's Great Western Terrace, one has no feeling of moving from one world to another; there is the same rigorous simplification, the same feeling for the weight and power of stone. The school is a stone building in a stone city, having risen, originally, out of the stone tenements of Renfrew Street and fitting naturally among them.

Mackintosh was also much influenced by the English or England-based Free Style architects, who liked their buildings to be bold and simple, who kept their roots in the past but felt free to diverge from it, who sedulously sketched old buildings but designed modest vernacular buildings as well as high-style ones, and who used their sketchbooks as a source for suggestion rather than copy. Mackintosh's own sketchbooks are fascinating evidence of what attracted his eye, always for visual rather than historical reasons, whether it was the curvaceous flow of a piece of Gothic tracery or the patchwork fenestration of a house in a country town. But he was amazingly creative; worthwhile though it is to analyse his sources, he always transformed them. Even when Mackintosh was doing the same kind of thing as W. R. Lethaby, Edward Prior, J. D. Sedding, C.F.A. Voysey, Henry Wilson, and their fellows in the Arts and Crafts movement, he was doing it in a different way. He had none of the interest in social theory or distrust of the machine-made. He designed in a different way from them, not so much building up mass sculpturally as enclosing it by line—that wonderfully sensitive living line that he shared with the other members of the Four but used with far more brilliance.[12] Much of his simplification is due to a desire to make this line tell more strongly.

THE EXTERIOR

The school is not a consistent work of art, a kind of Glasgow Taj Mahal. It is of a piece only insofar as it was all designed by Mackintosh, down to the last detail. From its conception in 1896 until its completion in 1909 it kept changing, partly in response to changing practical needs, partly because it was built in two stages, and partly because Mackintosh himself was changing and because it was his habit to detail and alter all through the course of construction. This gives the school an ad hoc quality and a feeling of growth, of having been designed as it went along—an effect strikingly different from that of Mackintosh's domestic and tea-room interiors but far from disagreeable. The plan and the main elements provided a framework that could easily absorb any additions that were hung on it.

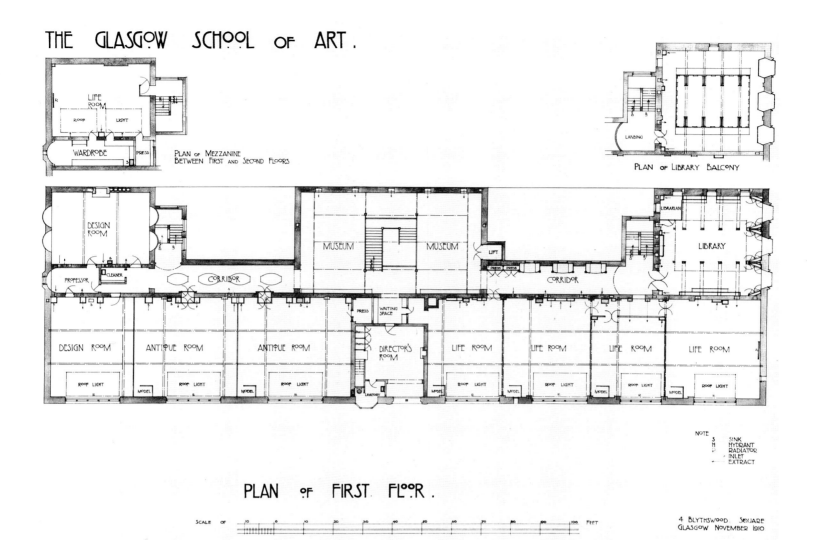

THE GLASGOW SCHOOL OF ART.

PLAN OF MEZZANINE
BETWEEN FIRST AND SECOND FLOORS

PLAN OF LIBRARY BALCONY

PLAN OF FIRST FLOOR.

SCALE OF ... FEET

4 BLYTHSWOOD SQUARE
GLASGOW NOVEMBER 1910

102. *Plan of First Floor,* November 1910. Ink, 23¹⁵⁄₁₆ x 43³⁄₁₆ in. (60.8 x 110.0 cm). Glasgow School of Art.

The changes can be followed in some detail, largely because of the survival of detailed plans, sections, and elevations made in 1897, 1907, and 1910. Those dating from 1897 consist of two sets, both recent discoveries: copies of the initial competition designs (recovered thanks to the researches of the historian Hugh Ferguson), from the archives of the Department of Science and Art now in the Scottish Record Office; and the slightly altered designs submitted later in the year for approval by the Dean of Guild.[13]

The plan (plate 102) was to receive only minor modifications over the years, because it closely followed the brief and was eminently sensible and straightforward: north-lit main studios along the front; miscellaneous accommodations at the back; two broad corridors for exhibiting students' work separating front from back and running into a central top-lit museum, filled with plaster casts; Newbery's room in the centre on the front, with the main entrance underneath them leading, by way of a vestibule and office, to a staircase rising up into the museum. Vestibule, stairs, museum corridors, and Newbery's own study (plate 103) provided a more highly finished core with which to show off the school, its work, and its director to visitors.

From the beginning, the design of the north front expressed the nature of the plan: the simplicity of the great studio windows contrasted with the complex asymmetrical design of the centre (plates 100 and 104). But there were continual changes. A subtle but important adjustment was made almost immediately and is shown in the Dean of Guild elevation: the big windows were slightly reduced in size, and as a result the ratio of wall to window was increased and both the corner and the centres strengthened, entirely to the benefit of the design. Additions or alterations made between 1897 and 1899 included the wrought-iron standards rising from the railings, the wrought-iron brackets strengthening the main studio windows, the six-foot projection of the cornice over them, and the wrought-iron lantern and arch over the entrance steps. These were not minor changes; the power of the north facade derives from the noble simplicity of the great wall of ashlar, the grid of the windows, the bold overhang of the cornice on the one hand and the subtle game of contrasting curves and straight lines that is played out against it on the other.

The south facade was the back of the building, and views of it were interrupted by the buildings in Sauchiehall Street. The facade was of some importance, however; since the school was on the crest of a hill, it rose above Sauchiehall Street and was conspicuous in the distance. This is the facade that has changed most since the original competition design (plate 105). The first view is disconcerting: three great masses of completely blank wall and very few windows, even in the two stretches of wall between them. The explanation is straightforward, however, for the design was brutally constricted by the brief, which laid down that "the south elevation may not have any lights in its walls, in a line with the building line, except perhaps in the upper floor." The reasons for this stipulation have not been investigated or even, I think, commented on; one suspects some legal constraint of "ancient lights," for it is hard to see how the blank walls could have had any practical advantage. The constraint explains the two recessed sections on this front; they set portions of it behind the building line and make windows allowable, permitting the addition of windows in the short return walls of the three projections to bring daylight to the rooms in them.

In the design as amended in the Dean of Guild drawings (plate 106), the windows in the centre have been moved around to the south and arranged symmetrically; the end projection remains as before. A newel-stair tower has been added in the angle of the west projection. The great masses of wall remain dominant, but less overpoweringly so. In this set of drawings the north elevation is dated March 1897; this suggests that in the intervening six months some kind of concession has been negotiated. The combination of the sweep of the great pitched roof, the stair tower, and the expanses of walls covered with harling (a

rough lime plaster), with windows only occasionally punched through them, suggests that Mackintosh now had Scottish castle architecture in mind.

The south elevation today (plate 107) is different even from this 1897 design, due to the way in which the school was completed in 1907–9. The western projection is now elaborately windowed; west and east staircases have been inserted—the former a replacement of a small original stair, the latter completely new. An extra storey has been added, served by a corridor on the south front; this is differently treated all the way along, first as a brick arched loggia, with projecting oriel windows, then as the glazed and panelled "hen-run," cantilevered out in order to get around the top of the museum and then inset within the new top storey. The end result of all these changes is in striking contrast to the formidable severity and near symmetry of the tender, or even more, of the competition elevation. One could say that it is the result of hand-to-mouth amendment of a back elevation that was not worth bothering about, except that it is reminiscent of Mackintosh's sketches of piecemeal-altered houses in towns in southern England and of his later watercolours of irregular townscapes in southern France. He clearly learnt to enjoy these kinds of combinations, and one suspects that he got pleasure from contriving the apparently haphazard nature of his south front as it finally developed.

▪▪ OPPOSITE
103. The director's room.
▪▪ ABOVE
104. The north front.

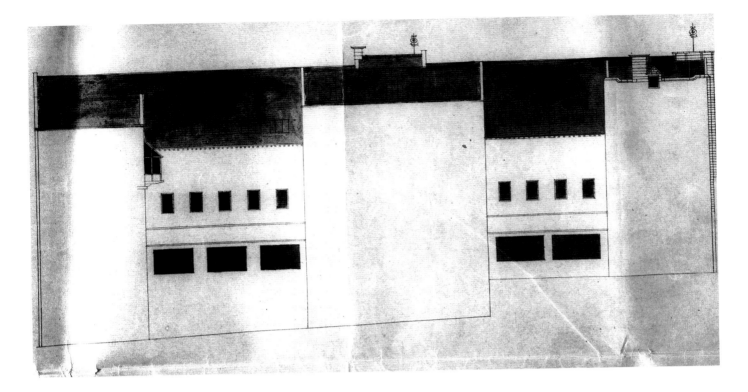

BACK ELEVATION

140 BATH STREET
GLASGOW SEPT 97.

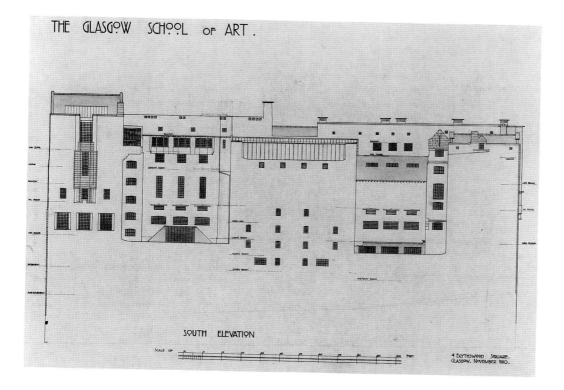

THE GLASGOW SCHOOL OF ART.

SOUTH ELEVATION

The Interior

The interior also underwent significant changes. According to a description made at the time of the opening in 1899, the internal woodwork was at that point painted an "artistic green."[14] The school in its first phase was in fact heading towards something with a much stronger element of what would have been called at the time "artistic." The existing ornamental ironwork and glass, outside and in, were to have been supplemented by other features that appear never to have been carried out. The Dean of Guild drawings show the main doors decorated with glass panels similar to, but larger and more elaborate than, those still seen elsewhere in the building (plate 108). Most important, the walls above the panelling in the museum are shown decorated with a figurative frieze (plate 109), drawn by Mackintosh in sufficient detail to suggest something in the style of the friezes in his Buchanan Street tea rooms. The trusses of the museum roof, with their uprights pierced by hearts (plate 110), strike a slightly discordant and whimsical note in the school as it is today because they are waiting for the frieze that never arrived.

The aestheticism of the Four had been looked at askance when it first appeared in the city and at the School of Art in the mid-1890s, but it seems likely that by the time the school was opened, that aestheticism and its derivatives had become acceptable, and even expected, in a suitably "artistic" ambience. They provided a desirable element of delicacy to offset the workmanlike

OPPOSITE, TOP
105. *Competition Entry: South Elevation* (detail), 1897. Ink and watercolour, 34 x 24 in. (86.4 x 61 cm), overall. The Keeper of the Records of Scotland, Scottish Record Office, Edinburgh.

OPPOSITE, BOTTOM
106. *South Elevation*, as submitted to the Dean of Guild, 1897. Mechanical copy with watercolour and ink, 22¼ x 35 in. (56.4 x 90.2 cm). Strathclyde Regional Archives, Glasgow.

ABOVE
107. *South Elevation*, as drawn in 1910. Ink, 23¹³/₁₆ x 33⅞ in. (60.5 x 86.0 cm). Glasgow School of Art.

The south elevation is virtually the same today.

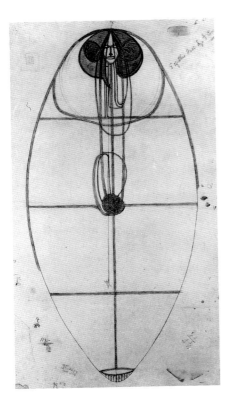

108. *Stained-Glass Panel for Glasgow School of Art Doors*, c. 1899. Pencil and watercolour, 40½ x 21¹³/₁₆ in. (103.5 x 55.4 cm). Hunterian Art Gallery, University of Glasgow.

109. *Proposed Decoration of the Museum* (detail) as submitted to the Dean of Guild Court, 1897. Mechanical copy with watercolour and ink, 21¼ x 35⅝ in. (54.0 x 90.5 cm), overall. Strathclyde Regional Archives, Glasgow.

robustness of the building as a whole, especially appropriate—as was commented on at the time—in a building where women were so much in evidence. This element of aesthetic delicacy is nicely epitomised in a pretty watercolour design by Mackintosh, much in the style of a drawing by E. W. Godwin, showing a dresser in the women teachers' sitting room, decorated with vases of flowers and blue-and-white porcelain.[15]

By the time the School of Art came to be completed in 1907–9, aesthetic curves had percolated down to saloon level, and there was an inevitable reaction. Unlike most of his contemporaries, Mackintosh himself could never express this by adopting a more academic classicism, along with a grammar the rules of which had to be obeyed. His development, as has so often been analysed, was to move from an ornamental language mostly made up of curves to one mostly made up of straight lines. There are forecasts of this in his earlier work, but the change was to be much stimulated by his contacts with Vienna from 1900 onwards. It can be seen on the large scale as well as the small; the building as a whole became more rectangular, largely as a result of the addition of an extra storey. The top-floor studios originally had huge open-timber roofs, similar to those over the museum. These were expressed externally by the deep and prominent slope of the crowning roofs, especially as seen from the south and in the slope of a gable end on the east elevation. All this disappeared with the addition of a floor above, entailing flat ceilings, supported on mighty iron beams in the second-floor studios, as in the lower studios. Almost all the new top floor was also given a flat roof, and the eastern gable end was squared off.[16]

It is interesting to watch Mackintosh's evolving use of simple rectangular elements to build up a decorative language. Perhaps this started as a way of doing something different using inexpensive elements, but it developed beyond that; he clearly became fascinated with working out the possible changes and devising gradations from the very simple to the obsessive intensity of the library. The beginnings are to be found in the first stage of the school, though here always offset by and played against his distinctive vocabulary of curves. The most obvious examples are the great rectangular grids of the studio windows, unrelieved by any form of moulding. Similar grids recur, on a smaller scale, in the balustrade of the main staircase, but here they play a subordinate role to another Mackintosh device, that of extended verticals. Not only are the staircase balusters, all of plain rectangular section, carried right up to a horizontal rail on the floor above—instead of ending in a sloping staircase rail, in the conventional fashion—but the newels that terminate the rails at the museum level are extended up to join with the timbers of the roof.

In the staircase also can be seen the origins of a form of joining that Mackintosh was often to use again. In two places the timbers supporting the staircase landing are extended to join up with newels extended vertically from the staircases below; but instead of the junction being made by one horizontal

butting up against the vertical, the horizontals are, as it were, split into two, joined to either side of the vertical, and carried on to project beyond it. Variations of this device, which are said to derive from Japanese joinery, were to become common in Mackintosh's work, in both wood and metal. One distinctive example is in the studio above the library, in the west wing (plate 111). Here Mackintosh played a simple but extremely effective game by piling up the junctions in a criss-cross one above the other; the slender verticals are, incidentally, made of steel, but all the other members are timber.

110. The museum.

111. The composition room, north studio above the library. Photographed by Bedford Lemere, 1910.

This type of junction can be found, combined with both grids and extended verticals, in the metal screens at the top of the east and west staircases (plate 112). These screens are extended stair rails, playing the same sort of game that is seen in the main staircase—but in metal, not timber, and in the form of a grid rather than with the verticals predominating. At the vertical end of the grid the uprights are doubled and the horizontals extended through them, to end (in typical Mackintosh fashion) each one in a slightly different curve or twist. In the east staircase the grid is carried up to join with the timbers of the roof, and finished off with a great horizontal circle of iron, fixed to the underside of the beams.

These modest utilitarian staircases are in fact wonderful places in which to observe Mackintosh's pleasure in combining curves and straight lines or in accepting ad hoc junctions in order to build up abstract compositions out of different materials (plate 114). The patterns of iron and timber at the top of the stairs are supplemented, all the way down, by a variety of very simple (and presumably very cheap) combinations of what appear to be standard square or rectangular tiles, set into the wall (plate 113). As one descends, the metal screen between the flights gives way to a wall made up of plastered arches, piled one above the other; these play against the zigzag profile of the stair treads seen through them; at the lowest level the wall itself is cut away in a zigzag that echoes the stair tread. As one looks down into the main corridor, this cutaway section rises to a cantilevered half-landing, its horizontal curve echoed by the curved vertical bracket that strengthens the landing railings. At this stage the staircase, which was a later addition, runs into the curved and originally external windows opening onto the original director's room. Rather than getting rid of these, Mackintosh let them play their part in the composition, accentuating them by adding a slithering in-and-out curve of plasterwork beneath them.

The culmination of Mackintosh's language of right angles, by now very subtly and at times almost imperceptibly combined with curves, is to be found in the library (plate 115) and in the west front (plate 117), in which the library windows are the main feature. The library is another feature with a history of ad hoc alteration, which Mackintosh let contribute positively to its design. As originally shown, in the plans drawn up in 1907, the library rose the whole height of the long strip windows in the projecting oriels on the west front. At some early stage it was decided to reduce its height, either for visual reasons or to obtain a bookstore in the resulting mezzanine between the library and the second-floor studio. Rather than blanking off the top stage of the oriels, Mackintosh left them open, so that the eye now follows them as they rise up through the library ceiling.

The library appears to be, and indeed is, an exceedingly complicated design, but its complications grow out of simple necessity, or at least structural good sense. An upper gallery was needed, which had to be supported, and the right place for the posts to support it was clearly on the line of the two great steel beams that hold up the library floor. But a gallery running up to these supports would have been larger than was required and would have uncomfortably reduced daylight at the main level.

Accordingly, the posts support beams that run back into the walls, and the gallery front is set back about two-thirds of the way along them. But nothing is simple here. The beams are in fact "split," made up of three vertical members butting up against each other (plate 115); the two outer members support the two halves of the split beam, while the central member rises up to the beams in the ceiling that follow the line of the gallery beams. The ceiling

112. Top of the east staircase, showing the grille roof detail.

 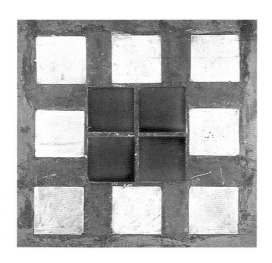 

is made of a simple coffered grid, between the beams, as though the window grids of the studios have been rotated to the horizontal. The tall posts are not structural, although they appear to be; the ceiling is actually suspended by iron ties from the steel beams in the ceiling of the bookstore above it.

The library is in fact made up of very simple elements put together in a very complex way, for aesthetic rather than functional reasons. The result is a composition in line, not mass; the dominant lines are provided by sharp arrises of sawn timber and are straight, but subtly set off by curves. These curves are conspicuous in the notched balusters that, for purely ornamental reasons, join the gallery balustrade to the posts; and they are conspicuous in the suspended panels of ornament, each one different, like a series of musical notations to

■■ OPPOSITE
113. Tiles from the staircases.
■■ ABOVE
114. The east staircase, photographed by T. and R. Annan Ltd., 1910.

115. The library.

which only Mackintosh had the key.[17] Even more subtle are the slightly curved facets or arches; one suspects that even the slight irregularities in the vertical lines of electrical cables would have appealed to Mackintosh.

What can one say about the exterior of the west wing? It relates closely to the design of the library, even if its curves, being of ashlar rather than wood, are more robust, its verticals more exaggerated, its grids more overpowering (plate 117). Its extended oriels relate to other oriels of the same date, in England and Glasgow, and back through them to sixteenth-century prototypes. The boldly modelled swell of its doorway was inspired by doorways designed by Mackintosh's Glasgow contemporary, John James Burnet. All this may be

true, but at the end of the day one has to stand back and wonder; the creative flash has taken place, and something original and amazing has been born.

Neither the west wing nor the library caused a ripple of interest, let alone shock, at the time. "Thoroughly business-like" has its merits as a description of the original design but seems entirely inapposite when applied to work so unique and powerful, so clearly and zestfully going beyond the merely functional. No explanation is entirely satisfactory, but the one put forward by Gavin Stamp in this volume is the most convincing: by 1909 it was buildings based on steel frames logically expressed (though clothed in disciplined classical details) that were catching the public eye. By contrast, Mackintosh's ad

117. The west front, photographed by T. and R. Annan Ltd., 1933.

hoc structural mixes and willful personal detail seemed old-fashioned. If this explanation is true, it is in curious contrast to the view of Mackintosh as a pioneer of the Modern movement. But this view, too, seems to distort what Mackintosh was doing. One can see why architects who wanted to reject or escape from the past adopted Mackintosh as an ancestor, but he has more to say to those who want to accept the past but develop from it. Most of all, he speaks to those who simply want to enjoy him for what he was and what he did as a creature of his time.

NOTES

1. Unattributed press clippings, scrapbooks, Glasgow School of Art Library. These scrapbooks, arranged chronologically, are full of interesting material, but many of the clippings are pasted in without source or date.

2. Unidentified clipping, May 25, 1899, scrapbooks; *Citizen*, October 11, 1899.

3. Scrapbooks.

4. Mackintosh to Hermann Muthesius, in William Buchanan, ed., *Mackintosh's Masterwork: The Glasgow School of Art* (Glasgow: Richard Drew Publishing, 1989), p. 36.

5. *News*, February 20, 1909; *Scotsman* (Edinburgh), December 10, 1909.

6. *Evening Times* (Glasgow), December 11, 1909.

7. The second stage had a more difficult passage; Alan Crawford suggests that the first stage went smoothly because Keppie, not Mackintosh, acted as the job architect.

8. The brief is published in full in Buchanan, ed., *Mackintosh's Masterwork*, pp. 205–9.

9. Mackintosh, in Pamela Robertson, ed., *Charles Rennie Mackintosh: The Architectural Papers* (Wendlebury, England: White Cockade Publishing, 1990), p. 184.

10. Illustrated in David Walker, "The Early Work of Charles Rennie Mackintosh," in *The Anti-Rationalists*, ed. Nikolaus Pevsner and J. M. Richards (London: Architectural Press, 1973), p. 134.

11. Mackintosh, in Robertson, ed., *Architectural Papers*, p. 207.

12. In an address on Mackintosh given at the Hunterian Art Gallery in 1990, the architect James Stirling said, "I've always tried for those thin line graphics and meaningful voids, the way he did it."

13. At the time of this writing the drawings are being restored in the Mitchell Library, Glasgow City Libraries, and their final destination is uncertain.

14. *Evening Times* (Glasgow), December 21, 1899.

15. The drawing is in the Hunterian Art Gallery, University of Glasgow.

16. It is perhaps worth wondering whether the flat roofs are there for legal or planning rather than aesthetic reasons—perhaps to comply with the daylight rights of the houses in Sauchiehall Street.

17. I am not qualified to discuss the fascinating but difficult question of the possible symbolism of these and other elements at the School of Art.

The Hill House

■■
JOHN McKEAN

Here is the house: it is not an Italian villa, an English mansion house, a Swiss chalet, or a Scotch castle. It is a dwelling house.

Charles Rennie Mackintosh to Walter Blackie,
on handing over The Hill House, 1904

Twenty-five miles down the Firth of Clyde, to the west of Glasgow, Helensburgh was a new nineteenth-century settlement, an idyllic seaside retreat for those whose mercantile wealth was being created in the dark, industrial city, the hellish engine room of the world's greatest empire. Henry Bell, the town's first provost, devised in 1812 the paddle steamer *Comet*, the first steamship to ply up to the metropolis and entice the Glaswegian bourgeoisie to commute from the smoke. By the 1860s, with the arrival of the railway, his little town's fashionable prosperity was assured. The south-facing fields that sloped up from Helensburgh's seafront were covered with a grid of generous roads and plots, and here some of Glasgow's most prestigious—and certainly most expensive—domestic buildings were erected through the second half of the nineteenth century.

Early in 1902 the Glasgow publisher Walter Blackie decided to join in; he purchased a plot (until recently a potato field) at the top edge of town, among the mansions of Upper Helensburgh. Almost next door to Blackie's site there already was a house by the well-known Arts and Crafts designer M. H. Baillie Scott; nearby were others by more-local architects but the majority appearing equally English—with foreign whitewash, half-timbering, and lots of red-tile roofs.

The publishing firm of Blackie had been founded in 1810, a half-century before Walter was born. It already had a tradition of excellence in design under his uncles John and Robert, each of whom had lived by now for thirty years in town houses designed for them by Alexander Thomson—Glasgow's best architect of the generation fifty years older than Mackintosh. In 1867 Uncle Robert's house in the magnificent Great Western Terrace had been designed down to the smallest detail of interior space and surface, with furniture, decoration, and carpets by Thomson. Robert Blackie continued to keep abreast of contemporary design ideas, and thirty years later, in the 1890s, he appointed as

118. The Hill House from the southeast.

119. Charles Rennie Mackintosh. *The Hill House: Perspective from the Southwest*, 1903. Ink, 13 x 21⅝ in. (33.0 x 55.0 cm). Glasgow School of Art.

his firm's art director the young English Arts and Crafts designer Talwin Morris. Morris quickly entered the circle of what the *Studio* would call the "Mac group," a remarkable, sizeable circle of talented craftsmen and designers in Glasgow. At the centre of the group was the close-knit quartet known as the Four: Mackintosh, Herbert McNair, and the Macdonald sisters, Margaret and Frances. The first collector of work by the Four was Talwin Morris, whose own designs were not limited to books and their decorative covers. He designed and made domestic hangings and interior fittings such as exquisitely wrought metal door handles and finger plates; a wall candle sconce by him is now outside the dining room in The Hill House.[1]

So, in 1902, we find Walter Blackie, a director in his family's firm but himself with no known interest in the arts or design, ready to move with wife and young children to a new house. His site at the top edge of Helensburgh (five minutes above the upper station from Glasgow) commands fine views away across the Clyde to the south. Lacking only an architect, he consults the company's designer. Talwin Morris recommends his friend and contemporary, Charles Rennie Mackintosh. Almost exactly two years later, in March 1904 (completion having been delayed only by a strike at the Ballachulish slate quarries), the Blackie family moves into The Hill House (plate 118), its final cost having come in under budget.

The Hill House is a bourgeois Edwardian mansion, with a considerable service wing and room for the staff of seven (plate 119). Its plan is absolutely within the commonsense tradition of such houses of the time; its form (seen from outside) has antecedents in Scottish history—Crathes Castle is often quoted as a model. That it has memories of Scots Baronial history is as obvious as that Mozart had memories of Handel. The Hill House, however, goes way beyond its sources, just as it is far more than a demonstration of competence in social planning. It fitted an affluent family very well; its convenience in detail was often remarked on. But that is no more significant than noting the way Mozart so often made great music that fitted perfectly under the fingers (which many fine composers, of course, do not). With Mackintosh much celebrated today in graphic imagery, with his decorative devices made into wonderful photographs that fill picture books and postcards, it must be added that this house is far more than a sum of its decoration and far from the icy perfection of the mere stylist.[2]

Though the surfaces and materials are beautifully formed, coloured, and joined, they enhance the place overall just as a musical cadence or its ornamentation enhances the melodic and harmonic whole, and each is based on an understanding of traditional formal structures. Therefore, it is as important that Mackintosh was a turn-of-the-century Scot as that Mozart was a late-eighteenth-century Austrian—and no more important than that.

THE WORLD OF INSIDE AND OUT

The Hill House balances between two poles, two extremes that are held in dynamic equilibrium and that are united through the making of interior spaces. At one end of this spectrum is the hard shell, characterised by the adjectives *strong, sober, empiricist, objective*; it is essentially a variant on the vernacular, on tradition. At the other end is the white interior (especially the master bedroom), which attracts adjectives such as *soft, decorated, idealist, fantastic, erotic*; this is essentially creative and modern.

Mediating between these extremes are the crucial intermediate spaces, which encourage reflection on such contrasts—potential sources of conflict and tension. Linking these extremes symbolically but also literally are the hallways and stair. Far from being just utilitarian connecting corridors, these intermediate spaces are the most fascinating places in the house. By performing this mediating role between the masculine, rather dour and tradition-conscious public world and the feminine, almost dreamlike, and freely creative private world, they are perhaps also the most important.

These sets of contrasting qualities do much more than simply reinforce the status quo or provide an embodiment of the place of women in Edwardian society. The design of Mackintosh, working with his wife and partner Margaret Macdonald, goes beyond a mapping of conventional values onto form; it implies a critique of those social assumptions.[3] His "femininity," for example, is seen as the locus of the avant-garde, formally creative qualities, and far more than a conventional femininity of pretty domesticity.[4]

We return with Mr. and Mrs. Blackie to their house, with the help of a private memoir that Walter Blackie wrote years later:

> The new School of Art was nearing completion. I had watched with interest its growth into the imposing structure that emerged, vaguely wondering who was architect, and when Morris named Mackintosh and recommended him as architect for my projected villa house I was at first taken aback, thinking so distinguished a performer would be too big a man for me. Morris, however, persisted in his recommendation and undertook to get Mackintosh to call upon me. He called next day. When he entered my room I was astonished at the youthfulness of the distinguished architect. . . .
>
> The conference didn't last long. I put to Mackintosh such ideas as I had for my prospective dwelling; mostly negative, I may say. I told him that I disliked red-tiled roofs in the West of Scotland with its frequent murky sky; did not want to have a construction of brick and plaster and wooden beams; that, on the whole, I rather fancied grey rough cast for the walls, and slate for the roof; and that any architectural effect sought should be secured by the massing of the parts rather than by adventitious ornamentation. To all these sentiments Mackintosh at once agreed and suggested that I should see a house he'd designed at Kilmacolm. . . . My wife and I were shown over the house and left convinced that Mackintosh was the man for us. Thus we got started.
>
> Mackintosh came to see us at [our house] to judge what manner of folk he was to cater for. . . . [And] before long he submitted his first designs for our new house—the inside only. Not until we had decided on the inside arrangements did he submit drawings of the elevation.[5]

How fascinating that the client's requirements were all to do with the outside—and luckily his masculine face was presented to the world in images with which Mackintosh easily concurred. The architect then responded with a design only for the inside, confirming the argument that inside and out are different worlds.

Here is a sharp contrast to contemporaries like Philip Webb, for whom every element on the outside, the articulation of shape and the change of material, makes the interior clear beyond the wall. For Arts and Crafts designers inspired by A.W.N. Pugin, John Ruskin, and William Morris, that was the only honest way to produce buildings. It had clarity and coherence. Perhaps the last great Arts and Crafts designer was Frank Lloyd Wright (Mackintosh's exact contemporary from the late 1860s). For Wright, designing masterly Prairie houses in Chicago's outer suburbs at the same time as The Hill House, every detail was conceived as a minor part of the overall fabric,

120. *Ground-Floor Plan*, as submitted to the Dean of Guild Court for building permission, 1902. Pencil, ink, and watercolour on linen, 17½ x 25¾ in. (44.4 x 65.5 cm). Dumbarton District Libraries, Dumbartonshire, Scotland.

The western half of the house contains the main rooms discussed in this essay; to the east a Z shape contains the dining room under a large guest bedroom and the second leg running back to the north. Here is the kitchen and service wing at ground level and the children's wing on the bedroom floor, with its corridor running from the spiral stair at the south to a tiny one at the north. On the east side, with its steep pitches and chimneys, is a third floor. Farther up the spiral are maids' rooms in the roof, and up the tiny stair at the north end of the bedroom corridor is a stunning, marvelously lit children's dayroom ("the school room"). This room, naturally, is the farthest possible from their father's study, at the opposite corner on the ground floor.

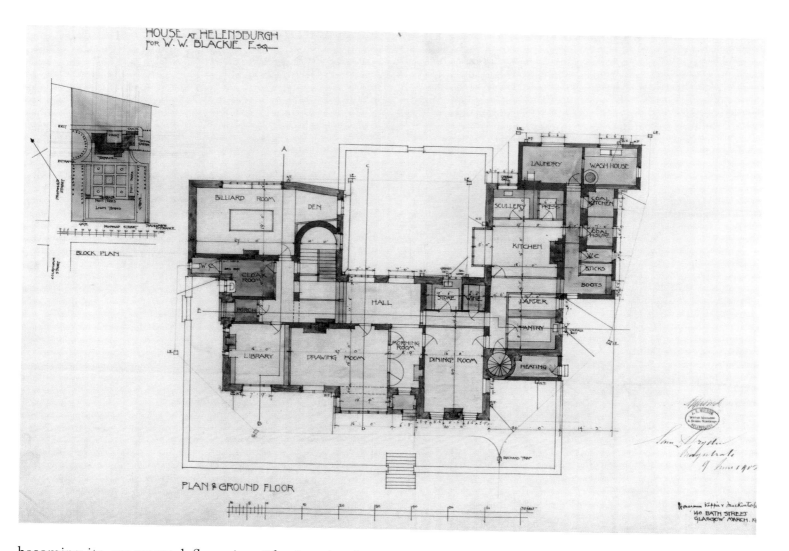

HOUSE at HELENSBURGH
for W. W. BLACKIE Esq

BLOCK PLAN

PLAN of GROUND FLOOR

becoming its ornamental flowering. The interior decoration was thoroughly architectonic—expressing, though at different scales and in varied materials, the architecture's basic motifs in plan and elevation. Those rare more modern architects able to handle decoration (such as the Venetian Carlo Scarpa) tend to follow Wright's unifying approach.

Mackintosh was taking quite a different line; he was not seeing either fitments or decoration as architecture in microcosm, nor was his inside a reflection of the out. For him, each place had its own specificity, whether a picturesque view of the house as you approach, a fireside you sit around, or the privacy of a bed recess. In its acceptance of this range of meaning from public to most private, the unity he achieved was more difficult. The Hill House is an essay in chamber music into whose depths one is gradually introduced, as Mackintosh linked inner and outer worlds through his complex, ambiguous intermediate spaces.

As we approach The Hill House, all is covered in silver grey harling (a typical Scottish rough plaster) under varied roofs of deep grey slate, and, likely

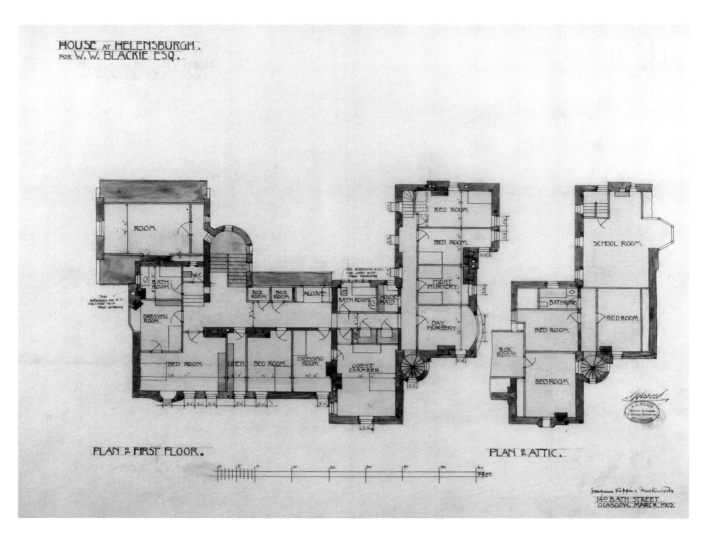

HOUSE at HELENSBURGH.
for W. W. BLACKIE ESQ.

PLAN of FIRST FLOOR.

PLAN of ATTIC.

121. *First-Floor Plan*, as submitted to the Dean of Guild Court for building permission, 1902. Pencil, ink, and watercolour on linen, 17½ x 25¾ in. (44.4 x 65.5 cm). Dumbarton District Libraries, Dumbartonshire, Scotland.

as not, a matching sky. The house recalls the Scots Baronial in outside image and even more in plan; but it would divert from understanding and enjoying Mackintosh's remarkable achievement to chase its origins to a fusion of the conventional Edwardian north-corridor house, on the west, and a seventeenth-century Z-plan Scots tower house, on the east (plates 120 and 121).[6] We note, however, that the spiral stair, like a hinge in the crook of the Z, is here a minor service connection, quite different from the Scots tradition of using the spiral as the main link between rooms in a building without corridors. At The Hill House, as already suggested, the other, much more generous connecting halls and their staircase are the essence of Mackintosh's creation.

This essay aims neither to overstress the typicality of The Hill House as architecture of its moment, nor to overstress its uniqueness as seen from the 1990s.[7] Some of the qualities of space and surface that attract us to this house are indeed typical of their moment, and today these deserve not to be submerged but to be seen alongside the other qualities that are unique to Mackintosh. So we pass the wrought-iron gates, sensing the balance of precise geometric order with a graphic, allusive, poetic decoration. (Perhaps they hint at something different within the building's dour exterior.) We approach this stately, solid house, clearly rooted in its place; knock at the dark door, absolutely plain apart from a square of nine small square lenses of clear glass; and enter.

THE LIBRARY

Having passed through an inner screen that is really a glazed thick trellis, and before rising four steps into the main hall glimpsed beyond, we see, to the right, the door of the library, Walter Blackie's study. As convention decreed, it is "thoroughly masculine,"[8] lined with dark-stained grainy-oak bookshelves and featuring simple, rather Arts and Crafts detailing, such as metal butterfly drawer pulls. But the door's four long purple inserts of sparkling handmade glass had intimated a less than conventional interior; the room's conservative order is offset by tiny inlaid squares of white enamel and purply blue glass broken into by an occasional single reed curving up the bookcase (plate 122). At 12½ feet, this is a tall room, kept down by the oak fittings whose low cornice line at 7½ feet links the fireplace with its little windows, the door, and all the bookcases between. Then, in a touch of pure Mackintosh, the southern window bursts upwards through this frieze (exactly as in his own homes[9]), adding a high light to the room and increasing its sense of being a contemplative *studiolo* (see plate 123, bottom left). Blackie would, I imagine, have received visitors here—the last of the world outside; only family and close friends could penetrate farther.

Consolidating the male domain on this entrance level, a billiard room was planned to be opposite this office, but was never built (though seen on plate 120). Above it is one other sober, masculine space, again with purple highlights: Walter Blackie's dressing room at the top of the stairs, next to the washroom with its wonderful shower (perhaps the first such shower in Scotland), in which horizontal jets spurt from a cage of chromed-copper pipes.

Although inventive and charming details appear throughout the house, we must resist imagining what is beyond the glowing glass squares in the various black doors we pass, for this brief essay can pause only in those few rooms where the designers put the most effort.[10] Much of the house was finished and filled quite conventionally. In the dark, panelled dining room, Mackintosh without a trace of condescension incorporated the Blackies' traditional Edwardian values. Their antique furniture and silver stands alongside his own remarkably apt light fixtures: sober bronze and white-glass shapes on the window wall and a magnificent fitting over the table, in which deep purple encloses a white-glass interior. The serious business of formal meals, with paterfamilias in place at the head of the table, was not to be dislodged by any creative shifts in the sexual politics of the Mackintosh milieu.

But the library, the drawing room next to it, the Blackies' own bedroom, and the hall and stairs are entirely to Mackintosh's design—furniture and fit-

122. Fitted furniture in the library, showing the squares of glass offset by the one bending, rising reed.

tings, carpets and wall decoration—and a large proportion of this is carefully in place today.[11]

THE HALLWAY

As we travel deeper from the entrance, towards the softest white at the house's heart, we first explore the stair and hall, those intermediate spaces that enable the whole allegorical journey to occur. This is a complex, mysterious space. To enter it, we must first rise four steps to the main ground floor (plate 124). It is an unusual experience to look upwards directly into a major space, having already negotiated two powerfully portcullis-like barriers. The sense of anticipation given by that platform's being raised two more feet accentuates the feeling that we are still outside, in the public realm of getting and spending, the sense that there is another threshold to be crossed before arrival at the heart.

What appears ahead is a palely lit clearing in the dark forest through which we now approach (plate 125). Such architectonic gestures are not bound by the decorative fashion of the moment. Alvar Aalto's masterly Villa Mairea (1938), which also has a rise of four steps at this point, offers a similar sense; moreover, Aalto's house can be seen to parallel the woody metaphor, though his stair rises within a more open Finnish birch forest. At The Hill House rectangular brass-framed light fittings above us glow through pink-and-white glass, the white squares cut by a brass stem and topped in a pink-and-white translucent circular flower head. The tungsten lamps cast weird orange-and-pink shadow patterns onto ceiling and walls. To our left, between the dark verticals, we glance up at a shadowy hidden seat (under the upper stair), from which we could be observed entering (see plate 121, lower centre).

Later, up in the top corridor, we will find another little "seat-room," up two steps from the hall floor, low ceiled, and enclosed with arms as if in the thickness of the wall (see plate 124, top right). Anne Ellis perceptively calls this alcove a "sit-ooterie," after the half-secret spaces where a girl could safely sit out a dance yet remain on the edge of the ballroom floor.[12] The Hill House abounds in such rooms within rooms—or rather in edge places, half in and half out of rooms, that playfully revel in ambiguity. They are natural spaces for children, who instinctively enjoy these boundary games as well as the changes of scale. Only a rare master architect can be in touch with such childlike experiences and yet hold them firmly within the adult's measured world. Many domestic corners by Edwin Lutyens have a similarly playful spatial charm, but they lack this order. On the other hand, Adolf Loos's Moller family house in Vienna (1928) is a comparable example of rigorous spatial skill—with its stair and study spaces, and particularly with its "sit-ooterie" alcove over the front door, which welcomes inhabitation. But in the Loos house, the elaboration of surface has been washed smooth, down to its material purity. Very rare is Mackintosh's elaboration of these little places so that their surfaces are appro-

OPPOSITE, TOP
123. Cross-section showing the front door in the centre and the library to the left, with its high windows. The stair (with its half-landing observation point), to the right, leads up to the main bedroom above the library.

OPPOSITE, BOTTOM
124. Long section from the front door (at left) to the inner hall (at right) with, between them, the stair beyond. Upstairs, Mr. Blackie's dressing room (with its "wrapped" furniture) is to the left and the "sit-ooterie" is to the right of the stairs.

priately worked to the scale of intimate occupation, attracting eye and hand close to the surfaces, while at the same time their spaces are unified by the larger formal or geometric ideas. Talwin Morris, before he ever suggested an architect to his boss, wrote how Mackintosh "frequently emphasised the fact that there should be no apparent break between construction and decoration of a house."[13]

As we move up and into the hall, dark and light glimpses, solid and void uprights divide the dynamic space. Tiny flashes of pink glass embedded in wood (glimpsed in plate 126) pass the eye.[14] We turn left to climb four more steps, and then we turn the other way into the stair drum. Its white walls, silvery grey with north light, are touched with spots of purple glass. We run our hands across the open hall timbers as we do forest trees. These are structure:

■■ OPPOSITE
125. The interior seen on entering.
■■ ABOVE
126. The hallway, looking up to joist ends sitting on the beam, showing the hall light and the glass inset in a vertical baluster.

strong, expressive, dark beams and posts and planks for stair balusters. Though explicitly constructional, this is no exercise in honest carpentry as advocated by the Arts and Crafts; it is certainly symbolic but no longer vernacular.

THE MAIN BEDROOM

Through the frame at the head of the stair, six little squares of glowing leaded glass in the dark door ahead invite us from the cool upper hall into the Blackies' bedroom (plate 127). Indeed, all around the house tiny accents are made by touches of colour—of glass, of ceramic, of mosaic—used like lipstick or earrings, only in places close enough to touch. Milky glass squares on the black door heighten expectation. It opens, the door jamb melts away in a curve, and we enter an ivory mist. (Not only is the other side of the dark door now white, but its little glass squares are enamelled pink inside.) Here materiality is disguised; wooden furniture is abstractly curvaceous, smoothly feminine, and thickly lacquered in ivory white—an extreme contrast to the structural clarity of stained timber in the library. The bedroom has an overall sleekness; it is all sensual surface, which you are induced to touch and caress—curves, sharpness, and extreme subtlety of form (plate 129). With the material and the carpentry obscured by the absence of a workman's touch, surfaces become ambiguous, forms blur, and our hands instinctively stretch out to run over surfaces.

This room, on plan, might at first appear irregular and poorly defined; in fact, the opposite is true (plate 128). It is exquisitely articulated into two spaces, with the bed recess beautifully contained under a low barrel ceiling. On each

127. Approaching the principal bedroom.

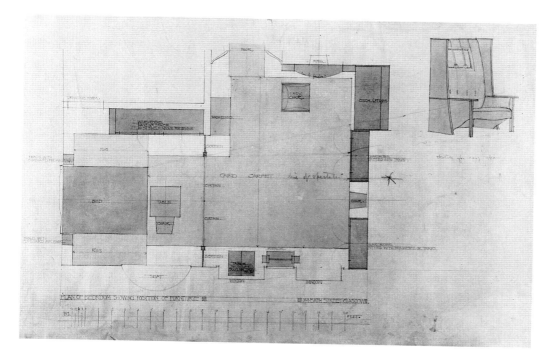

■■ LEFT

128. *The Principal Bedroom: Plan,*
1903. Pencil and watercolour, 13 x
21³/₁₆ in. (33.0 x 53.8 cm). Hunterian
Art Gallery, University of Glasgow.

This plan of furniture, fitments,
and spatial enclosure shows the precision of the block geometry in this
most sensuous room.

■■ BELOW

129. Surfaces in the principal bedroom.

side of the bed white-lipped alcoves are lined with deep purple shiny tesserae in black leading. The shallow, enclosing vault springs from wardrobe doors on one side and from a gentle bow, echoing the vault itself, on the other (plate 130).[15] This bedside space bellies out to one tiny, low window at its centre (see plate 123, top left, which cuts through this little bay). Here the whole thickness of the protective bedroom wall seems scooped dangerously thin; it is a riskily exposed moment in this womblike place. Safely thick curving interior shutters, each with three milky pink glass squares in them, when opened admit the morning sun to hit the pillow. Almost as a joke on Arts and Crafts "honesty," other little shutters appear outside this window, but only as flat, vestigial shapes slightly moulded in the curving exterior bay surface.

Mackintosh intended this intimate vault to be separated—by gossamer veils edged with bejewelled glazed screens—from the rest of the room, which itself is two little places. One is the dressing area, under the light fitting (an open metal rectangle with white glass enamelled pink inside) and in front of the tall ivory mirror that stands between the two windows. This mirror's silky smoothness—its canopy held on four prongs, its strangely curved shelves and backbone—is matched by that of two ivory white wardrobes (see plate 177). Their formalised botanical patterns, all smoothly white lacquered, hold milky pink glazed insets and silvered handles. The symmetry of the mirror between the windows is balanced by a tall, ladderback black chair between the wardrobes. Moreover, the space is unified almost imperceptibly by the fact that the top 2½ feet of the room is an enclosing band, formed by the line of the light fixture and the window head, as well as by the tops of wardrobes and the fireside seat hollowed into the wall beneath this band.

The other little place within the bedroom is around the fireplace by the door. Its cosy, built-in settle opposite the washstand snuggles into the wall thickness as if it were an inglenook, the seat's top aligning with the fireplace. In the use of naturally coloured materials—the pewter water jug, the untreated fabrics, the mirror glass, the enamel and pinkish tiles, and the naked polished sheet-steel fire surround—and with the widespread ivory white lacquer, the effect is innovative, daring, and bright, with a mood of more or less open eroticism. A small white table (which can be seen in plate 176) epitomises the mood. It is square topped, with four legs more like leaves than stems, paper thin but curving down, facing each other diagonally and joined by a little square timber with four square holes cut from it. Such a geometric description belies the extreme elegance of this delicate, dynamic, and satisfying object.

Onto the geometric order of this room, built up of cubes and two shallow cylindrical curves, is layered a veil of decoration. The ivory walls are all delicately stencilled as a rose bower in mauve and green; between the wardrobes, roses climb through the black grid of the trellis-backed chair. This frieze is light and uninhibited (in contrast to the more polite and formal beauty seen in the drawing room below); flower heads flying, and long leaves blowing like hair in the wind.[16] Here is a nudity not of masculine *structure*—as in the hall—but of sensual feminine *surface*. Any tension within this space is in the polarity of masculine and feminine, the dynamic equilibrium of geometry and nature. It lacks the threat that seems to lurk in the contemporaneous eroticism of, say, Edvard Munch or more obviously in Gustav Klimt and turn-of-the-century Vienna. In this deepest interior of the house, all hint of historical reference or vernacular has vanished.

Leaving the bedroom, we are gently squeezed by the narrowing of the ogee-curved door jambs, out of which are cut little rectangular niches for flower vases at face level. As we close the door behind us, it is worth stressing that Mackintosh designed the *room*. In drawings he placed all the moveable furniture as well as the immoveable (plate 128). This was not to fix them in an inviolable stage setting. Indeed, the chairs call out for elegant lingerie to be strewn over them, the cheval mirror's shelves to be cluttered with too much jewelry; the fireside table awaits a good book, the bed invites bodies. The room is fresh and awaits inhabitation.

Today, in a critical climate polarised between architecture historians who conceptually reduce such work to an underlying structure (often with eyes only for a Modernist form beneath the decorative and superficial veil) and fine-art-object historians who reify and fetishise each crafted gesture, it is difficult to keep hold of the range of orchestrated sounds that together build into the experience of these interior places. Carlo Scarpa has pointed out that in old Italian dictionaries *arredo* is defined as "to supply what is necessary"; *arredamento* (normally "furniture" or "furnishings" today) therefore means "the necessities" (although the etymology also includes the Gothic word *ga-reda*,

130. The rooms within the bedroom.

meaning "to take care," and the Spanish *a rear*, "to adorn"). Such adornments are indeed necessary—necessary for our bodies to be welcomed into the embodied space.

DOWN THE STAIRS

Back downstairs, the dynamic space in this direction is perceived quite differently. Prominent now is the stair light (plate 131). One of Mackintosh's most remarkable little objects, it epitomises his geometric concerns at The Hill House—and it can be seen only by moving diagonally past. At first it is below eye level, its form revealing itself as we spiral down underneath it. A structure of nine cubes, it has an openwork metal cage with light bulbs in four corner cubes; each side of each cube is glazed with nine purply blue leaded-glass squares. We then pass, at eye level, the deep crossbeam above which the exposed joists of the upper hall are carried on the tapering newel post (see plate 126). And we descend into the timber cage again, the hall–living room—the place of rendezvous and the dynamic fulcrum of the house.

It is surrounded with an almost Japanese black-and-white geometrical order. In this forest clearing we are surrounded by Mackintosh's metamorphosis of a classic frieze, the triglyphs and metopes of the Greek temple. The figurative metopes are now pale blue stencilling, with pink-and-black chequerboard patterns and one carefully placed touch of green. The elegant abstract pattern breaks through the bottom of its square format with one remarkable, sinuous gesture. The triglyphs between, articulated strictly geometrically and framed in dark oak, are sets of three tall, thin strips of pale purple enamelled glass (in fact, white hand-blown opalescent glass fused with a layer of enamel containing the colour).[17] Here the heart of the house mediates between the polar extremes emphasised in the rooms we have already seen—that dialectic of tradition and modernity, rough and smooth, black and white, nature and artifice, masculine and feminine, yin and yang. It is here that Mackintosh's theme of dynamic unity becomes clear.

THE DRAWING ROOM

From this evenly north-lit platform, a dark door—with six glowing little opal white squares—opens to the sun, into the most brilliant distant view. This is a Japanese trick far stronger than the graphic use of black and white or of simple geometrical shapes offset by a single curve. The quality here is an active visual experience: every visitor must draw breath on opening this door. Directly facing you is a glazed rectangular bay (diminutive under a lowered ceiling that acts like the brim of a cap), which captures the stunning panorama across the distant water of the Firth of Clyde (see plate 171).

Like the Blackies' bedroom, this drawing room on plan appears irregularly shaped. In fact, it is experienced as perfect sense and, just like the bedroom, is formed of precise geometric shapes[18] (plate 132). To the left another small rectangle is cut in the wall; darker than the window space ahead and similarly separated by the horizontal planes, this space is for music. To the right, within the room's large rectangle, is the fireplace and opposite it a small window.

The space is thus graduated from the winter fireside to the garden, via the music alcove, which is one of the tiny rooms within a room, with its own

132. The space and geometry of the drawing-room window bay, in plan (left) and section (right).

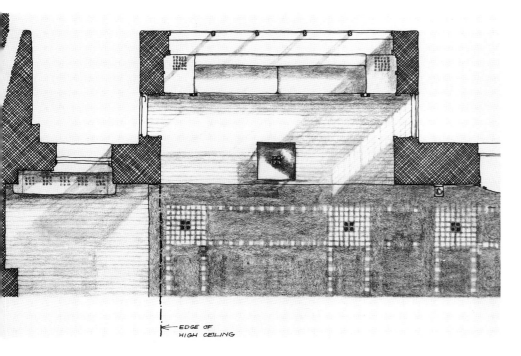

133. The rooms within the drawing room.

little window and window seat. The main window bay is a bower, an arbour, slightly mysteriously enveloping as we approach. It is surprisingly deep, a real little summer room, with its own threshold layers—through the wall thickness, across the light strip, to the little columns that define the seat space. Translucent curtains touched with rose cover the small geometric leaded panes; the full-width window seat and elegant built-in slits for books or magazines are flanked on each side by floor-length windows (one is a French door to the garden). There is a sense of fragility, of vulnerability, stepping into this space—we have broken through the great solid harled mansion wall,[19] we find glass down to our feet on both sides, and yet we are safely held close. In turning and sitting on the window seat, we touch the delicate white columns that frame it, with their little square holes and their form opening into stylised flower petals at the head. High on the white panelling at the sides are geometric rectangles of pink-and-green leaded glass, across which bends a single bluish reed; like the pink leaded-glass inset in the ceiling above the seat, they subliminally add to this impressionistic space.[20]

As in the bedroom, Mackintosh's strictly geometric armature carves three-dimensional spaces as precisely as any Purist master. Look at the southeast corner of the room, where the music and window rooms meet (plate 133). This articulation is aided by the carpet, whose geometric lines form different areas within the main rectangle, whether around the fireplace or by the door. The main rectangle of the room is held within a light, encircling band unified by a low cornice, which forms the door and fireplace head and the ceiling height of the music alcove and the window bay. Up to this (low) height, the walls are a trellis of white and shiny silvery stripes—which catch and throw the light differently as we move—decorated with pink roses, pale green foliage, and occasional falling petals. The window seat's white colonnettes repeat the rose design, as do the rectangular wall sconces in metal geometry offset by leaded glass.[21] Above this shimmering rose trellis, the space rises another three feet. The shape, disappearing into darkness, is ambiguous, for both walls and ceiling are the same deep damson—a colour made by adding rose madder to dark grey. It was then stippled with buttermilk, giving a low-gloss sheen when dry.[22]

The slightly concave fireplace, with its mosaic surround and oval mirror inserts behind the fire irons, is surmounted by a gesso panel by Margaret Macdonald (see plate 170). This place, centred on the fire, would be unsettled by the rival focus of a large window. So at this end of the room there is a smallish domestic window, whose detail shows Mackintosh's never-ending inventiveness with light and space. The darkest place in any room is the one immediately next to the glare of the window. Here, at the sides, the wall seems to continue across very slightly, as if gently pulled apart to make space for the window. On each side of this white framing, which curves ever so slightly into the room, are inserted seven little pink glass squares and a longer slit beneath, through which the light glows—mediating between light and dark, as does the white, translucent curtain between them, with its row of pink squares along the bottom (plate 134). The sill below the window forms an elegant light table, with two additional front legs and a shelf. (Like all the best architectonic effects, this experience cannot be adequately conveyed in photographs, which may be why I've never seen it described.)

All the moveable furniture by Mackintosh here is dark, stained, or ebonised. (The beautiful desk is discussed by Pat Kirkham, "Living Fancy," in

134. Window case and fitment in the drawing room, opposite the fireplace.

this volume; see plate 175.) In direct counterpoint to the little table we saw in the bedroom, a small black table here epitomises the mood as well as restates a geometric motif seen throughout the house (see plate 172). This key piece, made for the room, is an ebonised cubic coffee table.[23] A geometrically pure essay in squares, its three-by-three-by-three structure is transparent and precise, unlike that of its white counterpart upstairs. Its material, however, is not transparent; unlike, say, the furniture of Gerrit Rietveld, this is no metaphor of construction. Its formal austerity is melted by the fairy godmother's wand touching the centre of the top with four mother-of-pearl inlaid squares—each comprising nine tiny squares set with their grains at right angles to each other, thus catching the light differently as we move past. Just as the white table above was not entirely feminine but softened from a conceptual, formal armature, so here the rigorous, abstract, black geometry is centred on this delicate, feminine, natural patina, its surface shifting with our changing viewpoint. As the client later wrote, "Every detail received his careful—I might say loving—attention."

In *Das englische Haus* (*The English House*), Hermann Muthesius found Mackintosh's interiors unbearably overrefined, demanding an artificial existence from the occupants. "Even a book in an unsuitable binding would disturb the atmosphere simply by being left lying on the table; indeed the man or woman of today treads like a stranger in this fairy-tale world."[24] If I counter that this is not so, my intent is not simply to praise Mackintosh for his practicality but to suggest how in the hands of a spatial master refinement and practicality need not be opposites. His intuition enabled him to touch archetypal feelings in our body's inhabitation of places, which can in turn produce not only a highly charged atmosphere but also very comfortable interiors. Places both serviceable and enriching, useful and invigorating, they are open to our interpretation and active occupation.

Half a century later Mackintosh and Macdonald's achievement was befogged by a generation of Modernists, led by Thomas Howarth, who never forgave Mackintosh for not being a Gropius-like functionalist. Howarth dismissed the glass, textures, and colours as "contradictions"—all of which were "little more than the flotsam of the 'nineties"—and blamed Margaret for this "trivia."[25] The art critic Nigel Gosling, in the *Sunday Times* (London) twenty-seven years ago, put it simply: "Mackintosh exemplifies perfectly the muddle in which art was swimming at the turn of the century, before the victory of the modern movement clarified affairs."[26] Such judgement is profoundly ignorant, but much of the rehabilitation of Mackintosh since then has equally lacked insight, relying on the power of his imagery to generate income in an age of mechanical reproduction.[27] The importance of Mackintosh as architect—that is, as maker of places—is quite different and equally easily lost in today's fashionable fog.

Built at a time of great cultural uncertainty, work like The Hill House displays a unique range of feeling, a humane poignancy that, undogmatically and unnostalgically, not only balances but unites the old formality and the new uncertainty. (Perhaps we hear echoes of similar strains in Richard Strauss and Hugo von Hoffmenstal's *Der Rosenkavalier.*) And it is glimpsed in quiet irony too: look at how Mackintosh wrapped a new mahogany wardrobe around Walter Blackie's antique chest of drawers in his dressing room (plate 124, top left).

As we close the drawing-room door behind us, ready to take leave of The Hill House, the influence of stylised Japanese art and design is clearest in the hall (plate 136). Throughout we have seen a delicate, atmospheric use of a few chosen elements, perhaps one major colour or form offset by a touch of the opposite—a black chair in a white room, touches of pink glass on dark oak. Now, on reaching the front porch, we see that this yin and yang had been intimated almost subliminally when we entered, in the stencil pattern just inside the front door. There, right on the threshold of the public world, the decoration in the porch is a very simple stencil: the shadow of a flower curves across a chequerboard ground (plate 135). It sums up the dynamic balance—so far from his contemporaries' obsessive and fetishised Art Nouveau unity, which is not just cloying but sometimes seems about to strangle us in its tendrils. Far from such homogeneity, at The Hill House, Mackintosh achieved a sense of poised tension.

The range of achievements in this house marks it being as poignantly classic as a Mozart string quartet.[28] It is commodious and comfortable, compact and cost effective. But it isn't only those; it is also a feast for the senses and, just as important, for the mind. (The one little square of green glass among the purples and pinks on the private service door off the hall is not there by chance.) This place is both gay and sober, touching our hearts in the remarkable depth and range of its experience. In allotting some space to an active ambiguity and openness within the haute bourgeois Edwardian provincial life, it resonates to the word *modern* much more richly than what has since become known as "modern architecture."

135. Simple stencil pattern around the front porch.

Finally, it is worth repeating that this is a family house of small and intimate spaces. Much is achieved by very little means. The bay window and the music bay in the drawing room are tiny, as is the vaulted bedchamber. No two little glass facets are the same, and each sparkles differently as we move and as the light changes. The problem for the architect today, said Mackintosh, is "the task of clothing in grace and beauty the new forms and conditions that modern developments of life . . . insist upon." His aim was the nurturing of a modern life, which could be protected within society by a strong, masculine shield—a life whose goal was (as he said, paraphrasing W. R. Lethaby) "sweetness, simplicity, freedom, confidence and light."[29]

The Hill House, though praised in Europe through publication within a year in *Deutsche Kunst und Dekoration*,[30] was little noted in Britain at the time. Mackintosh himself seemed to lack that protective shield in the social world, and his architectural career ended tragically. This house was almost his first, and certainly his last, domestic masterpiece. Only a decade later, after a last visit to Mackintosh (still in his mid-forties), Walter Blackie would write:

> I found him sitting at his desk, evidently in a deeply depressed frame of mind. To my enquiry as to how he was keeping and what he was doing he made no response. But presently he began to talk slowly and dolefully. He said how hard he found it to receive no general recognition; only a very few saw merit in his work and the many passed him by. . . . During the planning and the building of The Hill House I necessarily saw much of Mackintosh, and could not but recognise, with wonder, his inexhaustible fertility in design and his astonishing powers of work. Withal he was a man of much practical competence, satisfactory to deal with in every way, and of a most likable nature. . . . Not many men of his calibre are born, and the pity is that when gone, such men are irreplaceable.

136. Interior hall, looking towards the front door.

NOTES

In this essay, an earlier version of which was published in 1995 by Giancarlo De Carlo in Spazio e società, *I am obviously indebted to David Brett's marvelously allusive study,* C. R. Mackintosh: The Poetics of Workmanship *(London: Reaktion Books, 1992). I particularly thank Anne Ellis at The Hill House for her hospitality, encouragement, and comments on my text in draft.*

I am also indebted to Aldo van Eyck, who thirty years ago gave the only lecture on Mackintosh to keep me awake right through, even though it went on so long that the Corporation caretakers of Glasgow's McLellan Galleries were trying to throw everyone out and get home to bed. Not long thereafter I first lingered in this house, which Campbell Lawson was putting up for sale, and for a mad moment I considered buying it.

Pace Alan Crawford ("The Mackintosh Phenomenon"), my memory is that Lawson considered asking £17,000 for The Hill House. The figure sticks because this is exactly what I paid a little later to build myself a new maisonette within an old London shell. In 1971 he formally offered The Hill House for sale for £25,000 to anyone prepared to keep its fabric and furnishings together; on March 13, 1972, the Royal Incorporation of Architects' decision to purchase was sealed.

1. Talwin Morris's metal frame for a watercolour that Mackintosh exhibited in 1896 is referred to in Pamela Robertson's essay in this volume.

2. The Ruskinian motto "There is hope in honest error, none in the icy perfection of the mere stylist" (the words are J. D. Sedding's) was used—in both German and English versions—by Mackintosh in 1901 to form some of his best-known calligraphic images (see plate 245).

3. This essay cannot open the illuminating, but here diverting, issue of design method. I have written elsewhere of design-personal partnerships, such as those of Ray and Charles Eames, Truus Schroeder and Gerrit Rietveld, and Macdonald and Mackintosh. Being rather less interested in the "gendering of their multivalent objects," which Pat Kirkham's essay so fascinatingly explores (see "Living Fancy" in this volume), I would argue, though not fundamentally disagree, with some of her gist.

4. Of course, his most consistent patron was Kate Cranston, whose tea rooms offered a locus for middle-class women safely to test the conventional bounds of their sexual roles, a subject Alan Crawford explores with much subtlety (see "The Tea Rooms" in this volume).

5. This and all other Blackie quotations in this essay are from a memoir found and published after his death as Walter W. Blackie, "Memories of Charles Rennie Mackintosh," *Scottish Art Review* 11, no. 4 (1968): 6. (The quotation at the start of this essay is also from this text.)

6. I am grateful to Robert Macleod for reading this essay enthusiastically and for drawing my attention to a house plan by W. R. Lethaby, published shortly before Mackintosh began designing Windyhill, which closely echoes it in ways developed in his next house, The Hill House.

7. That is, seen by a generation ignorant of the subtle and often charming domestic design typical of those illustrated almost a century ago in *Das englische Haus*. Hermann Muthesius's book, published in Germany in 1904–5, did not appear in English until Janet Seligmann's abridged translation, edited by Dennis Sharp, was published as *The English House* (London: Crosby Lockwood Staples, 1979). It includes The Hill House and the Baillie Scott house down the road. There is no space in this essay to argue for Mackintosh and Macdonald's place within their contemporary milieu, which was rich with studies on man and nature, on growth and form, on the evolution of sex, the *arbor saeculorum*, and, indeed, on architecture, mysticism, and myth.

8. The conventional arrangement was spelled out (and these actual words used) by Robert Kerr, in G. Sutcliffe, ed., *Principles and Practice of Modern Home Construction* (London and Glasgow: Blackie, 1899), vol. 1, p. 39. James Macaulay's uncovering of this text (in *Charles Rennie Mackintosh: Hill House* [London: Phaidon, 1994]), and the lovely coincidence that it was published by Blackie (in 1899) inside a cover by Talwin Morris, led Macaulay to overstate the conventional in The Hill House.

9. But there the aim, of course, was to lower the space—which, being converted from standard Glasgow blocks of the second half of the nineteenth century, typically had ceilings up to fourteen feet high.

10. Blackie in his memoir named these as the rooms that I discuss here.

11. Many of the present surfaces are replacements, including carpets, curtains, and some light fittings; see Richard Carr, "The House That Mac Built," *Building Design*, May 29, 1987. The debate about authenticity, and then *whose* authenticity, is rather sterile. For the former, it is 2,500 years since the question was first cleverly raised, when Kimon brought Theseus's ship back to be displayed at Athens, beginning its public life of continual renewal until eventually every bit had been replaced. For the latter, debate contrasting the Blackies' house with Mackintosh's creation simply drains any remaining life from a corpse that had been created and inhabited in active dialogue. (See Roger Billcliffe, "International Appeal of The Hill House," *Heritage Scotland* [National Trust for Scotland] [summer 1987]: 13.)

12. Anne Ellis is resident representative of the National Trust for Scotland, which now owns the house.

13. Talwin Morris, *Concerning the Work of Margaret Macdonald, Frances Macdonald, Charles Mackintosh and Herbert McNair: An Appreciation*, c. 1897; Glasgow Museums archives.

14. They are *only* glimpsed out of the corner of the eye, as you have to have reached them before they become visible, brightly backlit from the stair windows.

15. The vault is centred on the end of the bed; the third of a cylinder that it creates within the virtual cubes of the room is a favourite Mackintosh shape, seen again in the order-desk chair at the Willow Tea Rooms (see plate 168).

16. Much of this quality has been recovered only in recent restoration.

17. *Triglyph* means "sliced in three." For details on the glass, I am indebted to Anne Ellis, "Glass at The Hill House," *Charles Rennie Mackintosh Society Newsletter* 62 (summer 1993): 13.

18. Kirkham (in "Living Fancy") observes that the drawing room is less than a unified whole. I would suggest that, rather than being one static set piece, it has an active strength that lies in its quality of "both/and"—both comprehensible and complex, and therefore potentially a locus for many different human actions rather than for the performance of one exclusive script.

19. This is reflected in the built reality; a section (plate 132) shows how insubstantial is this bay construction.

20. Any verbal description like this will tediously overstate the motifs, like the bore who always points out how Claude Debussy creates an effect, rather than trusting listeners' ears.

21. All light fittings were originally for gas—except in the study, which was lit by oil, as Helensburgh had no electricity. But they

were easily adapted in the 1920s. The various stencilled decorative details mentioned have only recently been revealed in conservation work.

22. At the start Mackintosh had this ceiling white—an utterly different effect; others, trying to be faithful to the stronger effect, later made it much more crudely black (as in many well-known photographs). His notebook clearly says "plum." Having been black for too long, it is now being painted to re-create the "plum."

23. This table, conceived for this location, was designed and made in 1908, developing Mackintosh's obsession with the cube, first seen in designs for the house itself in 1903–4.

24. Muthesius, *English House*, p. 52.

25. Thomas Howarth, *Charles Rennie Mackintosh and the Modern Movement* (London: Routledge and Kegan Paul, 1952), reprinted 1977 and still in print today (3d ed., 1990), quoted from 1977 ed., p. 145.

26. I quote from "A Founding Glaswegian," Gosling's review of the Edinburgh Festival Mackintosh exhibition, August 25,

1968. By the end of the 1960s Mackintosh was being more firmly located by historians of the generation of David Walker and Robert Macleod, soon followed by the brilliant (inevitably object-fixated) archaeology of Roger Billcliffe.

27. The risky relationship of reproduction and authenticity is expanded on by Alan Crawford, in "The Mackintosh Phenomenon" in this volume. See also my "Unpredictable Weather: Keep Hold of Your Mackintoshes," *Architectural Design* (February 1979): 50, which discusses William Whitfield's reconstruction of the Mackintosh-Macdonald house at the Hunterian Art Gallery, University of Glasgow.

To suggest one simple path: I own a curved settle, looking identical to the order-desk chair in plate 168, which has been well used at home (and repaired) over a quarter of a century. It is neither a fetishistic original (so astutely hoarded by Howarth, so priced by Billcliffe), nor an acquisitivistic collectible (so authentically reproduced under Billcliffe or Filippo Alison's imprimatur). In fact, the last

time I saw its original, made for a tea-room cashier, it had become reified into a trophy in the director's office of Glasgow School of Art. The craftsman who around 1970 made mine (and three others, including one for David Hockney) charged me less than £70; Mackintosh was charged £4.2.6d in February 1904. Mine clearly is handmade; Cassina's (based on Alison's measured drawings) are, of course, better made not only than mine but than the original.

28. The subtle delicacy of the spaces as well as the surfaces reinforces the effect of chamber music. Lutyens, on the other hand, seems to have managed a comparable achievement only at the orchestral scale.

29. Mackintosh, from the manuscript notes of his lecture "Architecture" (1893), published in Pamela Robertson, ed., *Charles Rennie Mackintosh: The Architectural Papers* (Wendlebury, England: White Cockade Publishing, 1990), p. 206.

30. Fernando Agnoletti, "The Hill-House, Helensburgh," *Deutsche Kunst und Dekoration* (March 1905): 337–68.

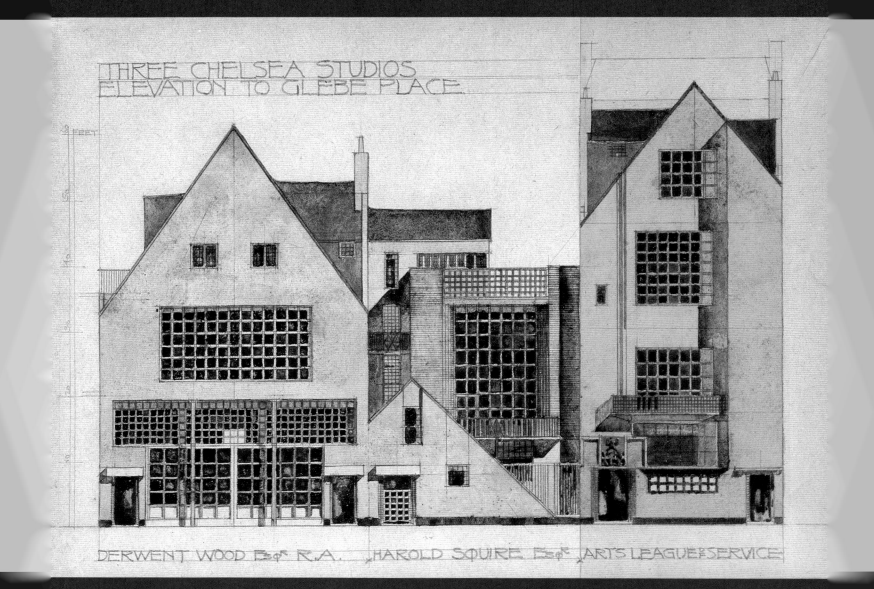

THREE CHELSEA STUDIOS
ELEVATION TO GLEBE PLACE

FEET

DERWENT WOOD Esq R.A.   HAROLD SQUIRE Esq   ARTS LEAGUE & SERVICE

The London Years

GAVIN STAMP

Just inside the elaborate front door of 185 Bath Street—the house that John Keppie, with assistance from the young Charles McIntosh, had converted for the Glasgow Art Club in 1893 (which, according to legend, he later ensured that his former assistant and now partner was not allowed to join)—is a memorial to those members who lost their lives in the Great War of 1914–18. And at the top of the list of names cast in bronze above the hall fireplace is that of Eugène Bourdon—"capitaine d'état, major de Réserve, chevalier de la Légion d'Honneur, Croix de Guerre"—the Beaux-Arts-trained French architect who had been invited to become Glasgow's first professor of architecture in 1904.

There is a deep and poignant irony here. Bourdon, two years younger than Mackintosh, was over the age for military service but, as a member of the French Army Reserve, had immediately returned to France at the outbreak of war. Along with so many of his own compatriots and the flower of Kitchener's British volunteer army—to which he was attached at the time—he was killed on July 1, 1916: the first day of the Battle of the Somme.[1] Mackintosh was then living in London. The preceding year he had been served with an expulsion order in Walberswick as he was considered a security risk by the military. A strange, outlandish figure in the sleepy Suffolk seaside town, he was rumoured to have connections with Germany and Austria. And, sure enough, when soldiers searched the cottage that Margaret and he were renting, they indeed "discovered some German & Austrian letters."[2]

Those letters, we must presume, were from the likes of Hermann Muthesius and Josef Hoffmann, "all some years old and all relating entirely to artistic and social affairs."[3] Mackintosh was outraged by his treatment in Walberswick, but to no avail; this was wartime England, xenophobic and paranoid, in which

137. Charles Rennie Mackintosh. *Three Studios in Chelsea: North Elevation,* c. 1920. Pencil and watercolour, 10⅞ x 14⅝ in. (27.6 x 37.2 cm). Trustees of The British Museum, London.

shops with German names were sacked and innocent dachshunds stoned in the open street. It was a wretched affair, a further assault on the architect's dignity following the collapse of his professional career in Glasgow and his pathetic exile from his native city in which all his finest work was achieved.

But it is possible to read into this melancholy coincidence of events a paradigm of the artistic tragedy of Mackintosh's career. On a simple level, it represents the conflict between the Austro-German influence acting on Glasgow through Mackintosh and the Franco-American ideal encouraged by Burnet and prompted by his protegé, Bourdon. This, at least, was the view of Bourdon's obituarist in the *Scots Pictorial:* "For it was to battle he came amongst us, to wage war upon sheer mediocrity and upon a strong cult of eccentricity in architecture which, strangely enough, emanated from Austria and Germany— enemies alike of freedom and justice and of the spirit of beauty which evolves through the age and carries forward the great work of tradition."[4]

Bourdon was one of several Belgian and French artists invited to teach at the School of Art, and he may well have been introduced to Glasgow by Burnet expressly to counter the Mackintosh influence. His appointment was also a reflection of a wider phenomenon: the replacement of the individualism of the Arts and Crafts movement by an academic and more rigorous form of training closely associated with the revival of interest in the discipline of classicism (in 1911 Bourdon wrote a report that was critical of design teaching methods in Germany[5]). But whereas the Architectural Association in London and the Liverpool School (under the direction of Mackintosh's bumptious enemy, Charles Reilly) adopted Beaux-Arts teaching methods at one remove, Glasgow opted for a real live Frenchman with experience of detailing skyscrapers in New York. This was the way forward.

Any account of Mackintosh's work after he left Scotland must take into account the architectural politics in Glasgow after the turn of the century. They transformed Charles Rennie Mackintosh, the youthful prodigy who attracted international attention, into a marginalised and increasingly despondent figure who could not come to terms satisfactorily with changing conditions—as all successful architects must. Certainly he failed to follow fashion by not shifting his artistic focus from Vienna to Paris. "Mackintosh is said to consider his Viennese journey the high point of his life!" reported an Austrian friend to Josef Hoffmann a decade after the Mackintoshes' triumph at the eighth Secession exhibition in 1900.[6] The relationship between Glasgow and Vienna is complex and subtle; Hoffmann's biographer, Eduard Sekler, agreed with Mackintosh's biographer, Thomas Howarth, that despite great mutual sympathy the Austrian was not directly influenced by Mackintosh.[7] It is clear, however, that the Glaswegian began to look to Vienna for inspiration when trying to cope with the changed conditions of the new century.

Not just in Britain but all over Europe in the years after 1900 there was a rejection of the mystical elaboration and curvaceous aesthetic of Art Nouveau

138. Josef Hoffmann (1870–1956).
Sanatorium, Purkersdorf, near
Vienna, 1904. From *The Art-Revival
in Austria*, special number of the
Studio (1906), plate C8.

and a move toward the rectilinear discipline and austerity of the classical tradition in its last vital phase. In the German-speaking world this was manifested in a revival of the Biedermeier aesthetic as well as in a move towards simplicity and the more rational use of materials. In Hoffmann's case, his work became increasingly abstract and geometric, culminating in the white classical simplicity of the Purkersdorf Sanatorium (plate 138) near Vienna and the restrained planar richness of the Palais Stoclet (1905–11) in Brussels. Mackintosh's work showed similar tendencies by 1903 and, even if he had not been in direct contact with Hoffmann and kept informed about developments in Germany through Hermann Muthesius, he would have been aware of the pure abstracted classicism realised at Purkersdorf from the illustrations in the 1906 special summer number of the *Studio*, *The Art-Revival in Austria*.

Mackintosh's supreme response to this changing artistic climate was, of course, the redesigned west wing of Glasgow School of Art, begun in 1907 (see plate 117). The greater rectilinearity of the design, in contrast to the east wing, has often been supposed to reflect a Viennese influence, although it is much more besides. Scottish castles as well as the streamlined Tudor style suggested by Charles Holden's Bristol Library design of 1903[8] are fused with a decorative style of Mackintosh's own, in which subtly modified classical details are integrated. But, in the Glasgow climate of 1910, this was not enough. In the *Vista* (the magazine of the Glasgow School of Architecture Club, started by Bourdon) an anonymous critic of the completed building "wondered if Mr. Mackintosh felt forlorn or relieved at having this child of his imagination off his hands. Of course that would depend on whether it was a child of joy or sorrow to him, a prodigy or a freak. In our opinion—but, silence is the better part of discretion."[9] If student opinion is a reliable guide to avant-garde fashion, then this deliberate ridicule must have been deeply painful to the once-fashionable architect.

> [If] Mr. Mackintosh aimed at doing something bizarre, we would congratulate him on his success while condemning it on principle. . . . While the strength of Mr. Mackintosh's architecture lies perhaps in its mystery, his system of decoration has its strength or weakness in its obviousness. His method is one of permutations and combinations of simple forms. This algebraic basis must account for the lack of romance in new art interiors. Coming fresh to the system, one finds interest in noticing that the details of a repeated ornamental motive are never the same, then it grows clear that the motive itself was selected in order that its internal arrangement might allow of endless different combinations, so that once the motive is selected an office boy or trained cat can do the rest.[10]

Such was the view of a student generation that dismissed symbolism as quaintly Ruskinian and Victorian, that did not mind repetitive ornament—providing it was based on historical models—and regarded steel-framed American classical skyscrapers as the acme of modernity. When those students who survived the Great War came to professional maturity in the 1920s, they successfully reproduced these models in the streets of Glasgow.[11] Never much interested in structural innovation (unlike his friend James Salmon Jr.) and antipathetic to conventional classical models, Mackintosh could not or would not go down this road; indeed, he could not go as far as Hoffmann in embracing and developing the classical tradition in his own way.

It is, however, highly misleading to see Mackintosh as a progressive figure out of sympathy with a reactionary revival of classicism, for men like John James Burnet and John Archibald Campbell—Beaux-Arts-trained architects with direct knowledge of American buildings—were erecting remarkable tall commercial structures in Glasgow that exploited new construction techniques. As David Walker long ago observed, "There were then *two* rival and quite independent schools of highly progressive architecture in the city."[12] Unfortunately, establishing a balanced picture of Glasgow in the Edwardian period has been rendered more difficult by the demolition of Burnet's McGeoch's Ironmongery Warehouse (plate 139), one of the most imaginative and modern buildings in the city and one that can be compared on favorable terms with any by Mackintosh.

139. John James Burnet (1857–1938). McGeoch's Ironmongery Warehouse, Glasgow, 1904–5. Demolished; photographed in 1969.

Some architects of Mackintosh's generation who had flourished in the 1890s—not just Hoffmann but Joseph Maria Olbrich, Edwin Lutyens, Victor Horta, Jože Plečnik, and, not least, Frank Lloyd Wright—were able to adapt and remain in command of their artistic destinies. Certain English Arts and Crafts architects, however—C.F.A. Voysey and C. R. Ashbee, for instance, as well as that expatriate Scot George Walton—saw their practices gradually subside. For Mackintosh the new century must have seemed increasingly alien and hostile; the consequence was psychological crisis, breakdown, and the collapse of his professional partnership. Although the brilliant career of James Salmon Jr. also expired in the years before the First World War, significantly, perhaps, he never became so marginalised and controversial that exile from Glasgow was the only course.[13]

THE FIRST LONDON DESIGNS

In discussing Mackintosh's work after his departure from Glasgow in 1914, certain important qualifications must be made before making comparisons with his earlier achievements. For a start, his (initially unintended?) exile coincided with the outbreak of a terrible world war. Almost a decade of bleak years followed, during which private architectural practice was very difficult. "We have had a hard struggle during the last 3 years of the war as no architectural work was possible," he complained in 1919.[14] Furthermore, even when Mackintosh was established in Chelsea, he was by himself—a lone middle-aged architect without established contacts working in an unfamiliar city, rather than a favored assistant or a partner in a well-known and successful Glasgow firm. Charles Rennie Mackintosh of Honeyman, Keppie and Mackintosh did not have to worry about the tiresome details of running a practice and could, in theory, concentrate on the pleasant task of designing. In London, on the other hand, undergoing wartime privations, it was difficult to find, let alone pursue, commissions.[15]

In the fourteen years left to him after 1914, Mackintosh erected only one complete new building to his designs, and that was a small studio in Chelsea much reduced in ambition from the original conception. His other built works consisted of alterations to existing buildings, while most of his designs remained on paper. Several of these projects are mysterious, and some could never have been built according to Mackintosh's surviving drawings. Immense interest rightly attaches itself to these last designs of a great artist, but it must be admitted that some of them would surely attract little attention if they were the work of another. Nonetheless, they all reflect a sincere attempt to come to terms with conditions very different from those in Glasgow.

Mackintosh's first post-Glasgow designs seem to be two long coloured elevations: *Shop and Office Block in an Arcaded Street* (plate 140) and *A Warehouse Block in an Arcaded Street*, which have only recently emerged. Very possibly they once belonged to the archives of the great Scottish urbanist and sociologist Patrick Geddes, for on July 21, 1915, Mackintosh wrote to William Davidson from London, "I am playing around with Professor Geddes at his Summer Meeting here." On August 5 he reported, "I have had a tentative offer from the Indian government to go out there for some 6 months . . . to do some work in reconstruction where they want me to do the architecture."[16]

Geddes had unsuccessfully proposed himself for the Delhi Planning Committee in 1912. He had gone out to India in 1914 with his Cities Exhibition, which unfortunately was sent to the bottom of the Indian Ocean by the German raider *Emden.* Lutyens, in India in January 1915, complained of "a certain Professor Geddes who has come out here to lecture on Town Planning. He seems to talk rot in an insulting way. I hear he is going to tackle me! A crank who don't know his subject."[17] After the Summer Meeting in London, Geddes went out to India for the second time to lecture and to make town-planning reports on Indian cities. It was presumably in connection with these that Mackintosh was asked to make model designs, although Geddes's precise status in relation to the British authorities in India remains uncertain.

Compared with, for example, R. T. Russell's colonnaded commercial blocks forming Connaught Circus in Lutyens's New Delhi, Mackintosh's designs are imaginative responses to the problem of designing buildings in a hot climate. No doubt he studied the exotic designs by other British architects, such as Charles Holden and Beresford Pite, but the greatest similarities are with the work of the official government architects in India. Such buildings as John Begg's Post Office in Agra and George Wittet's Central Offices in Poona demonstrate an analogous abstracted, arcaded, and colonnaded treatment, although the closest parallel is H. S. Goodhart-Rendel's first building, Gillander House (1908–9) in Calcutta, which sports a similarly Glaswegian eaves gallery with small cylindrical columns.[18] What makes Mackintosh's designs distinctive, however, is his use of an Egyptian colonnade at ground level in the shop and office block and the framing of both facades by a flat linear decorative frieze. This last is pure Vienna.

78 DERNGATE

That black year, 1915, also saw the genesis of Mackintosh's most significant realised post-Glasgow commission. By now established in Chelsea, Mackintosh was asked by W. J. Bassett-Lowke to adapt his terraced house in Northampton as a future marital home. Bassett-Lowke was an engineer who specialised in making scale models of machines and who promoted miniature railways for gardens (plate 141). During the war, his Northampton factory produced precision instruments. Bassett-Lowke was clearly a man with an original mind and independent judgement—why else would he have sought out Mackintosh in 1915? As a client, he clearly had decided opinions and exerted a profound influence on the form of the project.

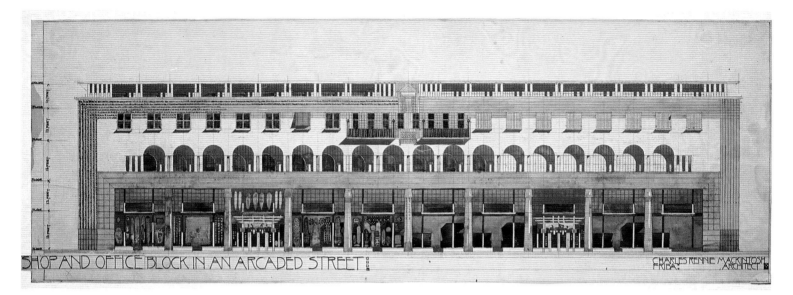

Much remains mysterious about this commission. For a start, all working drawings were signed not by Mackintosh but by another Scot, Alexander Ellis Anderson, a Glasgow-trained Northampton architect who was the younger brother of Mackintosh's predecessor as winner of the Alexander Thomson Travelling Studentship, William J. Anderson. He may, or may not, therefore, have known Mackintosh earlier.[19] And when the house was illustrated in an article in the *Ideal Home* in August 1920, Mackintosh's name was not once mentioned, although this may reflect his client's vanity rather than the architect's obscurity (in England).

No. 78 Derngate (plate 142) stands in the middle of an early-nineteenth-century (*not* "Victorian," as some have written) terrace of typically plain three-storey redbrick houses. The Scotsman clearly did not share the growing admiration for the uniform severity of the Georgian urban terrace, which was manifested both by avant-garde English architects and by Europeans like Adolf Loos.[20] Mackintosh's intervention broke the regularity of the street facades and made no. 78 different—thus betraying the classicist principle of reticent repetition. The ground-floor window was pushed forward into a rather twee vernacular bay, with pitched roof and leaded-light windows, while the balancing blank window on the first floor was ineptly pierced by a small new window to light a lavatory. Happiest is the new front door, which, with its stepped moulding and mannered guttae, looks as if it had been removed bodily from one of Miss Cranston's later tea rooms. (Indeed, Mackintosh's last Glasgow commission, for the Dug-Out [1916–17] in the Willow Tea Rooms, is almost contemporary; see plate 199).

Equally Glaswegian and appropriately ingenious was Mackintosh's alteration of the tight interior of the terraced house. On the ground floor the wall between the staircase hall and the parlour was removed to make a larger

BASSETT LOWKE LTD.... MAKERS OF ENGINEERING MODELS.... NORTHAMPTON LONDON ADDRESS 112 HIGH HOLBORN WC

lounge hall opening off the street (plate 144). The new staircase was placed laterally and divided from the new room by a timber grid—part filled, part open—that was echoed by the forms of doors and furniture. This originally dark space was enlivened by a bright stencilled pattern using a repeated triangular motif (see plate 179), something that seems reminiscent of Viennese interiors of a decade earlier, particularly those, as Howarth pointed out, by Josef Urban illustrated in that *Studio* special Austrian number of 1906[21] (plate 143). Similarly Austrian in character was the guest bedroom on the second floor (see plate 181), whose walls and ceiling were decorated with parallel black lines in 1919. George Bernard Shaw stayed in this room in 1923 and, when his host commented, "I trust the decor will not disturb your sleep," retorted, "No, I always sleep with my eyes closed."[22]

The aspect of 78 Derngate that has attracted most attention is Mackintosh's treatment of the rear elevation. Here, because of the fall in the ground, the house was four storeys high. In response to his client's requirements, Mackintosh extended this south-facing facade with a projecting bay that

144. Charles Rennie Mackintosh. Lounge hall, 78 Derngate. Photographed c. 1920.

rises three storeys to create a generous open balcony for the guest bedroom and a covered balcony for the principal bedroom on the first floor. The back of the house, like the front, was originally of brick, but Mackintosh covered both the old wall and his extension with a smooth cement render. It is this surface that has made the unassuming and largely unseen rear facade seem so close in spirit to the white concrete flat-roofed houses of a decade later in Britain, thus adding to the myth of Mackintosh as a pioneer of the Modern movement.

Certainly the rear extension, with its wide rectangular openings and lack of any mouldings, is remarkable for its austere simplicity. This may reflect the taste of the client, who on January 14, 1917, wrote to his architect (about a door) that "in any case the design must be *severe and plain.*"[23] It is clearly the use of a smooth painted surface that gives the impression of modernity—as with George Walton's White House at Shiplake (1908)—but the closest parallel to this elevation is surely the rectilinear austerity of Hoffmann's Purkersdorf Sanatorium of 1904. The design also has affinities with the severe rectilin-

145. Charles Rennie Mackintosh. Rear elevation of 78 Derngate, with Mrs. Bassett-Lowke, photographed c. 1920.

earity that characterised the work of Adolf Loos, notably the Scheu house (1912) in Vienna.

The photograph of the garden front of 78 Derngate taken about 1920 with Mrs. Bassett-Lowke standing by the trellised wall suggests, perhaps, an answer to this art-historical conundrum (plate 145). On the terrace in front of the extension stands a rectangular tree tub painted with black rectangles on white. This surely gives the whole composition a hint of prewar Vienna. Bassett-

Lowke, a man of independent judgement who admired fine craftsmanship and precision engineering, clearly had a taste for modern German design. In 1913, as his niece recalls, he had given her parents a room in their own house in Northampton as a wedding present—known as "the German room." "The walls were covered with a greenish paper with discreet stripes, the paintwork was skillfully changed to represent light oak, in harmony with the furniture arriving from Germany. Each piece was constructed on straight lines without any curves, eminently practical and beautifully made."[24] And when, in 1924, Bassett-Lowke wanted to build a completely new and modern house, he again looked to Germany, securing designs from the famous Peter Behrens for his "New Ways." In 1915, of course, it would have been impossible to commission a German architect; perhaps Mackintosh was the next best thing.

CHELSEA

For his remaining commissions Mackintosh looked not to Vienna but to England for inspiration. In 1919, with the war over, he was asked by his friend E. O. Hoppé to enlarge his house in Sussex. Hoppé was the German-born photographer who took several portraits of Mackintosh about 1920, including one of the artist in his rather pretentious long cloak (see plate 11). Hoppé owned a cottage (now called Little Hedgecourt) near East Grinstead, which Mackintosh extended using the appropriate Home Counties vernacular (plate 146). The only part of the new work that was distinctly Mackintosh in style was the woodwork of the interiors. Most of this survives, although the history of the house is confusing: Hoppé sold it in 1920 to André Simon, founder of the Wine and Food Society. In about 1926 Simon added another large extension beyond the one built by Mackintosh, whose pebble-dash render on the first floor walls (a hint of Scots harling?) he replaced with tile hanging to blend in with the surface both on the original cottage and on the new wing.[25]

Before he sold Little Hedgecourt, Hoppé asked Mackintosh to prepare designs for a much larger extension (plate 147). This would have included a classical colonnade between two gabled bays—a composition, inspired by Lutyens or M. H. Baillie Scott, of a type that any competent English domestic architect could have achieved at the time—as can be seen in the pages of the three volumes of Lawrence Weaver's *Small Country Houses of Today* (1910, 1919, and 1925). Which is not to deny that Mackintosh's scheme was a good and appropriate one, with Viennese and Glaswegian tendencies held in restraint in darkest southern England.[26]

Mackintosh had met Hoppé in the artistic milieu of Chelsea, to which he and Margaret naturally gravitated in 1915, finally taking adjoining studios there in Glebe Place. And it was here that Mackintosh's principal opportunity to build in London arose, although little would come of it. The site was that of Cheyne House, a Georgian building in Upper Cheyne Row whose large garden ran through to a row of small cottages at the eastern corner of Glebe Place. It

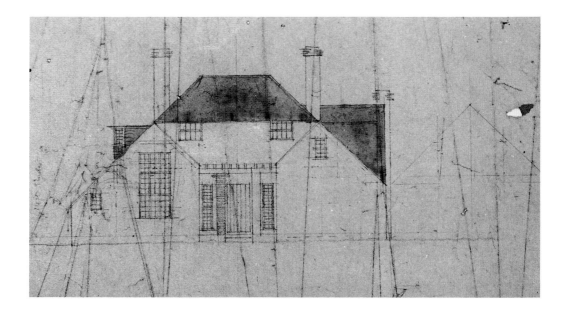

had all been owned by Dr. John Samuel Phené, eccentric architect and scientist, who "converted the garden and house into a repository of architectural curios, and so much was the place neglected that part of the roof and floors of Cheyne House have fallen in."[27] Dr. Phené died in 1912 and the property was offered for sale in 1914, but the outbreak of war postponed any redevelopment until 1919, when interest in the site resulted in the possibility of several commissions for Mackintosh.

Subdivision of the property allowed three houses to be built along Glebe Place to replace the two-storey cottages, plus a fourth building behind on the site of Cheyne House, running through to Upper Cheyne Row. Francis Derwent Wood, the sculptor who had taught in Glasgow in the late 1890s, took the easternmost plot, 50 Glebe Place; the middle plot, no. 49, was bought by the painter Harold Squire; and another painter, Arthur Cadogan Blunt, took an interest in no. 48, to the west. The site of Cheyne House itself was later considered by the Arts League of Service, which had been established in 1919 "To Bring the Arts into Everyday Life" and which now proposed a large block containing twenty-seven studio flats.

Mackintosh's proposals for these sites are known from the series of coloured elevations now in the British Museum (plates 137, 148, and 149). Much reproduced, his designs present an exciting geometrical composition of varied and abstracted triangular gable forms. It is now clear, however, that an integrated development of the whole site was never possible. Furthermore, the model constructed for the 1994 exhibition *C. R. Mackintosh: The Chelsea Years* at the Hunterian Art Gallery (plate 150) revealed that the various elevation designs were not resolved. Alan Crawford has established a chronology for Mackintosh's several and contradictory schemes for each of his putative clients during the course of 1920, efforts that culminated only in

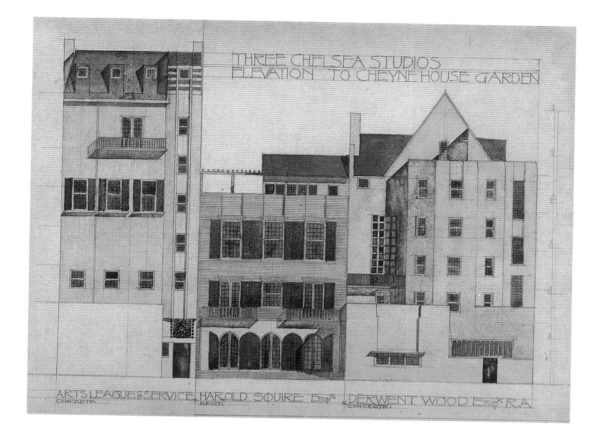

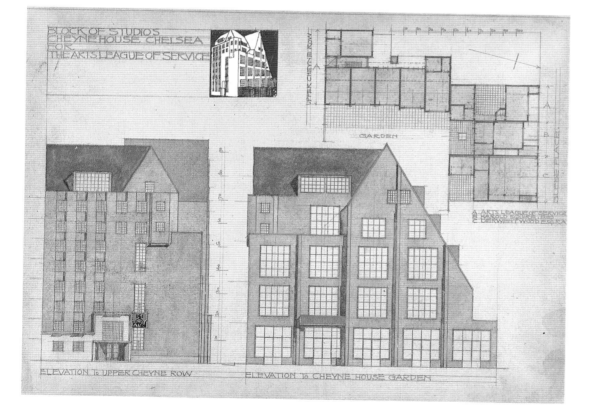

the erection of a much-reduced design for a studio for Harold Squire, completed in 1921.[28]

In considering an appropriate treatment for studio houses in this part of London, Mackintosh had many useful models close at hand. He may not have had any great respect for the sober early Georgian houses that gave the character to this part of Chelsea, but he surely would have admired the big redbrick house just along Glebe Place designed by the great Philip Webb and built in 1869–76 for the artist G. P. Boyce. Also, a number of new houses built nearby in the years before 1914 exploited in diverse and imaginative ways the various vernacular domestic styles—Tudor or Georgian—current in London. For a Scottish architect who had subscribed, albeit at a distance, to the ideals of the Arts and Crafts movement, Chelsea should have been a most rewarding home.

North of the King's Road, the area around Chelsea Park Gardens and the Vale had begun to be redeveloped after about 1909 with new houses, several of them for artists. The architects most involved—E.F.M. Elms and Sydney Jupp, and Alfred Cox and F. E. Williams—are not names to conjure with, but Leonard Stokes had built himself a house in Mulberry Walk, a new building by Halsey Ricardo was in Old Church Street, and one by W. D. Caroë in Mallord Street. The most distinguished new work in Mallord Street was, however, Mallord House by Ralph Knott (architect of London's new County Hall) with E. Stone Collins—a tall, urbane brick building in a smooth, abstracted Tudor manner of which hints can be glimpsed in Mackintosh's Chelsea studio designs.[29]

The building in Mallord Street that must surely have interested Mackintosh was the studio house built by the painter Augustus John in 1913–14; the two artists had met, and John would later ask Mackintosh to consider

150. Schematic model of the Chelsea studio proposals, made by Stephen Perry for the exhibition *C. R. Mackintosh: The Chelsea Years, 1915–1923*, at the Hunterian Art Gallery, University of Glasgow, 1994. Painted MDF, ¼ in.: 1 ft.; base size: 68½ x 64½ in. (174.0 x 163.8 cm). Hunterian Art Gallery, University of Glasgow.

designing another studio for him. The story goes that when John first decided to build, he walked into a Chelsea pub and asked if there was an architect in the house. If this is true, he was fortunate in his drinking habits, for he thus met Robert van t'Hoff, an enigmatic Dutch architect later associated with the De Stijl group, who was then living in the King's Road while attending the Architectural Association. Van t'Hoff is known principally for two neighbouring houses in Huis ter Heide near Utrecht, the Netherlands—one, dating from 1911, was palpably inspired by Lutyens's Homewood, and the other, the Concrete House completed four years later, was in the style of Frank Lloyd Wright. For John, however, he designed a two-storey brick building rather like a Dutch farmhouse, with a steep-pitched roof and a large studio at the back, lit by a large and unusual polygonal window. Its internal details were sufficiently exotic to be mistaken for the work of Mackintosh in the 1960s.[30]

Of all the new buildings in Chelsea, the ones that Mackintosh cannot have failed to notice and that do seem to have had a considerable influence on his designs for Glebe Place were those built in Cheyne Walk (plate 152) by C. R. Ashbee, the Arts and Crafts designer who, like Mackintosh, was known and admired in Vienna. Between 1893 and 1913 Ashbee, a longstanding Chelsea resident, had built seven houses facing the Thames along Cheyne Walk; sadly, only two of these survive today. As Ashbee's biographer, Alan Crawford, has written, "He thought in streetscape terms, creating a medley of buildings next door to each other, some in a bare Arts and Crafts style, others neo-Georgian, all various in form and mock-modest in detail; anyone who looked carefully would see a difference between inside and out, a playing with appearances, such as informed some of the best of Mackintosh's Glasgow buildings."[31] The Mackintoshes would have passed some of these buildings every day as they went to dinner at the Blue Cockatoo restaurant next to Ashbee's own house, 37 Cheyne Walk, better known as the Magpie and Stump.

In his several designs for the group of three buildings he proposed in Glebe Place, Mackintosh demonstrated something of Ashbee's ability to create both unity and variety in terms of picturesque streetscape, and he was happy to play with several styles—including Tudor half-timber (plate 151). In the garden elevation of Harold Squire's studio (plate 153) he even employed the fashionable neo-Georgian manner associated with architects like Oliver Hill in the 1920s, while the polygonal bay on Derwent Wood's studio next door (plate 148) is reminiscent of Lutyens at Little Thakeham. There are also echoes of Upmeads (1908) at Stafford (plate 154), that remarkable flat-roofed brick house designed by Edgar Wood in an austere streamlined Tudor style that was another—and most relevant—response by an innovative fin de siècle architect to changed conditions.[32] The basic vocabulary in Chelsea, however, was that of tall gabled houses with big rectilinear windows like those on Glasgow School of Art. Ashbee had used a big white gable on his studio house next to the Magpie and Stump, a form consciously reminiscent of the old

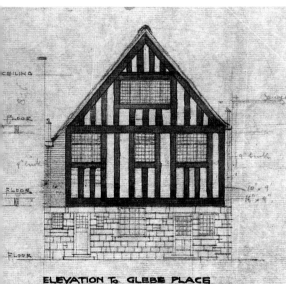

ELEVATION TO GLEBE PLACE
LOWER STOREY PORTLAND STONE
ABOVE OLD TIMBERS CEMENT FILLING.

BELOW

151. Charles Rennie Mackintosh. *Studio for Arthur Cadogan Blunt, Chelsea: North Elevation Using "Old Timbers,"* May 1920 or later. Pencil, ink, and watercolour on cream tracing paper, 8¾ x 8¼ in. (22.2 x 21.0 cm). Hunterian Art Gallery, University of Glasgow.

RIGHT

152. C. R. Ashbee (1863–1942). 71–75 Cheyne Walk, Chelsea, 1897–1913. Photographed by Anthony Kersting in 1938.

OPPOSITE, TOP

153. Charles Rennie Mackintosh. *Studios for Harold Squire and Arthur Cadogan Blunt, Chelsea: North and South Elevations,* 1920. Pencil and green wash on brown tracing paper, 12 x 19¹¹⁄₁₆ in. (30.5 x 50.0 cm). Hunterian Art Gallery, University of Glasgow.

OPPOSITE, BOTTOM

154. Edgar Wood (1860–1935). Upmeads, Stafford, England, 1908. From Lawrence Weaver, ed., *Small Country Houses of Today* (London: George Newnes; New York: Charles Scribner's Sons, 1910).

London houses of Holborn and the Strand, which were then disappearing. Mackintosh made the form much more abstract and austere—too austere, it seems, for Mr. W. E. Clifton, Surveyor to the Glebe of Chelsea, who, according to the architect, "maintains that my elevations are not architectural enough and must be more elaborate."[33]

The most remarkable and presumably least palatable of these designs were those Mackintosh made for the block of studios for the Arts League of Service (plate 149), first envisaged running north from Upper Cheyne Row in 1920 and later proposed to replace Blunt's house in Glebe Place. With its huge double-height studio windows facing the gardens and its eight storeys piled up along Upper Cheyne Row, this overambitious building would have resembled a large Hanseatic warehouse in a Baltic port, although more likely is that the tall tenements of Edinburgh were in the back of Mackintosh's mind. Certain details, like the stepped-back fenestration of the north elevation, recall the similarly industrial-looking fenestration on his Scotland Street School (see plate 72). But all this clever composing of triangular forms, juxtapositions of different windows, and contrived irregularity came to nothing. By the end of 1920 all that Mackintosh was building was a sorely economised design for Harold Squire: an awkwardly planned, single-storey house in Glebe Place with a big, north-lit studio behind it. The artist was initially very pleased but moved out after two years—largely, it seems, owing to the ghostly legacy of Dr. Phené—and the building has since been altered.[34]

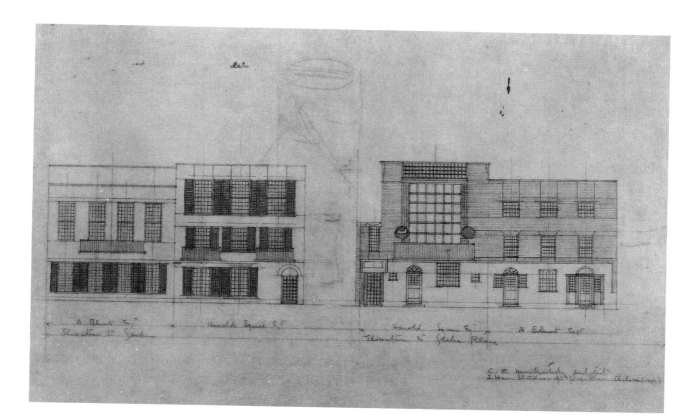

Rough plans and sketches for several projects from this period survive among Mackintosh's drawings, but only one other complete scheme merits discussion. This was associated with the Cheyne House development and is also one of the most puzzling of all the architect's designs (plate 155). It is a project for a small theatre-cum-cinema commissioned in 1920 by the Mackintoshes' old friend the dancer Margaret Morris, partner of the Scottish painter J. D. Fergusson. It was probably designed to go next to Harold Squire's studio—in Dr. Phené's old garden—although it was entirely alien in style to the proposed surrounding buildings. It is a curious and most unsatisfactory project, with a disturbing lack of resolution between the central entrance feature, flanked by domed towers, and the internal arrangements; as Howarth justly remarked, "Unlike the majority of Mackintosh's designs this project will not bear close analysis."[35] Although the splayed and stepped entrance surround might seem related to the Art Deco of the 1920s, the motif of a rectangular stepped recession ("multiple framing") around a door was a favourite motif of Hoffmann's at least as early as 1903[36]; the oval plan of the auditorium recalls Mackintosh's designs for the 1901 International Exhibition in Glasgow.

So, at the end of his professionally disappointing period of practice in London, Mackintosh seemed to revert to the past. To others, indeed, he seemed just a relic of the past. In 1922 he submitted his drawings *Three Studios in Chelsea* and the *Block of Studios* to the Exhibition of Contemporary British Architecture at the Royal Institute of British Architects; in reviewing it, H. S. Goodhart-Rendel wrote, "Two exhibits sent by Mr C. R. Mackintosh looked curiously old-fashioned, and recalled to mind the illustrations which one finds in turning over the pages of the early volumes of *The Studio*."[37] All these ambitious schemes had come to nothing, and all that Mackintosh managed to achieve in 1920–21 were Harold Squire's studio and the conversion of some cottages near Burgess Hill in Sussex for Miss Florence Brooks, which have since been destroyed.[38] This was a bathetic conclusion to the architectural career of Charles Rennie Mackintosh. Most of the income he earned in

155. Charles Rennie Mackintosh. *A Theatre: Front Elevation and Sections*, 1920. For Margaret Morris, Chelsea, London. Pencil, ink, and watercolour, 17⁵/₁₆ x 28³/₈ in. (44.0 x 72.0 cm). Hunterian Art Gallery, University of Glasgow.

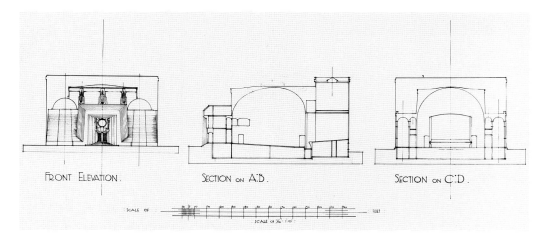

FRONT ELEVATION.   SECTION ON A:B.   SECTION ON C:D.

these years came from designing textile patterns. By 1923 he was so disillusioned that he let his studio and left for the south of France where, fortunately for posterity, he chose to perfect his extraordinary talent as a painter.

It has usually been assumed that Mackintosh decided to give up architecture altogether and that his old client in Northampton went to Behrens in 1924 because Mackintosh had disappeared abroad. In his memoir, written in 1939, Bassett-Lowke recalled:

> After the war I purchased a piece of land . . . on the outskirts of Northampton of which the garden was already laid out. Mr. Mackintosh was to have designed me a house on this site but he went away to live in the Pyrenees and I lost touch with him. I could not find any other architect with modern ideas in England, and when looking through a German publication called "Werkbund Jahrbuch" of 1913 I saw some work by Professor Peter Behrens which I thought very simple, straightforward and modern in its atmosphere. I obtained Dr Behrens address from the German consul and got in touch with him. This was the year 1924.[39]

It is also likely that, as Howarth suggested, Bassett-Lowke abandoned Mackintosh as he "found him quite impossible to work with" and always wanted to employ an avant-garde German architect.[40] In 1924, only six years after the Armistice, that was a characteristically unusual and independent course to take.

Nineteen twenty-four was also the year Mackintosh received some unexpectedly favourable publicity through being lauded in the book *Modern English Architecture* by Charles Marriott, art critic of the *Times* (London). This broad and catholic survey of recent British architecture was the first to publish a photograph of the completed Glasgow School of Art, which, wrote Marriott, "is important because of the great influence of Mr. Mackintosh's work on the Continent—in Germany, Holland and Sweden. It is hardly too much to say that the whole modernist movement in European architecture derives from him." Marriott's book is also interesting because it contains a list of living architects with their works, and the long entry for "Mackintosh, Charles Rennie, F.R.I.B.A., Corresponding Member der Kunstlers Osterreiche, Vienna. *Born* 1869 [*sic*] . . ." can only have been supplied by the architect himself. Again, if Mackintosh really intended to give up architecture for good in 1923, it is odd that he allowed his name and professional address—"2, Hans Studios, 43a, Glebe Place, Chelsea S.W."—to be retained in the 1926 edition of *Who's Who in Architecture*.[41] Perhaps he was still keeping his options open.

In surveying what Mackintosh achieved after 1914, it is hard not to agree with Robert Macleod that "the one definite impression of these works subsequent to his departure from Glasgow, is of a man who has lost his way."[42] Scots, of course, have long left their native land in search of fame and fortune. John James Burnet provides a telling example: in 1905, at the age of forty-eight, he had been invited to set up an office in London to extend the British Museum, and he remained a confident innovator for two more decades. But Burnet, trained at the Beaux-Arts, was working in an international style and could demonstrate his talents in any modern city. Mackintosh's architecture, in contrast, was deeply rooted in Glasgow and in Scotland. For all his receptivity to English (and Austrian) ideas, he was essentially working in a Scottish tradition, and it is difficult to imagine his School of Art standing anywhere else but Renfrew Street. Only Glasgow could have produced and sustained such a talent—as with "Greek" Thomson before him—and, despite all the frustrations that Mackintosh suffered there, only in his native city could he really flourish. Sadly, after the Edwardian decade Glaswegians seemed no longer to be impressed by what Mackintosh—or, for that matter, his friend James Salmon Jr.—had to offer.

The tragedy of Mackintosh is in part that the presumed authors of those letters found by the military in his cottage in Walberswick—Hermann Muthesius and Josef Hoffmann—made a brilliant but naive Glaswegian believe that he could play the role of an international figure, thus making him impatient with the environment that had made and sustained him. If he really had to leave Glasgow, perhaps he should have taken up those flattering invitations to work in Austria, although by 1914 it was surely too late to go abroad. Instead, like so many Scots before him, he went to London. It was an inevitable but, in his case, disastrous choice.

NOTES

The author wishes to acknowledge the help of Bruce A. Bailey, Pamela Robertson, and David Walker in the preparation of this essay.

1. The career of Bourdon (1870–1916) remains to some extent a mystery; the present writer is currently undertaking research for the catalogue of an exhibition of his drawings to be mounted at Glasgow School of Art in 1996 and then in Paris.

2. Mackintosh to William Davidson, July 21, 1915, Hunterian Art Gallery, University of Glasgow.

3. Ibid.

4. *Scots Pictorial*, July 29, 1916, p. 387; this was presumably written by one of Bourdon's former students.

5. Eugène Bourdon, "Report on German Art Education," July 1911, Minutes of the Governors of the Glasgow School of Art, Book VI, 1911–13, pp. 33–37, Glasgow School of Art Library.

6. Eduard Wimmer to Josef Hoffmann, n.d.; in Eduard Sekler, *Josef Hoffmann: The Architectural Work* (Princeton, N.J.: Princeton University Press, 1985), p. 39.

7. Ibid., p. 40; Thomas Howarth, *Charles Rennie Mackintosh and the Modern Movement*, 3d ed. (London: Routledge and Kegan Paul, 1990), p. 268.

8. Holden's designs for the Bristol Library were published in 1905; John Summerson was the first to point out Mackintosh's debt to Holden in "The British Contemporaries of Frank Lloyd Wright" (1963), reprinted in Summerson, *The Unromantic Castle* (London: Thames and Hudson, 1990), p. 240. In *The Turn of the Century: Architecture in Britain around 1900* (Glasgow: University of Glasgow, 1976), p. 24, Summerson observed, "This free Tudor . . . was everybody's property and a good case could be made for calling it the most profoundly characteristic and most distinctly unifying architecture in Britain around 1900."

9. *Vista*, no. 5 (summer 1910): 7. David Walker suggests that the anonymous author may have been Herbert Honeyman, who had been excluded from his father's old firm (though by Keppie, not Mackintosh).

10. *Vista*, no. 4 (autumn 1909): 100–101.

11. For example, the Head Office of the Union Bank of Scotland (now the Bank of Scotland) in St. Vincent Street, 1924, by Richard Gunn, chief assistant to James Miller, and E. G. Wylie's Scottish Legal Assurance Society building in Bothwell Street of 1927–31. See Alan Powers, "Edwardian Architectural Education: A Study of Three Schools of Architecture," *AA Files* (Architectural Association School of Architecture), no. 5 (1984); and Gavin Stamp, "Neo-Classicism in Late Victorian and Early 20th Century Scotland," in the proceedings of the conference "The Neo-Classical Town in Scotland," held at the Scott Sutherland School of Architecture, Robert Gordon University, Aberdeen, Scotland, December 1994, to be published 1995.

12. David Walker, "The Greet [*sic*] Modernist of Glasgow," in the *Times Literary Supplement*, December 9, 1977, p. 1450; see also Gavin Stamp, "Mackintosh, Burnet and Modernity," in *Architectural Heritage*, vol. 3, *The Age of Mackintosh*, ed. John Lowrey (Edinburgh: Architectural Heritage Society of Scotland, 1992), pp. 8–31. In his review of Howarth's biography in *New Statesman and Nation*, December 27, 1952, p. 784, John Summerson argued, "It is permissible, I think, to doubt whether Mackintosh was really a better or more progressive architect than, say, his contemporary Glaswegian, Sir John Burnet; and to wonder whether our present adulation of him has not more in it of self-justification than of sincere obeisance to greatness."

13. David Walker notes (in "The Partnership of James Salmon and John Gaff Gillespie," in Alastair Service, ed., *Edwardian Architecture and Its Origins* [London: Architectural Press, 1975], pp. 236–49) that Salmon's last major building in Glasgow was the reinforced-concrete Lion Chambers of 1905–6 and that he built virtually nothing in the decade before his death in 1924.

14. Mackintosh to William Davidson, April 1, 1919, Hunterian Art Gallery, University of Glasgow.

15. David Walker has pointed out, however, in a letter to the author, that "Mackintosh's difficulty in coping with the tiresome details after he became a partner and had to do it himself was part of the problem."

16. Mackintosh to William Davidson, August 5, 1915, Hunterian Art Gallery, University of Glasgow; the writing paper bears the printed heading "Summer Meeting at King's College, July 12–31"; what remains of the Geddes archives is at the University of Strathclyde, Glasgow.

17. Edwin Lutyens to Emily Lutyens, January 3, 1915, *The Letters of Edwin Lutyens to His Wife Lady Emily*, ed. Clayre Percy and Jane Ridley (London: Collins, 1985), pp. 307–8.

18. Although such Indian buildings were not well known, they were published in the *Annual Report on Architectural Work in India . . . by the Consulting Architect to the Government of India* (Calcutta, 1914 and 1915), which Mackintosh might well have consulted.

19. What little is known about this itinerant and shadowy figure, who had a successful practice in and around Northampton, has been discovered by the late Victor Hatley and Bruce A. Bailey. It is not known if Alexander Ellis Anderson (1866–1935) was at Glasgow School of Art, as was his brother William J. Anderson (whom he worked with at one time), but he practised in Northampton from 1893 until about 1931 and was a pioneer motorist, who designed the first recorded "motor house" in the city in 1901. He would have been known to Bassett-Lowke both because he had designed a large warehouse in Kingswell Street in 1903 for his father and because he lived in 72 Derngate during the First World War; his chief assistant, Keightley Cobb, was living in no. 70 in 1919.

20. For example, the neo-Regency terraces of the Duchy of Cornwall estate (1911–14) in Kennington, London, by Adshead and Ramsay, and the book by A. E. Richardson and C. Lovett Gill, *London Houses from 1660 to 1820* (London: Batsford, 1911): "Externally the houses of the late eighteenth and early nineteenth centuries in London present to the critical observer a beauty of proportion so subtle and refined as to be at first glance almost unapparent. True art is to conceal art."

21. Howarth, *Mackintosh*, p. 202.

22. Shaw, in ibid., p. 203; and in Janet Bassett-Lowke, "A Memoir of W. J. Bassett-Lowke," in Bassett-Lowke and Alan Crawford, *C. R. Mackintosh: The Chelsea Years, 1915–1923* (Glasgow: Hunterian Art Gallery, University of Glasgow, 1994), p. 28.

23. W. J. Bassett-Lowke to Mackintosh, January 14, 1917, Hunterian Art Gallery, University of Glasgow. For Bassett-Lowke, see Louise Campbell, "A Model Patron: Bassett-Lowke, Mackintosh and Behrens," *Journal of Decorative Arts* 10 (1986).

24. Janet Bassett-Lowke, "Memoir," p. 22.

25. Roderick Gradidge, "The Last of Mackintosh," *Field*, December 8, 1984, pp. 11–13.

26. In this context it is interesting to find that Lawrence Weaver, in his preface to the second edition of *Small Country Houses of Today*, vol. 2, 1921, wrote: "A new method of design is incredible, simply because it is not feasible. We had our misfortunes a few years ago in that pursuit, but even before the war the 'New Art' which pleased Germany and Austria so vastly was 'dead and damned' in Great Britain. It is far more likely that we shall signify our essential sympathy with Latin culture by developing a national school of design inspired by a classical spirit."

27. L. Gomme and P. Norman, eds., *Survey of London*, vol. 4, *The Parish of Chelsea (Part II)*, p. 72; Cheyne House is illustrated in plate 69 and the cottages in Glebe Place in plate 78.

28. Summarised in Bassett-Lowke and Crawford, *Chelsea Years*, p. 28.

29. Illustrated in Charles Marriott, *Modern English Architecture* (London: Chapman and Hall, 1924), p. 208.

30. Michael Holroyd, *Augustus John*, vol. 2, *The Years of Experience* (London: Heinemann, 1975), p. 36. By 1916 John was

complaining about "the damned Dutch shanty," and in 1920 he was talking to Mackintosh about a new studio on another site. Sketch plans survive in the Hunterian's collection, and on the basis of these a number of Mackintosh enthusiasts visited 28 Mallord Street and concluded that Mackintosh had been involved (see the file in the Hunterian Art Gallery, University of Glasgow). For Robert van t'Hoff, see Joseph Buch, *A Century of Architecture in the Netherlands 1880/1990* (Rotterdam, the Netherlands: NAi Publishers, 1994), pp. 130–34. (In the 1930s Augustus John would commission a Modern movement studio house in Hampshire from Christopher Nicholson.)

31. Crawford, in Bassett-Lowke and Crawford, *Chelsea Years*, p. 14; see also Alan Crawford, *Charles Robert Ashbee: Architect, Designer and Romantic Socialist* (New Haven, Conn., and London: Yale University Press, 1985).

32. Lawrence Weaver illustrated Wood's house in the first volume of *Small Country Houses of Today*, 1910. "Though the merits of Upmeads are considerable, it will be generally agreed that the house is unusual to the point of oddness," p. 186.

33. Charles Rennie Mackintosh, diary, June 22, 1920, Hunterian Art Gallery, University of Glasgow.

34. The haunting is recounted by Howarth, *Mackintosh*, p. 209.

35. Ibid., p. 214.

36. Sekler, *Josef Hoffmann*, p. 54; examples of Hoffmann's "multiple framing" include the interior of the reception room

illustrated as plate C18 in *The Art Revival in Austria*, special number of the *Studio* (1906).

37. *Architectural Review* 53 (1923): 31, and referred to in H. S. Goodhart-Rendel, *English Architecture since the Regency* (London: Constable, 1953), p. 223. Alan Crawford (Bassett-Lowke and Crawford, *Chelsea Years*, p. 16) notes with justice that "he might have written that the other exhibits recalled the early volumes of *Country Life* and *Architectural Review*, the arbiters of Edwardian architectural taste in whose pages Mackintosh's work had never appeared."

38. Correspondence accompanying drawings acquired from the contractors, Norman and Burt Ltd., now at the British Architectural Library, Royal Institute of British Architects, reveals that Mackintosh knocked two cottages together and added a new entrance, staircase, scullery, and bathroom on the north side, and also that Leigh Farm Cottages were destroyed by a German V1 flying bomb in August 1944.

39. W. J. Bassett-Lowke, "A Memoir," in Alistair Moffat and Colin Baxter, *Remembering Charles Rennie Mackintosh: An Illustrated Biography* (Lanark, Scotland: Colin Baxter Photography, 1989), p. 100.

40. Howarth, *Mackintosh*, p. 215.

41. Marriott, *Modern English Architecture*, pp. 129, 241; Frederick Chatterton, ed., *Who's Who in Architecture* (London: Architectural Press, 1926), p. 195.

42. Robert Macleod, *Charles Rennie Mackintosh* (London: Country Life, 1968), p. 150.

III

ART AND DESIGN

"Living Fancy": Mackintosh Furniture and Interiors

PAT KIRKHAM

Furniture was a major aspect of Charles Rennie Mackintosh's work. He designed over four hundred pieces between 1893 and 1919, and it is on these and their related interiors that his reputation as a designer rests.[1] As an architect Mackintosh was concerned about the inside as well as the outside of buildings, and much of his furniture was conceived as integral elements of carefully composed interiors. Only once did he work directly for a furniture-making firm; in all other cases his furniture was produced for commissioned buildings and rooms, including exhibitions and tea rooms, as well as for his own homes.

Neither Mackintosh nor his wife and sometime collaborator, Margaret Macdonald, was trained in furniture or interior design, although Macdonald had benefitted from the broad curriculum at Glasgow School of Art. Mackintosh's connections with the decorative arts increased rapidly after his association, starting in 1893, with Margaret, her sister Frances Macdonald, and Herbert McNair. Each of the Four had a considerable influence upon the others, but most relevant here are the mutual design influences of Charles and Margaret.[2] This essay is premised upon recognition of Margaret's talents and her influence on Charles, but because the focus of this book is Charles and because this brief chapter must cover much material, it is not possible for me to detail their collaboration. This essay does not attribute separate elements of a piece of furniture or room design to one or the other, nor does it establish a fifty-fifty input in order to prove an "equality"; rather, it insists that the mutual influences were both complex and compound. Even when Mackintosh was working "separately" from Macdonald, his work would be influenced by ideas already absorbed from and discussed with her. However strong that influence and however extensive their collaboration, I have nevertheless sometimes resorted

156. Charles Rennie Mackintosh. *Washstand*, 1904. For the Blue Bedroom, Hous'hill, Glasgow. Oak, with ceramic tiles and leaded and mirror glass, 63 1/4 x 51 1/4 x 20 3/8 in. (160.7 x 130.2 x 51.8 cm). The Metropolitan Museum of Art, New York; Purchase, Lila Acheson Wallace Gift, 1994.

to the shorthand terminology of "Mackintosh furniture" or "Mackintosh interiors." This book is a critical celebration of a multitalented man. Recognising that he worked in a complex collaboration with a multitalented woman does not diminish his prodigious talents.

As Alan Crawford points out in his essay "The Mackintosh Phenomenon," there are many Mackintoshes in the Mackintosh story. Here I concentrate on the furniture in some of the main interior schemes (my discussion of which is restricted largely to wall and surface decoration), but I hope that readers will be encouraged to discover other Mackintoshes, particularly those of the early and late years. The tendency to regard Mackintosh as a "pioneer" and to evaluate his work in terms of how Modernist or proto-Modernist it was is less pronounced today, but within Mackintosh studies originality and individuality remain privileged at the expense of the traditional, and many continue to search for a "pure" or essential Mackintosh. These Modernist approaches have marginalised both the early work, which is viewed with Modernist hindsight and found wanting because it "still has" features that Mackintosh would later discard, and the last commissions for interiors and furniture, which, at the time they were designed, were hardly at the cutting edge of avant-garde design.

I also discuss the gender coding of Mackintosh interiors and furniture, which were produced at a time when certain rooms in upper- and middle-class homes were considered to be "masculine" or "feminine." In the case of the Mackintoshes, some qualification is needed of the binary oppositions female/male, light/heavy, white/dark that have been used in recent feminist scholarship to suggest new ways of understanding interiors and their furnishings.[3] This issue is complex. The Mackintoshes did not draw neat distinctions between public ("male") and private ("female") interiors, and many individual pieces of furniture also defy simplistic categorisation as "masculine" or "feminine." In order to go beyond the identification of Macdonald with the feminine, new scholarship must acknowledge the complexities within and between masculine/feminine and related "oppositions."[4] The classification of a design or object as either "feminine" or "masculine" can be fruitful, but binary oppositions run the risk of marginalising or masking elements that do not fit one of the polarities. For example, by describing a particular ladderback chair in the billiard room at the Argyle Street tea rooms as a "solid-looking" item designed for an exclusively masculine preserve, attention is taken away from its elegance, linearity, and delicately tapering posts.[5] In other words, the object may well be a "hybrid" (to use a "postmodern" but rather obvious term) rather than exclusively "masculine" or "feminine."

Mackintosh furniture and interiors are the creation of one, often two, very creative minds working within the broad parameters of the avant-garde Free Style movement in European architecture and design, which flourished at the turn of the century and embraced the idea of the unified artistic interior. Such highly aestheticised designs are rooted in the Aesthetic movement, which propounded "art for art's sake," and in the Arts and Crafts movement, which emphasised the importance of "commonplace" as well as "state" furniture.[6] Some Mackintosh furniture and interiors are unmistakably commonplace and workaday; some are unmistakably state and special; and some combine elements of the ordinary and the special, the common and the exotic. In their variations on a known type—be it a piece of furniture or a room—they also offer the pleasures of the familiar at the same time as those of the new.

The Mackintoshes were more closely associated with the production of artistic interiors for "progressive" clients than with the democratisation of design. (The latter was central to the European design-reform movements at the turn of the century, particularly those in Austria and Germany, which themselves drew heavily on Arts and Crafts ideas.[7]) Nevertheless, they sometimes used—and quite deliberately so—commonplace and relatively inexpensive materials, techniques, finishes, and decoration in their efforts to achieve a desired effect. However, theirs was not the evangelical approach to cheaper materials or to working closely with manufacturers espoused by the design reformers; the Mackintoshes were, or at least Charles was, prepared to sacrifice quality of materials and construction for aesthetic effect.

Mackintosh's consummate skill as a designer was his ability to compose rooms that play on complementarity, repetition, harmony, and contrast. He sought a "synthesis or integration of myriads of details" and emphasised the necessity for "a discriminating thoughtfulness in the selection of appropriate shape, decoration, design for everything no matter how trivial."[8] Sometimes the room designs are enhanced by the inclusion of freestanding furniture, sometimes not. The tensions between the apparently randomly (though actually studiously and "artistically") placed objects and the often rhythmic, modular, and multilayered patterning of the room and wall furniture are more evident in some interiors than in others. Not every Mackintosh scheme was the seamless, harmonious whole that many Mackintosh enthusiasts maintain.

Mackintosh was a rich ornamentalist as well as a furniture designer adept at shaping three-dimensional form. He sought to develop an appropriate ornamentation, free from the restrictions of faithfully reproducing "antiquarian detail," and he aimed to "clothe modern ideas with modern dress—adorn our designs with living fancy."[9] The lifeblood of many Mackintosh designs, "living fancy" implies decoration; whimsy, fantasy, and imagination made material in vibrant contemporary forms, as opposed to the "dead" ones of the past. Embraced yet carefully controlled, the decorative elements in his work—be they witty, sensuous, relaxing, or disconcerting—can produce strong responses. Much of the affective power of Mackintosh interiors and furniture comes from the interplay of varied patterns and from an aesthetic of addition, permutation, and juxtaposition.

EARLY FURNITURE

The unjustly neglected furniture designed by Mackintosh between 1893 and 1896 needs reassessing and elevating to a more prominent position within the Mackintosh canon.

Mackintosh's first known furniture designs date from 1893 and fall well within the parameters of the Arts and Crafts movement, then at its height. Roger Billcliffe has suggested that the young McNair's practice of tracing over furniture designs in commercial catalogues and magazines "probably accounts for the somewhat traditional shapes" of early Mackintosh furniture. He has argued that by "reducing commercial designs to their basic outlines, he [Mackintosh] would have arrived at the plain, simple massing of elements" evident in the furniture and that "machine-made ornamentation has been entirely eliminated."[10] The picture of McNair and Mackintosh ridding vulgar commercial products of machine-made ornamentation fits the Modernist Mackintosh myth, but just because McNair (half a century later) claimed to have done this, there is no reason to assume that Mackintosh ever did. There was a well-established output of "art" or "aesthetic" furniture within the commercial furniture trade in late-nineteenth-century Britain, Glasgow included; it was not all complex forms and machine-produced decoration. Furthermore, Mackintosh—aged twenty-five, keen to make himself known as a "progressive" designer, and about to spend the next four summers sketching vernacular buildings and artefacts in England—was well aware that the Arts and Crafts movement applauded design *without* reference to popular commercial styles.

One source for Mackintosh's green-stained oak dressing table, washstand (plate 157), and wardrobe was Ford Madox Brown's green-stained "cottage" furniture of the 1860s, made for Morris and Company, and his chest of drawers exhibited in 1887 and 1890.[11] The Mackintosh washstand and wardrobe draw on eighteenth-century sources and equal, if not surpass, the "Simple Bedroom Furniture" designs by Ambrose Heal from 1893.[12]

Although Billcliffe regards this Mackintosh furniture as "not particularly successful,"[13] it does show him working confidently within an established progressive movement and displaying a preference for elegant and well-proportioned pieces. It was sufficiently successful for one of Glasgow's leading "artistic" firms, Guthrie and Wells, to put into production a range of bedroom furniture designed by Mackintosh. The resultant dark-stained cypress-wood wardrobes were in the "Simple Furniture" mode and decorated with brass ornamental hinges terminating in a heart shape more usually associated with C.F.A. Voysey.[14] This furniture had no unusual or stylised decoration of the type later associated with Mackintosh, although the 1893 wardrobe was ornamented with a small stylised bird's head—a near-abstract motif that recurred later in his work.

157. Charles Rennie Mackintosh. *Washstand*, 1893. For David Gauld. Oak, stained green, 35⅞ x 27¹⁵/₁₆ x 20⁹/₁₆ in. (90.0 x 71.0 x 52.0 cm). Hunterian Art Gallery, University of Glasgow.

The year 1894 saw a bolder use of stylised forms in a witty, if somewhat esoteric, cabinet made for William Davidson's house at Gladsmuir, Kilmacolm. It features a large cutout apple shape in the top doors as well as carved apple pips and apple shapes in the leaded glass (the significance of the apple is not known). A more restrained and beautifully proportioned piece, which reflects the elegance and quality of mid-eighteenth-century cabinetmaking, was the French-polished cypress-wood bookcase with glazed doors—the detached *cyma recta* capitals of which add emphasis as well as detail to the top. I do not see it as a problem that "Mackintosh was not yet able to rid his designs of all traditional forms of decoration"[15]; the bookcase is an elegantly modern update of a familiar Georgian Neoclassical item and should be appreciated as such.

In 1895 Mackintosh designed a green-stained cypress linen cupboard (plate 159) in the Arts and Crafts manner, with elongated hinges and two beaten-lead panels with stylised human figures that show the influence of the Macdonald sisters. More influenced by the Aesthetic movement was his settle in dark-stained oak (plate 158), also designed in 1895 and shown at the Arts and Crafts Exhibition Society in London in 1896.[16] The front legs of the settle develop into thin stylised columns and support an entablature that encloses the settle, thus forming a rectangular box. While adding weight to the top, Mackintosh also lightened the traditional form by cutting away the sides in a sweeping curve. The stylised plant designs in the stencilled back panels add to the "aesthetic" nature of this piece of art furniture.

Billcliffe considers that the decorative panels "contradicted the effect of the rest of the settle, with its sturdily utilitarian appearance."[17] This, however, is no simple utilitarian settle but a sophisticated piece of furniture, similar to a Voysey piece (Victoria and Albert Museum, London) in the same exhibition— at least as sophisticated as the settle designed about 1886 by Arthur Mackmurdo (William Morris Gallery, Walthamstow, England), who was one of the main influences on both Mackintosh and Voysey in the early 1890s. Praised by the *Builder* for its logical use of decorative construction, the Mackintosh settle required the talents of a skilled furniture maker to effect the subtle shapings and crisp detail of the capitals.[18] The decorative beaten-lead panel featuring three peacocks adds to the self-conscious aestheticising of Arts and Crafts forms; the peacocks, the stencil decoration, and the classical elements all signal the influence of the Aesthetic movement.

The furniture designed for the Argyle Street tea rooms in 1898–99 was also in the Arts and Crafts manner; many of the simple yet subtly shaped pieces were made of oak—sometimes scrubbed or varnished but mostly dark-stained. Some were stout and sturdy, but the dining chair with a subtly curved top rail and three central back slats offered customers an elegant simplicity in keeping with George Walton's panelling and screens (see plate 188). The slender, elegant, tapering uprights add a Japanese touch to this variation on the

158. Charles Rennie Mackintosh. *Hall Settle*, 1895. Made by Guthrie and Wells, Glasgow. Oak, stained dark, with beaten-lead panel and stencilled linen upholstery, 71 1/2 x 55 7/8 x 25 11/16 in. (181.5 x 142.0 x 65.0 cm). Trustees of the National Museums of Scotland.

■■ OPPOSITE

159. Charles Rennie Mackintosh.
Linen Cupboard, c. 1895. For John
Henderson, Glasgow. Cypress, originally stained green, with brass-and-
metal fittings, and beaten- and
coloured-lead panels, 72$^{1}/_{16}$ x 52$^{3}/_{16}$ x
15$^{7}/_{16}$ in. (183.0 x 132.5 x 39.2 cm).
Glasgow School of Art.

■■ ABOVE

160. Charles Rennie Mackintosh.
High-Backed Chair, 1898–99. For
Miss Cranston's tea rooms, Argyle
Street, Glasgow. Oak, stained dark,
reupholstered with horsehair, 53$^{7}/_{8}$ x
19$^{7}/_{8}$ x 18$^{3}/_{16}$ in. (136.8 x 50.5 x 46.2
cm). Glasgow School of Art.

"traditional" ladderback form, as had those designed by Ford Madox Brown
(for Morris and Company, London) and by Ernest Gimson.

Mackintosh's well-known high-backed chair with pierced oval decoration
(plate 160) was first designed for this tea room. It is audacious in the degree to
which its linear tapering forms are extended, in the use of an abstractly shaped
form to join the four back stiles, and in its symbolism. In my opinion, the oval
palette shape signals the artist, but there are as many readings of this "text" as
there are readers, and the shape is also reminiscent of an all-seeing eye or a

human head atop an androgynous body (a shape seen in drawings and watercolours by the Four). When these chairs are placed at a table, the anthropomorphic references intensify; even with no one sitting in them, the chairs appear peopled. A similar "talking heads" effect is obtained when the silvered highbacked chairs of the Salon de Luxe at the Willow Tea Rooms are placed around a table. The flat forms curve their backs and lean forward in intimate conversation (see plate 193).

One of the most interesting of the Argyle Street pieces is the low-backed armchair used in the billiard and smoking rooms, with elongated rear posts that terminate in small knobs and resemble billiard cues. (Both this lowbacked chair and the high-backed Argyle Street chairs were also used in the Mackintoshes' own home—see plate 161.) Several stood in a row in the billiard room, like sentinels guarding the male rituals enacted therein. With its references to billiard cues and to guns or bayonets clasped against the shoulder, the armchair has a strong male coding. As geometric and boxlike as anything to come out of Vienna at the turn of the century, it (like the high-backed chair) is far from solid. Open spaces cut into the shapes; elongated uprights or overstretched arms extend into space. Both this and the high-backed chair are "hybrids"—neither completely "masculine" nor "feminine."[19]

EARLY INTERIORS

Early examples of Mackintosh's excellence as a room designer are the 1898 dining room in the Munich home of Hugo Bruckmann, publisher of *Dekora-*

tive Kunst, and the bedroom of the same date at Westdel, 2 Queens Place, Glasgow, for the publisher Robert Maclehose. In Munich the wall decoration, fitted wall furniture, a freestanding cabinet, and the main doors to the room were all integrated (the commission for the other freestanding furniture went to Karl Bertsch). The integration of wall decoration and wall furniture at Westdel was enhanced by painting everything white. Mackintosh was learning lightness—from George Walton, whose interiors of the 1890s helped establish the domestic style of the Glasgow tea rooms, and from Margaret Macdonald, whom he would marry in 1900.

In 1900 Charles and Margaret decorated their Glasgow flat at 120 Mains Street. The bedroom furniture was white, that in the dining room was dark. The drawing room, a soothing space in grey and white dotted with purple and pink, mixed white and dark furniture—including the first Mackintosh white-painted chair. A large double bookcase with stylised flowers in leaded glass, a square table, and a desk were also painted white. The dark-stained high-backed chairs with pierced oval backrails were used in both the ("female") drawing room and the ("male") dining room but not in the bedroom, suggesting that the latter was more overtly coded as feminine. Photographs of the drawing room in 1900 (plate 161) and 1902 show slightly different arrangements of the freestanding furniture, which stood in carefully composed "informal" groupings incorporating subtle permutations of colour, form, and finish. Each of the chairs could in some way or other be described as both "masculine" and "feminine," suggesting that it might be more useful to consider this furniture, and the room in which it was placed, as "hybrid," though not necessarily androgynous.

The dining room (see plate 5) accorded with conventional notions of the dark "male" room, but the light ceiling and frieze, the elegance and linear lightness of the furniture, and the Japanese-looking candelabra counterbalanced those elements that suggested solidity (the dark colours and the stained wood) and traditionalism (the dresser, which was an earlier design, of 1896). By contrast, the small bedroom (see plate 68) was crowded with white furniture, including a four-poster bed, a large wardrobe, a washstand, and a cheval mirror, much of it enriched with expressively modelled organic decoration and inlays of coloured glass. The room has been described as a romantic and sensuous bower,[20] and when sunlight would shine through the coloured glass, delicate spots of colour would dapple the interior of the bed, enhancing the lyricism of this magical space. But it was a fairy-tale space in a room that was also somewhat claustrophobic and inhabited by a strange, robotlike creature that also functioned as a cheval mirror.

In 1900 the Mackintoshes also collaborated on the interior design of and furniture for two rooms at Miss Cranston's Ingram Street tea rooms. One was the Ladies' Luncheon Room (see plate 183). By conventional coding, dining rooms were male, yet this room (more petite in scale than photographs suggest) was specifically for women—and for it the Mackintoshes produced a design that incorporated both "masculine" and "feminine" elements. This fusion befitted a public ("male") place, part of whose attractions involved the presentation, in idealised or fantasy forms, of the comforts, pleasures, and aesthetics of the "female" domestic and private sphere.

At their Mains Street flat the Mackintoshes had produced an elegant and sparse version of the conventional dark dining room, but in the Ingram Street luncheon room they chose to make the surroundings light and the seat furniture dark (the tables were covered in standard white cloths). This dining room was as spacious, light, and airy as any living room, and if, as recent conservation work suggests, there was a considerable amount of silver in the decoration, then it must have shimmered in certain lights. Silvered-lead panels alternated with white ones on the walls directly beneath the magnificent gesso panels (one each by Mackintosh and Macdonald), which themselves contained silver detailing; in addition, there was the reflective sheen of the light fittings and the silvered-lead panels. The entrance screen picked out the white and green of the wall stencils.

The soft "feminine" forms of the organic ornament and the depictions of women in the gesso and silvered-lead panels confirmed the room as a place for women and womanly pursuits and contrasted with the verticality of the structural elements of the room (many of which are swept, curved, and tapered), the screen, and the upright, stiff-backed dining chairs. The latter are almost military in their bearing, and when shown in sequence, their uprightness and uniformity suggest the regimentation of soldiers on parade.

Although the dark chairs were open, they helped weigh down a light and lightly decorated room, whose impact came less from unity of effect than from a series of layers (the entrance wall of gesso, the staircase bannister/screen, and the leaded-glass screen) and from a dialectic between geometric forms (in both light and dark tones) and more obviously decorative, ornamental, and organic ones (in white, pink, green, and silvered tones). Not until (and only in) the Willow Tea Rooms were silver chairs designed to go with the silvered tones of an interior.

For their exhibit at the 1900 Secession exhibition in Vienna, the Mackintoshes produced a wall-and-furniture ensemble that mostly, but not exclusively, suggested the interior of a living room (see plate 63). The three enclosing walls were white; the gesso panels (later installed in the Ingram Street tea rooms) acted as a decorative frieze on the two facing walls. The only other wall decoration was a series of tapered posts attached to a narrow wooden frieze, inset with squares of coloured glass, which unified the exhibit. Dark furniture—most notably a tall writing desk and cabinet-sideboard (each with beaten-metal panels) and high-backed chairs and armchairs—was incorporated into the light and delicate scheme, but with less success than the flowing forms of the white cheval mirror. Before the striking oak cabinet-sideboard was shown at Turin in 1902, it too was painted white.

EMPFANGS==RAUM UND MUSIK==ZIMMER PANELS VON MARGARET MACDONALD MACKINTOSH

Amongst the most unified Mackintosh designs for interiors are those he drew (they were never realized) for the House for an Art Lover competition, sponsored by the Darmstadt publisher Alexander Koch in 1901. The hall and dining room were dark and panelled. The latter included a new high-backed chair with a single back splat that tapered down from the "head," reinforcing the suggestion of a human form. The white rooms were the bedroom and the music-cum-reception room (plate 162), the latter a multilayered tour de force. The organic forms of the decorative panels, the carving on the table, and the top of the piano contrast with the geometric forms of the chairs, table, piano case, flower stands, and shades on the light fittings but do so within an harmonious and tightly integrated design featuring complementary and repeating as well as contrasting forms, patterns, and colours. It is a symphony in white, grey, silver, pink, blue, green, and purple.

Some of the furniture for Windyhill, the house Mackintosh designed for William Davidson in 1900, was firmly in the Arts and Crafts mode. Some of the hall furniture, in particular, was extremely simple, rectangular, and plank-

162. Charles Rennie Mackintosh. *A House for an Art Lover Competition Entry: Perspective of the Reception and Music Room*, 1901. *Empfangs Raum und Musik Zimmer*, plate 7 from *Meister der Innenkunst: Charles Rennie Mackintosh, Glasgow: Haus eines Kunstfreundes*, edited by Hermann Muthesius (Darmstadt, Germany: Alexander Koch, 1902). Lithograph, 15$\frac{1}{2}$ x 20$\frac{13}{16}$ in. (39.4 x 52.9 cm). Hunterian Art Gallery, University of Glasgow.

like—commonplace in a crude sort of way. However, the variation on a peasant-style, high-backed, rush-seated oak chair developed for the hall (plate 163) was as sophisticated a version of the commonplace chair as any in contemporary Europe or the United States. The rushing of the seat is enclosed by wood to protect it in the traditional way, and the tapered back of the seat is similar to the traditional Scottish *caqueteuse,* or gossip's chair. But the extension of the plain, concave, and tapered wooden back to a height far beyond that of a headrest makes this a far from traditional piece.

The large dark-stained double-cabinet bookcase with leaded-glass panels featured plain full-plank-size pieces of wood at the front of the bookcase sections, concealing the shelves; this was less a reference to peasant furniture than a conscious witticism that added to the sophistication of this batlike piece. A small white-painted table for the main bedroom (similar ones, stained dark, were made for the children's bedrooms) also illustrates the Mackintosh wit and what Crawford calls "the games of direction" played. Crawford also notes the use of "planks about half an inch thick instead of ordinary legs, making the legs and carcase into a single plane," and comments: "The side view seems like a different table. It was a simple trick, but the dislocation was real. Davidson might read the plank style as simple and honest; but for his architect it was wit and contradiction."[21]

The visual impact of a double cabinet was also achieved in the drawing room at 14 Kingsborough Gardens, designed in 1901–2, where two adjacent white-painted cabinets appeared to form a single unit when the doors of each were opened. (Plate 164 shows the similar cabinet designed for the Mains Street flat.) Much of the immediate impact came from the inside doors, which were inlaid with pink, white, and purple glass in the form of a boldly stylised woman holding an enormous rose. Thereafter, the eye is caught by the subtlety of the curves—on the bottom of the doors, on the moulding between them, and on the lower shelf—and by the interplay between them. This is Mackintosh furniture at its most subtle and sophisticated.

"Rose leaf" wall stencils were used at Kingsborough Gardens, and related ones appeared in the Rose Boudoir—a white, pink, green, and silver room setting exhibited by the Mackintoshes at the *International Exhibition of Modern Decorative Art* held in Turin in 1902 (see plate 67). The rose theme of two magnificent gesso panels by Margaret Macdonald (see plate 64 for one of these), which hung at either end of the ensemble, was echoed in the inlaid table, the linen banners, the light fittings, the stencilled chair backs, the panels (of metal and glass and of gesso) of the ebonised writing cabinet, and the leaded-glass panels on the flanking screens. The interiors were becoming "more colourful, luxurious, feminine and intense, and the furniture likewise."[22]

The backs of the two white armchairs that faced each other across a small oval table each had two layers of canvas stretched between the top rail and the seat so that both front and back could be stencilled with a rose motif (plate

163. Charles Rennie Mackintosh. *Hall Chair,* 1901. For Windyhill, Kilmacolm. Oak, stained dark, with rush seat, 52⅝ x 28¹³⁄₁₆ x 21½ in. (133.7 x 73.2 x 54.5 cm). Hunterian Art Gallery, University of Glasgow.

165). This transposed a type of decoration associated with walls to a piece of furniture that, from the back, functioned as a frame for hanging stencilled linen panels—complementing the elaborate appliqué linen banners (by Macdonald) hanging on the wall and the tall stencilled banners (by Mackintosh), which hung free.

The two elegant high-backed stencilled chairs—one black, one white—with dramatically lowered seats and backs that stretch higher than almost any other Mackintosh piece (plate 166) were as mannered as the Windyhill hall chairs. The idea of using a simple and traditional decorative technique such as stencilling to adorn upholstery was in keeping with the Glasgow School of Art's emphasis on using everyday materials and techniques to aestheticise the middle-class home. By the application of two-dimensional decoration to three-dimensional form, Mackintosh found a cheap and effective way of translating the curves and swirls of Art Nouveau into furniture design. The stylised carved top panel is both the chair's weakness (in terms of visual unity) and its crowning glory. It is difficult to wrest a specific representation from its abstract forms, which have been variously read as a human face, a Halloween ghost, a ripe fruit, a petal, an ovary, and a testicle.[23]

What is one to make of an image that evokes both female and male genitalia (although the female imagery strikes me as the more powerful here)? How does one begin to think about the gendering of such multivalent objects? Are they primarily gendered through colour, as the linking of male/female and dark/light suggests? Are they "his" and "her" chairs? If so, why are the two by the table both white? The ebonised writing cabinet (see plate 51), the

■■ OPPOSITE
164. Charles Rennie Mackintosh. *Cabinet,* 1902. For 120 Mains Street, Glasgow. Oak, painted white, with doors finished inside with aluminium leaf and coloured glass, and silver-dipped brass fittings, 60³/₄ x 39³/₁₆ x 15⁵/₈ in. (154.3 x 99.3 x 39.7 cm). Hunterian Art Gallery, University of Glasgow.

■■ LEFT
165. Charles Rennie Mackintosh. *Armchair,* 1902. For the Rose Boudoir, *International Exhibition of Modern Decorative Art,* Turin, 1902. Oak, painted white, with upholstered seat, originally in rose silk, and stencilled loose canvas back, 44⁹/₁₆ x 27⁵/₈ x 22⁷/₁₆ in. (113.5 x 70.2 x 57.0 cm). Hunterian Art Gallery, University of Glasgow.

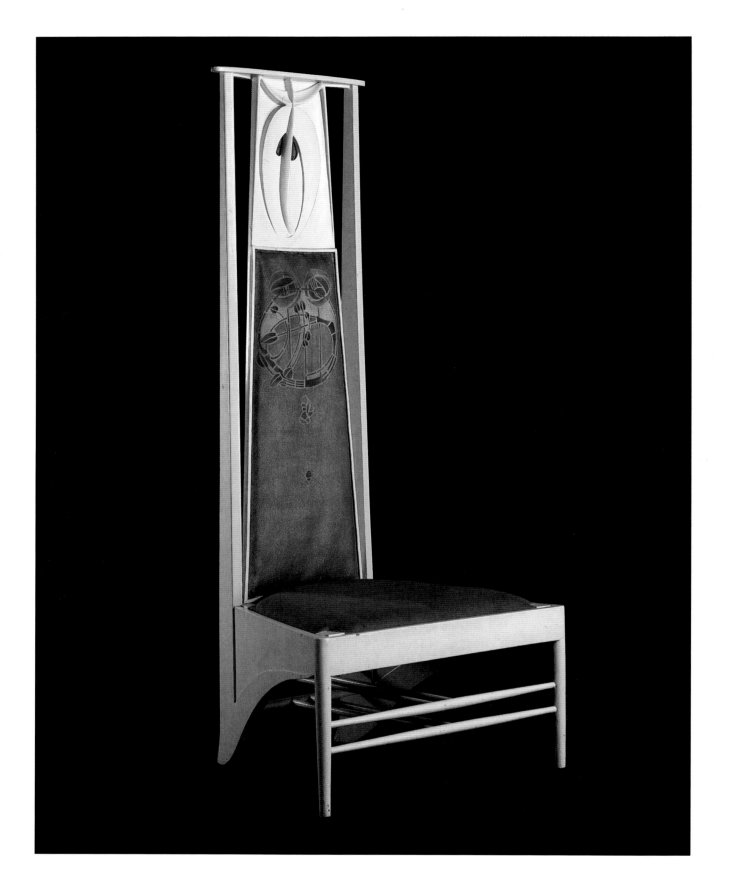

only such Mackintosh item to have gesso panels (and presumably used to complement the larger gesso panels of stylised women and flowers), cannot be coded as "male" simply because it is black. This elegant and stylish piece was probably the first black (as opposed to dark-stained) piece of Mackintosh furniture, reflecting the influence of both the Vienna Secession and the Aesthetic movement.

The Willow Tea Rooms had two main "white" rooms—the ladies' tea room and the Salon de Luxe, both reserved for women. The light, spacious, workaday front tea room was peopled with simple, dark furniture (plate 167 and see plate 192). Different chairs were used in different spaces: solid small chairs in the centre of the back saloon and, at the sides, the taller ladderbacks, elegant and open, in which the tensions between horizontal and vertical are beautifully resolved. Beyond these was the order-desk chair (plate 168), which featured another Mackintosh play on the horizontal and the vertical, including the formation of a stylised tree. In terms of colour, these dark pieces could be conventionally coded as masculine, but it is a masculinity that complements rather than disrupts the light "feminine" room. The deceptively simple order-desk chair, which also functions as a screen, might have proved most disruptive because of its large size and dark colour, but in some ways it is the most "feminine" of the furniture designed for the ground floor—being at once open and enclosing, even womblike.

There was no dark furniture to disrupt the cultural associations between lightness and femininity in the Salon de Luxe, with its decorative glass frieze and windows (see plate 193), magnificent gesso panel by Macdonald (see plate 70), equally magnificent doors of coloured and leaded glass (see page 2), and an exotic chandelier of coloured-glass balls reminiscent of Christmas baubles (see plate 69). The darkest colour was the vibrant rich purple of the silk fabric on the lower part of the walls and of the sensuous velvet upholstery of the silvered seating. The effect of the purple and the silver was dramatic. The silver-painted furniture with coloured insets played an important role in the creation of the overall fantasy setting. As with stage furniture, there is never any doubt that this is "imitation" silver, and its audacity and slight vulgarity dazzles and delights.

The taller chairs, which draw on the geometry, linearity, and stylisation of the Vienna Secession, have both human and robotic qualities—the latter enhanced by the silvering and the abstraction of form. They are flamboyant, excessive, and witty—even camp in their sheen, androgyny, and masquerade. When they are grouped around a table or placed at an angle that reveals the curve of the back panel, their anthropomorphic associations are difficult to avoid. However, viewed across the room as a group, particularly when seen front on and against the patterning of the window, frieze, or doors, they evoke tall, slender trees and enhance the tea room's willow symbolism. Smaller, plainer silvered chairs with tall, narrow backs that finish in an elegant

■■ OPPOSITE
166. Charles Rennie Mackintosh. *High-Backed Chair*, 1902. For the Rose Boudoir, Turin. Oak, painted white, with glass insets, stencilled linen back, reupholstered with silk, 60$^{1}/_{16}$ x 26$^{3}/_{4}$ x 25$^{11}/_{16}$ in. (152.5 x 68.0 x 65.2 cm). Hunterian Art Gallery, University of Glasgow. See also detail of stencilled back, plate 31.
■■ ABOVE
167. Charles Rennie Mackintosh. Willow Tea Rooms, Glasgow. View of the ground-floor tea room seen from the balcony. From *Dekorative Kunst* (April 1905): 266.

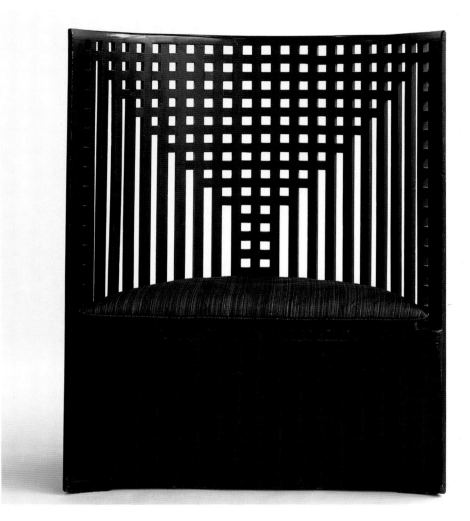

168. Charles Rennie Mackintosh. *Chair*, 1904. For the order desk, Willow Tea Rooms. Ebonised oak, reupholstered with horsehair, 46⁹/₁₆ x 37 x 16½ in. (118.2 x 94.0 x 42.0 cm). Glasgow School of Art.

inverted-V shape complement the higher ones (indeed, they are virtually the inner core of the larger ones).

Mackintosh, or the Mackintoshes, here displayed an audacious ability to handle excess, to add layer upon layer to their creation, and to push the novel and the unexpected, yet still contain them within a framework of complementary colours and patterns. One of the pleasures of the Salon de Luxe is that it offers too much to take in at one glance, or even several. The excess comes from density and detail of decoration and association, especially on the doors and the frieze. This is an aesthetic of addition, of accumulation; this is not Mackintosh the minimalist.

THE HILL HOUSE AND HOUS'HILL

The furnishings of The Hill House, Helensburgh (1903–4), with hall furniture as angular as any in Vienna (see plate 136), and of Hous'hill, Nitshill, Glasgow (plates 156 and 169), reveal a greater use of geometric form, but the organic

elements did not entirely disappear. A comparison of the drawing-cum-music rooms of these two houses and the music salon designed for the House for an Art Lover competition in 1901 (plate 162) reveals differing blends of the geometric and the organic, as well as differing solutions to the problem of integrating a piano into an interior scheme. The competition music salon has a more profuse and direct use of the female form in the decoration, much of which is organic, but the room is also laden with linearity, resulting in a beautiful fusion of "male" and "female" shapes.

The Hill House drawing room has an equally light, though not so intense or dense decorative scheme (in white, pink, green, silver, and grey). It is "feminine" in its lightness and in its prolific use of organic plant forms, which have led to its being read as an indoor garden. It has three main sections, with the elongated and narrow window bay area (plate 171) forming a more unified design than the others. That space could more easily be treated as a two-dimensional wall design, and its superior quality again suggests that,

169. Charles Rennie Mackintosh. *Dresser and Mirror*, 1904. For the White Bedroom, Hous'hill, Glasgow. Wood, painted white, with ebony handles with mother-of-pearl inlay. Dresser: 30¼ x 40 x 18 in. (76.8 x 101.6 x 45.7 cm); mirror: 40½ x 18¾ x 9¾ in. (102.8 x 47.6 x 24.7 cm). Royal Ontario Museum, Toronto.

▪▪ RIGHT, TOP
170. Charles Rennie Mackintosh. The fireplace area of the drawing room, The Hill House, Helensburgh. From *Deutsche Kunst und Dekoration*, no. 6 (1904–5): 356.

▪▪ RIGHT, BOTTOM
171. Charles Rennie Mackintosh. The window-seat area of the drawing room, The Hill House. From *Deutsche Kunst und Dekoration*, no. 6 (1904–5).

in terms of interiors and furniture, Mackintosh was at his best when handling wall or window decoration and related furniture. This section of the room was the only part not to have any dark furniture in the original scheme; in 1908 a small black cube table (plate 172), a sophisticated play on the simple square, was placed there, possibly to provide a better visual link with the rest of the room.

In the scheme for A House for an Art Lover the white piano was specially designed for the music room, whereas at The Hill House and Hous'hill, dark pianos had to be incorporated. They look heavy, awkward, and out of place, even at Hous'hill, where Mackintosh cleverly distanced the piano (designed by George Walton for Kate Cranston) from the main living area yet integrated it with the furniture by placing it behind an open screen (plate 173). The shape of the screen echoed that of the apse at the end of the room and, like a chancel screen in a church, marked a more sacred space behind. The screen, like the rest of the room, was white, and like the cabinet, it was adorned with decorative glass; it was further integrated into the room design by its circular candelabra, which complemented the nearby ceiling light. Having softened the visual disruption of the piano, Mackintosh proceeded to link it visually with the rest of the room by placing on the other side of the screen some dark-stained chairs (see plate 224), the backs of which complemented the screen.

By means of this ensemble of dark and light elements, the piano was better integrated into the overall decorative scheme at Hous'hill than at The Hill House. There it was located in a small, low-ceilinged alcove to the left of the drawing-room door as one entered, separate from a large rectangular space with a fireplace to the far right. It was into the latter, light, "feminine" living area that several items of dark furniture (some stained, some ebonised) were introduced (plate 173). They provided a link with the piano in terms of colour but little else. It seems that the Mackintoshes were prepared to admit dark objects into light areas as long as they knew their place within the greater artistic scheme and were suitably aestheticised.

The dark furniture in The Hill House drawing room is disparate in design. The combination of dark frame and lighter upholstery—which applied only to the seat furniture—provided a link between dark and light elements of the room. The large dark-stained couch with high back and sides (probably elongated to offer protection from draughts) contrasted with the light, almost delicate ebonised armchairs based on the white ones at Kingsborough Gardens. The black-lacquered, high-backed desk chair was more open than the couch or armchair and, with its play on squares and rectangles, more obviously reliant on geometry for effect.

In 1905 Mackintosh designed an easy chair, presumably to replace the period wooden armchair belonging to Walter Blackie (owner of The Hill House) seen in early photographs of the drawing room. Reminiscent of work by the German designer Richard Riemerschmid, this angular and somewhat

172. Charles Rennie Mackintosh. *Table*, 1908. For the drawing room, The Hill House. Sycamore, lacquered black, with mother-of-pearl inlay, 25$^1/_{16}$ x 26$^{15}/_{16}$ x 26$^3/_4$ in. (63.6 x 68.5 x 68.0 cm). The National Trust for Scotland.

squat "masculine" form had an ebonised frame, but it also had light-coloured upholstery in velvet, a material associated with the luxurious, the sensuous, and the feminine. We do not know exactly which pieces were intended to be placed in this fireplace area, but—despite recent evidence that the decorative stencilling was more subtle and pervasive than previously imagined—this area appears to have achieved less unity of effect than the window seating area.[24] The drawing room at The Hill House is one Mackintosh interior where the sum of the parts adds up to an impressive but less than unified whole.

Besides the seating, the room contained two fine pieces of cabinet furniture: an ebonised writing cabinet (plates 174 and 175) inlaid with mother-of-pearl, metal, and glass (which so pleased the Mackintoshes that they had a similar one made for their own use) and an ebonised cabinet inlaid with squares of mother-of-pearl and stained sycamore and with glazed upper doors leaded in squares. When the doors of the writing cabinet were open, the mother-of-pearl squares (composed of smaller squares) that punctuated the inside of the doors combined with the inlay over the interior arches to form a pattern across the top of the cabinet. The centrepiece of the cabinet is a panel with an inverted heart or bulb shape adorned with a tiny heart and stylised flowers, buds, leaves, dewdrops, and falling petals—the latter echoed in carved form near the top of the cabinet legs.

The cabinet made for the Mackintoshes' own use differed from that at The Hill House only in that fruitwood was used instead of mother-of-pearl for the inlay, the central section was slightly taller (for the storage of drawings), and the central panel featured a large single rose and falling petals. In that the cabinets are dark and sturdy, they could be classified as "masculine"; but their smooth, clear, and shiny skins suggest the feminine, as do the delicately and deliciously sensuous central panels, which look like beautiful pictures in enormous frames. Part of the symbolism of the cabinet lies in the fact that a dark and mysterious object is opened up to reveal a jewel-like feature, suggesting the hidden nature of female sexuality. The desk is suitable for male or female use; one could imagine either of the Blackies or either of the Mackintoshes at such a desk. Yet the complex dialectic between user and object would surely be different in each case; it would be a very different matter for a man to unlock a cabinet to reveal a sensuous inner jewel than it would be for a woman to do the same.

▪▪ ABOVE
173. Charles Rennie Mackintosh. The drawing room, Hous'hill. Photographed by T. and R. Annan Ltd., c. 1904. The piano is behind a white-painted screen with insets of coloured glass.

▪▪ OPPOSITE, TOP
174. Charles Rennie Mackintosh. *Design for a Writing Cabinet*, 1904. For The Hill House. Pencil and watercolour, 11⅝ x 17¼ in. (29.4 x 43.9 cm). Hunterian Art Gallery, University of Glasgow.

▪▪ OPPOSITE, BOTTOM
175. Charles Rennie Mackintosh. *Writing Cabinet*, 1904. For The Hill House. Ebonised oak, with ivory-and-mother-of-pearl inlay, glass insets, metal fitments, and a leaded-glass-and-metal panel, 44⅜ x 37 (71⅜ open) x 18⅜ in. (112.6 x 94.0 [181.2 open] x 46.7 cm). Private collection.

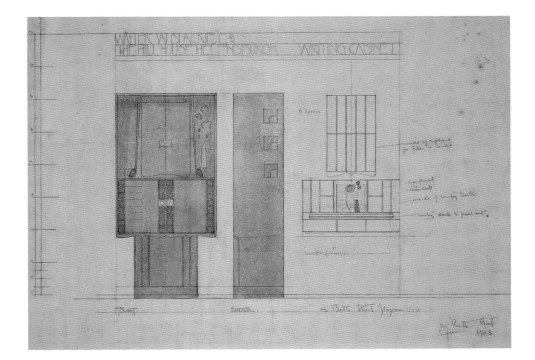

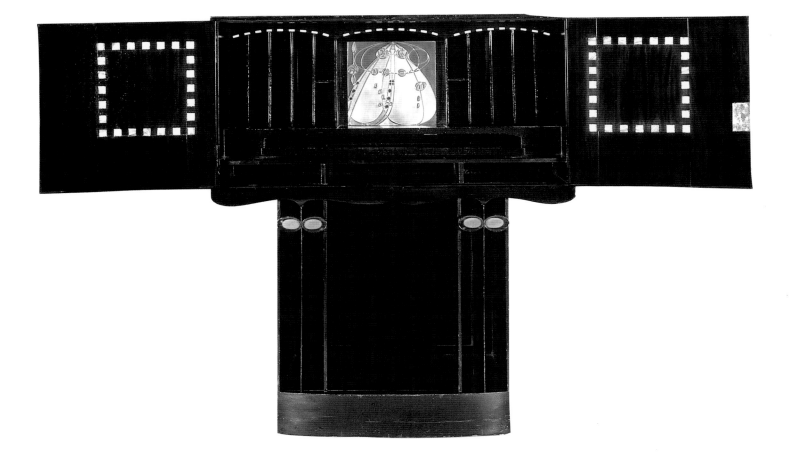

■ ABOVE
176. Charles Rennie Mackintosh.
The principal bedroom, The Hill
House.
■ OPPOSITE
177. Charles Rennie Mackintosh.
The wardrobes and a black (ebonised)
ladderback chair with upholstered
seat in the principal
bedroom.

Only three dark pieces were designed for the principal white bedroom at The Hill House (see plate 130): a stool and the two black, very elongated, and very mannered ladderback chairs, the top "rungs" of which form part of a lattice pattern (plates 176 and 177). These stark and startling designs dramatically accentuate the whiteness of the rest of the room and help highlight the geometric elements of a decorative scheme that fuses the organic and the geometric. One of the two chairs—which stands between two white fitted wardrobes decorated with elongated and stylised carved organic flowers with coloured-glass inserts—is more closely integrated into the complex patterning of the room. Its "trellis" back forms the central panel of three panels in the alcove between the wardrobes. The other two are rose-and-trellis wall stencils that, in turn, complement the design on the rugs. Taken together, the chair and the wardrobes emphasise the verticality of that section of the wall design, as opposed to the more horizontal feel of the seating alcove next to the fireplace.

It has been argued that the combination of the rose motif with the lattice marks a shift away from the feminine,[25] presumably because the rigidly geometric lattice is seen as masculine, although it is also open and light. However, if one takes the lattice as masculine, then is the feminine motif (the rose) not *more* feminised by being designed to cling to a trellis and more sexualised by being intertwined with a male motif? Different versions of stylised flowers and petals link the wardrobes, the washstand, the fireplace, the upholstery of the seating alcove, and the curtains to the wall stencils; trellis or geometric grids link the ladderback chairs, the bedhead panels, the washstand, the cheval mirror, and the rugs. The geometric predominates over the organic, and the eye is constantly caught by different permutations of lines that form squares and rectangles, not all of which are necessarily in harmony with each other. This room is a curious mix of harmony and disruption. The soft white, pink, green, and grey colour scheme is peaceful; the bed was originally adorned with embroidered hangings of dreaming women. Yet at the same time disruption results from the contrasts caused by the black ladderbacks in the white room and also from the competing squares and rectangles of different sizes.[26]

What then of the gendering of the furniture in this Mackintosh interior generally regarded as one of his most "feminine"? The geometric white wardrobes, which are part of the wall furniture, act less as masculine forms than as a plain backdrop for the elegant flower forms, which might also be the heads (roses), bodies (the rectangles composed of ten squares), legs, and feet (the edging of joining mouldings) of female or androgynous figures. These white wardrobes are altogether more solid and bulkily masculine than the dark chair that sits between them, which is more delicate and emaciated than any other piece of furniture in the room. If the top square of the chair back is read as a head and the painfully thin "ladder" as the ribs of a body, this chair comes as close as Mackintosh furniture ever gets to resembling the anorexic women in the work of Margaret and Frances Macdonald. However black and severe its form may be, the chair's lightness, delicacy, openness, and slenderness all work to characterise it as feminine, and the tensions between its "masculine" and "feminine" elements greatly add to the interest of this mannered and stylish piece of furniture.

THE VIENNESE INFLUENCE

The white bedroom designed by Mackintosh in 1903–4 for the exhibition presented by Dresdener Werkstätten für Handwerkskunst (Dresden Workshops for Arts and Crafts) was more harmonious, unified, and uniformly geometric than the one at The Hill House (plate 178). The predominant decorative motif was the square, used singly or in groups to form other squares—as in the back of a high-backed white chair that makes the black one at The Hill House look positively robust. It may well be that the Mackintoshes' awareness of the popularity of more severely geometric form in progressive design circles in

Germany and Austria encouraged their greater emphasis on the right angle as opposed to the curve. (The contemporaneous work at Hous'hill, from late 1903 to 1904, indicates less commitment to the Vienna Secession style.)

Their greater emphasis, at Dresden, on geometric form (particularly the right angle and the square) raises the important issue of the relationship between the Mackintoshes' work and the Vienna Secession. Central to this issue is a consideration of the commission for 78 Derngate, Northampton, England (1916–19), in which Austrian influences are strong (plates 179 and 181). We still do not know precisely how and when knowledge of new developments in design spread in Europe and the United States at the turn of the century, although the role of progressive magazines was undoubtedly important. We know something about the connections between the Mackintoshes and Viennese and German designers, critics, and patrons, but the picture is far from complete. In Britain scholars have tended to view Mackintosh as the originator of the cross-fertilization between Glasgow and Vienna, but Billcliffe's claim that "the increasing appearance of geometrical motifs in the Secessionists' designs was inspired by Mackintosh" has been challenged by Eduard

178. Charles Rennie Mackintosh. *A Bedroom: Fireplace Wall Elevation*, c. 1903. For a Dresdener Werkstätten für Handwerkskunst exhibition. Pencil and watercolour, 13³⁄₁₆ x 20¹⁄₄ in. (33.4 x 51.3 cm). Hunterian Art Gallery, University of Glasgow.

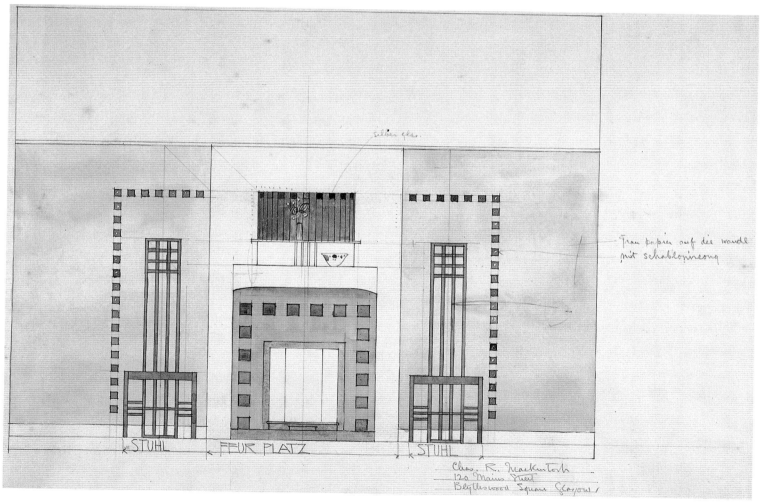

Sekler.[27] What is clear is that from 1903 on, Mackintosh's designs increasingly revealed the stylistic influence of the Viennese art- and design-reform movement generally known as the Vienna Secession.

Given the Mackintoshes' close contact with Vienna from 1900 and the considerable influence of certain Viennese designs on those of Mackintosh in the years 1916–19, one might ask why the influence was not more intense sooner and why it was at its strongest a decade and more after the first major impact of the Vienna Secession in Britain. For those progressive designers in Britain who did not already know about the Vienna Secession from German-language illustrated magazines or from word of mouth during the years 1899–1903, the English-language magazine the *Studio* featured Austrian cane furniture in the Secession style in January 1904. At least one piece of this furniture was copied in Scotland and, at some time, painted black.[28] There was sufficient interest in Austrian art and design for the *Studio* to publish a special issue, *The Art-Revival in Austria*, in 1906, by which date the work was reasonably well known to anyone with a serious interest in interior or furniture design.

What is fascinating about the Derngate designs of 1916–19 is that, of all the Mackintosh designs, these are the ones that most closely resemble the work illustrated in that special edition—far more than his work made between 1906 and 1911. Mackintosh had few opportunities to design either interiors or furniture after 1911, and it is impossible to guess whether the Derngate lounge hall (1916; see plates 144 and 179) and guest bedroom (1919; plate 181) would have been quite so strongly "Secessionist" in style had it not been for the admiration of the client, W. J. Bassett-Lowke, for Austrian and German design.

The Viennese influences are discussed below, but the Derngate designs should also be seen against the continuing influence of the Arts and Crafts movement, including the more exotic furniture produced in the early twentieth century by Ernest Gimson and others, which featured contrasts of dark and light materials, geometric forms, and lattice patterns. Furthermore, as might be expected of Bassett-Lowke, who was a prominent member of the Design and Industries Association (DIA)—which favoured "fitness for purpose" and simple, "rational" designs as well as the infusing of the modern with some of the best practices of the traditional—the neo-Georgian revival was not without influence.[29] The latter was revealed not only in the restrained classicism of some of the Derngate furniture but also in the touches of chinoiserie.

Mackintosh's earlier Chinese Room, designed in 1911 for the Ingram Street tea rooms (see plate 197), had marked the beginning of a particularly exotic episode in his design work. Colourful geometric motifs had been used in the Glasgow School of Art library in 1909, but they had been restricted to the scalloped edges of the gallery balusters. Thereafter, colour came to dominate and dazzle in certain interiors. In the Chinese Room a fantasy environment was created within the existing interior by erecting a wooden latticework structure, complete with "roof." With more concern for spectacle than for

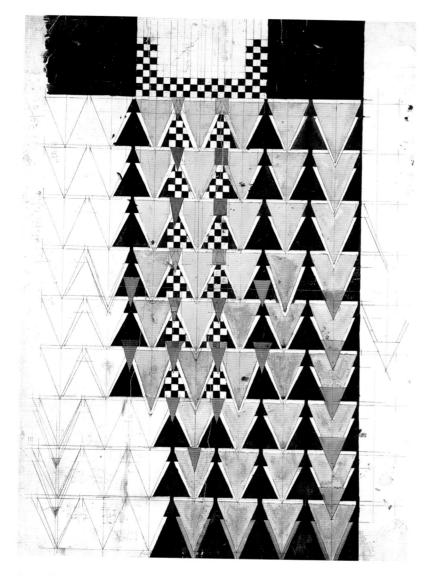

authenticity, this structure was painted bright blue. Pagoda-style finials decorated one of the screens, but the rectangular pay desk relied as much on the repetition of the square as it did on fretwork and "Chinese" beams for decorative effect. Also painted blue, the desk provided a link between the latticework structure and the elegant black-lacquered Chinese-style chairs with fretted backs, whose design featured rectangles and squares. Like the Salon de Luxe at the Willow Tea Rooms, this was a highly theatrical room, a make-believe stage-set for Glasgow's middle class.

In 1917 the same client, Kate Cranston, called upon Mackintosh to work his magic on another interior, this one patriotically named the Dug-Out (in reference to the trenches of World War I) (see plate 199). This dark basement room at the Willow Tea Rooms was painted black, but any reference to the gloom of the trenches ended there. The focal point was a memorial fireplace, decorated with inlaid glass and paintings of flags, which stood beneath a

179. Charles Rennie Mackintosh. *Design for Stencilled Mural Decoration,* 1916. For the lounge hall, 78 Derngate, Northampton, England. Pencil and watercolour, 31 1/2 x 22 1/4 in. (80.0 x 56.5 cm). Hunterian Art Gallery, University of Glasgow.

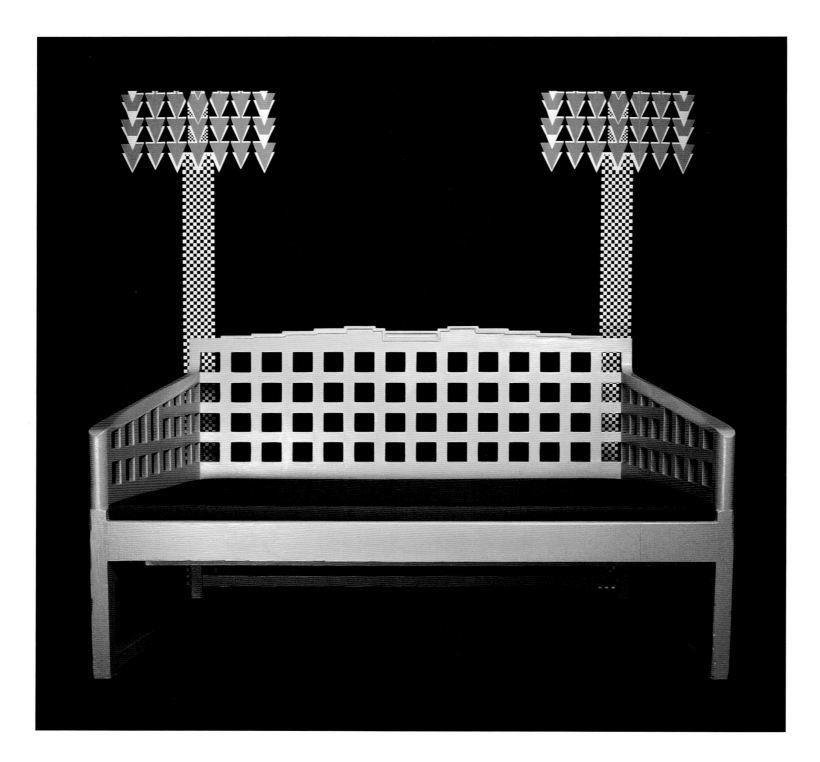

brightly coloured decorative panel of triangles, diamonds, and cheques in red, blue, and green. The rest of the room was equally exotic; a square-lattice wooden settee (plate 180) was painted bright yellow and upholstered in purple (the cushion was trimmed with green) and set against wall decorations of thin vertical black-and-white stripes, thin blue horizontal stripes on black, and bright red and green triangles. Once again, the wall ensemble reveals Mackintosh at his most freely inventive. Although one "decidedly conventional" small, painted, wooden, bobbin-turned table is almost indistinguishable from the "period" Jacobean-style tables produced in large numbers in the commercial trade, the alternation of small cubes with bobbins on one of the other tables indicates Mackintosh's ability to update and transform a conventional piece of furniture into something that amuses the mind and delights the eye.[30]

The Dug-Out drew on the darkly dramatic and colourful design for the hall at Derngate, designed a year earlier, which took to extremes the conventional dark-male coding of such a room but then played extremely clever games with the decoration. At Derngate the latticework settee was painted black, as were the room itself and the chairs therein (the backs of which referred both to the traditional ladderback and to a lattice of squares).[31] This potentially sombre scheme was enlivened by a multitude of small patches of colour. Some of the solid panels in the black square-latticed staircase screen were filled with geometric shapes (squares, triangles, and chevrons) in yellow and clear glass. Gold, grey, blue, green, vermilion, and white were used in the frieze (plate 179) that bordered the black walls and that was divided vertically at regular intervals by thin strips of black-and-white chequerwork. The resultant patterns have been likened to stylised trees (as at the Willow Tea Rooms), but they also suggest thin, sticklike people with all-seeing eyes. These androgynous (and, as at the Willow, almost robotic) stencil images and the dazzling jewel-like decoration shatter the male sobriety of the hall. So, too, is the male coding of the smoker's cabinet tempered, if not disguised, by its colourful decorative plastic inlay, which transforms something ordinary into something exotic.

With its door screen of black lacquered wood and purple and yellow silk panels, the hall would have made the perfect setting for a masquerade; it doubled as a living area and as a setting for domestic entertainments. As a place dedicated to social discourse and relaxation, however, it was a far cry from the light and delicate Mackintosh living rooms of earlier years. It is difficult to tell how well it fulfilled its hybrid function of hall and living area, but the green-painted standard lamp, the only item of furniture not painted black and the one that most clearly signals domesticity, looks curiously out of place.

The furniture in the main bedroom at Derngate was quite different, comprising fairly severely rectilinear, "modern," and "rational" versions of traditional items of the sort endorsed by the DIA. The sharp vertical edges were highlighted by a simple black inlay, but revealing the delicate grain of the

180. Charles Rennie Mackintosh. *Settee,* 1917. For the Dug-Out, Willow Tea Rooms. Wood, repainted yellow, 31¼ x 53¹⁵⁄₁₆ x 27¾ in. (79.5 x 137.0 x 70.4 cm). Glasgow School of Art.

181. Charles Rennie Mackintosh. *Bedroom Furniture*, 1919. For the guest bedroom, 78 Derngate; seen here in a reconstructed room setting at the Hunterian Art Gallery. Oak with painted edging. Hunterian Art Gallery, University of Glasgow.

sycamore and staining it grey to match the wallpaper reduced the severity. The furniture, the grey walls, and the mauve edging suggest a relaxing room—possibly as relaxing as the white bedrooms of earlier years. The furniture in the guest bedroom was also severely rectilinear but much darker, being made in mahogany. It was also even more modern looking, with inset squares of mother-of-pearl and aluminium—the latter material relatively new to furniture making and associated with the Viennese avant-garde.

It was the redesign of this guest bedroom three years later, in 1919, that produced Mackintosh's most exotic and most Viennese-influenced bedroom design (plate 181). It was also his last commission for furniture and interior design. Like the hall, the bedroom took the theatricality of certain tea-room interiors into the domestic sphere. On a room conventionally coded as feminine, Mackintosh unleashed a strongly masculine design that included a bold, almost overpowering, partial enclosure of black-and-white stripes edged and

decorated with bright ultramarine. The striking pattern runs up the wall behind the beds and over the ceiling, forming a two-dimensional canopy over the bed before continuing to the window wall, where the curtains take the vertical stripes down to the windowsill. The colour scheme was continued in the bedspreads, which, like the curtains, had edgings of emerald green. For the furniture of this predominantly black-and-white scheme, neither black nor white nor even a complementary or contrasting colour was chosen. A light oak was used, and the warm tones of the revealed grain provided an effective contrast to the cool black, white, and blue scheme. The wood, the high standard of craftsmanship, and the restraint of the design all signify quality and a sensitive blend of more traditional forms, materials, techniques, and values with modern ones.

The ultramarine silk upholstery on the seat furniture provides one link between the wall decoration and the oak furniture, and the painted small blue

182. Josef Urban (1872–1933). Boudoir with walls of purple silk and mahogany inlaid with mother-of-pearl, Vienna, c. 1905–6. From *The Art-Revival in Austria*, special number of the *Studio* (1906), plate C59.

squares on the black strip edging provide another. The horizontal rails of the oak chairs contrast with the verticality of the black-and-white stripes, while both horizontals and verticals feature in the cutout squares on the beds and the square lattice design of the stool. This is a bold and assured room design. The excess is beautifully contained—or is it? There are odd moments when the eye is literally dazzled.[32]

Mackintosh's use of stripes and small geometric motifs on wooden furniture owes a great deal to the Vienna Secession, particularly to the work of Hans Ofner, Robert Orley, Otto Prutscher, Josef Urban, and Otto Wagner. Wagner's designs for the dining room in his own apartment at 3, Kostlergasse, Vienna, in 1898 included striped wall hangings that complemented the plasterwork on the ceiling. Also designed for that room was a walnut cabinet inlaid with mother-of-pearl circles arranged in straight lines to add vertical emphasis. Illustrated in *Ver Sacrum* in 1900, the year the Mackintoshes visited Vienna, these designs would surely have been known to them. Wagner's more elaborate decoration on an armchair in oak, which involved mother-of-pearl and aluminium used in thin strips and small circles, was possibly a source for some of Gimson's more exotic furniture, particularly his ecclesiastical furniture in ebony inlaid with ivory for Roker Church, Sunderland, 1906, and St. Andrew's Chapel, Westminster Cathedral, London, 1914.[33] Gimson, who also used bold chevron designs, fielded panels, and string inlay and designed lattice-backed settees, may have been a source for this later Mackintosh work, and at the very least the Derngate designs should be seen within the context of the late Arts and Crafts movement as well as the Vienna Secession.[34] Both Mackintosh and Gimson must have known the bedroom suite with fielded panels in elmwood inlaid with mahogany and ebony designed by Otto Prutscher and illustrated in the 1906 special edition of the *Studio*. That volume also featured interiors by Josef Urban that appear to have influenced those of Mackintosh for Derngate. The three most important were a boudoir with walls of purple silk and panels of vertical stripes of mahogany and mahogany furniture inlaid with mother-of-pearl (plate 182); a library with triangles on the fireplace and down the front legs of the flanking armchairs; and a dining room decorated with triangular inlay and patterning (see plate 143). The designs produced for the Derngate commission show that, despite having not designed any interiors or furniture for five years, Mackintosh had lost none of his inventive eclecticism. He remained able to draw upon a wide range of sources while reaching far beyond them to produce aesthetically powerful interiors and furniture of individuality.

NOTES

I was delighted to be asked to contribute to this catalogue but acutely aware that any scholar would need to draw heavily on the work of Roger Billcliffe and Alan Crawford. I would like to acknowledge those debts and thank them both. I am particularly grateful to Alan Crawford for his constant courtesies, help, and encouragement throughout this and other projects and to Wendy Kaplan, Pamela Robertson, Juliet Kinchin, Janice Helland, and Annette Carruthers for their help in the preparation of this chapter.

1. See Roger Billcliffe, *Charles Rennie Mackintosh: The Complete Furniture, Furniture Drawings and Interior Designs*, 3d ed. (London: John Murray, 1986); and Billcliffe, *Mackintosh Furniture* (Moffat, Scotland: Cameron and Hillis, in association with Newton Abbot, England: David and Charles, 1990). I have not cited Billcliffe references for specific pieces of furniture or interiors, which are easy to locate because they are each cited by date.

2. See Janice Helland, "Collaboration among the Glasgow Four," in this volume. See also Pamela Robertson, "Margaret Macdonald Mackintosh (1864–1933)," and Timothy Neat, "Tinker, Tailor, Soldier, Sailor: Margaret Macdonald Mackintosh and the Principle of Choice," both in Jude Burkhauser, ed., *"Glasgow Girls": Women in Art and Design, 1880–1920* (Edinburgh: Canongate, 1990), pp. 109–16 and 117–22, respectively.

3. See David Brett, *C. R. Mackintosh: The Poetics of Workmanship* (London: Reaktion Books, 1992); Juliet Kinchin, "The Gendered Interior: Nineteenth-Century Essays on the 'Masculine' and the 'Feminine' Room," in *The Gendered Object*, ed. Pat Kirkham (Manchester, England: Manchester University Press, 1996, forthcoming); Perilla Kinchin, *Tea and Taste: The Glasgow Tea Rooms, 1875–1975* (Wendlebury, England: White Cockade Publishing, 1991); and Alan Crawford, *Charles Rennie Mackintosh* (London: Thames and Hudson, 1995).

4. I am grateful to Judy Attfield and Beverley Skeggs for discussing this point with me. See Judy Attfield and Pat Kirkham, "Towards the Introduction of Gendered Objects," in *Gendered Object*, ed. Kirkham.

5. Billcliffe, *Mackintosh Furniture*, pp. 28–29.

6. For the Arts and Crafts movement, see Gillian Naylor, *The Arts and Crafts Movement: A Study of Its Sources, Ideals and Influ-ence on Design Theory* (London: Trefoil, 1990); and for the Aesthetic movement, see Mark Girouard, *Sweetness and Light: The "Queen Anne" Movement, 1860–1900* (Oxford: Clarendon Press, 1977); and Elizabeth Aslin, *The Aesthetic Movement* (London: Elek, 1969).

7. For the Austrian and German design-reform movements, see Elizabeth Cumming and Wendy Kaplan, *The Arts and Crafts Movement* (London: Thames and Hudson, 1991), chap. 6.

8. Mackintosh, "Seemliness (1902)," lecture reputedly given to the Northern Art Workers Guild, Manchester, England, on January 6, 1902; in Pamela Robertson, ed., *Charles Rennie Mackintosh: The Architectural Papers* (Wendlebury, England: White Cockade Publishing, 1990), p. 221.

9. Mackintosh, in Robertson, ed., *Architectural Papers*, p. 207.

10. Billcliffe, *Mackintosh Furniture*, p. 14.

11. For Morris and Company, see Paul Thompson, *The Work of William Morris* (London: Quartet Books, 1977), especially pp. 91–93. The chest of drawers is illustrated in Mary Comino, *Gimson and the Barnsleys: "Wonderful Furniture of a Commonplace Kind"* (London: Evans Brothers, 1980), p. 53, fig. 26.

12. For Heal, see Susanna Gooden, *A History of Heal's* (London: Heal and Son, 1984), pp. 20–35.

13. Billcliffe, *Mackintosh Furniture*, p. 14.

14. Like Mackintosh, Voysey had not produced much furniture by 1893. David Gebhard, *Charles F. A. Voysey, Architect* (Los Angeles: Hennessey and Ingalls, 1975), pp. 98–99, illustrates two fireplaces with heart shapes, both dating from about 1890, and two designs for hinges that terminate in what approximates a heart shape similar to that adopted by Mackintosh. *British Architect* published Voysey designs for strap hinges in 1892, and Mackintosh probably saw them there.

15. Billcliffe, *Mackintosh Furniture*, p. 14.

16. Gebhard, *Voysey*, p. 17. Mackintosh had exhibited at the Arts and Crafts Exhibition held in Glasgow in 1895.

17. Billcliffe, *Mackintosh Furniture*, p. 17.

18. *Builder*, October 17, 1896, p. 301.

19. Another interesting hybrid is the large dark-stained high-backed oak armchair with wings. The most solid—and therefore most "masculine"—of the Argyle Street chairs, it has an elegance and cosiness appropriate to the ladies' reading room for which it was designed.

20. Crawford, *Mackintosh*, p. 70.

21. Ibid., p. 86.

22. Ibid., p. 96.

23. I asked twenty different people to "read" these abstract forms, and these were the results.

24. See Anne Ellis, "Recovery of the Original Drawing Room Scheme in The Hill House," *Charles Rennie Mackintosh Society Newsletter* 65 (autumn 1994): 6–7.

25. Billcliffe, *Mackintosh Furniture*, p. 123.

26. There are squares of 5 x 5 units (the ladderback chair and the larger rug), 21 x 21 (the central panel of the washstand within which the rose is set), 3 x 3 (the cheval mirror and the central panel of the larger rug), and 2 x 2 (the cheval mirror and the square table), as well as rectangles of 3 x 5 (the smaller rug), 1 x 3 (the central panel of the smaller rug), and 2 x 5 (the fitted wardrobes).

27. Billcliffe, *Mackintosh Furniture*, p. 69; and Eduard Sekler, *Josef Hoffmann: The Architectural Work* (Princeton, N.J.: Princeton University Press, 1985), p. 508 n. 37.

28. Gerald Larner and Celia Larner, *The Glasgow Style* (Edinburgh: Astragal Books, 1979), pl. 19. See also Pat Kirkham, "Willow and Cane Furniture in Austria, Germany and England, c. 1900–14," *Furniture History* 21 (1985): 127–33.

29. For the DIA, see Pat Kirkham, *Harry Peach Dryad and the DIA* (London: Design Council, 1986).

30. Billcliffe, *Mackintosh Furniture*, p. 208.

31. For Derngate, see Janet Bassett-Lowke and Alan Crawford, *C. R. Mackintosh: The Chelsea Years, 1915–1923* (Glasgow: Hunterian Art Gallery, University of Glasgow, 1994).

32. For a version of the frequently and variously quoted story of George Bernard Shaw's visit to Derngate, when he stayed in that room, see Gavin Stamp, "The London Years," in this volume.

33. See Charles Holme, ed., *The Art-Revival in Austria*, special number of the *Studio* (1906), pl. 32; and Comino, *Gimson and the Barnsleys*, pp. 177–78. The extent to which some of the Prutscher furniture in the 1906 volume resembles a type and design favoured by Gimson brings to the fore the complexities of the international cross-references in design at this time. It was only a few years later that W. R. Lethaby, the grand old man of the British Arts and Crafts movement, noted, in reply to statements about the supremacy of German design in terms of machine products, that there were a lot of Gimsons working in Germany.

34. Holme, ed., *Art-Revival in Austria*, pls. C53–64, especially pls. C53–C54 (Prutscher) and C57–58 (Urban).

The Tea Rooms: Art and Domesticity

■■
ALAN CRAWFORD

Mackintosh is famous for his tea rooms, and he deserves to be. The Willow Tea Rooms in Sauchiehall Street were among his most original buildings and the most complete in their scheme of decoration and furniture. In the Salon de Luxe, the inner sanctum of the Willow, the waitresses even wore chokers and dresses designed by Mackintosh.[1] If they were still flourishing as tea rooms in their original state, the Willow Tea Rooms would stand beside Glasgow School of Art and The Hill House as one of a trio of Mackintosh masterpieces.[2] And they were only the finest of a dozen or so tea-room interiors that Mackintosh worked on between 1896 and 1917. With one unimportant exception, they were all designed for one client, Kate Cranston, who provided Mackintosh with a steady flow of commissions over two decades, including the difficult years when he had almost no other work coming in.[3]

Mackintosh was a consummate stylist, and most of the writing about him is concerned with style, and style alone. But his tea rooms, which were spread over most of his career and belong to a specialised building type, provide an opportunity to look at him in a different way. Although this essay presents Mackintosh's tea rooms in chronological order and tells a stylistic story, it also takes account of the building type—the tea room as a place of public refreshment.

EATING OUT IN LATE VICTORIAN BRITAIN

A visitor to London's Great Exhibition of 1851, seeking something more than the light refreshments sold there, would not have had much to choose from.[4] In the 1850s the capital's most typical places of refreshment were gentlemen's clubs, dining rooms, and public houses. (From the 1860s the latter were known as "pubs.") The clubs were confined to their upper-class members. Dining

183. Charles Rennie Mackintosh. The Ladies' Luncheon Room in the Ingram Street tea rooms, as reconstructed by Glasgow Museums, 1992–95. In the frieze is a beaten-metal panel by Margaret Macdonald Mackintosh (1864–1933), *The Dew*, and a large gesso panel by Mackintosh, *The Wassail.*

184. The restaurant of the Queen's Hotel, Leeds, designed by Charles Trubshaw, architect. Photographed by Bedford Lemere, c. 1900. The walls and servery were clad in Burmantofts faience, a glazed constructional material made by the Leeds Fireclay Company.

rooms were typically long, bare rooms with tables and fixed benches forming compartments down either side, and they served very basic fare—beef, potatoes, and beer.[5] The pubs were almost entirely confined to the working class and sold little besides alcoholic drink. All three were virtually closed to respectable women. Fifty years later, a visitor would have been spoilt for choice.[6] By the turn of the century, the centres of British cities were full of crowds and spectacle, rich in new, specialised building types, and geared to consumption.

Restaurants on the French model, serving the middle class, were the earliest of the new places of refreshment. Simpson's Grand Divan Restaurant in the Strand, opened in 1848, was the first substantial restaurant in London. The Criterion at Piccadilly Circus, opened in 1874, was arguably the best appointed; the timidest lady, it was said, might eat in its east room.[7] The restaurant of the Queen's Hotel in Leeds (plate 184) shows the difference from the old dining rooms. The walls are richly decorated; the tables are laid with clean linen and plated cutlery; and compartments have been replaced by separate tables freely arranged around the room.

Since the old compartments were often shared by people who might, at least at first, have been complete strangers to each other, the new arrangement of separate tables created a different kind of social space: the table was more

segregated and private, the room more public and open. This suited a middle class that was both drawn apart into family units and drawn together for public display. Restaurants of this kind could be found in all British cities by 1900, though their early development outside London is hard to trace, for lack of research.[8]

The origins of cafés and tea shops, serving light refreshments and non-alcoholic drinks, are also difficult to discover. They were a little beneath the attention of the architectural press, and no one has brought the research and insight of Perilla Kinchin's *Tea and Taste: The Glasgow Tea Rooms, 1875–1975* to bear on any other British city.[9] They probably began to be common in the 1880s and 1890s. Middle-class cafés were sometimes much like restaurants, but lighter and less formal. The Vienna Café (plate 185), opened near the British Museum in about 1885, had a Continental air, with bentwood chairs, piles of cakes and chocolate, and newspapers, chess, and billiards to encourage customers to linger.[10]

For the working class there were many small dining rooms where you could get steak pudding and potatoes for fivepence, with tea at a penny or a penny-halfpenny.[11] These were supplemented when the Aerated Bread Company, established in 1862, began to open cafés-cum-bakeries in and around the City of London; it had about sixty by 1893.[12] They were fitted out more plainly than middle-class cafés, and the food was plainer too; tea came ready mixed with milk at the ABC.[13] Then, between 1894 and 1898, J. Lyons and Co. opened the first sixteen of their tea shops, with standard shop fronts in white and gold. Inside, the decorations were more French than English, with marble-topped tables, red plush seats, silk damask on the walls, and waitresses in grey uniforms; and the menu was lighter and more sophisticated.[14] *The Caterer and Hotel-Keepers' Gazette* reported of Lyons's first tea shop at 213 Piccadilly: "The whole appearance of the place reminds one of a high-class café in Paris or Brussels, so lavish and tasteful are the fittings."[15] Partly by operating economies of scale, Lyons brought restaurant sophistication within reach of the respectable working class.

These new places of refreshment reflected changes in British cities and society. City centres were increasingly places of middle-class resort, with new theatres, museums, exhibitions, shops, and department stores—places where eating out was a ritual of bourgeois pleasure. Not by accident was the Criterion at Piccadilly Circus, arguably the finest of London's late Victorian restaurants, only a stone's throw from the Royal Academy, the Geological Museum, and the shops of Regent Street. At the same time, a large number of the workers who travelled in from increasingly distant suburbs needed to buy lunch in the middle of the day, and many of these—respectable artisans, clerks, and shop assistants—would not look to the pub for refreshment. And women were increasingly a normal part of this urban crowd, whether for the sake of work or pleasure. The centre of cities had become both safer and more desirable for women. In 1902 the author of *The Night Side of London* reported, "Men don't dine at their clubs nowadays; they go with their wives or the wives of others to partake of the Restaurant Dinner."[16]

The temperance movement was important, not so much for the temperance coffee houses, which were opened in the 1870s and 1880s as alternatives to the demon drink (most of them did not last long), but for the many commercial undertakings that, without strict temperance principles, exploited the new respectability of nonalcoholic drink. It was said that Joe Lyons, of tea-shop fame, "did more for the cause of temperance than almost anyone," including the temperance reformers themselves.[17] A significant number of cafés belonged to chains such as Lyons's, which were often run by catering companies that distributed factory-made food from central depots. To this extent, the new refreshment rooms were also part of the late Victorian retailing revolution.

Two aspects of late Victorian catering are of particular interest in relation to the tea rooms Mackintosh designed for Kate Cranston. One is a sense of conflict or tension. An element of parade is often part of eating out. Setting out separate tables across an open room preserved the immediate privacy of a family or group of friends while allowing them to see others and to be seen, thereby creating tension between private and public. Some features, such as clean linen and plated cutlery, echoed the standards of a middle-class household, offering the reassurance of being at home, in known social territory. Other features, usually the interior decoration, created surroundings whose attraction was precisely that they were grander or stranger than the middle-class home. The more sumptuous, exotic, or novel the decoration, the more it underlined the excitement of eating out. Another tension, therefore, was between domesticity and excitement. These conflicts arose from the experience of a dominant, moralising, and domestically oriented middle class enjoying itself away from home. They hold the key to understanding much of the architecture, layout, and interior decoration of restaurants and cafés.

The second aspect is the role of tiles in places of public refreshment. The walls of restaurants and cafés were often covered with tiles, usually the richly glazed, coloured, and modelled type known then as "majolica ware," or with similarly glazed terracotta, known as "faience." Sometimes wall paintings would be incorporated within the tile scheme. Much of this can be seen in plate 184.[18] Not only were these tiles useful, because they could be washed easily, but they also had important meanings. They signified "away from home," since majolica ware was hardly ever used in houses. They fell on the side of excitement rather than domesticity.

They also signified "artistic." In 1865 the South Kensington Museum (now the Victoria and Albert) commissioned artists to decorate a suite of refreshment rooms in the museum. The middle room, now the Gamble Room, was designed by Godfrey Sykes, James Gamble, and Reuben Townroe in a Renaissance manner and decorated with stained glass, mirrors, and tilework of several kinds, but overwhelmingly of white-and-yellow majolica ware. The Grill Room was designed by the painter Edward Poynter and decorated with panelling to the lower walls, the panels inset with tiles painted blue in the Dutch manner (the room was sometimes known as the Dutch Kitchen in consequence); the upper walls were covered with tile paintings of maidens symbolising the seasons and the months.[19]

The point is not that the Gamble Room and the Grill Room influenced later places of refreshment, let alone those designed by Mackintosh, though they may have done; it is that, by their early date and their location in the South Kensington Museum, they created an association between tiles and art that can be felt over and over again in late Victorian places of refreshment.

In these places, which were characterised by tension, art was a liberator. It answered to, and perhaps to some degree resolved, the tension between domesticity and excitement. It was unusual, elevated, something you went to an art gallery to see. And yet, especially during the 1870s and 1880s when the Aesthetic movement was at its height, it was closely associated with women and the domestic world; art and the home were made into a woman's realm. It does not come as a surprise that the tiles in the Grill Room at the South Kensington Museum were painted by middle-class ladies, students at the National Art Training School nearby (later the Royal College of Art). It does not matter that Mackintosh hardly ever used tiles in his tea-room interiors. What matters is the kind of art he used instead of tiles, to resolve the tensions characteristic of places of public refreshment.

THE GLASGOW TEA ROOMS

Glasgow's catering history followed the British pattern. Restaurants appeared in the 1860s, tea rooms flourished in the 1880s and 1890s.[20] ("Tea rooms" was the common Glasgow name for places of light refreshment that might elsewhere be called cafés, tea shops, refreshment rooms, coffee shops, coffee houses, or, indeed, tea rooms.) In fact, Glasgow's very peculiarities made the city typical in catering history. The temperance movement was strong, as one would expect in a Presbyterian city with a reputation for hard drinking. The food industry was also strong: late Victorian Glasgow rivalled London in the import and blending of tea and coffee, and there was a tradition of fine, sweet baking. And light refreshments were strong; the lunch rooms where businessmen could take a light meal were famous beyond the city.

The Glasgow tea rooms have a clear starting date. In 1875 Stuart Cranston, a retailer of dry tea, set out tables for sixteen customers in his sample room at 2 Queen Street and advertised a cup of tea for twopence, with "bread and cakes extra."[21] Three years later his sister Kate opened the Crown Tea Rooms at 114 Argyle Street, serving lunches as well as teas. For ten years after that, only a few tea rooms appeared. But Glasgow's International Exhibition of 1888 enhanced the sense of spectacle and leisure in the centre of the city, and tea rooms opened in increasing numbers, reaching a peak in 1897. Stuart Cranston, operating as Cranston's Tea Rooms Ltd., ran a chain of six tea rooms by then, but there were also many small, individual premises, often in basements and often run by women.

At first the tea rooms were mostly concentrated in the merchants' quarter, south of George Square and east of Buchanan Street, but in the 1890s they spread westwards, perhaps drawn by the new department stores around Sauchiehall Street. These newer tea rooms were just as likely to cater for women as for men and, as Perilla Kinchin has written, "it was really the deftness with which the tea rooms met the separate needs of both men and women that wove them so inextricably into the fabric of middle-class life."[22] Places of refreshment in other cities were, perhaps, less evenhanded.[23]

The larger tea rooms were usually divided into lunch rooms—serving substantial food such as cooked meats, fried fish, ham and eggs—and tea rooms, where the basic fare was tea, coffee, or cocoa. This was plain, cheap food, but the tea rooms were proud of the quality of their cooking. General eating rooms, where men and women ate together, were common, but there might also be rooms that catered for each sex, men's lunch rooms, ladies' tea rooms, and so on, as well as the traditional male preserves of billiard rooms and smoking rooms.

Some tea rooms were laid out and decorated in a conventional manner. Stuart Cranston's premises at 28 Buchanan Street, opened in 1889, had a long, austerely decorated room for men and women, with tables in three rows, against the walls and down the middle, almost like a mid-Victorian dining room.[24] But others, especially the westward tea rooms that catered for women, were decorated according to the latest fashions in the decorative arts. Miss Cranston's Ingram Street tea rooms of 1886 (plate 186) had tables in rows against the walls, but the decorative scheme included wallpaper, a stencilled frieze, a modelled sunburst on the ceiling, stained glass, and ornate gasoliers—all in the style of the Aesthetic movement. The vocabulary of these artistic tea rooms was domestic: panelling, stencilled friezes, and fireplaces such as might have come from a middle-class house; male rooms decorated in dark tones, female in light, according to the domestic code; loose carpets and chequered tablecloths; vases of fresh flowers. In this respect, Glasgow's artistic tea rooms struck a different note from places of refreshment in London, and perhaps elsewhere. They operated between the poles of domesticity and excitement, but they came down firmly on the domestic side.[25] Where a Lyons's tea shop in London offered marble-topped tables and waitresses in grey uniforms, the luxury of the unfamiliar, Glasgow offered homely waitresses and chequered tablecloths.

186. Miss Cranston's tea rooms, Ingram Street, Glasgow, decorated in 1886. From *Miss Cranston's*, a brochure published in 1898 or later, p. [28].

The small, energetic, and upright figure of Kate Cranston stood at the head of the feminine/artistic/domestic tradition in Glasgow tea rooms. She wore odd hats, and her clothes were deliberately about thirty years out of date, but she was not just an eccentric. She was a hardworking, independent-minded businesswoman, who knew the power of interior decoration. In 1878 she opened her first tea rooms, at 114 Argyle Street. In 1886 she opened a tea room at 205 Ingram Street, in the merchants' quarter. And in 1888 she added a lunch room at 209 Ingram Street and redecorated her original rooms in Argyle Street. For the Ingram Street rooms she used established decorators working broadly in the manner of the Aesthetic movement; but she put the redecoration of Argyle Street in the hands of a young unknown, George Walton, whose light, spriggy decorations were in tune with the latest Arts and Crafts taste.

Tea Rooms by Mackintosh

In 1895–97 Kate Cranston built large new tea rooms at 91–93 Buchanan Street, Glasgow's most prestigious shopping street.[26] The building was designed by George Washington Browne, and most of the interior decoration and furniture was designed by George Walton. Mackintosh was invited to design mural decorations on three floors at the back of the building. He had scarcely done any mural decoration before, and we do not know why he was chosen. But he had designed posters on a similar scale, and Cranston, in her enthusiasm for the latest decorative fashion, may have been attracted by the notoriety that had surrounded the Four when they exhibited in Glasgow in 1894–95.

187. Charles Rennie Mackintosh. *Design for Stencilled Mural Decoration*, 1896. For the lunch gallery, Miss Cranston's tea rooms, Buchanan Street, Glasgow. Pencil and watercolour, 14¼ x 29¾ in. (36.2 x 75.6 cm). Hunterian Art Gallery, University of Glasgow.

The Buchanan Street building was four storeys high and two rooms deep. At the back, on the first floor, was a general lunch room, with a lunch gallery above it and a smoking gallery above that, around four sides of a light well. From the lower gallery you could get a sense of all three floors, and Mackintosh unified his scheme by colouring it green at the bottom, greyish-greenish-yellow in the middle, and blue at the top, suggesting the levels of lower earth, middle earth, and sky.[27] For the lunch room at the bottom, he designed stylised, plantlike forms flanked by peacocks; for the lunch gallery in the middle, haloed women enmeshed in rosebushes with a phallic or plantlike form between them (plate 187); and for the smoking gallery, stylised totem poles and a sun or moon with wavy, cloudlike lines running across them.

How did these designs look to the customers? The top level was straightforward: clouds and totem poles are male whimsy appropriate to a smoking gallery. But the lower designs were much more like the symbolic and slightly scandalous watercolours produced by the Four in the mid-1890s. As such, they probably gave a little shock of the new, as Kate Cranston wanted. But it is hard to believe that they were fully understood. Timothy Neat has argued that the traditional imagery of the middle design signifies "cosmic and human oneness."[28] Would Glaswegians taking tea in 1900 really have grasped such recondite meanings? If they did not, Mackintosh's designs must have quickly become just a puzzling accompaniment to the rituals of eating out.[29] In his first tea-room work, Mackintosh seemed to demonstrate the difference between the world of the tea rooms and the world of his imagination.

About two years later, in 1898–99, Miss Cranston enlarged and redecorated her tea rooms in Argyle Street, which now consisted of the ground-floor premises at 114 Argyle Street, which she had opened in 1878, plus the first, second, third, and attic floors across the whole length of the former tenement block known as 106–14 Argyle Street.[30] The architectural work was by Hugh and David Barclay, the decorations and fitted furniture by Walton, and the new moveable furniture and some of the light fittings by Mackintosh. For the public rooms Mackintosh produced at least sixteen designs for armchairs, settles, stools, tables, hatstands, and dining chairs. Sturdy-looking, simply shaped and constructed, and yet extraordinarily subtle in form, the Argyle Street work marks the beginning of Mackintosh's maturity as a furniture designer.

The most memorable piece was the first of Mackintosh's high-backed chairs. In almost the only surviving views of Argyle Street (plate 188), a group of them stands halfway down the first-floor lunch room, which was punctuated by structural uprights and divided on one side into compartments in the old-fashioned way.[31] The design for the chairs is inscribed "DRAWING OF/CHAIRS FOR/CENTER [sic] TABLES," as if Mackintosh meant them for exactly that spot, to break up the repetitive vista and create a sense of enclosure.[32]

It has been said that the sturdiness of some of the Argyle Street furniture was appropriate because it was used by men.[33] But in fact, all the Argyle Street furniture looks sturdy, and not all of it was designed for men. One of the most massive pieces was an armchair for the ladies' reading room. In her essay in

188. Miss Cranston's tea rooms, Argyle Street, Glasgow. The first-floor lunch room looking west. From the *Studio* 39 (October 1906): 34.

this volume, Pat Kirkham has warned against forcing Mackintosh's furniture into the middle-class code of dark-masculine or light-feminine, and it may be that at Argyle Street, Mackintosh was influenced more by the style of contemporary furniture, and specifically by the ostentatious simplicity of some joiner-made Arts and Crafts furniture.[34]

Mackintosh's work at Buchanan Street and Argyle Street was introductory. Both interiors owed more to Walton than to Mackintosh, and in both Mackintosh seemed slightly at odds with the building type. Around 1900, however, Kate Cranston asked him to design complete new interiors at her Ingram Street tea rooms. This work, which was carried out at the time of his marriage to Margaret Macdonald, was both more substantial and more sensitive to the building type.

Over the next twelve years Mackintosh designed five separate interiors at Ingram Street, so it is worth introducing plans of the building at this stage (plate 189). Cranston eventually occupied the whole of the basement and ground floor of 205–17 Ingram Street, a corner block with offices and warehousing on the upper floors. No. 205 contained the tea room and smoking room opened in 1886; 207 gave access to the upper floors; 209–11 was a galleried lunch room opened in 1888. No. 213–15 was two shops that had been thrown into one, leaving a metal stanchion holding up the walls above. In this last space Mackintosh designed a (male) smoking room and billiard room in the basement, panelled in dark wood, and the Ladies' Luncheon Room on the ground floor, filled with veiled light from new, full-height windows.[35]

The Ladies' Luncheon Room was panelled to a height of about ten feet, and the recent reconstruction of this room by Glasgow Museums (plate 183) has revealed that the panelling, previously thought to have been white, was painted silver. A screen divided the tables from the entrance; a curious tracery of wood and coloured glass was hung across the windows; and large panels of coloured gesso filled the frieze on either side. (These were called *The Wassail* and *The May Queen* [see plate 61], suggesting pagan nature festivals, but since they were not titled at Ingram Street and since *The Wassail* carried no visual reference to wassailing, their meaning was probably lost on the customers, as at Buchanan Street.[36]) In this silvery white interior, full of exquisitely original mouldings and little spots of colour, the chairs stood out, dark and rectilinear, giving the room the hybrid character that Pat Kirkham discusses.

These Ingram Street interiors were executed between August and November 1900.[37] Thus they were probably designed at the same time as, or shortly after, the flat at 120 Mains Street in which the Mackintoshes lived when they were married. This flat is important in Mackintosh's work because it was his first substantial domestic interior; because it was not just his but Macdonald's also; and because there they raised the light-feminine, dark-masculine code to a level of almost spiritual intensity.

Tea Room Plans

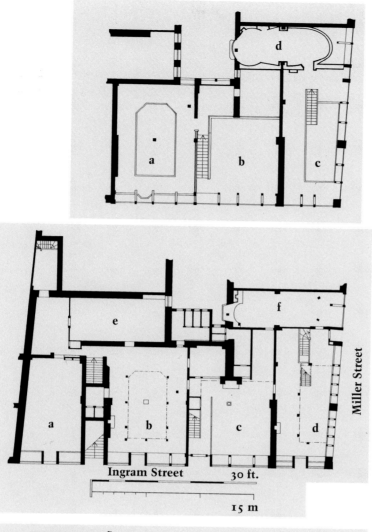

Miss Cranston's Tea Rooms
205–217 Ingram Street, Glasgow

MEZZANINE
a upper part of lunch room
b upper part of Ladies' Luncheon Room
c upper part of Oak Room
d Oval Room, 1909–10

GROUND FLOOR
a tea room, 1886
   Chinese Room, 1911
b lunch room, 1888
c Ladies' Luncheon Room, 1900
d Oak Room, 1907
e Cloister Room, 1911–12
f ladies' rest room, 1909–10

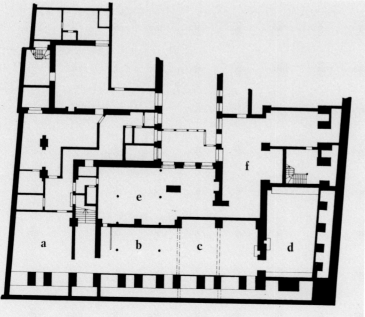

BASEMENT
a smoking room, 1886
b smoking room, 1900
c billiard room, 1900
d billiard room, 1907
e kitchen
f storage

189. Ingram Street tea rooms. Plans of the basement and the ground and mezzanine floors, showing the phases of Mackintosh's work. The details of the kitchens and storage areas at the back of the basement are conjectural.

190. The street front of the Willow Tea Rooms, Glasgow, as reconstructed in the late 1970s.

In 1900 the Mackintoshes were engaged on the extraordinary project of turning domestic life into art; that was what their lives, their marriage, and their flat at 120 Mains Street were about. The significance of this project for tea-room design is obvious. Art and domesticity were the themes of Glasgow's newer tea rooms, and it was their domesticity that distinguished them from places of refreshment elsewhere. When Kate Cranston offered a major tea-room commission, it could not have been more timely. The Mackintoshes simply transposed the project to Ingram Street, creating interiors that were more domestic *and* more exciting, for they were based not on the comfortable language of panelling and tablecloths, but on the challenging and intimate language of gender. Domesticity and excitement, the old opponents, went hand in hand.

The Mackintoshes' transformation of the Glasgow tea-room interior was continued on a larger scale in 1903, when Kate Cranston opened new tea rooms in Sauchiehall Street, among some of Glasgow's newest shops and largest department stores. They were called the Willow Tea Rooms, from the Celtic meaning of Sauchiehall, "a boggy place full of willows." Cranston had acquired an existing building, no. 217, consisting of a basement, four storeys at the front, and one at the back—part of a uniform, stuccoed mid-Victorian terrace.[38]

Mackintosh remodelled the front, stripping away the existing mouldings to create an irregular, abstractly modelled composition of shallow curves to the wall face, exaggeratedly deep reveals to some of the windows, and a border of little squares around the edges (plate 190). On the ground floor he set the entrance back with a long, small-paned, and curtained window, expressing a discreet welcome. This front was startlingly new in Glasgow and must have helped to advertise the tea rooms. It was also new in Mackintosh's work, though the modelled forms perhaps owe something to the soft geometry of Scottish vernacular houses, which Mackintosh had learned to handle at Windyhill and The Hill House.

The section (plate 191) shows how the different rooms were arranged. On the ground floor was a ladies' tea room at the front and a general lunch room at the back, with a tea gallery above it. The vaulted room at the front of the first floor was a more exclusive ladies' room, with the men's billiard and smoking room on the floor above. The section also shows a gap of about three feet between the floor level of the gallery at the back and the ceiling of the ground floor at the front. Mackintosh filled this gap with an open screen of

191. A section through the Willow Tea Rooms, looking east.

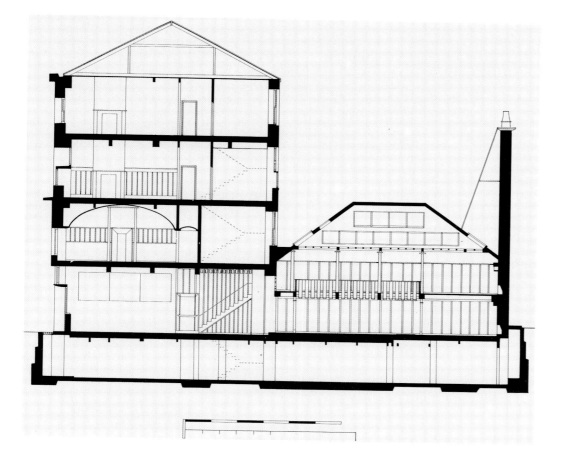

decorative metalwork and designed another for the stairs; both can be seen in plate 192.

The resulting sense of interconnected spaces delighted Modernist admirers of Mackintosh such as Nikolaus Pevsner, who wrote that these "fascinating vistas" revealed Mackintosh as "the European counterpart of Frank Lloyd Wright and one of the few true forerunners of the most ingenious juggler with space now alive: Le Corbusier."[39] This was not, however, just juggling with space for its own sake. By combining a sense of enclosure with glimpses of distance, the Mackintoshes gave physical shape to the private and the public elements in a place of refreshment. This was the first time that their tea-room designs had acknowledged the specially public character of eating out.

The different rooms were decorated according to the light-feminine, dark-masculine code (plate 194). The ladies' tea room at the front was white, silver, and rose; the general lunch room at the back was panelled in oak and grey canvas and was probably quite dark except in the middle, where light fell from the top-lit gallery above; that was decorated in pink, white, and grey on the theme of a rose bower. The curious structure in the foreground of plate 192 was a rectilinear framework of wood with an elaborate wrought-iron flower-stand on top of it, and a circular wrought-iron corona above that. It is not easy to give it a name; it was an open cage in which four customers could sit, and as such it suggests the interplay, once again, of private and public. It realised in wood the boundaries that people would bring with them and across which they would move psychologically when enjoying themselves in a public place.

▪▪ OPPOSITE
192. Charles Rennie Mackintosh. The Willow Tea Rooms. The front tea room, looking towards the lunch room and tea gallery at the back of the building. From *Dekorative Kunst* (April 1905): 260.

▪▪ ABOVE
193. Charles Rennie Mackintosh. The Salon de Luxe in the Willow Tea Rooms. From *Dekorative Kunst* (April 1905): 269.

The vaulted room upstairs (plate 193) was called the Salon de Luxe.[40] It was a white, intimate, richly decorated room such as tea-room work had not required from the Mackintoshes before. There was a long window in the outer wall, with the double doors facing it. One side wall contained the fireplace, and the other a gesso panel by Macdonald on a sad theme by Rossetti, *O Ye, All Ye That Walk in Willowwood* (see plate 69). The dado was upholstered in silk and the fixed seating in purple velvet. A frieze of coloured glass, mirror glass, and decorative leading ran around the room, culminating in the virtuoso display of the double doors (see page 2). A chandelier of almost myriad coloured-glass balls hung over silver tables and silver chairs; eight of the chairs were high-backed and were used at the central tables, forming another kind of enclosure.

The luxury of this room can be understood in terms of the Mackintoshes' stylistic development. From 1900 onwards their interiors—which were either for private houses, tea rooms, or exhibitions—followed a pattern. The Mackintoshes would develop a particular style in domestic work and then apply it to tea rooms and exhibitions. The spare white interior with spots of colour was developed at 120 Mains Street and then applied to the Ladies' Luncheon Room at Ingram Street and to the room setting exhibited with the Vienna Secession in 1900. A more colourful and luxurious style was developed in their designs for the House for an Art Lover competition (1900–1901), in 14 Kingsborough Gardens (1901–2), and in the music salon for Fritz Wärndorfer (1902–3), and applied to the Rose Boudoir exhibited in Turin in 1902 and to the Willow Tea Rooms. The Salon de Luxe is the most substantial surviving evidence of this second, luxurious phase. The luxury also makes sense in terms of the building type. It would have been too great, perhaps, for a domestic setting. Even in their House for an Art Lover designs, the Mackintoshes did not propose anything so enclosed, elaborate, and self-conscious. But in public places of refreshment, fantasy and overstatement can be appropriate. In the Salon de Luxe they created a fantasy for afternoon tea. It can be seen, perhaps, as a commercial version of the idea, more prevalent in Europe than in Britain, of the room as a work of art—the idea that the architect or designer should control all the details of an interior in the name of artistic unity.

The Willow Tea Rooms were opened on October 29, 1903, and were acclaimed in the local papers. The *Evening News* (Glasgow) reported that the city had plenty of tea rooms that were "plainly comfortable" or "quaintly or daintily artistic," but "until the opening of Miss Cranston's new establishment in Sauchiehall Street today the acme of originality had not been reached."[41] The *Bailie*, Glasgow's fashionable weekly, described the Salon de Luxe as "simply a marvel of the art of the upholsterer and decorator."[42] The public was impressed. A little over a year later Macdonald wrote to Hermann Muthesius that "the whole town is getting covered with imitations of Mack-

194. Charles Rennie Mackintosh. *Clock*, 1903. For the Willow Tea Rooms, Glasgow. Oak, stained dark, with polished-steel face, brass numerals, metal and coloured-glass insets, and glazed door, 74 1/8 x 27 13/16 x 6 7/16 in. (188.3 x 70.6 x 16.4 cm). Glasgow School of Art.

It is not known where this clock stood in the tea rooms, but its materials and its dark colour suggest that it may have come from the general lunch room or the men's billiard and smoking room.

intosh tea rooms, Mackintosh shops Mackintosh furniture &c—it is too funny."[43]

The opening of the Willow Tea Rooms marked the end of an important phase in the Mackintoshes' tea-room work. Six more jobs were to come, spread over the next thirteen years, but they were of a different character.

The first was the Dutch Kitchen (plate 195), which Mackintosh designed for the basement of the Argyle Street rooms, probably around the beginning of 1906. Nothing was particularly Dutch about it beyond some Delft tiles in the fireplace, and its name may have alluded, remotely, to the Grill Room or "Dutch Kitchen" at South Kensington. Mackintosh painted the ceiling black and applied a black-and-white chequer in diminishing sizes to the floor, the dado, and the structural uprights down the middle of the room.[44] The chairs were painted emerald green. This was very different from earlier tea-room designs, the most remarkable of which had been curvilinear and delicately coloured, feminine in the conventions of the time. This was something harder—perhaps *chic* is the right word. The pattern of development in the Mackintoshes' interiors, which we have already seen, explains the change.

After the second, luxurious phase, squares, clarity, and black-and-white began to displace organic ornament, symbolic overtones, and delicate greens, pinks, greys, and silver. This happened confusedly at The Hill House in 1903–4, and then austerely at Hous'hill in 1904–5. (*If* organic ornament, symbolism, and delicate colours were particularly associated with Macdonald, we should ask whether her influence, too, diminished.) The new style was used at the exhibition organised by the furniture manufacturer A. S. Ball in Berlin in 1905, where Mackintosh exhibited a dark, rectilinear dining room—a room with masculine associations—and an Austrian reviewer noticed the absence of "mysterious suggestions in the ornament."[45] And the new style was applied to the Dutch Kitchen.

In 1907 Miss Cranston took over no. 117, the last space on the ground floor of the Ingram Street block; it was on the corner, with a long frontage to Miller Street. In the summer of that year Mackintosh designed a billiard room in the basement and the Oak Room on the ground floor (plate 196). The Oak Room was long and narrow compared with the others at Ingram Street; Mackintosh introduced a gallery on three sides of the room, giving the long side considerable depth, as the plan (plate 189) shows. At this stage he was designing austere, right-angled forms in dark woods, sparsely decorated with spots of colour and wavy lines that read as embroidery of the orthogonal forms. Here squares of blue glass were set in the screen below the staircase, and wavy laths of wood were bent over the uprights springing from the columns supporting the gallery, creating a clever interplay of curves and straight lines.

The Oak Room was designed at the beginning of the painful phase in Mackintosh's career when he was getting little work, and it is not surprising that the fruitful relationship that we have observed among domestic, exhibi-

195. Charles Rennie Mackintosh. The Dutch Kitchen, 1906, in the Argyle Street tea rooms. Photographed by T. and R. Annan Ltd., 1906.

tion, and tea-room interiors should have broken down. The interior to which the Oak Room most nearly relates is the library of Glasgow School of Art (see plate 115), designed in outline in 1907 and completed in 1909. Both rooms have a gallery and ornament of wavy lines. And in the Oak Room, Mackintosh carried the front (and only the front) of his gallery around a fourth side, hanging it like a great rigid banner across the face of the Miller Street windows, presumably blocking out some of the light. This was a dress rehearsal for the strangest feature of the School of Art library, where not only the front but the whole fourth side of the gallery runs across the great oriel windows.[46]

In the summer of 1911 Mackintosh redesigned the first room that Miss Cranston had opened at Ingram Street, twenty-five years before (plates 186 and 197). The crucial element in the design was a lattice screen of squares, painted a powerful blue. The high ceiling was painted black. The walls were covered with heavy canvas painted blue with lattice screens placed against them; where the wall projected for structural reasons, the lattice squares were scooped out as concave niches lined with mirror glass or a newly invented plastic. The pay desk and two more freestanding screens divided the room down the middle, supporting more screens slung across the room at intervals, as an intermittent false ceiling. Although it was called the Chinese Room and although there were pagoda-like motifs on the screens and hanging lamps, projecting beams on the pay desk, and a fretwork canopy over the entrance to the servery at the back of the room, these details were no more essential to the

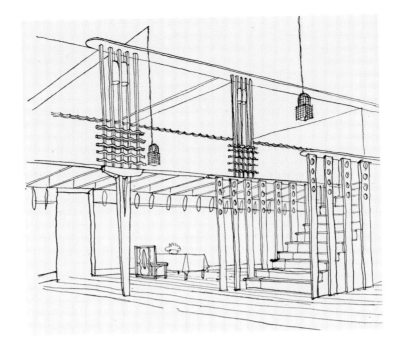

design than the Dutch tiles in the Dutch Kitchen. While exotic or thematic names and styles were common in places of refreshment at this time, Mackintosh's design hung exceedingly loose to the theme that Kate Cranston (presumably) had given him. The special quality of the Chinese Room did not come from China but from Mackintosh's passion for squares and his ability to create a complex interior from a few simple elements, light and dark, open and enclosed, abstract yet luxurious.

The same is true for the Cloister Room, which he designed at the back of the Ingram Street site about six months later (plates 189 and 198). It had no cloisters in it. The detailed decoration was based on regular wave forms, or meanders. The walls were covered with smoothly waxed wood picked out in panels by meanders painted red, green, and blue and outlined in black; the meanders are so angular that they look like lozenges. At intervals, panels of diminishing size were superimposed on each other, like a stepped frame that projects instead of receding. The barrel-vaulted plaster ceiling was decorated with ribs modelled in shallower curves that gave the effect of chamfering. And over the doors Mackintosh set overlapping strips of wood, scalloped and chamfered to create a canopy of extraordinary and repetitive intricacy. Many of these motifs may have been influenced, as so much of Mackintosh's later work was, by the work of progressive architects and designers in Vienna—the meanders by Otto Prutscher and Marcel Kammerer, the multiple frame by Josef Hoffmann.[47]

Kate Cranston commissioned her last tea-room interior late in 1916. It was part of the Willow Tea Rooms but actually located in the basement of the property next door, and it was called the Dug-Out, a reference to the trenches of the Great War (plate 199). No photographs of this room survive, but plans,

198. Charles Rennie Mackintosh. The Cloister Room, 1911–12, in the Ingram Street tea rooms. Photographed by Eric Thorburn, 1971, shortly before it was dismantled.

elevations, and some reminiscences record that the ceiling and part of the walls were painted black and that the interior included blue latticed screens like those in the Chinese Room and stepped frames like those in the Cloister Room. It was also very like the roughly contemporary lounge hall at 78 Derngate, Northampton (see plate 144). Both rooms were decorated with black ceilings and walls, bright primary colours, lattice screens, stepped frames, and chequerwork. But this was not a return to the pattern of the early 1900s, when domestic interiors were the seedbed for tea-room designs. The roles had been reversed. According to the domestic code, the lounge hall at 78 Derngate should have been light and feminine. Instead Mackintosh had it painted black and decorated in the vibrant but quite undomestic style he had developed in his later tea rooms.

We should not underestimate these late tea rooms, from the Dutch Kitchen onwards. In the sad passages of Mackintosh's life—when he was getting little work, drinking heavily, and suffering from depression—they stand out as episodes of brilliant invention. His talent was not diminished. And, in the absence of other work, they represent much of the development of his formal imagination at this date towards intensity and a preoccupation with small, repetitive motifs. Intensity could be an asset in a tea room, where fantasy and exaggeration were appropriate—the black-and-white chequers in the Dutch Kitchen, the intricate meanders in the Cloister Room, the dazzling frames of the Dug-Out.

At the same time, we have to grasp the paradox that these late tea rooms, which played a central role on the diminished stage of Mackintosh's later work, actually had a looser relationship to the building type than those of the early 1900s, whose character derived so obviously from domestic work. The Oak Room would not have been out of place in a school or a public library. The Chinese Room was appropriate to a tea room as Oriental, but that was simply a convention that Mackintosh had picked up. And the Cloister Room and the Dug-Out seem to be cases of style operating on its own, with Mackintosh designing in the way that suited him. His designs were, of course, entirely appropriate and successful. Roger Billcliffe has described the Cloister Room as "moodily atmospheric," and strangeness and novelty were just what tea rooms needed.[48] But there was no sense of transformation. The interiors of 1900–1903 had embraced both domesticity and excitement, and had resolved with extraordinary élan the tensions involved in eating out during the late Victorian era. Those of 1905–17 fell consistently on the side of excitement. They did not embrace the opposites, perhaps because they were, in some very loose sense, more masculine, instances of Mackintosh's designing by himself.

In all this Kate Cranston played the part of the beneficent patron. The tea rooms were very much hers, in their originality, their high standards, and their attention to detail. But, so far as one can tell, she did not intervene much, placing the commissions in Mackintosh's hands and trusting his judgement. After 1900 she did not give much work to other architects. But in October 1917, a few months after the Dug-Out was completed, her husband, John Cochrane, to whom she was devoted, died unexpectedly. She was sixty-eight, and the shock was very great. Within a few years she had given up all her tea rooms. She lived on until 1934, and her diminutive figure could sometimes be seen, in a cloak and a big black sombrero, on the streets of Glasgow.[49] But the story of the Cranston-Mackintosh tea rooms was at an end.

They were, taken as a whole, very different from other places of refreshment at that time. It is difficult to know what to compare them with. Other Glasgow tea rooms of the early twentieth century had none of Mackintosh's

199. Charles Rennie Mackintosh. *The Dug-Out, The Willow Tea Rooms: West Wall of the Staircase and Vestibule,* 1917. Pencil and watercolour, 15¹³⁄₁₆ x 30⅛ in. (40.2 x 76.5 cm). Glasgow School of Art.

urbanity. They developed the homely theme in obvious ways and so, increasingly, did those in England. The wicker chairs and gleaming copper hearths hinted at a nostalgia that would soon transform "tea shop" into "tea shoppe."[50] One might expect to find comparisons among the work of progressives in Germany and Austria, and the alcohol-free Jungbrunnen restaurant at the Düsseldorf Garden Festival of 1904, designed by Peter Behrens, had ladderback chairs modelled on Mackintosh's.[51] Stylistically, Mackintosh had been most at home among the progressive designers of Vienna, but in that city, famous for its coffee houses, Adolf Loos's Café Museum (1899) and Café Capua (1913) and Josef Hoffmann's Graben-Café (1912) were in a different spirit from the tea rooms of Mackintosh—spare, marble-lined places without a hint of fantasy.[52]

The closest comparison seems to be with Art Nouveau restaurants in Paris, such as Maxim's (1899) and Lucas-Carton (1904–5). Apart from the fact that they had a good deal of tilework, the decorative formula was comparable: walls decorated with mirrors, decorative plasterwork, and paintings of women; spaces subdivided by elaborate woodwork (glistening coils instead of Mackintosh's subtle curves); and a distinct sense of modernity.[53] Mackintosh's tea rooms, with their novel mouldings and elegant subdivisions of space, were the equal of these in sophistication of design, and much more original. The comparison seems strange only because the interiors in Paris were a setting for *haute cuisine* and in Glasgow for hot mutton pies, scrambled eggs, and pots of tea.

The relationship between Mackintosh's stylistic development and the requirements of the Glasgow tea rooms moved through three stages. In the beginning,
at Buchanan Street and Argyle Street, his work was slightly at odds with the
tea rooms. Then came the stage of collaboration with his wife, at Ingram
Street in 1900 and at the Willow, where the Mackintoshes created a subli-
mated domesticity so new and so appropriate that it completely transformed
the themes of Glasgow tea rooms. In the long last stage, Mackintosh's designs
were appropriately novel, varied, and atmospheric, but they lacked the transforming interplay of light and dark that had been so important between 1900
and 1903. The alchemy was over.

The relationship between style and building type was not an equal one.
Almost always, it is to the development of Mackintosh's style that one turns
for explanation of the character of a tea room. Only once, in the spatial dis-
criminations of the Willow (especially in the overstated luxury of its Salon de
Luxe), do the special requirements of the tea rooms seem to have shaped his
designs. I do not mean that the other interiors were inappropriate; they were
wholly appropriate and far more inventive than other work of the time. But
that was just because tea rooms suited Mackintosh's style.

This story of Mackintosh's involvement with a particular building type
only serves to underline how independent of building-type considerations his
inspiration was. His imagination was autonomous. His creative life was a
journey made, in the first place, along the paths and byways of his mind,
among colours and shapes and abstract forms, and only then, as occasion
demanded, in the world of architecture and interiors.

NOTES

1. Perilla Kinchin, *Tea and Taste: The Glasgow Tea Rooms, 1875–1975* (Wendlebury, England: White Cockade Publishing, 1991), p. 111.

2. The Willow Tea Rooms were the subject of an extensive restoration scheme in 1979–80, and the Salon de Luxe is once more in use as a tea room; but the rest of the building has been adapted to retail use. For an account of the history of Miss Cranston's various tea rooms after they left her hands, see my essay, "The Mackintosh Phenomenon," in this volume.

3. The exception is that in 1905 Mackintosh designed the plan (only) of the Wellesley Tea Rooms at 145 Sauchiehall Street, for the trustees of the late Dr. Walker.

4. This section is heavily indebted to Robert Thorne, "Places of Refreshment in the Nineteenth-Century City," in *Buildings and Society: Essays on the Social Development of the Built Environment,* ed. Anthony King (London: Routledge and Kegan Paul, 1990), pp. 228–53.

5. For an illustration of such dining rooms, see ibid., pl. 7.1.

6. The *Post Office Directory* listed 345 dining rooms in London in 1848, and 1,000 dining rooms and 800 refreshment rooms and cafés in 1902. See D. J. Richardson, "J. Lyons & Co. Ltd.: Caterers & Food Manufacturers, 1894–1939," in *The Making of the Modern British Diet,* ed. Derek Oddy and Derek Miller (London: Croom Helm, 1976), p. 161.

7. Thorne, "Places of Refreshment," p. 234.

8. The Pavilion Restaurant, William Street, Liverpool, designed by Edwin Kirby and opened in 1878, may be an early example of a grand restaurant outside London; parts of its principal dining hall were modelled on the refreshment room in the House of Lords. See *Builder,* April 27, 1878, p. 427.

9. For Kinchin, *Tea and Taste,* see note 1 above. Donald Tate, *A History of Cafés and Restaurants in Leeds* (Leeds, England: published by the author, 1988) is a less ambitious work. One of the few articles on cafés in the architectural press held up the cafés of Vienna as a model, holding that Parisian cafés were tainted by the recent "rage for

absinthe"; see "Cafés and Coffee-Houses," *Builder,* June 30, 1883, pp. 873–74.

10. See Priscilla Boniface, *Hotels and Restaurants: 1830 to the Present Day* (London: Her Majesty's Stationery Office, 1981), pl. 38.

11. Richardson, "J. Lyons & Co.," p. 163.

12. The manuscript reports of the directors of the Aerated Bread Company refer to ninety "depots" in 1897, but I have taken the figure of sixty cafés from Richardson, "J. Lyons & Co.," p. 164, as not all the depots may have been cafés. I am grateful to Robert Thorne for information on the reports.

13. Kinchin, *Tea and Taste,* p. 58.

14. For the interior decoration, *Caterer and Hotel-Keepers' Gazette,* October 15, 1894, p. 456; and Stuart Gray, *Edwardian Architecture: A Biographical Dictionary* (London: Duckworth, 1985), p. 65; for the menu, Richardson, "J. Lyons & Co.," p. 165.

15. *Caterer and Hotel-Keepers' Gazette,* October 15, 1894, p. 456.

16. R. Machray, *The Night Side of London* (1902), p. 69; in Richardson, "J. Lyons & Co.," p. 166.

17. Evidence to the Royal Commission on Licensing, 1929–31; in Thorne, "Places of Refreshment," p. 235.

18. For the development of majolica ware or faience, see Michael Stratton, *The Terracotta Revival* (London: Victor Gollancz and Peter Crawley, 1993), pp. 100–104. Paul Atterbury and Louise Irvine, *The Doulton Story* (London: Royal Doulton Tableware, 1979), pp. 90–98, provides details of Doulton's faience and tiles in various restaurants and cafés; and *Burmantofts Pottery* (Bradford, England: Bradford Art Galleries and Museums, 1983), pp. 70–72, does the same for Burmantofts.

19. See John Physick, *The Victoria and Albert Museum: The History of Its Building* (Oxford: Phaidon; London: Christie's, 1982), pp. 131–42. There were direct connections between the South Kensington Museum and restaurant design. The architect Frank Verity worked in Francis Fowke's architectural office at South Kensington until 1871, when he won the competition for the Criterion restaurant; as executed, the Criterion contained "a dazzling display of ceramic decoration in the South Kensington manner." (F.H.W. Sheppard, ed., *Survey of London,* vol. 38, *The Museums Area of South Kensington*

and Westminster [London: Athlone Press, 1975], p. 88.)

20. This section is particularly indebted to Kinchin, *Tea and Taste.*

21. Ibid., p. 17.

22. Ibid.

23. One cannot generalise, for lack of evidence, but a series of articles about local "snackeries" in *Liverpool Review,* November 8, 1890, to January 31, 1891, reflects a male clientele.

24. Kinchin, *Tea and Taste,* pl. 19.

25. My descriptions are based on Kinchin, *Tea and Taste,* passim, and a small booklet, *Miss Cranston's,* probably published in 1898, which illustrates her tea rooms up to that date; but there is not a great deal of visual evidence. J. Jeffrey Waddell, "Some Recent Glasgow Tea Rooms," *Builders' Journal and Architectural Record,* April 15, 1903, pp. 126–31, illustrates several tea rooms that are thoroughly domestic in character, but they are of late date, c. 1902. By that time English tea rooms had taken the same path, and the contrast between Scotland and England was less.

26. The building still stands, but Kate Cranston sold it in about 1917, and the work by Walton and Mackintosh seems not to have survived its subsequent refitting as a bank.

27. The colour scheme and its association with earth and sky are given by Gleeson White, "Some Glasgow Designers and Their Work," part 1, *Studio* 11 (July 1897): 95. It has associations with Igdrasil, the "World Tree" of Scandinavian mythology, which was a favourite image among progressive decorators.

28. Timothy Neat, *Part Seen, Part Imagined: Meaning and Symbolism in the Work of Charles Rennie Mackintosh and Margaret Macdonald* (Edinburgh: Canongate, 1994), p. 117.

29. In the autumn of 1896 Gerald Moira and F. Lynn Jenkins completed frieze decorations in the hall of Lyons's new Trocadero restaurant in Shaftesbury Avenue, London, to considerable acclaim. They painted scenes of feasting, romance, and chivalry from Tennyson's *Idylls of the King,* and it is arguable that their apotheosis of eating out and beefy English honour, though less intellectually ambitious than Mackintosh's symbolism, was more suitable to a restau-

rant. See *Caterer and Hotel-Keepers' Gazette,* October 15, 1896, p. 491, and J. Harold Watkins, *The Art of Gerald Moira* (London: E. W. Dickens, [1922]), pp. 12–14.

30. Mackintosh's work at Argyle Street has traditionally been given the date of 1897, following Thomas Howarth, *Charles Rennie Mackintosh and the Modern Movement,* 3d ed. (London: Routledge and Kegan Paul, 1990), p. 124. However, the Dean of Guild's "Reports on Buildings," in Strathclyde Regional Archives, Mitchell Library, Glasgow City Libraries, and a report on the completed work in the *Glasgow Advertiser and Property Circular* for October 20, 1899, show that the reworking of the building, including Walton's decorations, took place between June 1898 and September 1899. It is not impossible that Mackintosh's furniture for these rooms was designed at an earlier date, but it is unlikely. And Howarth (*Mackintosh,* p. 124) states that the archives of Francis Smith, now destroyed, showed furniture designed by Mackintosh being sent to Argyle Street in 1898–99.

The building still stands, but Kate Cranston sold it in 1918, and almost no trace of her tea rooms survives today.

31. *Glasgow Advertiser and Property Circular,* October 20, 1899.

32. Roger Billcliffe, *Mackintosh Furniture* (Cambridge: Lutterworth Press, 1984), p. 48, entry 1897.24.

33. For example, see ibid., p. 44, entry 1897.9.

34. For instance, the oak table by Charles Spooner exhibited with the Arts and Crafts Exhibition Society in 1896 and illustrated in *Builder,* October 17, 1896, on the same page as a hall settle by Mackintosh.

35. He also designed some stencilling and a screen in the room later decorated as the Cloister Room.

36. *Studio* 28 (May 1903): 287–88.

37. Dean of Guild, "Reports on Buildings."

38. It is possible that Mackintosh designed the single-storey building at the back; but the plans submitted to the Dean of Guild, now in Strathclyde Regional Archives, suggest that this part of the property was already standing in 1903.

39. Nikolaus Pevsner, *Pioneers of Modern Design: From William Morris to Walter Gropius,* 4th ed. (Harmondsworth, England: Penguin Books, 1975), pp. 168–69.

40. It is now usually called the Room de Luxe, but I have not seen any early evidence for this name, and the contemporary sources cited in notes 41 and 42 below both use the less mongrel "Salon de Luxe."

41. *Evening News* (Glasgow), October 29, 1903, p. 7.

42. *Bailie* (Glasgow), November 4, 1903, p. 6.

43. Macdonald to Hermann Muthesius, Christmas 1904, Hunterian Art Gallery, University of Glasgow.

44. Josef Hoffmann had used tiny black-and-white chequers in a similar way in a vestibule at the eighteenth exhibition of the Vienna Secession, in 1903. See Frank Russell, ed., *Art Nouveau Architecture* (London: Academy Editions, 1979), p. 230.

45. *Kunst und Kunsthandwerk* 8 (1905): 198.

46. Two years later, Mackintosh designed two small rooms to go behind the Oak Room: a ladies' rest room on the ground floor and the Oval Room on the mezzanine (see plate 189). It is impossible to get a full sense of these rooms as the only surviving photographs show them scarred and empty before they were dismantled in 1971.

47. See Prutscher's design for a crypt, illustrated in Anthony Alofsin, *Frank Lloyd Wright: The Lost Years, 1910–1922* (Chicago: University of Chicago Press, 1993), p. 295; and Kammerer's interior for the 1908 Kunstschau in *Moderne Bauformen* 7 (1908): 394. For Hoffmann, see Alofsin, *Wright,* p. 182.

48. Billcliffe, *Mackintosh Furniture,* p. 216.

49. Kinchin, *Tea and Taste,* pp. 79, 121.

50. For Glasgow, see Waddell, "Some Recent Glasgow Tea-Rooms," passim. For England, see the descriptions of the Old Oak Tea Rooms in Bond Street, London, in *Kunst und Kunsthandwerk* 5 (1902): 174–75, 177–80; of Ridgways' Café, St. Ann's Square, Manchester, England, designed by T. Arnold Ashworth, in Boniface, *Hotels and Restaurants,* pls. 64–66; and of the Kardomah Tea Rooms at 186 Piccadilly, London, also by Ashworth, in *British Architect,* November 29, 1901, pp. 381–82. Ashworth's cafés were indebted to George Walton's tea-room work.

51. Alan Windsor, *Peter Behrens: Architect and Designer, 1868–1940* (London: Architectural Press, 1981), pp. 56–58.

52. *Das Wiener Kaffeehaus: Won dem Anfängen bis zur Zwischenkriegszeit* (Vienna: Historisches Museum der Stadt Wien, 1980), entries 224–30, 235–56, and 257–58. The Café Ronacher in Vienna, by Richard Seifert, is comparable with Mackintosh's work in type, levels of decoration, and some techniques of decoration, but not in style; see "Ein modernes Wiener Kaffeehaus," *Das Interieur* 3 (1902): 49–56.

53. See Charlotte Ellis, "Nouveau Richesses," *Designers' Journal* 16 (April 1986): 71–79; and Bruno Girveau, *La Belle Epoque des cafés et des restaurants* (Paris: Hachette; Réunion des Musées Nationaux, 1990).

The Making of a Painter

PAMELA ROBERTSON

It is not often that an architect is also master of the art of landscape painting.

Evening Citizen (Glasgow),
May 4, 1933

In the early summer of 1933, a few months after the death of Mackintosh's widow, Margaret Macdonald, a Mackintosh memorial exhibition was organised in Glasgow by friends and admirers. Drawn principally from the couple's estate, it covered the full spread of Mackintosh's career. Though it was nearly twenty years since Mackintosh had left the city, much would have been familiar, or at least not unexpected, to friends and colleagues who remembered his work from before the Great War. But one aspect of the exhibition came as a revelation. Scattered among other works were over thirty landscapes of sun-baked rocks and hills, architecture, and seashore from the south of France. Painted in seclusion, at the end of Mackintosh's life, these had rarely been exhibited, never published, and never before seen in Scotland.

EARLY ARCHITECTURAL AND BOTANICAL DRAWINGS

Mackintosh's training as an apprentice architect in the 1880s and 1890s had been technical rather than "fine art." His professional language was drawing. It was a skill founded on years of painstaking study, seven of these at Allan Glen's Institution, a progressive school in Glasgow that aimed to provide a practical education for prospective engineers and scientists. This experience had been consolidated by an additional eleven years of evening classes at Glasgow School of Art—a Government School of Design. The school followed the centralised South Kensington curriculum, with an emphasis on draughtsmanship and, above all, line and with technical classes in mathematics, mechanics, building construction, geometry, perspective, sculptural modelling, and ornament. Mackintosh excelled as a student, winning prizes at both the local and the national levels and progressing swiftly within the practice of Honeyman and Keppie, which he had joined in 1889 as junior draughtsman.

200. Charles Rennie Mackintosh. *Port Vendres, La Ville,* c. 1925–26. Pencil and watercolour, $17^{11}/_{16}$ x $17^{11}/_{16}$ in. (45.0 x 45.0 cm). Glasgow Museums.

THE HERALD BUILDING
MITCHELL ST. GLASGOW. JOHN HONEYMAN AND KEPPIE

His early perspective drawing of the Glasgow Herald building (plate 201) well illustrates the fluidity and assurance of his draughtsmanship by the end of his formal training. The representation of the tower block is transformed into an arresting composition through the use of dramatic foreshortening, a low viewpoint, strong contrasts of light and shade, and Mackintosh's virtuoso handling of the sky. Such tricks were standard devices of skilled perspectivists of the period but individualised here through Mackintosh's decorative penmanship.[1]

Alongside such office and competition work, Mackintosh used his graphic skills on "field work"—shorthand studies of architectural forms and details as well as plants—with which to develop a reference portfolio for his design work. Through the 1880s and 1890s he travelled in and around Glasgow and the north of Scotland, and into England, to Dorset, Norfolk, Suffolk, Devon, Somerset, Worcestershire, Gloucestershire, and elsewhere. Five architectural sketchbooks survive from this period.[2] They are filled with drawings of the native architecture that he admired—including Scottish tower houses and English vernacular cottages or parish churches—and of eclectic details, such as the profile of a pew, the plan of a table, or the outline of a weather vane. Interspersed with these are pages of exquisite studies of plant forms. All of these reveal his early preference for line, not shading or hatching, to express form. His line was economic but eloquent and unhesitating, his draughtsmanship a demanding process that required rigorous analysis and editing of the subject prior to placing any mark on the sheet.

Mackintosh's skills were stimulated and enriched by a formative study trip to Italy in 1891, funded by the Alexander Thomson Travelling Studentship.[3] Mindful of the scholarship's requirement that he submit sketches and drawings at the conclusion of the tour, Mackintosh focussed exclusively on historical architecture and ornament; little time was left for visits to the great treasure houses of Italian painting. He sketched intensively and used the opportunity to develop his skills in watercolour. By the end of the tour, the tight mechanical line of his early studies from Pompeii and Naples had eased into an expressive and vibrant contour. Though artistically impressive, the body of work he took back to Glasgow was treated as no more than an adjunct to his architectural career, to be used as a valuable tool in career advancement.

His sketches and watercolours were exhibited at the Glasgow School of Art Club annual exhibition in the autumn and at the Glasgow Institute of the Fine Arts in 1892 and 1893; submitted for the 1892 Pugin Studentship (unsuccessfully, but to critical acclaim in the *British Architect* and *Builder*); and published in the *Glasgow Architectural Association Sketchbook* of 1894. Mackintosh was using these works to establish a name for himself in architectural circles, something he could not otherwise do as a junior employee with Honeyman and Keppie. These works, though technically precocious, were entirely within the mainstream in terms of subject matter and interpretation. At the institute, Mackintosh's topographical watercolours hung comfortably in

201. Charles Rennie Mackintosh. *Extension to the Glasgow Herald Building: Perspective from the Northwest*, 1894. Ink, 35$^{15}/_{16}$ x 23$^{15}/_{16}$ in. (91.2 x 60.8 cm). Hunterian Art Gallery, University of Glasgow.

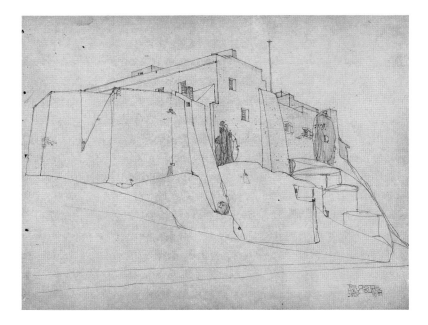

202. Charles Rennie Mackintosh. *The Castle, Holy Island*, 1901. Pencil, 8 x 10¼ in. (20.3 x 26.0 cm). Hunterian Art Gallery, University of Glasgow.

the company of works by other architects, including his senior, John Keppie, and his close friend, James Salmon Jr.

Throughout the following years Mackintosh continued to record architecture and plants, but the role of the sketches changed. Following his marriage to Margaret Macdonald in 1900, sketching became a leisure activity, carried out on the couple's trips away from Glasgow to England, Portugal, or the Scilly Isles. Direct connections between his architectural designs and the sketches of the 1900s are less easily made. Mackintosh's greater concern now was to develop self-contained compositions. In his studies of Holy Island Castle (plate 202), for example, he was preoccupied with the architecture in its setting, exploring the relationship of castle and rock, of light and shade, of the curvilinear and the angular patterns of landscape and fortifications, or the concentrated detail of a sea pink set against the mass of a castle wall or buttress. Increasingly watercolour was used, particularly in the botanical studies. This sketching was largely a private activity; after the mid-1890s none of his botanical or architectural studies were exhibited, nor were they published, or even displayed on the walls of his own Glasgow homes, as far as contemporary photographs show.[4] There are only rare instances, in the Glasgow years, of Mackintosh's creating watercolours as works of art for a wider audience, and this was confined to a few years in the 1890s.

THE SYMBOLIST WATERCOLOURS

Though topographic painting was a natural and accepted activity for architects, the crossover between architecture and painting was less usual, as Glasgow's *Evening Citizen* was to remark in 1933.[5] Even though it was a short-lived episode in Mackintosh's career, his paintings of the mid- to late 1890s are significant for suggesting an early interest in purely painterly concerns and for having allowed him to experiment with imaginative subject matter. Such preoccupations might be expected, for Mackintosh's immediate circle at that time, the self-styled Immortals, principally comprised student painters from the school: Janet Aitken, Katherine Cameron, Jessie Keppie, Margaret and Frances Macdonald, Herbert McNair, and Agnes Raeburn. The talented and individualistic painters David Gauld and John Quinton Pringle were close friends. Moreover, painting was a live issue in the city, the centre for the "Glasgow Boys"—a group of local painters acclaimed in Europe and America from the 1880s.[6] The city centre was the hub of an expanding and lively group of dealers, studios, and galleries that surrounded the school and Honeyman and Keppie's office. Further stimulus must have come from the example of Mackintosh's ally and patron, Francis Newbery—an educator who championed creative individuality and was himself an able painter.

Mackintosh's work of the 1890s is characterised by its wide-ranging experimentation. In addition to his office work, he was also producing metalwork, furniture, and interior design, as well as taking up stencilling, mural decoration, and graphic and poster design. In all of this Mackintosh seems to have been seeking an individual language through exploring diverse media and styles. Ambition played its part. Mackintosh confided his frustration at his anonymity within the architectural practice to Hermann Muthesius: "Although the building in Mitchell St here [the Glasgow Herald extension] was designed by me the architects are or were Messrs Honeyman & Keppie— who employ me as assistant. So if you reproduce any photographs of the building you must give the architect's name—not mine. You will see that is very unfortunate for me, but I hope when brighter days come, I shall be able to work for myself entirely, and claim my work as mine."[7] Startling posters, exaggeratedly tall chairs, large-scale tea-room murals, and a distinctive style for his perspective drawings were all means of getting himself noticed.

At times Mackintosh's ideas emerged in almost overwhelming profusion. An early library scheme of 1894 buzzes with decorative leaded glass, beaten metal, stencil decoration, and wall panelling.[8] At Queen's Cross Church, Glasgow, flying buttresses, multiple window types, a varied roofline, an engaged turret, and a battered tower are all crowded onto a corner site. The form of the tower is a direct borrowing from Mackintosh's sketches of All Saints Church, Merriott, Somerset. Similar borrowings occur elsewhere. The forms of catalogue furniture were reputedly used as templates for his early furniture designs.[9] Recently published writings by W. R. Lethaby, J. D. Sedding, and David MacGibbon and Thomas Ross, among others, were liberally raided as Mackintosh sought to formulate a convincing expression of his architectural philosophy for his student lectures.[10] His painting and graphic designs benefitted in a similar way. Alexandre Cabanel's nude from his then well-known Salon picture of 1863, *The Birth of Venus* (Musée d'Orsay, Paris),

appears in *The Harvest Moon* (plate 203); Michelangelo's Delphic and Erithraean sybils adorn graphics for the Glasgow School of Art Club. Stylistic vocabularies, specifically those of innovative contemporaries, were also adopted as Mackintosh experimented with alternative watercolour techniques.

The Lido (plate 204), possibly executed on his Italian tour, shows a distant view of Venice across the lagoon. In the middle ground a gondola passes in silhouette against the vast expanse of the grey sea, which is punctuated by mooring posts. The work is clearly indebted to the hero of the Glasgow Boys, James McNeill Whistler, in subject matter, composition, technique, even the style of framing. Like Mackintosh, Whistler followed a process of close analysis and reduction of the subject matter. But Whistler's technique, emulated here, in which the subject is realised through colour and brushwork, was alien to Mackintosh's draughtsman's training and was quickly abandoned.

Different painterly preoccupations informed Mackintosh's *Wareham* (plate 205). Rather than present a straightforward topographical view, Mackintosh used the architecture of the street and church as one element in the composition, locking it between the open expanses of sky and lawn and punctuating it with highly simplified trees. In its disciplined composition, fine detailing, and delicacy of tonal variations and application of watercolour, *Wareham* is closely related to the work of Mackintosh's friend and fellow student, John Quinton Pringle. A different technique is used for the whimsical *Cabbages in an Orchard* (plate 206). The outlines of the highly stylised vegetables and trees were lightly marked in pencil, then watercolour washes were floated over the dampened paper to the outlines of the composition, achieving a seemingly random but in fact highly manipulated finish. The resultant chance effects of tonal variations are central to the decorative character of the whole. This mannered and decorative use of the medium is

■■ OPPOSITE
203. Charles Rennie Mackintosh. *The Harvest Moon,* 1892. Pencil and watercolour, 13⅞ x 10⅞ in. (35.2 x 27.6 cm). Glasgow School of Art.

The winged figure hovers above, but not quite touching, the streaming hair of Cabanel's Venus. The latter's upturned elbow can be seen silhouetted against the bottom-left section of the moon. A second elbow, from a repeat of the reclining figure, appears at the left-hand edge.
■■ ABOVE
204. Charles Rennie Mackintosh. *The Lido,* c. 1891. Watercolour, 4⅝ x 13½ in. (11.7 x 34.3 cm). Hunterian Art Gallery, University of Glasgow.
■■ BELOW
205. Charles Rennie Mackintosh. *Wareham,* c. 1895. Watercolour, 12³⁄₁₆ x 14⅛ in. (31 x 35.8 cm). Private collection.

akin to the bravura technique developed by Arthur Melville, one of the Glasgow Boys.

Cabbages was submitted for inclusion in the handwritten "Magazine" compiled by Lucy Raeburn, one of the Immortals, while she was a student at the School of Art. Only four unique numbers of "The Magazine," dating from 1894 to 1896, survive. These contain watercolours, fairy tales, drawings, and commentaries by the Immortals, and seven watercolours by Mackintosh, of which *Cabbages* was the first. With these works Mackintosh was continuing his experimentation, here with symbolic content and decorative stylisation, influenced by the example of his immediate circle—McNair and the Macdonald sisters—and the wider example of fin de siècle artists such as Carlos Schwabe and Jan Toorop.[11] The images created by these contemporaries used abstracted elements of the real world to illustrate allegorical and literary themes of life and death, decay and renewal, night and day, good and evil, as well as the world of dreams and the imagination. Human or plant forms, particularly in the work of the Macdonalds and McNair, were transformed into linear ciphers and then often integrated into abstract patterns or reconfigured into mutant forms.

"The Magazine" provided a stimulating vehicle for such experiments. Though no more than an informal album, it attracted innovative work by other Glasgow artists, including photographs by the Photo-Secessionist James Craig Annan and a rare Symbolist print, *Night*, by D. Y. Cameron. Though their imagery is not as daring as that of the Macdonalds or McNair, Mackintosh's "Magazine" watercolours are virtually unprecedented in his work. All incorporate plant forms, and three also use stylised figures. Mackintosh's imagery generally provides straightforward illustrations of his titles: *Autumn, Spring,* and the self-referential theme of ambition in the pair *The Tree of Personal Effort The Sun of Indifference* (plate 207) and *The Tree of Influence—The Tree of Importance—The Sun of Cowardice* (Glasgow School of Art).[12]

CHARLES RENNIE MACKINTOSH · JANUARY · 1895

THE TREE OF PERSONAL EFFORT · THE SUN OF INDIFFERENCE ::

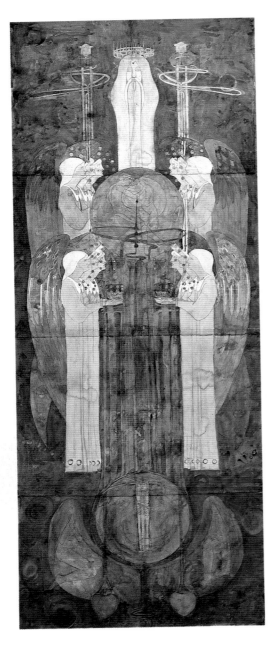

208. Attributed to Charles Rennie Mackintosh and James Herbert McNair (1868–1955). *The Creation and the Fall*, c. 1893. Pencil and watercolour, 104 x 40¾ in. (264.2 x 103.5 cm). Hunterian Art Gallery, University of Glasgow.

The one significant precedent is *The Harvest Moon* (plate 203), exhibited at the Glasgow Institute exhibition of 1894. In it a wraithlike band passes before the full golden moon, against which stands a winged figure. The band contains a repeated image of Cabanel's reclining Venus. In the foreground is a decorative tangle of thornbushes. The iconography is not certain, but it may well deal with the opposing themes of chastity and abandon, of Christianity and paganism. The picture's decorative finish, and its probable religious content, relate the work less to the Macdonald-McNair group (and Mackintosh may not have encountered the Macdonalds' work at this early date) and more to the innovative paintings of the Glasgow Boys E. A. Hornel and George Henry. Their major painting *The Druids* (1890; Glasgow Museums) had been recently exhibited in London and Munich and widely reviewed in the art press. A more intimate picture, Hornel's *Brook* (Hunterian Art Gallery, University of Glasgow), which deals with the related theme of spiritual choice, had been owned by McNair from 1891, the year the picture was painted.[13]

There is one other possible forerunner to Mackintosh's "Magazine" paintings—an ambitious but unsigned, undated, and untitled watercolour that depicts the creation of Eve and the Fall (plate 208). In it the narrative flows downward from the godhead through an illustration of the emergence of Eve from Adam's rib to an illustration of the Temptation. Stylistically and technically, the composition relates to work of the early 1890s by both McNair and Mackintosh. The figures in the creation, for example, are closely related to McNair's watercolour *The Lovers* (1893; private collection), while the temptress Eve conforms in every detail to Mackintosh's female figure in his diploma design of c. 1893 for the Glasgow School of Art Club. The whole is another experiment with content and style, this time indebted to William Blake. If, as is probable, the two men worked together on the composition, it is a rare early graphic collaboration by Mackintosh (and the only one known in watercolour) and a rare example of a collaboration by him with an artist other than Margaret Macdonald. Above all, it is significant for illustrating the close artistic and intellectual communion that existed between the two young architects, one that must have stimulated Mackintosh's contributions to "The Magazine."[14]

The evidence suggests that Mackintosh's experimentation with Symbolist watercolours was a private episode never intended for public consumption. Unlike the other members of the Four, Mackintosh neither exhibited nor published his paintings ("The Magazine's" circulation would have been confined to contributors and friends). He was, for example, the conspicuous absentee from the issue of the *Yellow Book* in 1896 that included work by the Macdonalds and McNair as well as by Katherine Cameron and D. Y. Cameron. That year saw the end of Mackintosh's experimentation. With the demise in 1896 of "The Magazine," he no longer had the opportunity, or perhaps the obligation, to contribute; he may have believed he had exhausted the possibilities of such work after the spectacular launch that year of one of "The Magazine" images as a poster.

Though he had no formal training in lithographic poster design, Mackintosh produced at least four poster designs in the mid-1890s, of which the large *Scottish Musical Review* is the most dramatic (plate 209). It is a reworking of *Autumn* from the November 1894 issue of "The Magazine." The poster presents characteristically idiosyncratic lettering (with the designer's name prominently set), unconventional stylisations of the human form and songbirds, and a rich colour scheme of purple, indigo, and green—perhaps symbolic of Scotland. An engaging piece of doggerel in the local magazine *Quiz* was typical of the popular response to Mackintosh's posters and comparable designs by McNair and the Macdonald sisters:

> One day as I gazed at a hoarding,
> My soul was filled with dread;
> For I looked on an Art School Poster,
> A Poster comprised of a head,
> With lines attached that seemed to fall
> In somewhat aimless ways—
> 'Twas the Crazy Aubrey Beardsley,
> No—the Aubrey Beardsley Craze.[15]

Despite trenchant backing from Newbery and the published support of the influential *Studio* editor, Gleeson White, Mackintosh did not take this Symbolist poster-making experiment further—though symbolism was to play an increasingly sophisticated role in his interiors of the early 1900s.[16] Instead he started to produce paintings of a more overtly decorative and popular character.

THE DECORATIVE WATERCOLOURS

Some ten watercolours dated between 1896 and 1898 are documented. These bear titles such as *Part Seen Imagined Part* (plate 210), *Princess Ess* (location unknown), and *Princess Uty* (location unknown), and usually depict a romantic female figure robed and garlanded with flowers, set against a nebulous background. This conscious reorientation was shared with, and perhaps led by, Margaret and Frances Macdonald, reflecting their reading of William Morris, Dante Gabriel Rossetti, the Ossianic writings of James Macpherson, and the plays of Maurice Maeterlinck. It reflects also a more conscious wooing of public and press. Romantic fairy-tale images would appeal to a Glasgow public enthusiastic for sentimental pictures such as those by the Dutch painter Matthijs Maris. Unlike "The Magazine" watercolours, these new compositions were exhibited by Mackintosh. *Part Seen Imagined Part* was mounted in a special metal frame designed and worked by Talwin Morris and sent to the important fifth show of the Arts and Crafts Exhibition Society in London in 1896. Others were submitted to the Royal Scottish Society of Painters in Water-Colours, the Glasgow Institute, and the 1899 Venice Biennale. By 1899, the *Evening News* (Glasgow) was able to report, with relief, on

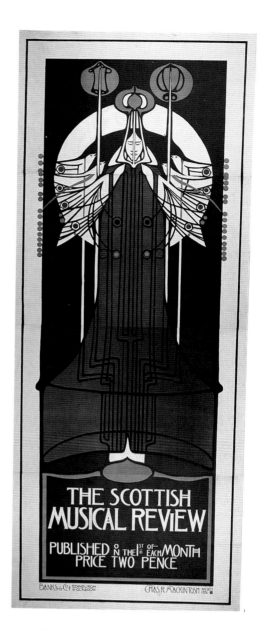

209. Charles Rennie Mackintosh. *Poster for the "Scottish Musical Review,"* 1896. Lithograph printed in four sections, 97¾ x 40 in. (247.8 x 101.5 cm). Hunterian Art Gallery, University of Glasgow.

the works by Mackintosh and the Macdonald sisters at the International Society of Sculptors, Painters and Gravers exhibition in London: "The pictures of each of them represent a vast improvement on anything I have previously seen of theirs. The desire to startle for startling's sake has passed away, and they now produce honest, mature work."[17]

These decorative watercolours blur the distinction between fine and applied art, demonstrating that Mackintosh did not view painting in a hierarchical way. He argued passionately, in his architectural writings and through his design work, for the equality of architecture, craft, and the fine arts. In the exhibition and domestic interiors of the early 1900s—at the 1900 Vienna Secession exhibition, his Glasgow flat at 120 Mains Street, and the Rose Boudoir (1902)—these watercolours fulfilled a decorative role equivalent to that of the embroidered hangings, metal and glass panels, and stencilled decoration. Subject matter and composition were freely transferred across the different media. Related stylisations of women appeared both in watercolours and in stencilled and gesso decorations. Conversely, designs for applied art, such as *Part Seen Imagined Part* and *The Wassail*, were exhibited in their own right. Mackintosh saw a relationship between painting and mural decoration (whether stencilled, in gesso, or later oil) that fulfilled the Arts and Crafts tenets of collaboration and a "commune" of all the arts. His early watercolour illustrating the creation of Eve and the Fall may well have been a youthful attempt at a scheme for a religious mural decoration inspired by his Italian trip.

One can conveniently, if simplistically, divide Mackintosh's graphic work of the early Glasgow years into two spheres. One encompasses his steady and independent evolution as an accomplished draughtsman and designer. The other comprises his short-lived painterly experiments of the 1890s, which formed part of his wider experimentation across the full range of his creative work. In terms of the latter, Mackintosh can be seen as part of two interrelated alliances, the Immortals and the Four, following their collective shifts in direction. He did not emerge, at this point, as an independent artist. Rather he was a restless, enquiring, talented young man, who would pick up and discard stylistic mannerisms. For him painting was just one of many skills—one that would increasingly be confined to the role of leisure activity.

By 1900 substantial changes in Mackintosh's personal and professional life further marginalised the role of painting. The Immortals had dispersed and the Four had fragmented, with McNair taking up a position in Liverpool in 1898, to be followed there a year later by his bride, Frances Macdonald. Professionally, Mackintosh was about to launch into the most intensively productive and successful years of his career. It is significant that at the *International Exhibition of Modern Decorative Art* at Turin, where Margaret Macdonald and the McNairs all exhibited new watercolour panels, Mackintosh had no new painting to present, showing instead primarily commissioned graphics and

210. Charles Rennie Mackintosh. *Part Seen Imagined Part*, 1896. Pencil and watercolour on tracing paper, 15⅜ x 7¹¹⁄₁₆ in. (39.0 x 19.5 cm). Glasgow Museums.

gesso designs, together with plates from the House for an Art Lover competition folio. He did not exhibit watercolours again until 1914.

ENGLAND

When things began to go badly wrong with Mackintosh's career in Glasgow, in the years before the First World War, Margaret Macdonald persuaded him to leave the city for a recuperative holiday over the summer of 1914. Their destination was an area already known to the Mackintoshes—the tiny village of Walberswick on the Suffolk coast, an artists' colony where the Newberys had holidayed since the 1890s.[18] Here, in lodgings next door to Newbery and his family—with their good friend the Glasgow Boy painter E. A. Walton at nearby Wenhaston, and in the company of the English painter Bertram Priestman—the talk would be of painting. According to contemporaries, the Mackintoshes spent their days working in a rented riverside studio[19]; this was the first occasion since the Italian tour over twenty years earlier that Mackintosh had the opportunity to concentrate exclusively on painting. He reputedly had a commission—for the exhibition or publication of a collection of flower drawings—and he worked hard, producing over forty exquisite studies between August 1914 and the early summer of 1915 (plate 211).[20] The process provided effective therapy and began a shift in Mackintosh's self-definition. He found new challenges in painting, and wrote to William Davidson of his "straightforward frank work . . . much thought of by the artist men who have seen them here—E. A. Walton, Bertram Priestman & others."[21] It was the first step in a reorientation that would lead finally to France.

Early in 1914, even before their move to Walberswick, Margaret Macdonald and Mackintosh had submitted work to an exhibition of British arts and crafts in Paris. Their exhibits were not craftwork but watercolours.[22] The hiatus in his architectural career allowed painterly ambitions to emerge—with these Mackintosh could be independent, needing neither client, budget, nor planning permission. Such ambitions had emerged relatively late—Mackintosh was now in his late forties. Yet painting had been a constant if informal part of his daily life for years. Each of the other members of the Four had already moved in that direction. Margaret Macdonald had been a member of the Royal Scottish Society of Painters in Water-Colours since 1898, a member of its council for several years, and a steady exhibitor. Almost every year between 1893 and 1924 she participated in an exhibition, whether in Glasgow, Edinburgh, London, Liverpool, on the Continent, or, in the late Glasgow years, in America. McNair's youthful ambition had been as a painter; he had spent a year in Rouen, France, studying watercolour with a M. Haudebert in the late 1880s, and in the mid-1890s he had given up architecture for painting and design.[23] Though much of his and Frances Macdonald's work was destroyed during their lifetimes, enough survives to document that the couple regularly painted and exhibited, at least until 1912. In 1911 they had produced enough work to mount a show exclusively of their watercolours and pastels at the Baillie Gallery in London. Other friends had also turned away from architecture and object design. The Scottish designer E. A. Taylor, for example, had largely given up interior design in favour of pattern designing and painting; from 1911 he was working in Paris with his wife, the artist Jessie M. King. Other friends, such as the versatile Austrian designer Koloman Moser, successfully combined design and painting.

By the summer of 1915 the Mackintoshes were in London, where they chose to settle in Chelsea—the painterly hub of the 1880s and 1890s and the former home of Whistler and E. A. Walton. Their circle came to comprise not

211. Charles Rennie Mackintosh. *Japanese Witch Hazel, Walberswick,* 1915. Pencil and watercolour, 10³⁄₈ x 8⁵⁄₁₆ in. (26.3 x 21.1 cm). Hunterian Art Gallery, University of Glasgow.

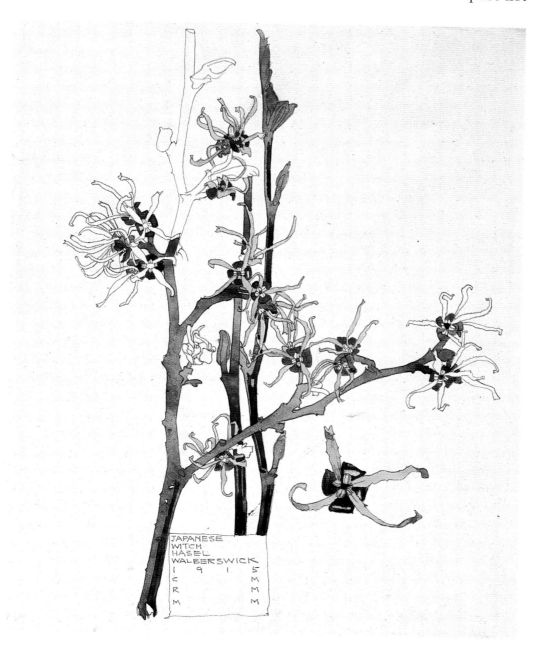

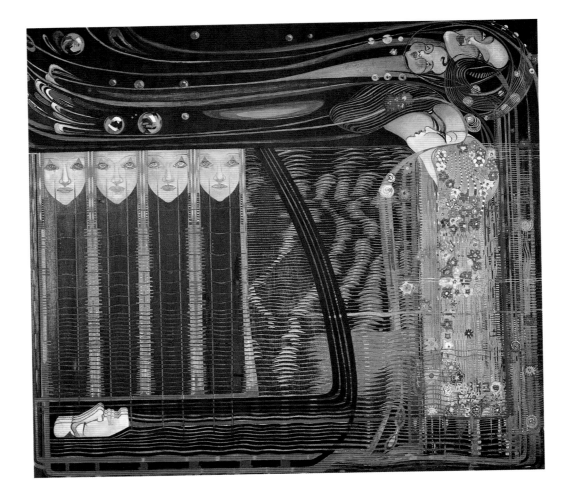

212. Margaret Macdonald Mackintosh (1864–1933) with Charles Rennie Mackintosh. *The Opera of the Sea*, c. 1916. Oil and tempera on canvas with *papier collé*, 56¾ x 63 in. (144.0 x 160.0 cm). Hessisches Landesmuseum, Darmstadt, Germany.

Pattern designs by Charles Rennie Mackintosh exist that are closely related to the female figure's flower-bedecked head; these were possibly working drawings for the oil. The combination of diced bands and richly coloured stylised flowers was developed for a number of his vivid textile designs.

architects but painters, musicians, writers, and sculptors: old friends from Scotland—J. D. Fergusson, Maurice Greiffenhagen, W. O. Hutchison, and James Pryde, all painters; and new friends Randolph Schwabe (lecturer at the Royal College), the young Slade School artists Edgar Hereford and Rudolph Ihlee, the painter-designers Claude Lovat-Fraser and George Sheringham, and the photographer E. O. Hoppé. The couple joined the theatrical groups the Plough and Margaret Morris's Theatre Club; they became involved in the Allied Artists Association and the London Salon of the Independents; and they ate regularly at the Blue Cockatoo on Cheyne Walk, an idiosyncratic restaurant frequented by artists. Their milieu was bohemian and artistic.

The joint ambition of the Mackintoshes to establish themselves quickly in London as painters is seen in their exhibit for the 1916 Arts and Crafts Exhibition Society show, held in the fine-art sanctum of the Royal Academy. In line with the major emphasis of the exhibition on mural painting, the Mackintoshes submitted a "wall decoration."

As only two months' notice had been given, the schedule may have precluded the possibility of designing and executing three-dimensional work. Nonetheless, the Mackintoshes produced a significant installation, *The Voices of the Wood*, a "wall decoration of panel and candlesticks." The "panel"—unillustrated and poorly documented—seems to have comprised two canvasses, *The Opera of the Sea* (plate 212) and *The Opera of the Winds* (location unknown) butted together.[24] This was a collaborative effort, based closely on the eponymous gesso panels designed in 1903 by Margaret Macdonald for a music room in the Vienna town house of art patron Fritz Wärndorfer. Margaret Macdonald probably executed the paintings, using her 1903 designs, while Mackintosh designed the overall colour scheme, the decorative details for the background, and the candlesticks. The format was clearly modelled on the double-panelled canvas *The Little Hills* (subsequently incorporated in Miss Cranston's Willow Tea Rooms and now in the Hunterian Art Gallery, University of Glasgow), which Macdonald had worked on in collaboration with Mackintosh in Walberswick.[25]

The launch of the exhibition was chaotic—many exhibitors, including the Mackintoshes, were not ready—and the catalogue was weeks late. This may in part explain the lack of critical attention their work received. In addition, theirs was just one exhibit among over two thousand objects, which ranged from large-scale murals to jewellery. And their exhibit did puzzle. For some the difficulty arose with the subject. The *Scotsman* opined, "Voices of the Wood is the name Mr. and Mrs. Mackintosh have given to a picture of wonderful colour, but of doubtful meaning." Other commentators sidestepped the issue, describing it as a "characteristic painting" or "unmistakable."[26]

The explanatory text in the catalogue did not immediately help: "*The Song of the Lovers, The Dirge of the Dead Mother, The Lament of the Little Child, The Song of Peace as she covers the Child with her Cloak of Comfort, The Songs of Joy, The Cries of the Lost Souls* and *The Great Silences.*" Yet the text may provide a key to the apparently disparate elements in the composition, the various "Voices of the Wood," as did the titles for Mackintosh's early *Tree* watercolours. The surviving right-hand panel (plate 212) can be read as containing *The Song of the Lovers* (right); *The Song of Peace* (top); *The Cries of the Lost Souls* (left); and *The Great Silences* (bottom). Stylistically, the exhibit did not easily fit into a recognised category. The *British Architect* commented, "It looks as though it was specially meant for execution in needlework, to which its very liney effect would be suitable."[27] The work clearly posed a problem for the hanging committee, who finally placed it alongside the stained glass, near the embroidery, in the inaccurately titled "Printing and Lithography Room."

The Little Hills and *The Voices of the Wood* show the continuation of Mackintosh's adherence to a collaborative integration of art, craft, and architecture. Such collaboration provided the central theme of the last exhibition in which he participated before leaving for France, the forty-eighth Royal Academy Winter Exhibition, which opened in January 1923. Entitled an *Exhibition of Decorative Art*, it specifically aimed "to draw attention to the impor-

tant part which the arts of Painting and Sculpture should take in architectural schemes."[28] The catalogue singled out the inspiring example of the frescoes of the Italian Renaissance. "By means of these decorations the arts were made a source of inspiration to everyone. Their influence was blended with the daily purpose and use of each building, and made itself felt by a quiet and habitual impression; they were thus accepted as an essential part of an aesthetic and social education which continued, as a matter of course, throughout the life of the ordinary person."[29] This was a programme that must have resonated with Mackintosh and surely stimulated memories of the early days of his career, in Italy. His exhibit, *A Landscape Panel*, is sadly unrecorded.

In the 1890s a duality had existed between Mackintosh's symbolic and decorative paintings, which he had originated as a member of a wider group, and his independent studies of nature and architecture, which recorded observed reality. A similar duality characterises the London years. Concurrently with his collaborative large-scale oils, Mackintosh was finding a new challenge—working independently on still-life paintings. Ten are documented, executed between 1916 and the early 1920s. These bouquets drew on his botanical knowledge but also display a hitherto unseen richness of colour. The tonal variations and colour harmonies of the still lifes (plate 213) are among the most sumptuous of his career and are closely related to his contemporaneous textile designs (plate 214).[30]

As early as 1916 Mackintosh was exhibiting the still lifes at the International Society of Sculptors, Painters and Gravers in London, with subsequent exhibits there in 1917 and 1918, at the Goupil Gallery, London, in 1923, and in the early 1920s at international exhibitions in Chicago and Detroit.[31] At the 1916 International Society exhibition he was in the company of a wide range of Scottish artists (some of them friends), including Lily Blatherwick, Norah Neilson Gray, Francis Newbery, James Pryde, Olive Carleton Smyth, and the Scottish Colourists F.C.B. Cadell and S. J. Peploe. Mackintosh had a particular admiration for the work of the Colourist J. D. Fergusson. Intensely productive years in France before the war had fired Fergusson's paintings of Paris, women, and the south of France with a rich colour and a bold line. Their impact remained with Mackintosh long after leaving Chelsea. "I still have such a vivid mental picture of them that I can pass them in review one by one making a sort of subconscious 'peep show' and see them quite clearly just as you showed them to us."[32] Their exuberance and concern with surface pattern making must have encouraged Mackintosh's experiments with still-life composition, even though the expressive means of the two artists differed widely.

Technically, Mackintosh's varied output as architectural draughtsman, Symbolist artist, and botanical and still-life painter remained rooted in the teachings of South Kensington and his professional training, with its emphasis on line and on the use of pen, pencil, and pure watercolour. Mackintosh was not experimental with his materials; there is little known use of pastel or char-

■■ OPPOSITE
213. Charles Rennie Mackintosh. *Anemones*, c. 1916. Pencil and watercolour, 19⅞ x 19½ in. (50.5 x 49.5 cm). Private collection.
  Mackintosh incorporated one of his textile designs in the background.
■■ ABOVE
214. Charles Rennie Mackintosh. *Textile Design: Stylised Flowers and Buds*, c. 1915–23. Pencil and watercolour, 18⅞ x 21⅝ in. (48.0 x 55.0 cm). Hunterian Art Gallery, University of Glasgow.

coal, for example, and he rarely worked in oil. But the confines of South Kensington's vocabulary were transmogrified by Mackintosh's inherent sense of pattern, his delight in the decorative potential of pure line. The vitality of compositions like *Japanese Witch Hazel, Walberswick* (plate 211) derives from the continuously moving outline, which crosses and touches and intertwines, defining space as eloquently as it does form; watercolour is used only in a subordinate role, as illustrative embellishment. Similar concerns inform the elaborately worked perspectives of the mid-1890s to early 1900s, in which one senses Mackintosh flaunting his artistic fluency. Equally virtuoso performances are found in the stencilled decoration of a room (see plate 130), the design of a gesso panel (see plate 183) or a leaded-glass door (see page 2). In such cases, line is used as the two-dimensional embellishment of a flat plane. But Mackintosh also drew in three dimensions, whether using the line of a picture rail to unify and define the disparate volumes of an interior or inscribing Glasgow's coat of arms in metal above Glasgow School of Art.

Mackintosh was not creative in terms of subject matter. His early experimentation in the 1890s with Symbolist watercolours had been brief and seems to have been stimulated by others. The later mural paintings looked back to the major gessos of the 1900s, while the origination of both murals and gessos had been a collaborative process. Where Mackintosh did work independently—on botanical studies and still lifes—his inspiration was nature. In this, again, he honoured the Arts and Crafts philosophy that underpinned his design training. Indeed, painting and design overlapped, for Mackintosh approached his sketches and watercolours with the analytical mind of the designer and pattern maker. He thought in terms of two-dimensional surface pattern as much as, if not more than, in terms of the inherent three-dimensionality of his subjects.

FRANCE

By the early 1920s, finding himself increasingly estranged from current architectural taste, with little prospect of establishing a practice in London, and financially hard-pressed, Mackintosh sublet the London studios and moved abroad with Macdonald. Their choice of France as a destination was not surprising. Mackintosh had long cherished the ambition to visit the south of France; life would be cheap, and the Francophile enthusiasm of Fergusson, as well as of Ihlee and Hereford, would have provided further encouragement. By then both Ihlee and Hereford were painting in Collioure, near the Franco-Spanish border.

The exact date of the Mackintoshes' arrival is not known, nor are their subsequent movements in and beyond France fully documented. On the evidence of the surviving watercolours and letters, it is known that from the beginning of 1924 to the early summer of 1927 they were based largely in the Pyrénées-Orientales, staying at Amélie-les-Bains, Ille-sur-Têt, Mont Louis

(plate 215), and Port Vendres. It appears that, from 1925 at least, the couple followed a routine of summering in Mont Louis and spending part of the rest of the year at Port Vendres, a few kilometres southeast of Collioure. Though the historic and picturesque fishing village of Collioure was the favoured destination for artists, the Mackintoshes appear deliberately to have chosen to settle on its fringes. Mackintosh preferred to paint the architecture and landscape of the bustling and expanding working port of Port Vendres: of his thirty-eight surviving French landscapes, nearly half show the harbour and environs of Port Vendres (plate 200), as opposed to only two of Collioure.

215. Charles Rennie Mackintosh. *Mixed Flowers, Mont Louis*, 1925. Pencil and watercolour, 10⁵/₁₆ x 8¹/₁₆ in. (26.2 x 20.5 cm). Trustees of The British Museum, London.

216. Charles Rennie Mackintosh. *The Rock*, 1927. Pencil and water-colour, 12 x 14¹⁄₂ in. (30.5 x 36.8 cm). Private collection.

In this seclusion, the Mackintoshes' life was modest—walking, harbour watching, reading the British papers or books supplied by Mudie's Lending Library, enjoying the local food and wine, and, in the case of Mackintosh at least, painting. Now he was free, virtually for the first time, to paint for himself.

His chosen subject matter was landscape—specifically, its interrelationships with man-made architecture and engineering. With the exception of the early *Wareham* (plate 205), an interest in landscape for its own sake had emerged relatively late, with a watercolour sketch of Kent oasthouses of 1910 (Hunterian Art Gallery, University of Glasgow). In Suffolk, between 1914 and 1915, landscape had been further explored; two watercolours, of Walberswick (see plate 71) and Blackshore-on-the-Blyth (George Smith), survive. Further encouragement would have come in London, through Mackintosh's close friendship with the highly skilled draughtsman and watercolour artist Randolph Schwabe. Two views of the gently rolling hillside outside Worth Matravers in Dorset, executed during a holiday there with the Schwabes in 1920 (Glasgow School of Art), are the sole survivors of what may have been a more substantial body of work. The last known work exhibited by Mackintosh in London was *Venetian Palace, Blackshore-on-the-Blyth* (George Smith) at the 1923 Royal Academy exhibition. But paintings of pure landscape were rare; in France only a couple were completed. The relationships of a hill town to its surrounding landscape, of a port to the sea and hills behind, or a fort to its rock and approaching roads, however, were rigorously explored from different vantage points. At least four different views of the hill town Fetges survive, and sixteen watercolours of Port Vendres, including four of the outlying Fort Mailly.[33]

Little is known of Mackintosh's working practice at any stage in his career, beyond the physical evidence of the pictures themselves. However, a continuous stream of letters, written to Macdonald over a six-week period in 1927, together with the watercolours, provide valuable insights into his technique.[34] Progress was slow and painstaking; *The Rock* (plate 216) was still unfinished even after five weeks of steady work.[35] A chosen subject would be closely observed and analysed in advance—the lack of any preliminary sketches suggests that this was largely a visual process—and then the picture made in front of the subject, never indoors. Mackintosh seems not to have worked from memory or sketches. Even the earlier flower studies and still lifes, though worked on in the studio, were painted from life.

Mackintosh appears to have used the minimum of equipment: a prepared paper-mounted millboard, collapsible lead tubes of watercolour paint, an enamelled sketcher's palette, mixing dish, rubber, ruler, brushes, pocketknife, water container, and a brush-washing cup. There is no indication of the bulkier accoutrements of umbrella, easel, or stool. Unencumbered, Mackintosh could scramble to the best locations on rocks or hillsides from which to secure his preferred vantage point. The principal areas of the composition, already predetermined, would be outlined in pencil, creating a framework that cannot have been dissimilar to his earlier architectural sketches, such as the Holy Island studies (plate 202). Watercolour would then be applied, and the pencil subsequently largely erased.

Subject matter was often boldly manipulated to achieve a balanced composition. Different views of different subjects would be dovetailed together. In *The Rock* the background view of Port Vendres was painted in first, from a vantage point in Anse Christine, a bay south of Port Vendres; Mackintosh then moved slightly to the west to a vantage point from which he would have the desired view of his principal subject, the rocky outcrop (plate 217). More dramatically, with *The Fort* (Hunterian Art Gallery, University of Glasgow), he must have pivoted through ninety degrees on the spot to fix a view of the lighthouse on the Redouté du Fanal and of the distant Côte Vermeille, with which to close off the left-hand section of the composition. In a similar way, in *Le Fort Mauresque* he closed up the wide bay that separates the main subject and the distant promontory by combining separate views of each.

Dramatic effect was intensified by the use of particularly high or low viewpoints, as in his Fort Mailly studies, or by slicing through foreground details, such as the road in *Fetges* (plate 218). Contrasts and tensions were often set up within the composition. In *The Rock*, for example, areas of dark and light play off against each other, while the angular architecture counter-

217. Rocks, Port Vendres, France. A walkway has now obliterated the shore at bottom left.

218. Charles Rennie Mackintosh. *Fetges*, c. 1925–26. Pencil and watercolour, 18¼ x 18 in. (46.4 x 45.7 cm). Tate Gallery, London; Presented by Walter W. Blackie, 1929.

points the sweep of the landscape. Spatial ambiguities are also established. At the left the harbour road, rue du Soleil, is cut sharply back into space; but, at the other edge of the composition, the vine terraces seem to rise heavenward with no attempt at recession, and the central rocks stand like two-dimensional theatre flats, with little sense conveyed of their actual solidity.

Despite, or perhaps because of, over forty years' experience, Mackintosh was finding it difficult to redefine his technique. Late in 1925 he confided to Newbery: "I am struggling to paint in watercolour—soon I shall start in oils— but I feel I have a great lot to learn, or unlearn. I seem to know far too much, and this knowledge obscures the really significant facts, but I am getting on."[36] Later letters to his wife speak of the need to get more light into the pictures, to restrain his passion for green, and he confides to her that he is experimenting a lot. One notable, if short-lived, experiment shows Mackintosh trying out a Vorticist-inspired manner. Four small watercolours present looser, more gener-alised studies of steamers and figures at Port Vendres's quayside.[37]

It is difficult to establish a secure chronology, for few of the French water-colours are dated, and what inscriptions do exist are not reliable since both signatures and dates are known to have been added later, both by Mackintosh and by Macdonald. However, it is possible to make general groupings on stylistic grounds between early and late: late watercolours related to *The Rock* of 1927 include *The Fort, Port Vendres, The Little Bay, La Rue du Soleil*, and others; less sophisticated earlier works are typified by *A Southern Port* and *The Road Through the Rocks*.

Some measure of Mackintosh's technical advances is provided by two nearly identical views of the mountain village of Fetges. Fetges sits due east of Mont Louis and could, in the 1920s, be clearly seen from the sixteenth-century fortifications of this military outpost, across the steep river gully that separates the two villages. *Fetges* (plate 218) shows a view of the town seen across this gully from the road beneath Mont Louis. Probably dating from the couple's summer trip to the mountains in 1926, it was one of the few pictures taken to London by Macdonald the next May; these presumably represented the finest examples of Mackintosh's most recent work. That month Mackintosh wrote to her that it was the best thing he had done, or was ever likely to do. *Slate Roofs* (plate 219) is taken from a near-identical vantage point; its central roadside block sits at the right-hand edge of *Fetges. Slate Roofs* is conceivably a preliminary study for *Fetges*, but given its stylistic relationship to other signed watercolours—notably the "Mountain Landscape" pictures—it must be an earlier, finished composition, perhaps from the summer of 1925. In the later work, through a sharper and tighter technique, based on disciplined draughtsmanship, and through the precisely controlled application of washes of pure, barely modulated colour and sharp contrasts of light and shade, Mackintosh so transformed the view that the two paintings have not previously been recognised as being of the same subject.

Mackintosh's interpretation of these Mediterranean subjects is not concerned with the moods or forces or textures of nature, or with the recording of human activity. Rather, his watercolours depict an immobilised world, unruffled and unpeopled. Out of mundane reality—a diminutive rock formation, a modest, ruined fort, or a roadside straggle of houses—Mackintosh formulated patterns from shadows, rocks, terraces, fields, and reflections that transformed the subject without sacrificing its identity. With the finest, such as *Fetges*, he purified his technique, expunging any flamboyant handling of the medium or use of line as a decorative means in itself. These pictures achieve an equilibrium of draughtsmanship, composition, and material.

In part these flat stylisations derive from the Vorticist experiments of his London graphics for W. J. Bassett-Lowke—a rare example of a Scot working in this language; the most notable other contemporary Scottish practitioner was the little-discussed printmaker and illustrator William McCance. Parallels can also be seen with earlier townscapes by the Viennese Egon Schiele and with contemporary paintings by the French artists Henri de Waroquier and Jean-Hippolyte Marchand and by the Dutchman Dirck Filarski. Mackintosh's frag-

219. Charles Rennie Mackintosh. *Slate Roofs*, c. 1925. Pencil and watercolour, 14$^{7}/_{16}$ x 10$^{15}/_{16}$ in. (37.0 x 27.8 cm). Glasgow School of Art.

The snaking road at the left forms the centrepoint of *Fetges* (plate 218).

mentation of form and manipulation of perspective give the watercolours a superficial relationship to Cubist aesthetics. But the origins of these pictures, which so astonished his contemporaries in Glasgow in 1933, lie in the work of the 1890s: the line is South Kensington and the manipulation of subject that of a skilled perspectivist of the turn of the century; the selective analysis and ordered pattern making can be found in work as early as his sketchbook studies of the 1890s. The skillful games that Mackintosh played with planes and viewpoints in his finest architectural designs are here reconfigured in watercolour.

Drawing and painting were a constant part of Mackintosh's life, often used concurrently as professional language and design tool and as a vehicle for symbolic ideas and decorative pattern. Mackintosh's sense of himself as a painter emerged as his design career receded. Yet "painter" and "designer" cannot be, and in Mackintosh's philosophy were not, treated as separate entities. As a designer, Mackintosh worked with colour and line and form and space in the pursuit of beauty. These same ingredients characterise his painting. The same discipline and artistry is apparent in his orchestration of a room or a facade as in his recording of a flower or a French hill town.

Ironically, those circumstances that provided Mackintosh's greatest opportunity to paint—the self-imposed isolation in France—also denied him public recognition. In his lifetime one landscape, *Collioure (Pyrénées-Orientales)*, was shown in Chicago at the sixth International Water Color Exhibition, and another painting, *Le Fort Mauresque*, was shown in Paris at the *British Artists Exhibition* of 1927. The Leicester Galleries, London, showed a few as part of a group exhibition in 1928.[38] But it was not until the memorial exhibition of 1933 that they were seen publicly as a group; thirty-one were shown. Four were lent by the Mackintoshes' long-standing friends Desmond Chapman-Huston, Francis Newbery, and Randolph Schwabe. Seven were acquired by William Davidson, Mackintosh's client at Windyhill and the principal organiser of the exhibition. Such loyalty typifies the strength of friendship and professional respect inspired by Mackintosh and his work. Though confined to a small group, it ensured the long-term survival of his work in the face of more general neglect. Five landscapes were distributed among the Mackintoshes' family and lawyers. One was bought by Glasgow Art Gallery. The rest were sold to private individuals, generally for between fifteen and twenty pounds. As a collected oeuvre the watercolours were to remain largely unseen for the next forty years, until the revelatory major survey exhibition held at Glasgow Art Gallery in 1978.

NOTES

The author gratefully acknowledges the financial support provided by The British Academy, The Paul Mellon Centre for Studies in British Art, and the University of Glasgow towards a research trip to Port Vendres and the surrounding area in 1993.

1. Mackintosh would have been familiar with the successful draughtsmanship of contemporaries such as Alexander McGibbon, employed by Honeyman and Keppie, and the Scottish architect James MacLaren, whose designs informed Mackintosh's work of the mid-1890s. The decorative architectural drawings by Richard Norman Shaw's pupil Reginald Barratt are also comparable—see, for example, his drawing of S. Maria del Carmine, Siena, illustrated in the *Architect* 38 (October 1886), between pages 196 and 197. I am grateful to Alan Crawford for drawing this to my attention.

2. Four sketchbooks are in the Hunterian Art Gallery, University of Glasgow; the fifth is in the National Library of Ireland, Dublin.

3. For a full account of Mackintosh's Italian tour, see Pamela Robertson, ed., *Charles Rennie Mackintosh: The Architectural Papers* (Wendlebury, England: White Cockade Publishing, 1990), pp. 64–125.

4. Mackintosh's architectural sketches were published only once in his lifetime: nineteen drawings were illustrated in three issues of the *British Architect* in 1895. The first feature was undoubtedly prompted by the argument currently being aired in the *British Architect* and the letters page of the London *Times* over the merits of current standards of restoration in relation to the churches of Wareham, Dorset. The quality of these drawings may well have encouraged the *British Architect* to request additional sketches for two subsequent issues. See *British Architect* 44 (November 1895): 326–27, 332–33, 359–61, 384–85, 388–89.

5. *Evening Citizen* (Glasgow), May 4, 1933, p. 10: "It is not often that an architect is also master of the art of landscape painting."

6. For a full and well-illustrated survey, see Roger Billcliffe, *The Glasgow Boys* (London: John Murray, 1985).

7. Mackintosh to Hermann Muthesius, May 11, 1899, Werkbund Archive, Berlin.

8. Roger Billcliffe, *Charles Rennie Mackintosh: The Complete Furniture, Furniture Drawings and Interior Designs*, 3d ed. (London: John Murray, 1986), D1894.4, ill. p. 257.

9. Ibid., p. 10. Billcliffe argues that the process of tracing the outlines of furniture from published images, known to have been followed by McNair, was probably also used by Mackintosh.

10. See Robertson, ed., *Architectural Papers*, for transcriptions of Mackintosh's two early lectures on architecture and for an introductory essay to those lectures by David Walker, "Mackintosh on Architecture."

11. In the foreword to *Charles Rennie Mackintosh: Exhibition Catalogue* (Glasgow: McLellan Galleries, 1933) Jessie Newbery, wife of Francis Newbery, recalled the impression made on the Four in the 1890s by Carlos Schwabe's illustrations to Emile Zola's *Le Rêve* (Paris: Librairie Marpon et Flammarion, 1892) and Jan Toorop's work published in the *Studio* 1 (1893): 247.

12. For an imaginative and at times illuminating account of Mackintosh's use of symbolism, see Timothy Neat, *Part Seen, Part Imagined: Meaning and Symbolism in the Work of Charles Rennie Mackintosh and Margaret Macdonald* (Edinburgh: Canongate, 1994).

13. For an exhibition history of *The Druids*, 1890, see Billcliffe, *Glasgow Boys*, pp. 292–99. For *The Brook*, see Christopher Allan, *A Guide to the Hunterian Art Gallery* (Glasgow: Hunterian Art Gallery, University of Glasgow, 1990), pp. 56–57.

14. The existence of this watercolour raises the possibility of the loss of other non-"Magazine" Symbolist watercolours by Mackintosh.

15. *Quiz* (Glasgow), February 21, 1895, p. 157; in Elizabeth Bird, "Ghouls and Gas Pipes: Public Reaction to Early Work of 'The Four,'" *Scottish Art Review* 14 (1975): 16. The poem was dedicated to Glasgow School of Art.

16. Ibid., pp. 16, 28. Gleeson White was author of the *Studio* articles cited by Bird.

17. *Evening News* (Glasgow), May 22, 1899, p. 5; in Janice Helland, "The 'New Woman' in *Fin-de-Siècle* Art: Frances and Margaret Macdonald" (Ph.D. diss., University of Victoria, Canada, 1991), p. 173.

18. Mackintosh is first known to have visited the area in 1897, and subsequent visits are likely, as the Newberys purchased a house in Walberswick in the early 1900s.

19. See Alistair Moffat and Colin Baxter, *Remembering Charles Rennie Mackintosh: An Illustrated Biography* (Lanark, Scotland: Colin Baxter Photography, 1989), pp. 79, 80.

20. See Pamela Robertson, *Charles Rennie Mackintosh: Art Is the Flower* (London: Pavilion, 1995), for a full discussion of Mackintosh's flower painting.

21. Mackintosh to William Davidson, June 18, 1915, Hunterian Art Gallery, University of Glasgow.

22. *Arts décoratifs de Grande-Bretagne et d'Irlande* (Paris: Palais du Louvre, 1914). Mackintosh exhibited *Le Jardin* (cat. no. 1320); Margaret Macdonald exhibited *Cinderella* (cat. no. 1577), *The Mysterious Garden* (cat. no. 1578), and *The Sleeper* (cat. no. 1579). I am grateful to Barclay Lennie for drawing my attention to this exhibition.

23. Thomas Howarth, *Charles Rennie Mackintosh and the Modern Movement*, 2d ed. (London: Routledge and Kegan Paul, 1977), p. 6 n. 1, refers to "M. Haudebert," who is still unidentified but probably Léon-Auguste-César Hodebert (1851–1914)—painter, printmaker, and teacher.

24. It has been speculated that this work comprised seven panels, each illustrating one of the seven lines of the accompanying text published in the catalogue. However, careful examination of the few published notices and consideration of the space available, supported by the catalogue description of the exhibit as "a panel," confirms that *The Voices of the Wood* was a smaller exhibit than has previously been suggested. *The Opera of the Wind* is illustrated in Lawrence Weaver, *The Smaller House* (London: Architectural Press, 1924), p. 52.

25. A preliminary drawing, annotated by Mackintosh and probably executed by him, exists for the right-hand panel of *The Little Hills* (both Hunterian Art Gallery, University of Glasgow).

26. *Scotsman* (Edinburgh), October 10, 1916. A useful album of press clippings for this exhibition is in the National Art Library, Victoria and Albert Museum, London, A.13 (14). Unfortunately, the clippings are not all fully identified.

27. "The Arts and Crafts Exhibition—II," *British Architect* 85 (November 1916): 138–39.

28. Preface to the catalogue *Exhibition of Decorative Art* (London: Royal Academy, 1923). I am grateful to Janice Helland for drawing my attention to this exhibition.

29. Ibid.

30. For a well-illustrated survey of the textile designs, see Roger Billcliffe, *Charles Rennie Mackintosh Textile Designs*, 2d ed. (San Francisco: Pomegranate Artbooks, 1993); and for a fuller discussion of the still lifes, see Robertson, *Art Is the Flower*, chap. 4.

31. Mackintosh exhibited still lifes and landscapes in Chicago at each annual International Water Color Exhibition between 1922 and 1926, inclusive, and two still lifes at the

1920 *British Arts and Crafts* exhibition in Detroit and U.S. tour.

32. Mackintosh to J. D. Fergusson, February 1, 1925; in Moffat and Baxter, *Remembering Charles Rennie Mackintosh*, pp. 109–10.

33. References are to Roger Billcliffe, *Mackintosh Watercolours*, 3d ed. (London: John Murray, 1992). Views of Fetges: *The Boulders* (cat. no. 177); *Fetges* (cat. no. 180); *Slate Roofs* (cat. no. 194); and probably *Mountain Village* (cat. no. 199). Views of Fort Mailly: *The Road Through the Rocks* (cat. no. 182); *The Fort* (cat. no. 184); *Port Vendres* (cat. no. 185); *Le Fort Maillert* (cat. no. 215). Views of Port Vendres and environs: *A Southern Port* (cat. no. 176); *Le Fort Mauresque* (cat. no. 183); *Port Vendres, La Ville* (cat. no. 186); *La Rue du Soleil* (cat. no. 208); *Port Vendres* (cat. no. 290); *Steamers* (cat. nos. 210–13); *The Little Bay* (cat. no. 214); *The Rocks* [sic] (cat. no. 216); and *The Lighthouse* (ex-Billcliffe; private collection).

34. The twenty-three letters (Hunterian Art Gallery, University of Glasgow), dubbed by Mackintosh his "Chronycle," spanned May 11 to the end of June 1927. The terms of the donor's gift do not allow direct quotation from them. I am grateful to my colleague Christopher Allan for his advice on the evaluation of Mackintosh's technique, which is based on references in those letters.

35. Mackintosh refers to the painting in the 1927 letters as "The Rock," and that form has been used in this essay. The painting was exhibited at the 1933 Mackintosh memorial exhibition as *The Rocks*, the title that has recurred in the subsequent literature. No title is inscribed on the work.

36. Mackintosh to Francis Newbery, December 28, 1925, National Library of Scotland.

37. See Billcliffe, *Watercolours*, cat. nos. 210–13.

38. Desmond Chapman-Huston bought two French landscapes from the exhibition at the Leicester Galleries. See Billcliffe, *Watercolours*, cat. no. 208 and cat. no. 214. No catalogue of that show has been traced.

IV

CONCLUSION

The Mackintosh Phenomenon

■■

ALAN CRAWFORD

In 1992 I spent six months in Glasgow doing the research for a short book on Mackintosh. I spent many days in the Hunterian Art Gallery, studying the University of Glasgow's unparalleled Mackintosh collection. On the way home, I would pass shop windows full of mugs and T-shirts and little roundels of stained glass, the giftware in the style of Mackintosh now happily dubbed "Mockintosh" or "Mockingtosh."[1] Outside my flat there were neo-Mackintosh streetlamps, and the brass doorplate was stamped with Mockingtosh lettering. In the Hunterian's reconstruction of the Mackintoshes' own house, I would eavesdrop on visitors who seemed to have been transported by those subtle, intimate interiors into the very presence of Mackintosh and Margaret Macdonald. And outside Glasgow School of Art I would overhear Glaswegians explaining the merits of the building to their weekend guests. Londoners do not do that in front of St. Paul's.

By the end of my stay I could see that there were two subjects, two Mackintoshes. One was the subject of my research, the man who was born in 1868. The other was the Mackintosh I found at large on the streets of Glasgow, the Mackintosh phenomenon. I wrote my book, which is a story of Mackintosh's life and work.[2] And now I write a story of the other Mackintosh.[3]

There have been three stages in the development of Mackintosh's reputation. During the first stage (1928–1960), his architectural work enjoyed a specialised reputation, chiefly among architects and architectural historians who saw him as a pioneer of the Modern movement. In the second stage (1960–1980), his work as an artist and designer came to the fore. His furniture and interiors were seen as an important variant of Art Nouveau, and museum curators, collectors, designers, and furniture manufacturers joined the ranks of his admirers. In the third stage (1980–1995), his reputation has been increas-

220. Tom Conti as Mackintosh and Kara Wilson as Macdonald in the television documentary *Dreams and Recollections* (1987); in the background, the buildings of the University of Glasgow.

ingly in the hands of commercial interests and of the media. His work is valued less for itself than as a source of images, and his reputation reaches millions of people who would be hard-pressed to name another architect. I have made sharp divisions between these stages but, of course, the transitions have been gradual.

1928–1960: The Age of the Architects

Mackintosh left Glasgow in 1914, and by the 1920s the city had almost forgotten him. John Summerson first went there in 1926 and found that "his works were remembered, if at all, only as something quite out-moded, and not worth a thought or glance."[4] In 1933 the contents of Kate Cranston's house, Hous'hill, were sold at auction. Only two buyers at the sale knew that the strange furniture was by Mackintosh, and a revolving bookcase (now in the Scottish National Gallery of Modern Art, Edinburgh) had fallen into several pieces, one of which was mistaken for a wireless aerial.[5] Mackintosh might have been completely forgotten if it had not been for William Davidson, for whom he had designed Windyhill. A few months after Margaret's death in January 1933, Davidson and the Glasgow architect Jeffrey Waddell organised a memorial exhibition of the Mackintoshes' work in Glasgow Corporation's McLellan Galleries (plate 221), at which many of Mackintosh's watercolours were sold for small sums to friends and colleagues.[6]

But just as his reputation was diminishing locally, it was growing on the printed page. Mackintosh had been rediscovered by architects and journalists associated with the Modern movement. In 1924 Charles Marriott, the art critic of the *Times* (London) and not a Modernist, published a thorough if insular survey entitled *Modern English Architecture.* He did not give Mackintosh prominence but reported in passing, "It is hardly too much to say that the whole modernist movement in European architecture derives from him."[7] In 1933 the *Listener* hailed Mackintosh as "this pioneer of the modern movement in architecture."[8] Scottish architects of the 1930s like Robert Hurd and Frank Mears, whose Modernism was based on the simple, harled masses of their native vernacular, looked back to Mackintosh's Windyhill and The Hill House as forerunners. And among the European leaders of Modernism, Walter Gropius, Eric Mendelsohn, and Le Corbusier knew of Mackintosh's work.[9] In 1935 the Royal Institute of British Architects held its annual conference in Glasgow, and all the talk was of Mackintosh and Alexander Thomson (as it is today).[10] In 1936 Nikolaus Pevsner's *Pioneers of the Modern Movement: From William Morris to Walter Gropius* appeared.

Pevsner's interpretation of Mackintosh was not new. He saw Glasgow School of Art as looking forward to the twentieth century, and Mackintosh as a master in the handling of space—both typical Modernist interpretations.[11] But he gave the authority of a scholarly historical narrative to the prevailing assessment of Mackintosh, whose place in history now seemed secure, at

221. The Mackintosh memorial exhibition at the McLellan Galleries, Glasgow. Photographed by T. and R. Annan Ltd., May 1933.

least for British and perhaps also European readers. In the United States, on the other hand, where the history of Modernism was shaped by Henry-Russell Hitchcock, Alfred Barr, and Philip Johnson around a purist machine aesthetic, Mackintosh had less standing. The progressives of around 1900, whose transitional role so fascinated Pevsner, were weeded out by Hitchcock if he thought their styles impure; and he thought that Mackintosh was "not of prime importance."[12]

The Modernists concentrated on Mackintosh's buildings, looking for functional expression, spatial innovation, and, in some cases, freedom from precedent. They felt uneasy with his decorative work and liked to edit it out. Raymond McGrath wrote, "His name has in it a suggestion of high-backed chairs and those little flowering trees which had a part in all his pen pictures. But these are details, signs of the 'art nouveau' and in no way representative of his serious art."[13] One technique was to identify the collaborative interiors with Margaret Macdonald and then dismiss them as feminine, trivial, and dated. Before the 1933 memorial exhibition, the Scottish Modernist critic P. Morton Shand wrote to Davidson urging that the exhibition should concentrate on "the abiding (the structural) qualities" of Mackintosh's work; he thought the decorative aspects were tainted by Margaret's "rather thin Aubrey Beardsley mannerism of the arty-crafty type."[14]

During the 1940s there was renewed activity around Mackintosh's reputation in Glasgow. Thomas Howarth, a lecturer at the School of Architecture, chose Mackintosh as a subject of research, registered for a Ph.D., sorted the piles of Mackintosh drawings stored in the basement of William Davidson's city warehouse, and interviewed anyone who could remember his hero. He found memories strangely split: a few close friends spoke of genius, others were reluctant to speak at all.[15]

Davidson had care of much of Mackintosh's former property, and after his death in 1945, his family was instrumental in the University of Glasgow's acquiring 78 Southpark Avenue (the house in which the Mackintoshes lived between 1906 and 1914), its Mackintosh contents, and the Mackintosh estate, including furniture, watercolours, and the drawings stored in Davidson's basement.[16] This was the origin of the Hunterian Art Gallery's collection. In 1947 Glasgow School of Art gave its former boardroom over to the display of Mackintosh furniture.[17] In 1948 Nikolaus Pevsner, who had been gathering material for a book on Mackintosh since 1934, was asked by the Milanese publishers Il Balcone to write about Mackintosh for their series of little books, "Architects of the Modern Movement." In 1949 Howarth completed his doctorate, and Pevsner, who still wanted to write a big book on Mackintosh, characteristically suggested that they might collaborate. Howarth declined.[18]

Pevsner's book, *Charles R. Mackintosh*, was published in Italian in 1950 and, short though it was, offered a fuller understanding of Mackintosh than the writings of the 1930s and 1940s. In *Pioneers* he had presented Mackintosh as a Modernist architect, neither denying nor affirming the decorative qualities in his work. But in the 1950 account, the decorative elements had an equal place. It is not clear why Pevsner changed his mind, but he wrote: "In order to understand Mackintosh, it is essential to grasp the fusion in his art of puritanism with sensuality. The enchanting curves of Art Nouveau have the same importance as the austere verticals of the incipient Modern Movement."[19] Hermann Muthesius had written a substantial article about the Mackintoshes in 1902 using similar polarities—male/female and rectilinear/curvilinear.[20] Perhaps Pevsner had not seen this article before.

Howarth's thesis was revised and published as *Charles Rennie Mackintosh and the Modern Movement* in 1952. It presented Mackintosh as a transitional figure, looking back to the traditions of the Scottish vernacular and forward to the twentieth century; the first phase of Glasgow School of Art was, Howarth wrote, "the first important architectural monument to the new movement in Europe."[21] His account of Mackintosh's buildings and designs followed Modernist lines. In the facade of the Willow Tea Rooms, for instance, he saw Mackintosh reaching out towards "an architecture of clean cut mechanical precision," while his mastery of the interior space of the Willow "draws the observer again and again . . . long after he has tired of the ornament, the hanging lamps, and the stencilled decoration."[22] Like most Modernists, Howarth regretted much of the decorative element in Mackintosh's work.

It was Howarth's account of Mackintosh's career that gave the book its persuasive force. He told a moving tale of a young Glasgow architect who was passed over in his native city, rejected by the English, and fully appreciated only in Vienna. Much of this came from Muthesius's article of 1902. I have argued elsewhere that this is a false account.[23] But there is no denying its romantic appeal, and it fitted snugly into Pevsner's Modernist art history, in which the loss of nerve in English progressive architecture about 1900, coupled with the emergence of Vienna as a centre of Modernism, were cardinal points.

Howarth's book was the first substantial monograph on a British architect of this date apart from Christopher Hussey's books on Edwin Lutyens. It was obviously the standard work, and its Modernism was in tune with mainstream attitudes in British architecture in the 1950s. But a different point of view was beginning to emerge at this time among those for whom the Modernist perspective did not work. John Summerson brought his irreverent insight to bear on the School of Art library when reviewing Howarth's book: "One has the odd feeling that if the whole room were turned upside-down, so that the light fittings grew upwards from the floor, it would be even more true to itself."[24]

People connected with the *Architectural Review*, such as John Betjeman, were interested in the very Victorians against whom Mackintosh was supposed to have reacted. In 1952 the Victoria and Albert Museum organised the exhibition *Victorian and Edwardian Decorative Arts*, in which Mackintosh appeared neither as genius nor as pioneer, but as one designer among many. In 1958 the Victorian Society was founded. These were the sort of people who would be interested in Mackintosh but who might think that, in Summerson's words, "His work can just as easily be esteemed an end as a beginning."[25]

It may help here to distinguish between two kinds of reputation. During his lifetime Mackintosh had a local reputation in Glasgow, based on direct and daily knowledge of his buildings. Shortly before his death, he began to acquire a reputation among architects and critics outside Glasgow, which was based on a knowledge of architectural movements and was fed by books and magazines. During this first stage, from 1928 to 1960, these two reputations were far apart. His local reputation had almost vanished by the time of his death and, but for William Davidson's loyalty, might have disappeared altogether. However, his reputation in architectural literature was just developing and was soon firmly established among a particular ideological group.

For the Modernists, it was the story of Mackintosh's career that mattered. One can easily see what Howarth and others admired in his work: the bareness of the studio windows that bulk so large in the north front of Glasgow School of Art, for instance. However, today one cannot so easily overlook the things that they overlooked: the loose relationship between plans and elevations, the wit, the preoccupation with mouldings, the spiritual and sensual intensity of the collaborative interiors. The fact is that Mackintosh's work did not fit the Modernist canon very well, and Henry-Russell Hitchcock, who was interested in stylistic correctness, edited him out. Mackintosh's story fitted the canon, and Pevsner, who was interested in historical development, edited him in. Modernists needed to write their own history while the movement was in progress, to give themselves heroes; and the story of Mackintosh, welcomed abroad and rejected at home, was perfect. In this story, success worked—he was a pioneer, welcomed by the most progressive circles in Europe; and, amazingly, failure worked too—he was a lonely genius, rejected by conservatives and Philistines at home.

1960–1980: The Age of the Enthusiasts

More of Mackintosh's work was seen in the 1960s, and by more people, thanks to the new enthusiasm for Art Nouveau. The first substantial Art Nouveau exhibition was at the Kunstgewerbemuseum, Zurich, in 1952, followed by a major show at the Museum of Modern Art, New York, in 1960; Mackintosh figured in both.[26] In the Council of Europe's massive exhibition in Paris in 1960–61, *Les Sources du XXe siècle*, he was the largest single exhibitor in the architecture and decorative-arts section.[27] And a stream of lavishly illustrated books appeared during the decade, many with a section on Mackintosh.[28] Although his rectilinear work was very different from the curvilinear Art Nouveau from France and Belgium, he was more at home with this decorative, brilliant, and short-lived movement than he was with the Modernists. It drew attention to his furniture and interiors, and it allowed his work to be understood in terms of his own time. And of course, this was the sixties, when Art Nouveau was part of popular culture and Jefferson Airplane posters dazzled the eyes with their flickering curves. For the first time, Mackintosh appealed beyond the earnest circle of Modernist architects and critics.

Mackintosh's centenary in 1968 was celebrated by a major exhibition of his work organised by Andrew McLaren Young, Richmond Professor of Fine Art at the University of Glasgow. It was shown at the Edinburgh Festival (plate 222) and at the Victoria and Albert Museum in London; then, in a reduced form and accompanied by a film about Mackintosh by Murray Grigor, it travelled to Zurich, Darmstadt, and Vienna. But it was not shown in Glasgow. McLaren Young, a specialist in the work of James McNeill Whistler, was a big, kindly, rumpled-looking man who brought his scholarship to bear on the university's Mackintosh collections. In the catalogue he quoted from letters he

had solicited from Ludwig Mies van der Rohe and Gropius, underlining Mackintosh's status within Modernism. But he also reported the new sense of Mackintosh as a leading exponent of Art Nouveau, arguing: "Any understanding of him must . . . reconcile the *fin-de-siècle* and the prophetically modern aspects of his work."[29] McLaren Young's exhibition changed people's understanding of Mackintosh, not by reinterpreting him but by bringing his decorative work, hitherto seen only in books, before a large public. Here were Mackintosh's strange creations, his tall chairs, his hanging banners of dreaming women, his reconstructed tea-room interiors; it was all much more colourful, and more covetable, than the School of Art on a rainy day.

Robert Macleod's lucid *Charles Rennie Mackintosh*, published in the centenary year, was the first attempt to write something corrective about Mackintosh, to oppose the current of interpretation. Macleod disputed that Mackintosh was "a lonely genius whose work suddenly emerged out of context, out of time."[30] Using Mackintosh's lecture notes, he argued that Mackintosh stood in the Victorian tradition of progressive architectural thought, championing modernity, individuality, function, *and* the value of the past, and that he worked in the same spirit as his progressive British contemporaries. Macleod's argument was perhaps too intellectual: architects' words do not always throw a clear light on their work, and Mackintosh's certainly do not. But it made good historical sense and was complemented by David Walker's article in the *Architectural Review* in the same year, which showed how many details in Mackintosh's early buildings were inspired by his contemporaries.[31]

In 1970 Murray Grigor made a second film about Mackintosh and asked the shoppers in Glasgow's Sauchiehall Street what the name meant to them. "Toffees," they said, "raincoats."[32] For the ordinary people of Glasgow, Mackintosh was still the forgotten man. His buildings were at risk in the changing city, and there were enough Mackintosh enthusiasts to make this an issue, but not enough to provide solutions. The Willow Tea Rooms had been incorporated in Daly's department store since 1927 and were much altered; now they were threatened by the closure of Daly's. The Ingram Street tea rooms, with their variety of Mackintosh interiors, lasted longer; Thomas Howarth used to eat there in the 1940s, pondering the mixture of "ordinary" and Mackintosh cutlery in front of him. Partly at his urging, Glasgow Corporation acquired the tea room in 1950, to preserve the fittings in situ; but this proved impractical and they were removed in 1971.[33] In 1963 the University of Glasgow caused a furore when it demolished Mackintosh's house, though the fittings were stored for re-erection.

These were the years when slum clearance and urban motorways cut swathes through the inner suburbs of Britain's cities. In the early 1970s Martyrs' Public School was threatened with demolition for a motorway, and both Queen's Cross Church and Scotland Street School were threatened with redundancy as road schemes decimated their catchment areas.[34] Outside Glasgow, the owner of The Hill House was offering it, with its furniture, for a modest twenty-five thousand pounds in the hope that it might be preserved. But no conservation organization would take it on, and nothing happened for most of 1971, until the Royal Incorporation of Architects in Scotland (RIAS), with great imagination, stepped into the breach.[35]

These were also the years, however, when conservation became a force in city planning and local people learned to resist environmental change. Mackintosh's champions fitted a familiar pattern: the people who had read the books were pressuring the people who ran the city. The fact that Mackintosh's reputation had burgeoned in the world at large in the 1960s, while Glasgow was understandably preoccupied with the problems of industrial decline, put a mighty weapon in their hands: Mackintosh was "world-famous," and what was Glasgow doing with his buildings?[36]

The first Mackintosh group was the Friends of Toshie, started by Murray Grigor and Bill Williams, a journalist, as early as 1964; the name was modelled on Barcelona's Amigos de Gaudí.[37] In 1972 Thomas Howarth flew in from Toronto and protested that Mackintosh's buildings did not belong to Glasgow but to the whole world.[38] Then the New Glasgow Society took up the cause of Mackintosh, and on October 4, 1973, the Charles Rennie Mackintosh Society was founded.[39] From the start it has been driven by the extraordinary energy of Patricia Douglas, first as honorary secretary and then as director. In 1976 the little society took a lease on Queen's Cross Church, boldly proposing to repair the building and use it as their headquarters. By 1980 there were a thousand members, half of them in Scotland, a quarter in England, and the rest all over the world; by the mid-1980s there were fifteen hundred members; there has been a chapter in Japan since the late 1970s, and there is one just starting up in New York.[40] The Mackintosh Society manages to be friendly and rooted in one place, like the best kind of local amenity society, yet at the same time it is an international network of Mackintosh scholars and enthusiasts. It is a pressure group in Glasgow's environmental politics, but it has also undertaken the heavy practical task of restoring and maintaining the fabric of Queen's Cross Church. Rarely does a conservation group combine these qualities.

In 1973, while the Mackintosh enthusiasts were struggling in Glasgow, careful facsimiles of some of Mackintosh's most striking chairs and tables were set on a gleaming dais at the Triennale in Milan.[41] They had been made under the supervision of Professor Filippo Alison of the University of Naples, and the exhibition launched a series of reproduction Mackintosh chairs and tables made by Cassina of Milan in collaboration with Alison. Cassina had been making furniture by well-known contemporary designers since the 1950s. In 1965 the company began reproducing the work of famous Modernists from the past, first Le Corbusier and Gerrit Rietveld, then Mackintosh, Gunnar Asplund, and Frank Lloyd Wright. From Mackintosh's work Cassina selected the pieces with the most powerful image, such as the order-desk chair from the Willow Tea Rooms (see plate 168) and the delicate little ladderback from The Hill House bedroom (see plate 177); since then, more than four thousand copies of the order-desk chair have been made.[42]

Most of the Mackintosh pieces made by Cassina are exact copies, and they pose a question in our age of mechanical reproduction. Are they Mackintosh or not? Faced with an original Mackintosh chair and an exact copy of it, we know the differences between them: one was made in 1904, for example, from Mackintosh's drawings, and is unique; the other was made in 1984, perhaps, from drawings of the original, probably using some new techniques of construction, and is one of thousands knocking around the design-conscious world. But they look the same. Do the differences matter? The exhibition that really put Mackintosh on the map in the United States was *Furniture by Charles Rennie Mackintosh* at the Museum of Modern Art, New York, in 1974–75 (plate 223). The museum owns an original Mackintosh chair, but that was not in the show. Every exhibit was a Filippo Alison facsimile.[43]

Andrew McLaren Young died in February 1975. As a memorial, Glasgow University hoped to buy the armchair (plate 224) from the drawing room at Hous'hill, which was coming up for auction at Sotheby's in London. Roger Billcliffe, McLaren Young's second-in-command at the Hunterian Art Gallery, assembled upwards of £6,500, roughly twice the estimate. The Hunterian had never spent so much at auction, and Billcliffe was nervous but hopeful. "Unbelievably," he has recalled, "the bidding just kept on going."[44] The chair was sold to American collectors for £9,200, a record for twentieth-century decora-

tive art at auction.[45] Mackintosh has gone on creating records ever since, and they have boosted his reputation more than almost anything else.[46] Of the 1975 episode, Thomas Howarth wrote ruefully, "Despite the efforts of scholars and others seeking to establish Mackintosh's place in history . . . it was in fact the sale of a single chair that, through the activities of the commercial world, made Mackintosh a household name."[47]

Roger Billcliffe's two particular interests were Mackintosh's furniture and his watercolours. With a wealth of drawings in his care at the Hunterian, he was well placed to trace, identify, and document Mackintosh pieces—and occasionally dart out and bid for the few that were still turning up unrecognised in Glasgow sales. Billcliffe combines a collector's appetite with an energy in research and a scrupulous sense of fact that collectors do not always have. In 1979 he published a catalogue raisonné, *Charles Rennie Mackintosh: The Complete Furniture, Furniture Drawings and Interior Designs*. It was the culmination of years of sorting and research by McLaren Young and himself, but it was also a starting point for collecting and research by others. The book is so detailed and complete that it could be called obsessive if it were not also informed by a sustained and open-minded analysis of Mackintosh's furniture style. Today, Mackintosh scholars and collectors stand on Billcliffe's shoulders. If we see farther, it is thanks to him.[48]

This second stage of Mackintosh's reputation was marked by two important developments. One was that portable objects came to the fore. The Mod-

ernists had been interested in Mackintosh's story and his architecture; the new enthusiasts were interested in his tables and chairs. The objects that they saw illustrated and exhibited in the 1960s, they copied, auctioned, and catalogued in the 1970s. The Modernist Mackintosh now seemed terribly austere, all high principles and black-and-white photographs, whereas his objects lent themselves to consumption and colour photography.[49]

The other was that Mackintosh came back to Glasgow. This was not a revival of his local reputation; the celebrity he had earned in architectural literature since his death was imported into the city. His buildings were championed as the work of a "world-famous" architect—that is, famous everywhere but Glasgow. The title of this chapter-section is a tribute to the peculiar innocence of this revival. Here were people who championed Mackintosh not to illustrate a Modernist argument or to exploit the Mackintosh image, but just because they admired him. Harry Jefferson Barnes, the modest and knowledgeable director of the School of Art and second chairman of the Mackintosh Society, was just such a figure, the éminence grise of Mackintosh lobbying at this time.[50] By bringing Mackintosh home, and by enlisting the urban dynamics of Glasgow in his cause, these people created much of the Mackintosh phenomenon of today.

1980–1995: MACKINTOSH AND THE MARKET

During the past fifteen years or so, control of Mackintosh's reputation has passed out of the hands of the enthusiasts and into those of advertising agencies, journalists, giftware manufacturers, and tour operators. A few media events in the 1980s will give a sense of the shift. In the February 1980 number of *House and Garden,* twelve pieces of Mackintosh furniture were illustrated, three in an article about identifying classic designers, one in a geometrical room setting, five in a piece on modernising a small Roman villa, and three in an advertisement for the General Trading Company of Sloane Street, Chelsea.[51] In March 1982 Ludovic Kennedy and Moira Shearer unveiled a Class 47 British Rail engine named "Charles Rennie Mackintosh"; the director of the Art School, media-sensitive Tony Jones, dressed up as Francis Newbery for the occasion.[52] In August 1987, Channel Four Television broadcast a ninety-minute dramatised documentary, *Dreams and Recollections,* starring Tom Conti as Mackintosh and Kara Wilson as Margaret Macdonald (plate 220).[53] Thousands of people in Britain who know nothing else about Mackintosh remember this film.

The media have made the Mackintosh phenomenon much more complicated. Mackintosh is now a part of popular as well as of academic culture, creating two sides to the phenomenon, the "popular" and the "serious." The story of his reputation can no longer be told in a single narrative, and so this section abandons chronology and deals with the phenomenon under three different headings: Mackintosh and Glasgow; the influence of Mackintosh's work; and the image of Mackintosh. In each case the serious shades off into the popular.

First, Mackintosh and Glasgow. Although many of Mackintosh's buildings were threatened in the early 1970s, by the early 1980s the situation had changed. The Willow Tea Rooms had been largely reconstructed inside and out by Arrowcroft Management Ltd. and the architects Keppie Henderson, in a scheme that was more complete than either the conservationists hoped or the planners required; in 1983 the Salon de Luxe became a tea room again. Martyrs' Public School was weathertight, though still empty; plans were developed to use Scotland Street School as a museum of education and have since been realised; and the repairs on Queen's Cross Church were well advanced.[54] The RIAS was struggling to maintain The Hill House, but their intervention had shown that Mackintosh should be taken seriously, and in 1982 the house was transferred to the National Trust for Scotland, with a substantial endowment from the National Heritage Memorial Fund.[55] The credit for these changes lies partly with the Mackintosh enthusiasts and partly with larger forces such as inner-city renewal, the shift to conservation in urban planning, and Glasgow's own "Renaissance."

In 1981 the University of Glasgow, so much the villain of the piece in 1963 when they demolished 78 Southpark Avenue, opened their reconstruction of its interior, calling it simply the Mackintosh House (plate 225). The outside of the building is a puzzling reinforced-concrete shell hung on the side of the new Hunterian Art Gallery: the front door opens into midair, for the structure re-creates the height and orientation of the original house, which

225. The Mackintosh House, Hunterian Art Gallery, University of Glasgow.

226. The House for an Art Lover, Bellahouston Park, Glasgow, by Andy Macmillan after designs by Charles Rennie Mackintosh.

stood about a hundred yards away. Inside, the staircase hall, dining room, studio-drawing room, and principal bedroom have been carefully reconstructed.[56] The Mackintosh House is not as important a work as Glasgow School of Art or The Hill House, for it is only an interior. But it is here that the public comes closest to Mackintosh and Macdonald.

In 1988 the Glasgow engineer Graham Roxburgh decided to build the House for an Art Lover—that is, the large house for a connoisseur that Mackintosh designed in 1900–1901 in a competition organised by a German publisher. (Mackintosh did not win, but his plans, elevations, and perspectives were published as a set of fourteen lithograph drawings.) Roxburgh did not want to live in this house; he just wanted to build it and then pay for it by renting part as offices. The building has gone up in Bellahouston Park, on Glasgow's south side, and at the time of writing it is a completed shell, awaiting internal finishes and final decisions about its use (plate 226). Of course, you cannot build a house from fourteen lithograph drawings, so Roxburgh turned to Andy Macmillan, then head of the Mackintosh School of Architecture in Glasgow, who interpreted Mackintosh's designs, altered them in places, and added extra accommodation on the top floor. The house was built on public land, and public funds were invested in it. After some difficulties in financing, it has passed into the hands of the local authority.[57]

Roxburgh's House for an Art Lover means different things to different people. To Roxburgh himself it is a fascinating experiment. "When I see a really good perspective of a turn-of-the-century building," he told me, "I get an urge to build it."[58] To the general public it is simply a new Mackintosh building that has somehow appeared on the Glasgow tourist route; enthusiasm for Mackintosh can be gullible. To someone who cares particularly about Mackintosh it is a mongrel—part Mackintosh, part Macmillan. To someone who cares not only about Mackintosh but also about Glasgow and its historic buildings, it is a diversion of money and effort that might have been spent on the real thing.[59]

The popular enthusiasm for Mackintosh is part of Glasgow's "Renaissance." Like other British cities that have lost their industrial base, Glasgow has sought to rebuild itself with the help of a clever marketing campaign, which sold the city as a desirable place to live in and visit.[60] Hence the posters on buses all over Britain: "Glasgow's Miles Better"; hence the Scottish Exhibition and Conference Centre, the beautifully housed Burrell Collection, a new concert hall, and an immense programme of stone cleaning; hence—because some of this has worked—the café-bar culture and the chic designer shops of the Merchant City. Mackintosh the designer of international reputation, portable, reproducible, buyable Mackintosh, is at home in this design-led phenomenon. And he is the perfect tourist package, new-old, clean, artistic, and manageable.

Mackintosh was a major presence at the Glasgow Garden Festival in 1988, when roof trusses from a Mackintosh building then being altered were used for the pavilion of the RIAS, and Councillor Danny Crawford, convener of the City of Glasgow Parks and Recreation Committee, named a rose "Charles Rennie Mackintosh" at the annual general meeting of the Mackintosh Society (plate 227).[61] Then came 1990, Glasgow's year as European City of Culture. The Post Office issued a stamp with the School of Art on it. Saatchi and Saatchi were employed to market "1990" and designed a new version of Mackintosh lettering for their slogan "There's a lot Glasgowing on in 1990." The Mackintosh House had record numbers of visitors. And, for architects and Mackintosh enthusiasts, an international array of luminaries including Ted Cullinan, Aldo van Eyck, Hans Hollein, Arata Isozaki, Leon Krier, and Stanley Tigerman was invited to the School of Art to design installations—visual commentaries on Mackintosh's work—and to take part in a symposium on Mackintosh's relevance today.[62]

The year 1990 was perhaps the climax of Glasgow's Renaissance so far as culture was concerned, but sometimes it felt as if the Mackintosh phenomenon had already peaked, perhaps at the garden festival. Roger Billcliffe talked of Saatchi and Saatchi's "bastardisation" of Mackintosh lettering; the architectural stars at the School of Art were perhaps the attraction more than Mackintosh; and the flood of Mockingtosh had grown so great that several Mackintosh enthusiasts were to be seen rather obviously getting *off* the bandwagon.[63]

The second aspect of the Mackintosh phenomenon we can consider is the influence of Mackintosh's work. It excites great admiration among modern architects. In 1984 the readers of *Building Design* voted Mackintosh the best

227. The Naming of the Rose. Councillor Danny Crawford, Patricia Douglas, and others at the annual general meeting of the Charles Rennie Mackintosh Society, Glasgow Garden Festival, June 1988. In the background, the Mackintosh-designed cupola from the demolished Pettigrew and Stephens department store in Sauchiehall Street.

architect of the last 150 years, and the School of Art the best building.[64] In 1985 Robert Venturi wrote of the School of Art, "The North facade is one of the greatest achievements of all time, comparable in scale and majesty to Michelangelo."[65] Thomas Howarth has written of the "profound effect" on architects of Mackintosh's "enduring principles of design."[66]

Some architects do owe a profound debt to Mackintosh. Sir Denys Lasdun, for instance, has described his Milton Gate office building in London (plate 228) as "partly a serious attempt to move architecture forward and partly a homage to one of the great masters of the modern movement, Charles Rennie Mackintosh."[67] He feels that it is the fundamentals of architecture, such as the handling of space and light, that count in Mackintosh's work, not mere decorative details.[68] But for many architects nowadays Mackintosh is attractive as a source of motifs and images. His work is full of idiosyncratic details, and modern architects like to quote. Yoshinori Mori has said that when he adapted the famous order-desk chair from the Willow Tea Rooms (see plate 168) to the portico of his art gallery in Tokyo (plate 229), he was just having fun. "Creativity does not necessarily demand bearing the heavy cross of a philosophical ism."[69] In Britain it has usually been ornamental ironwork and glazing patterns that reveal the Mackintosh afflatus, and the stepped glazing of

■■ OPPOSITE
228. Milton Gate, Chiswell Street, London, by Denys Lasdun, Peter Softley and Associates, Architects, 1988–90. This speculative office building, with its three tall oriel windows, is sheathed in green glass half an inch thick, as if Glasgow School of Art had been transported to the bottom of the sea.
■■ ABOVE
229. Yoshinori Mori and CORE Architectural Association, 1985. Art Space KEIHO, Hachioji, Tokyo.

▪▪ ABOVE, LEFT
230. Arata Isozaki, *The Marilyn Chair*, 1974; front and side views.
▪▪ ABOVE, RIGHT
231. Wendy Maruyama, *Mickey Mackintosh*, 1986.

the stair towers of Scotland Street School can now be seen in several parts of Glasgow.[70]

The powerful imagery of the Mackintosh style lends itself to restaurants and café-bars more than it does to domestic interiors, though Thomas Howarth has designed a luxurious flat in a Mackintosh style in Toronto.[71] The most powerful image of all is that ultimate Mackintosh icon, the high-backed chair. This is a theme on which almost any variation can be played; the two examples in plates 230 and 231 show how effectively Mackintosh imagery operates in a world of international design where the distinctions between high and popular culture no longer apply. Arata Isozaki took his curves from a nude photograph of Marilyn Monroe, but could not make a chair out of them until he saw Mackintosh's work at Glasgow School of Art. "If Marilyn Monroe was my muse in the 1950s of my youth," he has said, "then Charles Rennie Mackintosh was one of my most important teachers in the 1960s. My chair pays homage to both."[72] Wendy Maruyama, a Californian furniture maker, says of her chair, "It is my personal homage to both Rennie and Mickey and a hybrid of two time zones!"[73]

It is as if the design of Mackintosh's chairs is so strong that it attracts images of equal power from the world of films. And the strange, ghostly quality of these chairs has earned them a niche in science-fiction and fantasy films. They have appeared in *The Addams Family*, *Ghost*, and *Batman*; televi-

sion sightings include *Star Trek: The Next Generation* and the British space comedy *Red Dwarf.* Oliver Stone's television series *Wild Palms* included an extraordinary scene with two high-backed chairs from the Argyle Street tea rooms floating in a swimming pool.

Some of Mackintosh's contemporaries thought that his chairs looked ghostly, and film appearances like these recognise the intrinsic power of his designs. The same cannot always be said of "Mockingtosh." That is a good word, in which scorn and endearment are equally mixed; and it is best applied to certain forms of lettering in the Mackintosh style, and to the mass of giftware, T-shirts, scarves, mugs, cards, panels of stained glass, jewellery, mirror frames, potpourri jars, and so on, to which Mackintosh motifs have been applied (plate 232). These things can be bought all over Britain; in Glasgow they cannot be avoided. A recipe for a successful Mockingtosh product would read something like this: first select two-dimensional Mackintosh motifs that can be easily printed or stamped out; manufacturers seem to prefer the organic ornament of the early 1900s, when Mackintosh worked closely with Macdonald. Then apply them to the giftware product; if possible choose a product that Mackintosh might have designed, for this brings the consumer closer to the real thing. Jewellery and picture frames are good. Finally, to enhance sales, identify Mackintosh as a thwarted genius. The Scottish firm Ortak produce Mockingtosh jewellery with a tiny biographical note in each box, stating that Mackintosh "left Glasgow in failure and died in London in 1928 in obscurity."[74]

It is easy to write about Mockingtosh in this lighthearted and superior tone, and to treat it as something different from, and inferior to, Mackintosh

232. "The Rennie Mackintosh Collection" of jewellery in the window of Henderson the Jewellers, 217 Sauchiehall Street, Glasgow. The display panel says that Mackintosh "shared the fate of many others in his field in failing to achieve recognition in his own city until many years after his death."

MACKINTOSH
MOCKINTOSH

233. Letraset's dry-transfer version of
Mackintosh lettering.

reproductions or serious work inspired by Mackintosh. But is it so different?
The story of Mackintosh lettering suggests that one leads helplessly into the
other.

Mackintosh never created an alphabet. He designed some letters for
posters, signs, and books, and he drew a great many as titling on his drawings.
In 1968 Henry Hellier, head of graphics at Glasgow School of Art, designed a
set of Mackintosh-style letters for the centenary exhibition in Edinburgh. He
based them on Mackintosh's hand-drawn letters, but standardising them
changed them into something like type, exact and repeatable. This was the
first step. In the 1970s Letraset produced a set of their familiar dry-transfer letters based on Hellier's work; the design was as close to Mackintosh as Hellier's. Although sold only through the Mackintosh Society, the transfer sets
were now available to graphic designers, printers, and everyone else who
wanted to purchase them (plate 233). Used on books, posters, packaging, car-
rier bags, and shop fronts, they became the most familiar of all Mackintosh
images, though perhaps not always recognized as his. This was the second
step. As time went by, the authentic Mackintosh element in the design was
emptied out, by sign painters who did not copy them exactly and by graphic
designers who wanted to vary them anyway: Saatchi and Saatchi cut their own
variant for the "Year of Culture." This was Mockingtosh, the third step.

Finally, let us consider the image of Mackintosh himself. In the first stage
of this story he was a Pioneer of the Modern Movement; in the second a
Master of Art Nouveau; what is he in the third, market-oriented stage of his
reputation? There is no single academic answer to this question. No one has
written a big book like Howarth's, but from a new perspective. Academic work
in the 1980s and 1990s has been concerned with reevaluating Mackintosh in
relation to his context or with particular insights. In 1984 Glasgow Museums
organised the exhibition *The Glasgow Style, 1890–1920*. Jessie M. King, illustrator, was represented by seventeen objects, and the designer E. A. Taylor by
nine, including a complete room setting; Mackintosh had four. "Charles
Rennie Mackintosh was not working in a vacuum," the catalogue said, "but in

a city which nurtured an abundance of creative talent at all levels of artistic activity."[75] Here, at least, was a richer and more accurate kind of history than the tale of heroes and geniuses that had nurtured Mackintosh's reputation.

Many Glasgow Style designers were women, and some recent work on Mackintosh has been feminist. For the Year of Culture, Glasgow Museums and Art Galleries put on an exhibition called *"Glasgow Girls": Women in Art and Design, 1880–1920,* curated by Jude Burkhauser, who also edited a book of the same title.[76] Feminism has had to re-create the identities of Margaret and Frances Macdonald, both in themselves and in relation to Mackintosh who, as genius and pioneer, has been seen as solitary and male. Mackintosh's reputation rejects Margaret. But, as Janice Helland has demonstrated in her essay in this volume, Mackintosh did not; they were collaborators for a significant part of their careers. This fact is at the heart of David Brett's *C. R. Mackintosh: The Poetics of Workmanship,* the most positive and thought-provoking book on Mackintosh for many years, which argues that the Mackintosh-Macdonald interiors are designed around sexuality. But Brett has not worked out the implications of his insight across the whole of Mackintosh's work. My own *Charles Rennie Mackintosh* is a short book, an attempt to tell the story of Mackintosh's life and work in a single narrative, and to free that story from some of the myths that have grown up around it.

A common, middlebrow image of Mackintosh is that he was one of a number of architects in Europe and America around 1900 who produced work of startling originality and who, though not necessarily in touch with each other, formed an international group. I once heard an American woman say to her little daughter in the Mackintosh House, "Yes, dear, this is the architect's own house, and if it had been in our country, he would have been Frank Lloyd Wright." Others with whom Mackintosh is sometimes linked include Antoní Gaudí, Greene and Greene, Hector Guimard, Victor Horta, Ödön Lechner, Joseph Maria Olbrich, Otto Wagner, and Josef Hoffmann.[77] The argument is attractive, for it seems to rescue Mackintosh from the wreck of Modernism. He is still a heroic figure, but his work can be understood in its own time. However, apart from the Austrians, these architects produced work very different from Mackintosh's, and some were wholly, or almost wholly, unaware of him.[78] The argument is hard to sustain unless you believe in a zeitgeist. It is probably not an historical argument at all, but the projection back into history of two phenomena of the late twentieth century: first, the adoption by certain cities of highly original but atypical turn-of-the-century architects as their patron saints (Horta adopted by Brussels; Gaudí by Barcelona; Wright by Chicago; and Mackintosh by Glasgow); and, second, the international star system in modern architecture, which brings together motley groups of luminaries, such as those who came to Glasgow in 1990.

As for the popular image of Mackintosh, it is obvious in some ways—it floats above Glasgow like a gas-filled publicity balloon; at the same time it is

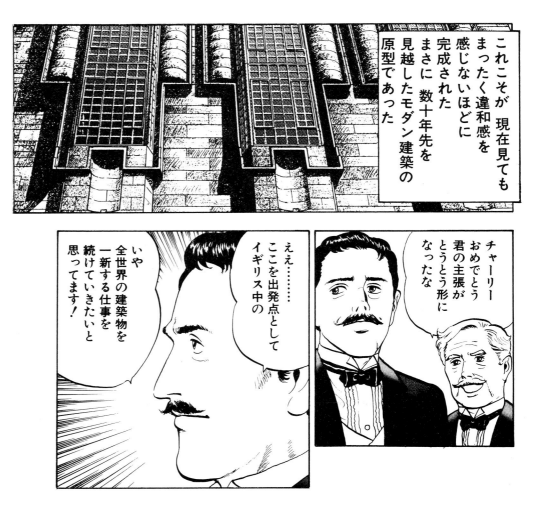

234. Frames from Morita Shingo, "Geniuses without Glory," new series, 8: "C. R. Mackintosh, The Architect Ahead of His Time," *Young Jump* 2 (c. 1993).

elusive, manifesting itself in many different forms.[79] The Japanese picture-book biography of Mackintosh by Morita Shingo (plate 234) expresses much of it; the frames illustrated, for instance, present Mackintosh as the pioneer of Modernism. "This is the original form of modern art, several decades ahead of its time," the speech bubble reads: "when we look at it, it has been so perfected that we don't feel any strangeness." Francis Newbery says, "Congratulations, Charlie, your idea has finally taken form." And Mackintosh replies, "Yes, I intend to make this a starting point, and to go on working to renew Britain's, nay the whole world's architecture."[80]

The Mackintosh image can be summarised as a series of propositions. He was unique; none of his contemporaries came near him. He was a liberator; houses were cluttered and dark until he came along with his light, modern interiors. He designed in a modern, honest way; he stripped away fussy Victorian detail, leaving structures that show what the plans and function are. He was ahead of his time; he designed chairs that look as good now as the day they were made. He was a lonely genius; rejected at home but successful abroad, he died in poverty. Until rediscovered by later generations, he was a forgotten man.

This picture is familiar. It is a crude version of the picture Thomas Howarth drew in 1952. The stereotypes of the lonely genius and the pioneer underpin them both. The Modernist version of Mackintosh may be discredited academically, but it is alive and well in Glasgow and Japan, and flourishing in the popular imagination. This bears much thinking about.

My story ends as I write, early in 1995. Mackintosh's does not. The exhibition that is the occasion for this book will surely be the biggest event of the Mackintosh phenomenon so far. And Glasgow has recently received the British Arts Council's prestigious designation as City of Architecture and Design in 1999. Mackintosh's Glasgow Herald building, which has been standing empty for almost twenty years, will be brought into use as the architecture and design centre, a hub of the year's activities.[81]

I hope that during these years there will be a reduction in the marketing hype and a return to good sense in the evaluation of Mackintosh. The Hunterian Art Gallery and the Charles Rennie Mackintosh Society are important here. Both promote the appreciation of Mackintosh's work through scholarly and accessible activities. Both have steered an honourable course through the reefs and shoals of Mockingtosh and marketing. Both have been active in caring for the buildings and objects that Mackintosh *did* design, with the help of public funds. The society finally completed repairs to Queen's Cross Church in 1990, and the Hunterian has raised six-figure sums towards Mackintosh acquisitions in recent years, to keep them in the public domain. If the future of Mackintosh's reputation lies with them, and with sympathetic institutions such as Glasgow School of Art, we may see a fourth stage in the story of the Mackintosh phenomenon, the Age of Good Sense.

NOTES

I would like to thank Roger Billcliffe, Patricia Douglas, Murray Grigor, James Macaulay, Pamela Robertson, Graham Roxburgh, Gavin Stamp, and David Walker for their memories of and comments on the Mackintosh story; Toshio Watanabe for help with Mackintosh and Japan; and Alison Brown for sightings of Mackintosh chairs in film and on television.

1. "Mockintosh" appears to be the common form nowadays, but the original form, coined by Murray Grigor in the early 1980s, was "Mockingtosh."

2. Alan Crawford, *Charles Rennie Mackintosh* (London: Thames and Hudson, 1995).

3. In this account I have drawn on sources cited in individual notes; on Thomas Howarth's invaluable recollections in *Charles Rennie Mackintosh and the Modern Movement* (3d ed.; London: Routledge and Kegan Paul, 1990), pp. xxi–xxxi, xliii–xlix, 292–94; and on the memories of those acknowledged above.

4. John Summerson, "On Discovering Greek Thomson," in *"Greek" Thomson*, ed. Gavin Stamp and Sam McKinstry (Edinburgh: Edinburgh University Press, 1994), p. 3.

5. Roger Billcliffe, "Some Thoughts on Collecting Mackintosh," *Charles Rennie Mackintosh Society Newsletter* 61 (spring 1993): 10.

6. *Charles Rennie Mackintosh: Exhibition Catalogue* (Glasgow: McLellan Galleries, 1933); Roger Billcliffe, *Mackintosh Watercolours* (paperback reprint, London: John Murray, 1979), p. 21. Fifty years later Roger Billcliffe re-created the exhibition for the Charles Rennie Mackintosh Society.

7. Charles Marriott, *Modern English Architecture* (London: Chapman and Hall, 1924), p. 129; see also John Summerson, *The Unromantic Castle* (London: Thames and Hudson, 1990), p. 237.

8. *Listener*, July 9, 1933, p. 98.

9. So they told Thomas Howarth; see Howarth, "Charles Rennie Mackintosh (1868–1928): Architect and Designer," *RIBA Journal* 58 (1950): 18.

10. See Charles McKean, "The Influence of Mackintosh in the 1930s," *Charles Rennie Mackintosh Society Newsletter* 47 (autumn 1987): 3–4; and the handbook, *British Architects Conference, Glasgow, June 19–22, 1935*, which has an essay on Mackintosh by Desmond Chapman-Huston.

11. Nikolaus Pevsner, *Pioneers of the Modern Movement: From William Morris to Walter Gropius* (London: Faber and Faber, 1936), pp. 158–65.

12. Henry-Russell Hitchcock, *Modern Architecture: Romanticism and Reintegration* (New York: Payson and Clarke, 1929), p. 87. See also Henry Matthews, "The Promotion of Modern Architecture by the Museum of Modern Art in the 1930s," *Journal of Design History* 7 (1994): 43–59.

13. Raymond McGrath, *Twentieth-Century Houses* (London: Faber and Faber, 1934), p. 78.

14. "Abiding qualities": Shand to Davidson, March 31, 1933; "thin Aubrey Beardsley": Shand to Macdonald Smith and Co., March 20, 1933, Hunterian Art Gallery, University of Glasgow. Shand's part in the story is complicated. In a 1935 article, while still deploring Macdonald's influence, he argued that Mackintosh was a decorator more than a constructor, and no true pioneer of functionalism. ("Scenario for a Human Drama, V: Glasgow Interlude," *Architectural Review* 77 [1935]: 23–26.)

15. Howarth, *Mackintosh*, pp. xxi–xxiii, 291–94.

16. 78 Southpark Avenue was originally 6 Florentine Terrace; its name and number were later changed to 78 Ann Street, and more recently Ann Street was renamed Southpark Avenue.

17. Howarth, *Mackintosh*, pp. 293–94.

18. I am grateful to Susie Harries for information about Pevsner's work on Mackintosh.

19. This appeared on pp. 31–32 of the Italian edition; the translation is from the revised English version published as "Charles Rennie Mackintosh" in Nikolaus Pevsner, *Studies in Art, Architecture and Design*, vol. 2, *Victorian and After* (London: Thames and Hudson, 1968), pp. 152–75.

20. Hermann Muthesius, "Die Glasgower Kunstbewegung: Charles R. Mackintosh und Margaret Macdonald-Mackintosh," *Dekorative Kunst* (March 1902): 193–221.

21. Howarth, *Mackintosh*, pp. 286–88.

22. Ibid., pp. 138, 146.

23. Crawford, *Mackintosh*, pp. 7, 41–42, 78–79, 81.

24. John Summerson, *New Statesman and Nation*, December 27, 1952, p. 784.

25. Ibid.

26. *Um 1900: Art Nouveau und Jugendstil* (Zurich: Kunstgewerbemuseum, 1952); Peter Selz and Mildred Constantine, eds., *Art Nouveau: Art and Design at the Turn of the Century* (New York: Museum of Modern Art, 1959).

27. *Les Sources du XXe siècle: Les Arts en Europe de 1884 à 1914* (Paris: Musée National d'Art Moderne, 1960–61), exhibits 1.065–1.104.

28. See, for instance, Robert Schmutzler, *Art Nouveau* (New York: Harry N. Abrams, 1962), p. 239; Maurice Rheims, *Flowering of Art Nouveau* (New York: Harry N. Abrams, 1966), p. 20; John Russell Taylor, *The Art Nouveau Book in Britain* (London: Methuen, 1966), pp. 122–24; Stephen Tschudi Madsen, *Art Nouveau* (London: Weidenfeld and Nicolson, 1967), pp. 123–36, 166–68; Mario Amaya, *Art Nouveau* (London: Studio Vista, 1968), pp. 50–55; and Renato Barilli, *Art Nouveau* (New York: Hamlyn, 1969), pp. 59–60, 76–77.

29. McLaren Young, in *Charles Rennie Mackintosh (1868–1928): Architecture, Design and Painting* (Edinburgh: Scottish Arts Council and Edinburgh Festival Society, 1968), p. 5.

30. Robert Macleod, *Charles Rennie Mackintosh* (Feltham, England: Country Life, 1968), p. 9.

31. David Walker, "Charles Rennie Mackintosh," *Architectural Review* 144 (November 1968): 355–63; reprinted as "The Early Work of Charles Rennie Mackintosh," in *The Anti-Rationalists*, ed. Nikolaus Pevsner and J. M. Richards (London: Architectural Press, 1973), pp. 116–35.

32. Grigor's film was *Mackintosh in Peril*.

33. For the later history of Mackintosh tea rooms, see Perilla Kinchin, *Tea and Taste: The Glasgow Tea Rooms, 1875–1975* (Wendlebury, England: White Cockade Publishing, 1991), pp. 79, 129, 169–70; and Howarth, *Mackintosh*, pp. xxii and 294.

34. For the threat to Martyrs' Public School, see *Architects' Journal*, March 20, 1974, p. 602.

35. Howarth, *Mackintosh*, p. xxiv.

36. See, for instance, Gordon Borthwick, chairman of the New Glasgow Society, letter to the *Glasgow Herald* dated March 24, 1973.

37. Murray Grigor and Richard Murphy, eds., *The Architects' Architect: Charles Rennie Mackintosh* (London: Bellew Publishing and the Charles Rennie Mackintosh Society, 1995), p. 15.

38. See Borthwick, letter to the *Glasgow Herald*.

39. Information from Patricia Douglas and James Macaulay.

40. *Charles Rennie Mackintosh Society Newsletter* 26 (summer 1980): unpaginated; Jan Burney, "Glasgow Record," *Building Design*, March 7, 1986, pp. 16–17; information from Patricia Douglas.

41. The catalogue of this exhibition, *Le Sedie di Charles Rennie Mackintosh*, was

published in English as Filippo Alison, *Charles Rennie Mackintosh as a Designer of Chairs* (London: Warehouse Publications, 1974).

42. See Murray Grigor's film, *The Fall and Rise of Mackintosh*, broadcast by Scottish Television in 1991. For Cassina, see Penny Sparke, *An Introduction to Design and Culture in the Twentieth Century* (London: Allen and Unwin, 1986), pp. 186–87, and the company's own brochure, *Charles R. Mackintosh* (Milan: Cassina, n.d.).

43. *New York Times*, November 14, 1974, p. 48, and November 14, 1974, sec. 2, p. 29. For informed comment on the reproduction of Mackintosh furniture, see Roger Billcliffe, *Charles Rennie Mackintosh: The Complete Furniture, Furniture Drawings and Interior Designs*, 3d ed. (London: John Murray, 1986), pp. 22, 256. For high-quality reproductions made by Josep Melo and marketed by BD Ediciones de Diseño of Barcelona, see Elizabeth Lyon, "A Quiet Perfectionist Recreates Mackintosh," *Craftwork* 50 (November–December 1982): 5. Howarth has had furniture from his collection reproduced; see Jim Strasman, "Elegance Recreated," *Canadian Architect* 30 (February 1985): 28–29. For Mackintosh's metalwork designs reproduced by Sabbatini Argenteria of Italy, see Nonie Niesewand, "How Mackintosh Stood the Test of Time," *House and Garden* (England) 40 (August 1985): 68–69. Textiles based on Mackintosh's designs are produced by Bute Fabrics of Scotland.

44. Billcliffe, "Some Thoughts on Collecting Mackintosh," p. 7.

45. It was sold to Sidney and Frances Lewis, who later presented it, with other Mackintosh pieces, to the Virginia Museum of Fine Arts, Richmond.

46. Other Mackintosh records at auction are as follows: in 1979 Mackintosh's own ebonised oak desk was sold at Sotheby's in London for £89,200; this was a record for British furniture of any date. In 1993 Mackintosh's poster for the Glasgow Institute of the Fine Arts was sold at Christie's South Kensington for £68,200, a record for a British poster. And, most sensationally of all, when the collection put together by Thomas Howarth in the 1940s was auctioned at Christie's in London early in 1994, an ebonised oak desk from The Hill House, virtually identical to that sold in 1979, fetched £720,000, a record for twentieth-century decorative arts; Howarth's collection as a whole grossed more than £2,000,000.

47. Howarth, in Patrick Nuttgens, ed., *Mackintosh and His Contemporaries in Europe and America* (London: John Murray, 1988), p. 55.

48. For a list of Billcliffe's publications on Mackintosh, see the bibliography in this volume.

49. The first of Mackintosh's many appearances in the Sunday colour supplements was in the *Sunday Times Magazine* (London), October 27, 1968, pp. 42–44, with photographs by John Goldblatt.

50. I am grateful to James Macaulay and Patricia Douglas for bringing Barnes's importance to my attention.

51. *House and Garden* (England) (February 1980): 3, 66–67, 70–73, and 88.

52. *Glasgow Herald*, March 23, 1982.

53. The documentary was written by Alistair Moffat and made by Scottish Television. Moffat's excellent research was also put to good use in the book he produced with Colin Baxter, *Remembering Charles Rennie Mackintosh: An Illustrated Biography* (Lanark, Scotland: Colin Baxter Photography, 1989).

54. Colin B. Kirkwood, "Notes on Mackintosh Buildings," *Charles Rennie Mackintosh Society Newsletter* 23 (autumn 1979): unpaginated; report of a visit to the Willow Tea Rooms, 26 (summer 1980): unpaginated; and Pamela Reekie, "The Buildings—A Survey: Part I: Glasgow," 35 (autumn 1983): unpaginated. For Scotland Street School, see also Gavin Stamp, "School Lessons," *Architects' Journal*, April 6, 1988, pp. 42–53; and Richard Carr, "History Lesson," *Building Design*, April 19, 1991, pp. 22–23.

55. *The Hill House* (Edinburgh: National Trust for Scotland, n.d.), p. [25]; information from David Walker.

56. Pamela Robertson, *Charles Rennie Mackintosh at the Hunterian Art Gallery* (Glasgow: University of Glasgow, 1991), p. 5.

57. *Charles Rennie Mackintosh Society Newsletter* 50 (winter 1988–89): 8; Joe Mulholland, "The House That Toshie Never Built," *Glasgow Herald*, February 11, 1989, p. 17; Daniel Robbins, "Art Lover's House," *Charles Rennie Mackintosh Society Newsletter* 54 (autumn 1990): 3.

58. Roxburgh, interview with author, October 24, 1994.

59. In 1990–92 Dr. Peter and Mrs. Maxine Tovell built a house at Strathnairn near Inverness, based on Mackintosh's sketch design of c. 1901 for An Artist's House in the Country. On this occasion the house was to be lived in; see Michael Hall, "The Artist's Cottage, Inverness," *Country Life*, November 26, 1992, pp. 34–37. On the fallacies that surround the House for an Art Lover and the Artist's Cottage, see Gavin Stamp, "Bits and Pieces with an Elevated Status," *Glasgow Herald*, July 24, Saturday sec., p. 7; and Luciano Semerani and Marco Dezzi Bardeschi, "Fragments of a Discourse on Falsehood," *Abitare* 303 (January 1992): 110–28.

60. Robert Cowan, "Back from the Brink," *Architects' Journal*, April 6, 1988, pp. 36–39, is an excellent report on the realities of the "Renaissance."

61. *Glasgow Herald*, March 11, 1988; *Charles Rennie Mackintosh Society Newsletter* 48 (spring 1988): 2; 49 (summer 1988): 5.

62. For an account of the conference and installations, see Malcolm Fraser and Roddy Langmuir, "Master Visions," *Architects' Journal*, August 22 and 29, 1990, pp. 26–29. Grigor and Murphy, *Architects' Architect*, includes interviews with the participating architects, accompanied by illustrations of their work and installations.

63. Richard Mellis, "There's a Lot of Mockintosh Going On," *Scotland on Sunday*, January 14, 1990.

64. *Building Design*, March 30, 1984, p. 1.

65. Venturi, letter to Anthony Jones; see Anthony Jones, *Charles Rennie Mackintosh* (London: Studio Editions, 1990), p. 88.

66. Howarth, *Mackintosh*, p. xlii.

67. Lasdun, in *Building Design*, January 8, 1988, p. 18; see also William J. R. Curtis, *Denys Lasdun: Architecture, City, Landscape* (London: Phaidon, 1994), pp. 181, 222–23.

68. Lasdun, conversation with author, February 9, 1995.

69. Mori, in *Japan Architect* 349 (May 1986): 60–62.

70. For instance, ornamental ironwork by Alan Evans on the extension to Cheltenham Art Gallery and Museum, Cheltenham, England, 1989. Stair towers in Glasgow: Murray Hall student accommodation, Strathclyde University, Townhead, by G.R.M. Kennedy and Partners, 1983–84; Craigen Court, Shakespeare Street, North Kelvinside, by Ken McCrae with McGurn, Logan, Duncan and Opfer, 1987–88; and housing in Langlands Road, Elderpark, Govan, by Simister, Monaghan, McKinney, MacDonald, 1984–86.

71. See Thomas Howarth, "Moses, Marilyn, Mackintosh . . . and Me," *City and Country Home* 12 (January 1994): 30–37. Mackintosh-style restaurants include the Tall House, 134 Southwark Street, London; the Mackintosh Restaurant in Stafford Street, Edinburgh, run by Eve Mackintosh (no relation); and the Pataka Indian Bengali Restaurant, Causewayside, Edinburgh.

72. Isozaki, in Grigor and Murphy, *Architects' Architect*, p. 80.

73. Maruyama, letter to author, January 3, 1995.

74. For a range of neo-Mackintosh pieces, some exactly reproduced, others not, see Siân Rees, "The Genius of Charles Rennie Mackintosh," *Woman and Home* (September 1987): 52–53, 55.

75. Brian Blench et al., *The Glasgow Style, 1890–1920* (Glasgow: Glasgow Museums and Art Galleries, 1984), p. [5].

76. Jude Burkhauser, ed., *"Glasgow Girls": Women in Art and Design, 1880–1920* (Edinburgh: Canongate, 1990).

77. See, for instance, Nuttgens, ed., *Mackintosh and His Contemporaries.*

78. The only known link between Wright and Mackintosh is that, according to Lloyd Wright's recollection in 1966, C. R. Ashbee had talked to his father about Mackintosh in 1900; see Anthony Alofsin, *Frank Lloyd Wright: The Lost Years, 1910–1922: A Study of Influence* (Chicago: University of Chicago Press, 1993), pp. 20, 329 n. 72. Charles Sumner Greene, on the other hand, may well have seen Mackintosh's work when he visited Glasgow in 1901 and 1909. (Information from Ted Bosley.)

79. Many elements of it can be found in Alison, *Mackintosh as a Designer of Chairs;* Jones, *Mackintosh;* and John Ennis, "Scotland's Neglected Giant of Architecture," *Reader's Digest* (May 1984): 86–91.

80. Translation by Toshio Watanabe. Picture books are a serious adult genre in Japan, and Mackintosh is very popular there. Arata Isozaki has said, "A Japanese person looking at the work of Charles Rennie Mackintosh is immediately struck by how very 'Japanese' his designs are. The simplicity needs no explanation." (Grigor and Murphy, *Architects' Architect*, p. 77.) Also, the Japanese are fascinated by heroes who fail, as Mackintosh is thought to have done. Morita Shingo's narrative ends with Mackintosh depressed and frustrated in Chelsea; the whole Port Vendres episode of 1923–27, which was arguably happy and certainly productive, is omitted.

81. Demetrios Matheou, "Glasgow: City of Architecture and Design 1999," *Architects' Journal*, November 24, 1995, pp. 16–17.

Bibliography

BOOKS AND CATALOGS

Alison, Filippo. *Charles Rennie Mackintosh as a Designer of Chairs.* London: Warehouse Publications, 1978.

Barnes, H. Jefferson. *Charles Rennie Mackintosh and Glasgow School of Art.* Vol. 1, *The Architecture, Exteriors and Interiors.* 3d ed. Glasgow: Glasgow School of Art, 1988.

———. *Charles Rennie Mackintosh and Glasgow School of Art: Furniture in the School Collection.* 2d ed. Glasgow: Glasgow School of Art, 1978.

———. *Charles Rennie Mackintosh and Glasgow School of Art.* Vol. 3, *Ironwork and Metalwork at Glasgow School of Art.* 2d ed. Glasgow: Glasgow School of Art, 1978.

Bassett-Lowke, Janet, and Alan Crawford. *C. R. Mackintosh: The Chelsea Years, 1915–1923.* Glasgow: Hunterian Art Gallery, University of Glasgow, 1994.

Billcliffe, Roger. *Architectural Sketches and Flower Drawings by Charles Rennie Mackintosh.* London: Academy Editions, 1977.

———. *Charles Rennie Mackintosh: The Complete Furniture, Furniture Drawings and Interior Designs.* London: John Murray, 1979; 2d ed. 1980; 3d ed. 1986.

———. *Mackintosh Furniture.* Cambridge: Lutterworth Press, 1984.

———. *Mackintosh Watercolours.* 3d ed. London: John Murray, 1992.

———. *Charles Rennie Mackintosh Textile Designs.* 2d ed. San Francisco: Pomegranate Artbooks, 1993.

Blench, Brian, et al. *The Glasgow Style, 1890–1920.* Glasgow: Glasgow Museums and Art Galleries, 1984.

Brett, David. *C. R. Mackintosh: The Poetics of Workmanship.* London: Reaktion Books, 1992.

Buchanan, William, ed. *Mackintosh's Masterwork: The Glasgow School of Art.* Glasgow: Richard Drew Publishing, 1989.

Burkhauser, Jude, ed. *"Glasgow Girls": Women in Art and Design, 1880–1920.* Edinburgh: Canongate, 1990.

Christie's, London. *The Dr. Thomas Howarth Collection.* Sale catalogue, February 17, 1994.

Cooper, Jackie, ed. *Mackintosh Architecture: The Complete Buildings and Selected Projects.* 2d ed. London: Academy Editions, 1980.

Crawford, Alan. *Charles Rennie Mackintosh.* London: Thames and Hudson, 1995.

Eadie, William. *Movements of Modernity: The Case of Glasgow and Art Nouveau.* London: Routledge and Kegan Paul, 1990.

Gomme, Andor, and David Walker. *Architecture of Glasgow.* 2d ed. London and Glasgow: Lund Humphries in association with John Smith, 1987.

Grigor, Murray, and Richard Murphy, eds. *The Architects' Architect: Charles Rennie Mackintosh.* London: Bellew Publishing in association with the Charles Rennie Mackintosh Society, 1995.

Helland, Janice. *The Studios of Frances and Margaret Macdonald.* Manchester, England: Manchester University Press, 1996.

Howarth, Thomas. *Charles Rennie Mackintosh and the Modern Movement.* London: Routledge and Kegan Paul, 1952; 2d ed. 1977; 3d ed. 1990.

Kinchin, Perilla. *Tea and Taste: The Glasgow Tea Rooms, 1875–1975.* Wendlebury, England: White Cockade Publishing, 1991.

Kinchin, Perilla, and Juliet Kinchin. *Glasgow's Great Exhibitions: 1888, 1901, 1911, 1938, 1988.* Wendlebury, England: White Cockade Publishing, 1988.

Larner, Celia, and Gerald Larner. *The Glasgow Style.* London: Astragal Books, 1980.

Macaulay, James. *Charles Rennie Mackintosh: Glasgow School of Art.* London: Phaidon, 1993.

———. *Charles Rennie Mackintosh: Hill House.* London: Phaidon, 1994.

McLaren Young, Andrew. *Charles Rennie Mackintosh (1868–1928): Architecture, Design and Painting.* Edinburgh: Edinburgh Festival Society and Scottish Arts Council, 1968.

Macleod, Robert. *Charles Rennie Mackintosh: Architect and Artist.* 2d ed. London: Collins, 1983.

Moffat, Alistair, and Colin Baxter. *Remembering Charles Rennie Mackintosh: An Illustrated Biography.* Lanark, Scotland: Colin Baxter Photography, 1989.

Moon, Karen. *George Walton, Designer and Architect.* Oxford: White Cockade Publishing, 1993.

Muther, Richard. *Studien und Kritiken.* Vienna: Wien-Verlag, 1900.

Muthesius, Hermann. *The English House.* London: Lockwood Staples, 1979, an abridgement of the second edition of Muthesius's *Das englische Haus* (Berlin, 1904–5; 2d ed. Berlin, 1908–11), edited by Dennis Sharp and translated by Janet Seligmann.

Neat, Timothy. *Part Seen, Part Imagined: Meaning and Symbolism in the Work of Charles Rennie Mackintosh and Margaret Macdonald.* Edinburgh: Canongate, 1994.

Nuttgens, Patrick, ed. *Mackintosh and His Contemporaries in Europe and America.* London: John Murray, 1988.

Pevsner, Nikolaus. *Pioneers of the Modern Movement: From William Morris to Walter Gropius.* London: Faber and Faber, 1936; 2d ed. retitled *Pioneers of Modern Design: From William Morris to Walter Gropius.* New York: Museum of Modern Art; 3d ed. Harmondsworth, England: Penguin Books, 1960; 4th ed. 1974.

———. "Charles Rennie Mackintosh." In Pevsner, *Studies in Art, Architecture and Design.* Vol. 2, *Victorian and After,* pp. 152–75. London: Thames and Hudson, 1968. A revision and translation of *Charles R. Mackintosh.* Milan: Il Balcone, 1950.

———. *The Sources of Modern Architecture and Design.* London: Thames and Hudson, 1968.

Reekie, Pamela. *Margaret Macdonald Mackintosh.* Glasgow: Hunterian Art Gallery, University of Glasgow, 1983.

Robertson, Pamela. *The Estate and Collection of Works by Charles Rennie Mackintosh at the Hunterian Art Gallery, University of Glasgow.* Glasgow: Hunterian Art Gallery, University of Glasgow, 1991.

———. *Mackintosh Flower Drawings.* 2d ed. Glasgow: Hunterian Art Gallery, University of Glasgow, 1993.

———. *Charles Rennie Mackintosh: Art Is the Flower.* London: Pavilion, 1995.

Robertson, Pamela, ed. *Charles Rennie Mackintosh: The Architectural Papers.* Wendlebury, England: White Cockade Publishing, 1990.

Savage, Peter. *Lorimer and the Edinburgh Craft Designers.* Edinburgh: Paul Harris Publishing, 1980.

Schweiger, Werner J. *Wiener Werkstaette: Design in Vienna, 1903–1932.* London: Thames and Hudson, 1984.

Sekler, Eduard. "Mackintosh and Vienna." In *The Anti-Rationalists,* edited by Nikolaus Pevsner and J. M. Richards, pp. 136–42. London: Architectural Press, 1973.

———. *Josef Hoffmann: The Architectural Work.* Princeton, N.J.: Princeton University Press, 1985.

Service, Alastair, ed. *Edwardian Architecture and Its Origins.* London: Architectural Press, 1975.

Stamp, Gavin. "Mackintosh, Burnet and Modernity." In *Architectural Heritage,* vol. 3, *The Age of Mackintosh,* edited by John Lowrey, pp. 8–31. Edinburgh: Architectural Heritage Society of Scotland, 1992.

Summerson, John. "The British Contemporaries of Frank Lloyd Wright." In Summerson, *The Unromantic Castle,* pp. 237–44. London: Thames and Hudson, 1990.

Vergo, Peter. *Art in Vienna, 1898–1918.* 3d ed. London: Phaidon, 1993.

Walker, David. "The Early Work of Charles Rennie Mackintosh." In *The Anti-Rationalists,* edited by Nikolaus Pevsner and J. M. Richards, pp. 116–35. London: Architectural Press, 1973.

———. "Scotland and Paris, 1874–1887." In *Scotland and Europe: Architecture and Design, 1850–1940,* edited by John Frew and David Jones. St. Andrews, Scotland: St. Andrews Studies in the History of Scottish Architecture and Design, 1991.

Williamson, Elizabeth, Anne Riches, and Malcolm Higgs. *The Buildings of Scotland: Glasgow.* Harmondsworth, England: Penguin Books, 1990.

PERIODICALS

Agnoletti, Fernando. "The Hill-House, Helensburgh." *Deutsche Kunst und Dekoration* (March 1905): 337–68.

[Agnoletti, Fernando.] "Ein Mackintosh-Teehaus in Glasgow." *Dekorative Kunst* (April 1905): 257–75.

Bedford, June, and Ivor Davies. "Remembering Charles Rennie Mackintosh: A Recorded Interview with Mrs. Mary Sturrock." *Connoisseur* 183 (August 1973): 280–88.

Billcliffe, Roger. "J. H. MacNair in Glasgow and Liverpool." *Annual Report and Bulletin* (Walker Art Gallery, Liverpool) 1 (1970–71): 48–74.

———. "Mackintosh and Cranston—A Pioneering Partnership." *Arts in Virginia* 26, no. 12 (1986): 14–29.

———. "Some Thoughts on Collecting Mackintosh." *Charles Rennie Mackintosh Society Newsletter* 61 (spring 1993): 5–12.

Billcliffe, Roger, and Peter Vergo. "Charles Rennie Mackintosh and the Austrian Art Revival." *Burlington Magazine* 119 (November 1977): 739–46.

Bird, Elizabeth. "Ghouls and Gas Pipes: Public Reaction to the Early Work of The Four." *Scottish Art Review* 14, no. 4 (1975): 13–16.

Brett, David. "The Eroticization of Domestic Space: A Mirror by C. R. Mackintosh." *Journal of Decorative and Propaganda Arts* 10 (fall 1988): 6–13.

Buchanan, William. "The Mackintosh Circle." Part 3, "Mackintosh, John and Jessie Keppie." *Charles Rennie Mackintosh Society Newsletter* 32 (midsummer 1982): unpaginated.

Charles Rennie Mackintosh Society Newsletter. 1973–present.

Cooke, Catherine. "Shekhtel in Kelvingrove and Mackintosh on the Petrovka." *Scottish Slavonic Review* 10 (spring 1988): 177–205.

Helland, Janice. "The Critics and the Arts and Crafts: The Instance of Margaret Macdonald and Charles Rennie Mackintosh." *Art History* 17 (summer 1994): 209–27.

Kossatz, Horst-Herbert. "The Vienna Secession and Its Early Relations with Great Britain." *Studio International* 181 (January 1971): 9–19.

McKean, Charles. "The Influence of Mackintosh in the 1930s." *Charles Rennie Mackintosh Society Newsletter* 47 (autumn 1987): 3–4.

Muthesius, Hermann. "Die Glasgower Kunstbewegung: Charles R. Mackintosh und Margaret Macdonald-Mackintosh." *Dekorative Kunst* (March 1902): 193–221.

Waddell, J. Jeffrey. "Some Recent Glasgow Tea Rooms." *Builders' Journal and Architectural Record* (April 15, 1903): 126–31.

Walker, David. "James Sellars." *Scottish Art Review,* n.s., 11 (1967): 1–2.

———. "The Honeymans." Parts 1–3. *Charles Rennie Mackintosh Society Newsletter* 62 (summer 1993): 7–12; 63 (winter 1993): 5–8; and 64 (spring 1994): 5–8.

White, Gleeson. "Some Glasgow Designers and Their Work." Part 1. *Studio* 11 (July 1897): 86–100.

Buildings and Collections

Many of Mackintosh's buildings and interiors are open to the public. These are listed below. Please note that opening times and admission charges vary widely and are subject to change. Advance booking for groups is essential for all properties. Full, up-to-date details are available from the Charles Rennie Mackintosh Society, 870 Garscube Road, Glasgow G20 7EL. Telephone: (0141) 946-6600.

GLASGOW

DAILY RECORD BUILDING
20–28 Renfield Lane
(exterior only)

GLASGOW HERALD BUILDING
60–96 Mitchell Street
(exterior only)

GLASGOW SCHOOL OF ART
167 Renfrew Street
Telephone: (0141) 353-4526
Mackintosh's major architectural achievement, the school remains a working educational institution. Important collection of furniture, objects, watercolours, and designs on permanent display. Access is by guided tour only and these may be subject to alteration due to academic commitments. Shop. Admission charge.

THE MACKINTOSH HOUSE
Hunterian Art Gallery
University of Glasgow
82 Hillhead Street
Telephone: (0141) 330-5431
The Mackintosh House comprises the principal interiors from Mackintosh's home, formerly 6 Florentine Terrace, complete with original fitments and furniture. Changing displays from the unrivalled Mackintosh Collection of objects, designs, and watercolours are shown in The Mackintosh House Gallery. Shop. Admission free.

MARTYRS' PUBLIC SCHOOL
11 Barony Street
(exterior only)

QUEEN'S CROSS CHURCH
870 Garscube Road
Telephone: (0141) 946-6600
Mackintosh's only executed church has been the international headquarters of the Charles Rennie Mackintosh Society since 1977. Information centre, reference library, small displays, light refreshments. Shop. Admission free.

RUCHILL CHURCH HALL
17 Shakespeare Street
Telephone: (0141) 946-0466
This busy hall plays an active part in the community life but welcomes visitors. Admission free.

SCOTLAND STREET SCHOOL
225 Scotland Street
Telephone: (0141) 429-1202
Mackintosh's magnificent building now functions as a Museum of Education. Varied exhibition programme and activities. Café. Admission free.

THE WILLOW TEA ROOMS
217 Sauchiehall Street
Phone: (0141) 331-2569
Mackintosh's most impressive suite of tea rooms was meticulously restored in 1980 and now houses a jewellers and gift shop. The Salon de Luxe has been refurbished as a tea room and provides light snacks.

OUTSIDE GLASGOW

THE HILL HOUSE
8 Upper Colquhoun Street
Helensburgh G84 9AJ
Telephone: (0143) 667-3900
Approximately 23 miles northwest of Glasgow, The Hill House is $1^{1}/_{4}$ miles uphill from Helensburgh Central Station. Mackintosh's domestic masterpiece has been carefully restored by The National Trust for Scotland. Displays, tea room. Shop. Admission charge.

Checklist of the Exhibition

Unless otherwise stated, all works are by Charles Rennie Mackintosh. Many of the architectural drawings were made by draughtsmen in the practice of Honeyman, Keppie and Mackintosh. These are identified as "Office drawing."

The practice records of Honeyman, Keppie and Mackintosh (Hunterian Art Gallery, University of Glasgow) identify which craftsmen made many of the pieces of furniture; all were Glasgow-based. That information is included in each relevant entry.

Many of the titles of Mackintosh's watercolours have been given posthumously. These are either descriptive or interpretive. To distinguish between lifetime and posthumous titles, those known to have been given by the artist are shown in inverted commas (quotation marks). Occasionally Mackintosh misspelt an inscribed title; such errors have been corrected for the checklist.

Dimensions are given height x width x depth. Unless otherwise indicated, the support for drawings and watercolours is cream-coloured paper.

▪▪ Glasgow only
❖ United States tour only

APPRENTICESHIP

▪▪ 1. *Sketchbook: Drawings of Building Construction Details*, c. 1890
Pencil and watercolour, 5¼ x 7⅛ in. (13.4 x 18.2 cm), single leaf
Hunterian Art Gallery, University of Glasgow

▪▪ 2. *Sketchbook: Drawings of Architecture in Scotland and Italy*, c. 1890–91
Pencil, 5¹/₁₆ x 5⅛ in. (12.8 x 13.0 cm), single leaf
Courtesy Trustees, The National Library of Ireland, Dublin
See plate 4

3. *Sketchbook: Drawings of a Tour to Italy, France and Belgium*, 1891
Pencil, 9⅛ x 6⅜ in. (23.1 x 16.2 cm), single leaf
Glasgow School of Art

❖ 4. *A Florentine Palace and Tower*, 1891
Pencil, 10¾ x 7 in. (27.3 x 17.8 cm)
Signed and dated
Charles Rennie Mackintosh Society; Presented by Dr. Thomas Howarth on the occasion of its Tenth Anniversary Conference Dinner, August 26, 1973

▪▪ 5. *"Certosa di Pavia," Italy*, 1891
Pencil and watercolour, 26⁹/₁₆ x 14¾ in. (67.5 x 37.5 cm)
Signed and dated
Glasgow School of Art

6. *Sketchbook: Drawings of Plants*, early 1890s
Pencil, 5¼ x 6¹⁵/₁₆ in. (13.3 x 17.6 cm), single leaf
Glasgow School of Art
See plate 236

▪▪ 7. *Sketchbook: Drawings of Architecture in England*, 1894
Pencil, 4⁹/₁₆ x 7 in. (11.6 x 17.8 cm), single leaf
Hunterian Art Gallery, University of Glasgow

▪▪ 8. *Sketchbook: Drawings of Architecture in Scotland*, mid-1890s
Pencil, 5¼ x 5⅛ in. (13.4 x 13.0 cm), single leaf
Courtesy Trustees, The National Library of Ireland, Dublin

9. *Sketchbook: Drawings of Architecture and Plants in Scotland and England*, c. 1894–1910
Pencil, 4½ x 6¹⁵/₁₆ in. (11.5 x 17.6 cm), single leaf
Hunterian Art Gallery, University of Glasgow

▪▪ 10. *Sketchbook: Drawings of Plants*, c. 1895
Pencil, 5⅛ x 5⅛ in. (13.0 x 13.0 cm), single leaf
Courtesy Trustees, The National Library of Ireland, Dublin

▪▪ 11. *Sketchbook: Drawings of Architecture in England*, c. 1896–1901
Pencil, 5¼ x 7⁵/₁₆ in. (13.4 x 18.5 cm), single leaf
Hunterian Art Gallery, University of Glasgow
See plate 237

▪▪ OPPOSITE
235. Charles Rennie Mackintosh. *The Grey Iris*, c. 1923.
▪▪ ABOVE
236. Charles Rennie Mackintosh. *Roses*, page from *Sketchbook: Drawings of Plants*, early 1890s.

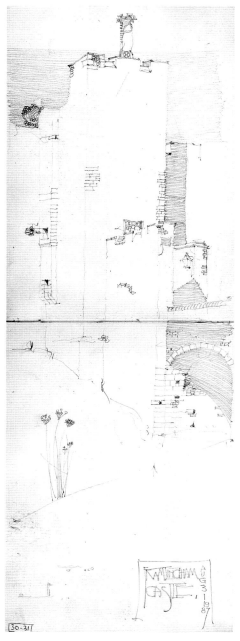

237. Charles Rennie Mackintosh. *Framling-ham Castle*, 1897, pages from *Sketchbook: Drawings of Architecture in England*, c. 1896–1901.

12. *Extension to the Glasgow Herald Building: Perspective from the Northwest*, 1894
Ink, 35¹⁵⁄₁₆ x 23¹⁵⁄₁₆ in. (91.2 x 60.8 cm)
Dated
Hunterian Art Gallery, University of Glasgow
See plate 201

■ 13. *Anatomical School, Queen Margaret College, University of Glasgow: Perspective from the Southwest*, c. 1895
Ink, 19¹¹⁄₁₆ x 31¹¹⁄₁₆ in. (50.0 x 80.5 cm)
Signed
William Hardie Ltd
See plate 84

■ 14. *Martyrs' Public School, Glasgow: Perspective from the Northeast*, 1896
Ink, 24¹⁄₈ x 36⁷⁄₈ in. (61.3 x 92.5 cm)
Signed and dated
Hunterian Art Gallery, University of Glasgow
See plate 85

❖ 15. *Lecture: "Seemliness,"* c. 1902
Ink manuscript, 13 x 8¹⁄₁₆ in. (33.0 x 20.4 cm), single leaf
Hunterian Art Gallery, University of Glasgow

■ 16. David Gauld (Scottish, 1865–1936)
St. Agnes, 1889
Oil on canvas, 24 x 14 in. (61.0 x 35.5 cm)
Signed
Andrew McIntosh Patrick

■ 17. Edward Atkinson Hornel (Scottish, 1864–1933)
The Brook, 1891
Oil on canvas, 16³⁄₁₆ x 20⁵⁄₁₆ in. (41.1 x 51.3 cm)
Signed and dated
Hunterian Art Gallery, University of Glasgow

■ 18. John Quinton Pringle (Scottish, 1864–1925)
Old Houses, Parkhead, Glasgow, 1893
Oil on canvas, 9 x 12 in. (22.8 x 30.5 cm)
Signed and dated
Private collection

"THE IMMORTALS"

19. *"The Harvest Moon,"* 1892
Pencil and watercolour, 13⁷⁄₈ x 10⁷⁄₈ in. (35.2 x 27.6 cm)
Signed and dated
Glasgow School of Art
See plate 203

20. Frances Macdonald (English, 1873–1921)
Ill Omen, 1893

Pencil and watercolour, 20¹⁄₈ x 16⁷⁄₈ in. (51.8 x 42.7 cm)
Signed and dated
Hunterian Art Gallery, University of Glasgow

21 i. Margaret Macdonald (English, 1864–1933)
Invitation Card for a Glasgow School of Art Club "At Home," 1893
Line block, 5¹⁄₄ x 6¹⁄₈ in. (13.1 x 15.6 cm)
Signed on block
Hunterian Art Gallery, University of Glasgow
See plate 34

21 ii. Frances Macdonald (English, 1873–1921)
Programme of Music for a Glasgow School of Art Club "At Home," 1893
Line block, 5¹⁄₈ x 4⁵⁄₈ in. (13.1 x 11.8 cm)
Signed on block
Hunterian Art Gallery, University of Glasgow

22. Margaret Macdonald (English, 1864–1933)
Summer, c. 1893
Pencil, ink, and watercolour, 20³⁄₈ x 8⁹⁄₁₆ in. (51.7 x 21.8 cm)
Hunterian Art Gallery, University of Glasgow

23. *Stylised Plant Form*, c. 1893
Pencil and watercolour, 10 x 4¹⁄₄ in. (25.5 x 10.7 cm)
From "The Magazine," November 1893
Glasgow School of Art

■ 24. Attributed to James Herbert McNair (Scottish, 1868–1955)
The Fountain, c. 1893–95
Pencil and watercolour, 16¹⁄₄ x 6³⁄₈ in. (41.3 x 16.2 cm)
Hunterian Art Gallery, University of Glasgow

25. Frances Macdonald (English, 1873–1921)
A Pond, 1894
Pencil and watercolour on grey paper, 12³⁄₈ x 10 in. (31.5 x 25.5 cm)
Signed and dated
From "The Magazine," November 1894
Glasgow School of Art
See plate 57

❖ 26. *"Cabbages in an Orchard,"* 1894
Pencil and watercolour, 3³⁄₈ x 9⁵⁄₁₆ in. (8.6 x 23.6 cm)
From "The Magazine," April 1894
Glasgow School of Art
See plate 206

❖ 27. Agnes Raeburn (Scottish, 1872–1955)
Cover for "The Magazine," 1894
Pencil and watercolour, 12³⁄₈ x 10 in. (31.5 x 25.5 cm)

Signed
From "The Magazine," April 1894
Glasgow School of Art

28. *Diploma for the Glasgow School of Art
Club*, c. 1894
Photogravure, 9¹/₈ x 11¹/₂ in. (23.2 x 29.2 cm)
Signed on plate
Hunterian Art Gallery, University of Glasgow

29. *"Design for a Library in a Glasgow
House": Four Wall Elevations*, c. 1894–95
Pencil and watercolour, 6³/₄ x 34³/₈ in. (17.1 x
87.3 cm)
Signed
The Metropolitan Museum of Art, New York;
Purchase, Edward Pearse Casey Gift, 1981

❖ 30. *Design for a Linen Cupboard*, 1895
For John Henderson, Glasgow
Pencil and watercolour, 11¹⁵/₁₆ x 19¹/₈ in. (30.4
x 48.6 cm)
Hunterian Art Gallery, University of Glasgow

31. *Linen Cupboard*, c. 1895
For John Henderson, Glasgow
Cypress, originally stained green, with brass-
and-metal fittings and beaten- and coloured-
lead panels, 72¹/₁₆ x 52³/₁₆ x 15⁷/₁₆ in. (183.0 x
132.5 x 39.2 cm)
Glasgow School of Art
See plate 159

32. *"The Tree of Influence—The Tree of
Importance—The Sun of Cowardice,"* 1895
Pencil and watercolour, 12¹/₂ x 9¹/₄ in. (31.8 x
23.2 cm)
Signed and dated
From "The Magazine," spring 1896
Glasgow School of Art

33. *"The Tree of Personal Effort The Sun of
Indifference,"* 1895
Pencil and watercolour, 12¹¹/₁₆ x 9¹/₄ in. (32.2
x 23.6 cm)
Signed and dated
From "The Magazine," spring 1896
Glasgow School of Art
See plate 207

❖ 34. *Washstand*, 1895
Cypress, stained green, with brass fittings and
ceramic tiles, 38⁵/₁₆ x 45¹/₄ x 23¹/₈ in. (97.3 x
115.0 x 57.8 cm)
Made by J. & W. Guthrie
Glasgow School of Art

❖ 35. Frances Macdonald (English,
1873–1921), Margaret Macdonald (English,

1864–1933), and James Herbert McNair
(Scottish, 1868–1955)
*Poster for the Glasgow Institute of the Fine
Arts*, c. 1895
Lithograph printed in four sections, 92¹⁵/₁₆ x
40⁷/₈ in. (236.0 x 102.0 cm)
Signed on plate
Glasgow Museums
See plate 53

■ 36. James Herbert McNair (Scottish,
1868–1955)
Smoker's Cabinet, c. 1895
Wood, stained dark, with brass fittings, 32 x
41 x 7¹/₂ in. (81.3 x 104.2 x 19.0 cm)
Signed
Private collection

❖ 37 i. Margaret Macdonald (English,
1864–1933)
The Annunciation, 1895–96
Pencil, watercolour, and gold paint on vellum
sheet folded in two with a sheet of brown
tracing paper inserted; stitched with gold
thread, 12⁵/₈ x 9⁷/₁₆ in. (32.0 x 24.0 cm)
Signed
From "The Magazine," spring 1896
Glasgow School of Art

❖ 37 ii. Frances Macdonald (English,
1873–1921)
The Star of Bethlehem, 1895–96
Pencil, watercolour, and gold paint on vellum
sheet folded in two with a sheet of brown
tracing paper inserted; stitched with gold
thread, 12⁵/₈ x 10¹/₄ in. (32.1 x 26.0 cm)
Signed
From "The Magazine," spring 1896
Glasgow School of Art

38. *Poster for the "Scottish Musical Review,"*
1896
Lithograph printed in four sections, 96¹/₂ x
39¹/₈ in. (245.0 x 99.4 cm)
Signed and dated on plate
Glasgow Museums

39. Frances Macdonald (English, 1873–1921)
Candlestick, c. 1896
Beaten brass, 20¹/₂ x 13 x 13 in. (52.0 x 33.0 x
33.0 cm)
Glasgow Museums

40. Frances Macdonald (English, 1873–1921)
Mirror: "Honesty," c. 1896
Beaten tin on a wood frame, 28³/₄ x 29 in.
(73.0 x 73.6 cm)
Glasgow Museums
See plate 39

41 i. *A Bedroom: South Wall Elevation,*
c. 1898
For Westdel, Glasgow
Pencil and watercolour, 9¹/₄ x 17 in. (23.6 x
43.1 cm)
Hunterian Art Gallery, University of Glasgow
See plate 46

41 ii. *A Bedroom: West Wall Elevation,*
c. 1898
For Westdel, Glasgow
Pencil and watercolour, 9¹/₄ x 13⁷/₁₆ in. (23.6 x
34.1 cm)
Hunterian Art Gallery, University of Glasgow

41 iii. *A Bedroom: North Wall Elevation,*
c. 1898
For Westdel, Glasgow
Pencil and watercolour, 9¹/₄ x 17 in. (23.6 x
43.1 cm)
Hunterian Art Gallery, University of Glasgow

42. *Wardrobe*, c. 1898
For Westdel, Glasgow
Cypress, painted white, with metal fittings
and beaten-metal panels, 81¹¹/₁₆ x 62⁷/₈ x 22³/₈
in. (207.5 x 159.8 x 56.8 cm)
Hunterian Art Gallery, University of Glasgow
See plate 238

238. Charles Rennie Mackintosh. *Wardrobe*,
c. 1898. For Westdel, Glasgow.

TEA ROOMS

43. *Design for Stencilled Mural Decoration,* 1896
For the lunch gallery, Miss Cranston's tea rooms, Buchanan Street, Glasgow
Pencil and watercolour, 14¼ x 29¾ in. (36.2 x 75.6 cm)
Hunterian Art Gallery, University of Glasgow
See plate 187

▪ 44. *Armchair,* 1898–99
For Miss Cranston's tea rooms, Argyle Street, Glasgow
Oak, stained dark, reupholstered with horsehair, 47⅞ x 26³⁄₁₆ x 25³⁄₁₆ in. (121.5 x 66.5 x 64.0 cm)
Glasgow School of Art

▪ 45. *Armchair,* 1898–99
For Miss Cranston's tea rooms, Argyle Street, Glasgow
Oak, stained dark, 33¹⁄₁₆ x 24¹³⁄₁₆ x 18⅛ in. (84.0 x 63.0 x 46.0 cm)
Private collection; courtesy The Fine Art Society plc, London

46. *Design for a High-Backed Chair and Tables,* 1898–99
For Miss Cranston's tea rooms, Argyle Street, Glasgow
Pencil and watercolour, 10½ x 8⁷⁄₁₆ in. (26.6 x 46.8 cm)
Signed
Hunterian Art Gallery, University of Glasgow

47. *High-Backed Chair,* 1898–99
For Miss Cranston's tea rooms, Argyle Street, Glasgow
Oak, stained dark, reupholstered with horsehair, 53⅞ x 19⅞ x 18³⁄₁₆ in. (136.8 x 50.5 x 46.2 cm)
Glasgow School of Art
See plate 160

▪ 48. *Design for a Ladderback Armchair,* 1898–99
For Miss Cranston's tea rooms, Argyle Street, Glasgow
Pencil and watercolour, 13½ x 12½ in. (34.3 x 31.8 cm)
Signed
Hunterian Art Gallery, University of Glasgow

▪ 49. *Ladderback Armchair,* 1898–99
For Miss Cranston's tea rooms, Argyle Street, Glasgow
Oak, stained dark, 53⅛ x 24¼ x 19½ in. (135.0 x 61.5 x 49.5 cm)
Private collection

50. *Design for Chairs,* 1900
For the Ladies' Luncheon Room, Miss Cranston's tea rooms, Ingram Street, Glasgow
Pencil and watercolour, 10⅝ x 17¾ in. (26.8 x 45.0 cm)
Signed and dated
Hunterian Art Gallery, University of Glasgow

51. *High-Backed Chair,* 1900
For the Ladies' Luncheon Room, Miss Cranston's tea rooms, Ingram Street, Glasgow
Oak, stained dark, reupholstered with horsehair, 59½ x 18⅝ x 17¹⁄₁₆ in. (151.0 x 47.3 x 43.3 cm)
Glasgow Museums

❖ 52. *Design for a Leaded-Glass Panel,* 1900
For Miss Cranston's tea rooms, Ingram Street, Glasgow
Pencil, 38¹⁄₁₆ x 20¹³⁄₁₆ in. (96.7 x 52.8 cm)
Signed
Hunterian Art Gallery, University of Glasgow

❖ 53. *Miss Cranston's Tea Rooms, Ingram Street, Glasgow: Ground-Floor Plan,* 1900
Ink and watercolour on linen, 24⁵⁄₁₆ x 19¹¹⁄₁₆ in. (61.8 x 50.0 cm)
Office drawing
Strathclyde Regional Archives, Glasgow

54. *Ladies' Luncheon Room, Miss Cranston's Tea Rooms, Ingram Street, Glasgow,* 1900
Interior comprising original fitments set with glass insets, stencilled and painted wood panels, and leaded-glass panels; restored 1992–95 with lead-white paint and aluminium leaf. The window seating, exterior window wall, tables, and table settings are modern reconstructions.
Overall room size: 14 x 24 ft. 1½ in. x 28 ft. 2¾ in. (4.27 x 7.35 x 8.60 m)
Glasgow Museums
See plate 183

The interior includes the following:

EAST WALL
The Wassail, 1900
Three panels of oil-painted gesso on hessian and scrim, set with twine, glass beads, thread, mother-of-pearl, and tin leaf, each panel: 62⅝ x 60⅝ in. (158.2 x 154.0 cm); total length: 15 ft. 1⅞ in. (4.62 m)

Margaret Macdonald (English, 1864–1933)
The Dew, c. 1900
Beaten lead, with painted aluminium finish, 49 x 12 in. (124.5 x 30.5 cm)
Signed

WEST WALL
Margaret Macdonald (English, 1864–1933)
The May Queen, 1900
Three panels of oil-painted gesso on hessian and scrim, set with twine, glass beads, thread, mother-of-pearl, and tin leaf, each panel: 62½ x 60 in. (158.8 x 152.4 cm); total length: 15 ft. (4.57 m)
See plate 61

Panel, c. 1900
Beaten lead, with painted aluminium finish, 49 x 12 in. (124.5 x 30.5 cm)
Signed

Chair, 1900 (22)
Oak, stained dark, reupholstered with horsehair, 41⅞ x 18¾ x 17¼ in. (106.4 x 47.7 x 43.8 cm)

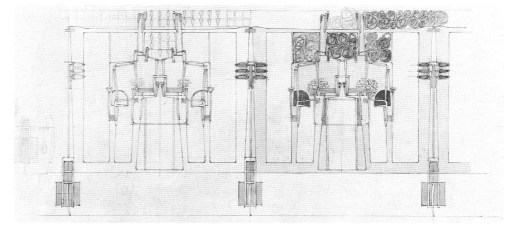

239. Charles Rennie Mackintosh. *Design for a Plaster-Relief Frieze,* 1903. For the Willow Tea Rooms.

■ *Fireplace,* 1900
Lead-clad wooden frame with glass insets, $78\frac{3}{4}$ x $78\frac{3}{4}$ x $16\frac{1}{2}$ in. (200.0 x 200.0 x 41.9 cm)

Hat, Coat, and Umbrella Stand, 1900
Oak, stained dark, with wrought iron, $77\frac{1}{2}$ x $20\frac{7}{8}$ x $13\frac{3}{8}$ in. (196.8 x 53.0 x 34.0 cm)

Hat, Coat, and Umbrella Stand, 1900 (2)
Oak, stained dark, with wrought iron, $77\frac{1}{2}$ x $13\frac{1}{4}$ x $12\frac{3}{4}$ in. (196.8 x 33.6 x 32.4 cm)

Light Fittings, 1900 (4)
Copper, with painted aluminium finish and leaded-glass insets, $9\frac{7}{16}$ x $14\frac{9}{16}$ x $14\frac{9}{16}$ in. (24.0 x 37.0 x 37.0 cm)

55. *Willow Tea Rooms, Glasgow: Model of Front Elevation as Completed in 1903*
Painted bextrine on a PVC core with painted photo-etched brass and acrylic; scale 1:20; $31\frac{1}{2}$ x $15\frac{1}{4}$ x $8\frac{1}{16}$ in. (80.0 x 40.0 x 20.5 cm)
Made by Brian Gallagher, B. G. Models Ltd, Glasgow, 1995
Glasgow Museums

56. *Clock,* 1903
For the Willow Tea Rooms, Glasgow
Oak, stained dark, with polished-steel face, brass numerals, metal and coloured-glass insets, and glazed door, $74\frac{1}{8}$ x $27\frac{13}{16}$ x $6\frac{7}{16}$ in. (188.3 x 70.6 x 16.4 cm)
Glasgow School of Art
See plate 194

■ 57. *Flower Stand,* 1903
For the Willow Tea Rooms, Glasgow
Wood, 15 x 6 x 6 in. (38.1 x 15.2 x 15.2 cm)
Private collection; courtesy The Fine Art Society plc, London

58. *Ladderback Chair,* 1903
For the Willow Tea Rooms, Glasgow
Ebonised oak, $41\frac{1}{4}$ x $17\frac{7}{8}$ x $16\frac{1}{4}$ in. (104.8 x 45.5 x 41.2 cm)
Made by Alex Martin
Art et Curiosité Inc. (Christopher Payne)

59. *Stool,* 1903
For the Willow Tea Rooms, Glasgow
Ebonised oak, with modern upholstery, 25 x 18 x $17\frac{13}{16}$ in. (63.5 x 45.6 x 45.2 cm)
Made by Alex Martin
Glasgow School of Art

60. *Table,* 1903
For the Willow Tea Rooms, Glasgow
Ebonised oak, $28\frac{13}{16}$ x $39\frac{1}{8}$ x $39\frac{1}{8}$ in. (73.2 x 99.3 x 99.3 cm)
Made by Francis Smith
Glasgow School of Art

61. *Design for a Plaster-Relief Frieze,* 1903
For the front tea room, Willow Tea Rooms, Glasgow
Pencil and watercolour, $9\frac{15}{16}$ x $17\frac{13}{16}$ in. (25.2 x 45.2 cm)
Hunterian Art Gallery, University of Glasgow
See plate 239

62. *Three Casts of a Plaster-Relief Frieze Panel,* 1903
For the front tea room, Willow Tea Rooms, Glasgow
Fibrous plaster, $65\frac{9}{16}$ x $71\frac{1}{16}$ in. (166.5 x 180.5 cm)
Made by David Fisher & Sons Ltd, Edinburgh
Glasgow Museums

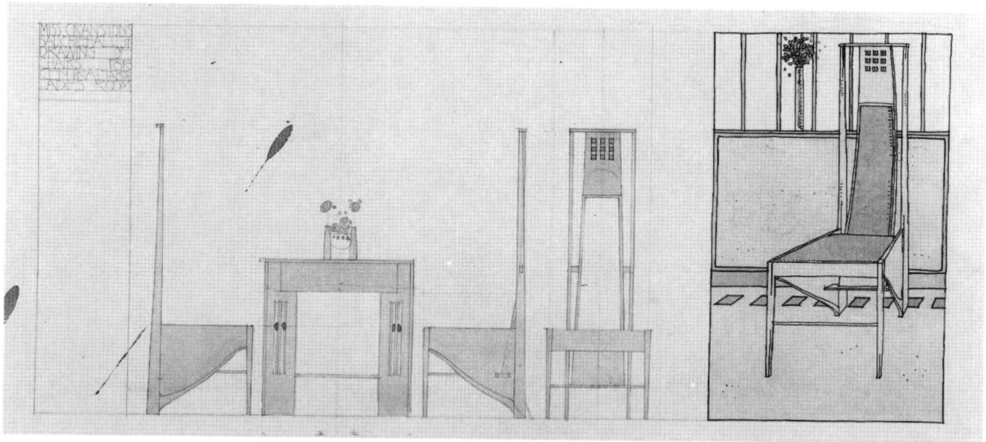

240. Charles Rennie Mackintosh. *Design for a Chair and Tables,* 1903. For the Willow Tea Rooms.

63. *Section of the Partition Screen,* 1903
For the front tea room, Willow Tea Rooms, Glasgow
Oak, painted white, with leaded-glass panels, 77 x $114\frac{3}{16}$ in. (195.6 x 290.0 cm)
Hunterian Art Gallery, University of Glasgow

64. *Banner,* 1903
For the rear lunch room, Willow Tea Rooms, Glasgow
Stencilled and painted linen, 63 x $15\frac{13}{16}$ in. (160.0 x 40.2 cm)
Hunterian Art Gallery, University of Glasgow

■ 65. *Design for a Chair and Table,* 1903
For the rear lunch room, Willow Tea Rooms, Glasgow
Pencil and watercolour, $13\frac{3}{4}$ x $19\frac{1}{4}$ in. (34.9 x 48.8 cm)
Hunterian Art Gallery, University of Glasgow

■ 66. *Chair,* 1903
For the rear lunch room, Willow Tea Rooms, Glasgow
Ebonised oak, reupholstered with horsehair, $28\frac{11}{16}$ x $21\frac{3}{4}$ x $17\frac{7}{8}$ in. (72.8 x 55.3 x 45.4 cm)
Made by Alex Martin
Glasgow School of Art

67. *Doors,* 1903
For the Salon de Luxe, Willow Tea Rooms, Glasgow
Pine, painted white, with leaded-glass panels and metal handles, 77 x 27 in. (195.5 x 68.5 cm), each leaf
Morgan Grenfell Property Asset Management Ltd
See page 2

68. *Design for a Chair and Tables,* 1903
For the Salon de Luxe, Willow Tea Rooms, Glasgow
Pencil and watercolour, $12\frac{15}{16}$ x $20\frac{1}{4}$ in. (32.8 x 51.4 cm)
Hunterian Art Gallery, University of Glasgow
See plate 240

69. *High-Backed Chair,* 1903
For the Salon de Luxe, Willow Tea Rooms, Glasgow
Oak, painted silver, with glass insets, reupholstered with velvet, $53\frac{7}{8}$ x $19\frac{3}{8}$ x $18\frac{7}{8}$ in. (135.0 x 49.2 x 48.0 cm)
Made by Francis Smith
Hunterian Art Gallery, University of Glasgow

■ 70. *Panel,* 1903
For the Salon de Luxe, Willow Tea Rooms, Glasgow

Leaded coloured and mirror glass, $31\frac{3}{8}$ x $9\frac{3}{4}$ in. (79.7 x 24.7 cm)
Hunterian Art Gallery, University of Glasgow

71. Margaret Macdonald Mackintosh (English, 1864–1933)
O Ye, All Ye That Walk in Willowwood, 1903
For the Salon de Luxe, Willow Tea Rooms, Glasgow
Painted gesso on hessian, set with glass beads, $64\frac{3}{4}$ x 23 in. (164.5 x 58.4 cm)
Signed and dated
Private collection
See plate 70

72. *Chair,* 1904
For the order desk, Willow Tea Rooms, Glasgow
Ebonised oak, reupholstered with horsehair, $46\frac{9}{16}$ x 37 x $16\frac{1}{2}$ in. (118.2 x 94.0 x 42.0 cm)
Made by Francis Smith
Glasgow School of Art
See plate 168

❖ 73. *Chair,* 1911
For the Chinese Room, Miss Cranston's tea rooms, Ingram Street, Glasgow
Ebonised pine, with modern upholstery, $32\frac{7}{16}$ x $17\frac{1}{4}$ x $16\frac{1}{16}$ in. (82.4 x 43.8 x 40.7 cm)
Made by Francis Smith
Glasgow Museums

■ 74. *Light Fitting,* 1911
For the Chinese Room, Miss Cranston's tea rooms, Ingram Street, Glasgow
Copper and painted wood, $29\frac{15}{16}$ x $10\frac{1}{2}$ x $10\frac{1}{2}$ in. (76.2 x 26.7 x 26.7 cm)
Glasgow Museums

■ 75. *Pay Box,* 1911
For the Chinese Room, Miss Cranston's tea rooms, Ingram Street, Glasgow
Pine, painted blue, $93\frac{1}{8}$ x $28\frac{3}{4}$ x $40\frac{1}{8}$ in. (236.5 x 73.0 x 102.0 cm)
Glasgow Museums

■ 76. *Section of the Chinese Room,* 1911
For Miss Cranston's tea rooms, Ingram Street, Glasgow
Pine, painted blue, with leaded- and mirror-glass panels and painted woven seagrass; glass panels each: 96 x $50\frac{1}{2}$ x $8\frac{3}{8}$ in. (243.9 x 128.3 x 21.2 cm); seagrass panels each: $74\frac{13}{16}$ x $37\frac{3}{4}$ x $\frac{3}{4}$ in. (191.0 x 95.8 x 1.9 cm)
Made by James Grant
Glasgow Museums

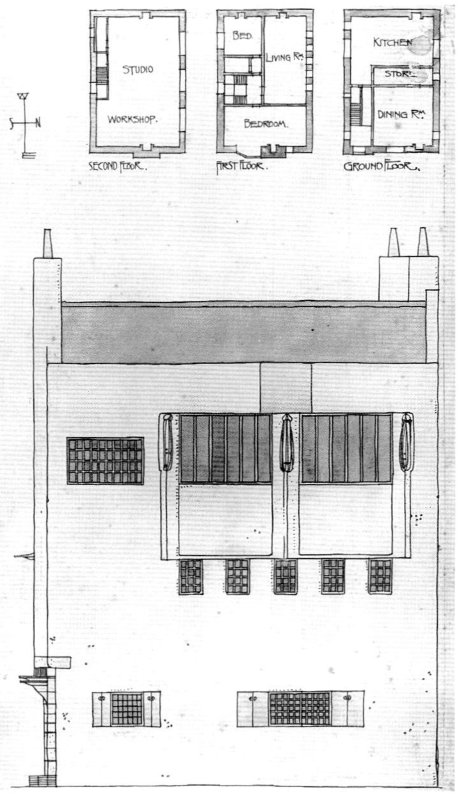

241. Charles Rennie Mackintosh.
An Artist's Town House: North Elevation and Plans, c. 1900.

77. Margaret Macdonald Mackintosh (English, 1864–1933)
Design for a Menu Card, 1911
For Miss Cranston's White Cockade tea rooms, Scottish Exhibition of National History, Art and Industry, Glasgow
Gouache and watercolour on black paper, $8\frac{5}{8}$ x $12\frac{1}{2}$ in. (21.8 x 31.6 cm)
Signed
Hunterian Art Gallery, University of Glasgow

HOUSES AND INTERIORS

78. *Gate Lodge, Auchenbothie, Kilmacolm: Elevations and Plans,* c. 1900
Pencil, ink, and watercolour, $13\frac{3}{8}$ x $17\frac{1}{16}$ in. (33.9 x 43.3 cm)
Signed
Hunterian Art Gallery, University of Glasgow

79. *Gate Lodge, Auchenbothie, Kilmacolm: Elevations, Plans, and Sections,* c. 1900
Pencil, ink, and watercolour, $13\frac{3}{16}$ x $17\frac{1}{16}$ in. (33.5 x 43.3 cm)
Signed
Hunterian Art Gallery, University of Glasgow

80 i. *An Artist's Cottage: East Elevation,* c. 1900
Pencil, ink, and watercolour, 8 x $9\frac{7}{8}$ in. (20.0 x 25.0 cm)
Hunterian Art Gallery, University of Glasgow

80 ii. *An Artist's Cottage: South Elevation and Plans,* c. 1900
Pencil, ink, and watercolour, 8 x $17\frac{9}{16}$ in. (20.2 x 44.6 cm)
Hunterian Art Gallery, University of Glasgow

80 iii. *An Artist's Cottage: West Elevation,* c. 1900
Pencil, ink, and watercolour, 8 x $9\frac{3}{4}$ in. (20.2 x 24.8 cm)
Hunterian Art Gallery, University of Glasgow

80 iv. *An Artist's Cottage: North Elevation,* c. 1900
Pencil, ink, and watercolour, $7\frac{7}{8}$ x $17\frac{1}{2}$ in. (20.0 x 44.5 cm)
Hunterian Art Gallery, University of Glasgow

81. *An Artist's Town House: North Elevation and Plans,* c. 1900
Pencil, ink, and watercolour, $19\frac{9}{16}$ x $10\frac{5}{8}$ in. (49.7 x 27.0 cm)
Glasgow School of Art
See plate 241

82. *An Artist's Town House: East Elevation,* c. 1900
Pencil, ink, and watercolour, $15\frac{1}{4}$ x $8\frac{1}{16}$ in. (38.7 x 20.4 cm)
Glasgow School of Art

83. *An Artist's Town House: South Elevation,* c. 1900
Pencil, ink, and watercolour, $15\frac{5}{8}$ x $19\frac{7}{8}$ in. (39.7 x 27.7 cm)
Glasgow School of Art

84. *Windyhill, Kilmacolm: Perspective from the Northwest,* 1900
Ink, $11\frac{3}{8}$ x $22\frac{1}{2}$ in. (28.9 x 57.2 cm)
Signed and dated
Glasgow School of Art

■ 85. *Windyhill, Kilmacolm: Perspective from the Southeast,* 1900
Ink, $11\frac{3}{8}$ x $22\frac{1}{2}$ in. (28.9 x 57.2 cm)
Signed and dated
Glasgow School of Art

■ 86. *Windyhill, Kilmacolm: North Elevation,* 1901
Pencil and watercolour, $15\frac{1}{4}$ x 22 in. (38.6 x 55.8 cm)

Signed
Hunterian Art Gallery, University of Glasgow

■ 87. *Windyhill, Kilmacolm: East Elevation,* 1901
Pencil and watercolour, $15\frac{1}{4}$ x 22 in. (38.6 x 55.8 cm)
Signed
Hunterian Art Gallery, University of Glasgow

88. *Windyhill, Kilmacolm: Ground-Floor Plan,* 1901
Pencil and watercolour, $15\frac{5}{16}$ x $22\frac{5}{16}$ in. (38.9 x 56.7 cm)
Signed
Hunterian Art Gallery, University of Glasgow

89. *Windyhill, Kilmacolm: First-Floor Plan,* 1901
Pencil and watercolour, $15\frac{3}{16}$ x $22\frac{3}{16}$ in. (38.6 x 56.3 cm)
Signed
Hunterian Art Gallery, University of Glasgow

❖ 90. *Design for Hall Furniture,* 1901
For Windyhill, Kilmacolm
Pencil and watercolour, $12\frac{3}{4}$ x $27\frac{3}{4}$ in. (32.4 x 70.5 cm)
Signed
Hunterian Art Gallery, University of Glasgow

91. *Design for a Hall Chair,* 1901
For Windyhill, Kilmacolm
Pencil and watercolour, $10\frac{1}{2}$ x $12\frac{3}{4}$ in. (26.6 x 32.3 cm)
Signed
Hunterian Art Gallery, University of Glasgow

92. *Hall Chair,* 1901
For Windyhill, Kilmacolm
Oak, stained dark, with rush seat, $52\frac{5}{8}$ x $28\frac{13}{16}$ x $21\frac{1}{2}$ in. (133.7 x 73.2 x 54.5 cm)
Made by Francis Smith
Hunterian Art Gallery, University of Glasgow
See plate 163

93. *Table for the Hall,* 1901
For Windyhill, Kilmacolm
Oak, stained green, $28\frac{3}{4}$ x $32\frac{1}{8}$ x $31\frac{1}{2}$ in. (73.0 x 81.5 x 80.0 cm)
Made by Francis Smith
Glasgow School of Art

94. *Cheval Mirror,* 1901
For the principal bedroom, Windyhill, Kilmacolm
Oak, painted white, with glass insets, 90 x $33\frac{7}{8}$ x $14\frac{15}{16}$ in. (228.6 x 86.0 x 38.0 cm)
Made by Francis Smith
Glasgow School of Art

❖ 95. *Design for a Pair of Cabinets,* 1902
For Mrs. Robert Rowat, 14 Kingsborough Gardens, Glasgow
Pencil and watercolour, $11\frac{9}{16}$ x $17\frac{3}{4}$ in. (29.4 x 45.1 cm)
Dated
Hunterian Art Gallery, University of Glasgow

96. *The Hill House, Helensburgh: Perspective from the Southwest,* 1903
Ink, 13 x $21\frac{5}{8}$ in. (33.0 x 55.0 cm)
Signed and dated
Glasgow School of Art
See plate 119

■ 97. *The Hill House, Helensburgh: Perspective from the Northwest,* 1903
Ink, $12\frac{13}{16}$ x $24\frac{3}{8}$ in. (32.5 x 62.0 cm)
Signed and dated
Kenneth Lawson Esq., Banffshire

98. *The Hill House, Helensburgh: Ground-Floor Plan,* 1902
Pencil, ink, and watercolour on linen, $17\frac{1}{2}$ x $25\frac{3}{4}$ in. (44.4 x 65.5 cm)
Dated
Office drawing
Dumbarton District Libraries, Dumbartonshire, Scotland
See plate 120

99. *The Hill House, Helensburgh: First-Floor Plan,* 1902
Pencil, ink and watercolour on linen, $17\frac{1}{2}$ x $25\frac{3}{4}$ in. (44.4 x 65.5 cm)
Dated
Office drawing
Dumbarton District Libraries, Dumbartonshire, Scotland
See plate 121

100. *The Hill House, Helensburgh: Model of the House, Lodge, and a Section of the Grounds as Completed in 1904*
Painted bextrine on a PVC core, with painted photo-etched brass and acrylic; scale 1:60; 18 x 60 x $48\frac{1}{4}$ in. (46.0 x 152.5 x 122.4 cm)
Made by Brian Gallagher, B. G. Models Ltd, Glasgow, 1995
Glasgow Museums
See plate 242

101. *Hall Chair,* 1904
For The Hill House, Helensburgh
Varnished oak, with rush seat, $28\frac{15}{16}$ x $26\frac{3}{8}$ x $23\frac{1}{4}$ in. (73.5 x 67.0 x 59.0 cm)
Made by John Craig
Virginia Museum of Fine Arts, Richmond; Gift of Sydney and Frances Lewis

102. *Stencil,* 1904
For the hall, The Hill House, Helensburgh
Card, $21\frac{1}{4}$ x $16\frac{3}{8}$ in. (54.0 x 41.5 cm)
Glasgow Museums

■ 103. *Design for a Writing Cabinet,* 1904
For The Hill House, Helensburgh
Pencil and watercolour, $11\frac{5}{8}$ x $17\frac{1}{4}$ in. (29.4 x 43.9 cm)
Dated
Hunterian Art Gallery, University of Glasgow
See plate 174

104. *Design for a Writing Cabinet, Chair, and Candlestick,* 1904
For The Hill House, Helensburgh
Pencil and watercolour, $10\frac{7}{16}$ x $18\frac{1}{8}$ in. (26.5 x 46.0 cm)
Signed and dated
Hunterian Art Gallery, University of Glasgow

105. *Writing Cabinet,* 1904
For The Hill House, Helensburgh
Ebonised oak, with ivory-and-mother-of-pearl inlay, glass insets, metal fitments, and a leaded-glass-and-metal panel, $44\frac{3}{8}$ x 37 ($71\frac{3}{8}$ open) x $18\frac{3}{8}$ in. (112.6 x 94.0 [181.2 open] x 46.7 cm)
Made by Alex Martin
Private collection; courtesy The Fine Art Society plc, London
See plate 175

106. *Writing Cabinet Chair,* 1904
For The Hill House, Helensburgh
Ebonised wood, with modern upholstery, $43\frac{11}{16}$ x 16 x $16\frac{1}{2}$ in. (111.0 x 40.6 x 42.0 cm)
Made by Alex Martin
Glasgow Museums

107. *Candlestick,* 1904
For The Hill House, Helensburgh
Ebonised wood with mother-of-pearl inlay and silver bowl, 12 x $5\frac{7}{8}$ x $5\frac{7}{8}$ in. (30.5 x 15.0 x 15.0 cm)
Made by Alex Martin; silver by David W. Hislop
Glasgow Museums

108. *The Principal Bedroom: South Wall Elevation,* 1903
For The Hill House, Helensburgh
Pencil and watercolour, $13\frac{5}{8}$ x $25\frac{1}{2}$ in. (34.6 x 64.7 cm)
Hunterian Art Gallery, University of Glasgow

109. *The Principal Bedroom: West Wall Elevation,* 1903

242. *The Hill House, Helensburgh: Model of the House, Lodge, and a Section of the Grounds as Completed in 1904.*

For The Hill House, Helensburgh
Pencil, watercolour, and gold paint, 12³/₈ x 17⁷/₈ in. (31.4 x 45.3 cm)
Hunterian Art Gallery, University of Glasgow

110. *The Principal Bedroom: Plan,* 1903
For The Hill House, Helensburgh
Pencil and watercolour, 13 x 21³/₁₆ in. (33.0 x 53.8 cm)
Hunterian Art Gallery, University of Glasgow
See plate 128

▪▪ 111. *Ladderback Chair,* 1903
For the principal bedroom, The Hill House, Helensburgh
Ebonised oak, with modern upholstery, 55¹/₈ x 15¹⁵/₁₆ x 13³/₁₆ in. (140.0 x 40.5 x 33.5 cm)
Made by Alex Martin
The National Trust for Scotland, The Hill House, Helensburgh

❖ 112. *Design for an Easy Chair,* 1905
For The Hill House, Helensburgh
Pencil and watercolour, 11⁷/₁₆ x 11¹³/₁₆ in. (29.1 x 30.0 cm)
Signed
Hunterian Art Gallery, University of Glasgow

❖ 113. *Design for a Lampshade,* 1904
For the dining room, Hous'hill, Nitshill, Glasgow
Pencil and watercolour, with swatch of coloured silks, 22¹/₈ x 15³/₄ in. (56.2 x 39.9 cm)
Hunterian Art Gallery, University of Glasgow

❖ 114. *Design for Stencil Decoration,* 1904
For the vestibule, Hous'hill, Nitshill, Glasgow
Pencil and watercolour, 23¹/₂ x 26⁵/₈ in. (59.7 x 67.5 cm)
Hunterian Art Gallery, University of Glasgow

115. *Design for Furniture and Screen,* 1904
For the drawing room, Hous'hill, Nitshill, Glasgow
Pencil and watercolour, 14¹/₂ x 34⁷/₈ in. (36.7 x 88.6 cm)
Hunterian Art Gallery, University of Glasgow

116. *Bookcase,* 1904
For the drawing room, Hous'hill, Nitshill, Glasgow
Wood, painted white, with glass insets, 48 x 18¹/₈ x 18¹/₈ in. (122.0 x 46.0 x 46.0 cm)
Made by Alex Martin
National Galleries of Scotland, Edinburgh (Glasgow, New York, and Chicago exhibitions only)

❖ 117. *Design for Chairs,* 1904
For the drawing room, Hous'hill, Nitshill, Glasgow

Pencil and watercolour, $12\frac{3}{4}$ x $16\frac{3}{4}$ in. (32.4 x 42.5 cm)
Dated
Hunterian Art Gallery, University of Glasgow

118. *Armchair,* 1904
For the drawing room, Hous'hill, Nitshill, Glasgow
Wood, stained dark, with glass insets and modern upholstery, 47 x 23 x 22 in. (119.4 x 58.4 x 55.8 cm)
Made by Alex Martin; glass by McCulloch and Co.
Virginia Museum of Fine Arts, Richmond; Gift of Sydney and Frances Lewis
See plate 224

■ 119. *Chair,* 1904
For the drawing room, Hous'hill, Nitshill, Glasgow
Wood, stained dark, with glass insets and modern upholstery, $31\frac{1}{2}$ x 23 x $21\frac{13}{16}$ in. (80.0 x 58.4 x 55.4 cm)
Made by Alex Martin; glass by McCulloch and Co.
Private collection; courtesy The Fine Art Society plc, London

120 i. *Furniture for the Blue Bedroom: North and South Wall Elevations,* 1904
For Hous'hill, Nitshill, Glasgow
Pencil and watercolour, $14\frac{5}{16}$ x $34\frac{1}{4}$ in. (36.2 x 87.0 cm)
Hunterian Art Gallery, University of Glasgow

120 ii. *Furniture for the White Bedroom: East and South Wall Elevations and Plan,* 1904
For Hous'hill, Nitshill, Glasgow
Pencil and watercolour, $13\frac{7}{8}$ x $34\frac{9}{16}$ in. (35.0 x 87.0 cm)
Hunterian Art Gallery, University of Glasgow

❖ 121 i. *Furniture for the Blue Bedroom: West Wall Elevation and Plan,* 1904
For Hous'hill, Nitshill, Glasgow
Pencil and watercolour, $14\frac{1}{4}$ x $34\frac{1}{4}$ in. (36.2 x 87.0 cm)
Hunterian Art Gallery, University of Glasgow

❖ 121 ii. *Furniture for the Blue Bedroom: East Wall Elevation,* 1904
For Hous'hill, Nitshill, Glasgow
Pencil and watercolour, $14\frac{11}{16}$ x $31\frac{11}{16}$ in. (37.3 x 80.5 cm)
Hunterian Art Gallery, University of Glasgow

122. *Washstand,* 1904
For the Blue Bedroom, Hous'hill, Nitshill, Glasgow
Oak, with ceramic tiles and leaded and mirror glass, $63\frac{1}{4}$ x $51\frac{1}{4}$ x $20\frac{3}{8}$ in. (160.7 x 130.2 x 51.8 cm)
Made by Francis Smith; glass by McCulloch and Co.
The Metropolitan Museum of Art, New York; Purchase, Lila Acheson Wallace Gift, 1994
See plate 156

■ 123. *Chair,* 1904
For the White Bedroom, Hous'hill, Nitshill, Glasgow
Ebonised sycamore, with modern upholstery, $28\frac{7}{8}$ x 16 x 16 in. (73.3 x 40.6 x 40.6 cm)
Made by Alex Martin
Musée d'Orsay, Paris

❖ 124. *Dresser,* 1904
For the White Bedroom, Hous'hill, Nitshill, Glasgow
Wood, painted white, with ebony handles with mother-of-pearl inlay, $30\frac{1}{4}$ x 40 x 18 in. (76.8 x 101.6 x 45.7 cm)
Made by Alex Martin
On loan from the Royal Ontario Museum, Toronto. Purchased by the Royal Ontario Museum with the assistance of a grant approved by the Minister of Canadian Heritage under the terms of the Cultural Property Export and Import Act
See plate 169

❖ 125. *Mirror,* 1904
For the White Bedroom, Hous'hill, Nitshill, Glasgow
Wood, painted white, with ebony handles with mother-of-pearl inlay, $40\frac{1}{2}$ x $18\frac{3}{4}$ x $9\frac{3}{4}$ in. (102.8 x 47.6 x 24.7 cm)
Made by Alex Martin
On loan from the Royal Ontario Museum, Toronto. Purchased by the Royal Ontario Museum with the assistance of a grant approved by the Minister of Canadian Heritage under the terms of the Cultural Property Export and Import Act
See plate 169

■ 126. *Table,* 1904
For the White Bedroom, Hous'hill, Nitshill, Glasgow
Wood, painted white, with ebony handle with mother-of-pearl inlay, 30 x $17\frac{1}{16}$ x $16\frac{13}{16}$ in. (76.3 x 43.3 x 42.7 cm)
Made by Alex Martin
Hunterian Art Gallery, University of Glasgow

❖ 127. *Washstand,* 1904
For the White Bedroom, Hous'hill, Nitshill, Glasgow
Wood, painted white, with leaded glass and metal panels and an ebony handle with mother-of-pearl inlay, 48 x $28\frac{1}{2}$ x $16\frac{1}{2}$ in. (121.9 x 72.3 x 41.9 cm)
Made by Alex Martin; glass by McCulloch and Co.
On loan from the Royal Ontario Museum, Toronto. Purchased by the Royal Ontario Museum with the assistance of a grant approved by the Minister of Canadian Heritage under the terms of the Cultural Property Export and Import Act

❖ 128. *Design for a Table,* 1909
For the Card Room, Hous'hill, Nitshill, Glasgow
Ink and watercolour on linen, $15\frac{5}{8}$ x $19\frac{1}{4}$ in. (39.6 x 49.0 cm)
Office drawing
Private collection

129. *Table,* 1909
For the Card Room, Hous'hill, Nitshill, Glasgow
Cypress, stained dark, with ebony and mother-of-pearl inlay, $30\frac{1}{4}$ x 48 x 29 in. (76.8 x 122.0 x 73.6 cm)
Glasgow School of Art

CITY ARCHITECTURE

❖ 130. Alexander McGibbon (Scottish, 1861–1938)
Glasgow School of Art: Perspective, c. 1899
Ink, $9\frac{5}{8}$ x $14\frac{7}{16}$ in. (24.5 x 36.7 cm)
Glasgow School of Art

131. *Glasgow School of Art: North Elevation,* 1897
Photo-mechanical copy with watercolour, $20\frac{11}{16}$ x $33\frac{7}{8}$ in. (52.5 x 86.0 cm)
Dated
Strathclyde Regional Archives, Glasgow

132. *Glasgow School of Art: South Elevation,* 1897
Photo-mechanical copy with watercolour and ink, $22\frac{1}{4}$ x 35 in. (56.4 x 88.8 cm)
Dated
Strathclyde Regional Archives, Glasgow
See plate 106

133. *Glasgow School of Art: East and West Elevations,* 1897
Photo-mechanical copy with watercolour, $21\frac{7}{16}$ x $34\frac{1}{2}$ in. (54.4 x 87.6 cm)
Dated
Strathclyde Regional Archives, Glasgow

243. *Glasgow School of Art: Model of the Building as Completed in 1909.*

■ 134. *Glasgow School of Art: Basement-Floor Plan,* 1897
Photo-mechanical copy with watercolour and ink, 22¹³/₁₆ x 34¼ in. (58.0 x 87.0 cm)
Dated
Strathclyde Regional Archives, Glasgow

■ 135. *Glasgow School of Art: Ground-Floor Plan,* 1897
Photo-mechanical copy with watercolour and ink, 22⁷/₁₆ x 33¹³/₁₆ in. (57.0 x 85.8 cm)
Dated
Strathclyde Regional Archives, Glasgow

■ 136. *Glasgow School of Art: First-Floor Plan,* 1897
Photo-mechanical copy with watercolour and ink, 22³/₈ x 34 in. (56.8 x 86.3 cm)
Strathclyde Regional Archives, Glasgow

■ 137. *Glasgow School of Art: Sections,* 1897
Photo-mechanical copy with watercolour and ink, 21¼ x 35⁵/₈ in. (54.0 x 90.5 cm)
Dated
Strathclyde Regional Archives, Glasgow
See plate 109

138. *Glasgow School of Art: Schematic Model of the Winning Competition Entry of 1897*
Painted bextrine on a PVC core with painted photo-etched brass and acrylic; scale 1:120;
15¾ x 31½ x 13³/₈ in. (40.0 x 80.0 x 34.0 cm)
Made by Brian Gallagher, B. G. Models Ltd,

Glasgow, 1995
Glasgow Museums

139. *Glasgow School of Art: North Elevation,* 1907
Ink and watercolour on linen, 27¼ x 41 in. (69.2 x 104.2 cm)
Dated
Office drawing
Strathclyde Regional Archives, Glasgow

140. *Glasgow School of Art: South Elevation,* 1907
Ink and watercolour on linen, 27⅛ x 40³/₁₆ in. (68.8 x 102.1 cm)
Dated
Office drawing
Strathclyde Regional Archives, Glasgow

141. *Glasgow School of Art: East and West Elevations,* 1907
Ink and watercolour on linen, 26¾ x 38³/₁₆ in. (68.7 x 97.7 cm)
Dated
Office drawing
Strathclyde Regional Archives, Glasgow

142. *Glasgow School of Art: Basement-Floor Plan,* 1907
Ink and watercolour on linen, 27¼ x 40¼ in. (69.2 x 102.2 cm)
Dated
Office drawing
Strathclyde Regional Archives, Glasgow

143. *Glasgow School of Art: Ground-Floor Plan,* 1907
Ink and watercolour on linen, 26¾ x 40¼ in. (68.7 x 102.2 cm)
Dated
Office drawing
Strathclyde Regional Archives, Glasgow

144. *Glasgow School of Art: First-Floor Plan,* 1907
Ink and watercolour on linen, 27⁵/₁₆ x 39⅜ in. (69.3 x 100.0 cm)
Dated
Office drawing
Strathclyde Regional Archives, Glasgow

145. *Glasgow School of Art: Second-Floor Plan,* 1907
Ink and watercolour on linen, 27 x 40¼ in. (68.5 x 103.4 cm)
Dated
Office drawing
Strathclyde Regional Archives, Glasgow

❖ 146. *Glasgow School of Art: Sections,* 1910
Pencil, ink, and watercolour, 25⁹/₁₆ x 33⁷/₁₆ in. (60.5 x 80.5 cm)
Dated
Office drawing
Glasgow School of Art

147. *Glasgow School of Art: Model of the Building as Completed in 1909*
Painted bextrine on a PVC core with painted photo-etched brass, acrylic, and resin;
scale 1:60; 31½ x 63 x 27 in. (80.0 x 160.0 x 68.5 cm)
Made by Brian Gallagher, B. G. Models Ltd, Glasgow, 1994–95
Donald and Eleanor Taffner
See plate 243

148. *Glasgow School of Art: Model of the Interior of the Western Tower as Completed in 1909*
Painted bextrine on a PVC core with painted photo-etched brass, acrylic, and resin;
scale 1:40; 36¼ x 13¾ x 13 in. (92.0 x 35.0 x 33.0 cm)
Made by Brian Gallagher, B. G. Models Ltd, Glasgow, 1995
Donald and Eleanor Taffner

149. *Studio Wall Clock,* 1910
For the Glasgow School of Art
Wood with stencilled numerals, 17 x 16¹³/₁₆ in. (43.2 x 42.7 cm)
Glasgow School of Art

150. *Glasgow International Exhibition Buildings Competition Entry: West and East Elevations for the Industrial Hall*, 1898
Pencil and watercolour, 35⁷/₁₆ x 60¹/₄ in. (90.0 x 153.0 cm)
Hunterian Art Gallery, University of Glasgow

151. *Glasgow International Exhibition Buildings Competition Entry: Elevations, Sections, and Plans for a Concert Hall, Bar, Dining Room, and Bridge*, 1898
Pencil and watercolour, 35³/₄ x 58¹/₂ in. (90.7 x 148.5 cm)
Hunterian Art Gallery, University of Glasgow

152. *Queen's Cross Church, Glasgow: Perspective from the North*, 1899
Pencil and ink, 22¹/₁₆ x 24³/₈ in. (56.0 x 61.8 cm)
Signed
Hunterian Art Gallery, University of Glasgow

∷ 153. *Design for a Notice Board*, 1897
For Queen's Cross Church, Glasgow
Pencil and watercolour, 15 x 8¹/₂ in. (38.1 x 21.5 cm)
Dated
Hunterian Art Gallery, University of Glasgow

154. *Communion Table*, 1899
For Queen's Cross Church, Glasgow
Oak, stained dark, 28⁷/₁₆ x 60 x 26¹¹/₁₆ in. (72.5 x 152.3 x 67.8 cm)
Made by Francis Smith
Congregation of Ruchill Parish Church and the Charles Rennie Mackintosh Society, Glasgow
See plate 244

155. *Daily Record Building, Glasgow: Perspective from the Southeast*, 1901
Pencil, ink, and watercolour, 46³/₈ x 14⁵/₈ in. (117.7 x 37.2 cm)
Signed and dated
Hunterian Art Gallery, University of Glasgow
See plate 93

∷ 156. *Daily Record Building, Glasgow: South Elevation*, 1900
Pencil, ink, and watercolour on linen, 20³/₁₆ x 27 in. (51.2 x 68.5 cm)
Dated
Hunterian Art Gallery, University of Glasgow

∷ 157. *Daily Record Building, Glasgow: North Elevation*, 1900
Pencil, ink, and watercolour on linen, 20³/₈ x 27 in. (51.8 x 68.6 cm)
Dated
Hunterian Art Gallery, University of Glasgow

∷ 158. *Anglican Cathedral, Liverpool, Competition Entry: West Elevation*, 1902
Ink and watercolour, 26¹³/₁₆ x 36³/₄ in. (67.8 x 93.4 cm)
Hunterian Art Gallery, University of Glasgow

159. *Anglican Cathedral, Liverpool, Competition Entry: South Elevation*, 1902
Ink and watercolour, 24³/₈ x 36 in. (62.0 x 91.5 cm)
Hunterian Art Gallery, University of Glasgow

160. *Scotland Street School: Perspective from the Northeast*, 1906
Ink, 21⁵/₁₆ x 43³/₈ in. (54.2 x 110.2 cm)
Signed and dated
Drawn by William S. Moyes
Hunterian Art Gallery, University of Glasgow

161. *Scotland Street School: South Elevation*, 1904
Ink and watercolour on linen, 17⁹/₁₆ x 25¹/₁₆ in. (44.6 x 63.7 cm)
Dated
Office drawing
Strathclyde Regional Archives, Glasgow
See plate 95

244. Charles Rennie Mackintosh. *Communion Table*, 1899. For Queen's Cross Church, Glasgow.

162. *Scotland Street School: Elevations, Plans, and Section of the Janitor's House*, 1904
Ink and watercolour on linen, 20¹/₁₆ x 26¹/₈ in. (51.0 x 66.4 cm)
Dated
Office drawing
Strathclyde Regional Archives, Glasgow

163. *Scotland Street School: Ground-Floor Plan*, 1904
Ink and watercolour on linen, 17⁵/₈ x 25¹/₁₆ in. (44.7 x 63.7 cm)
Dated
Office drawing
Strathclyde Regional Archives, Glasgow

164. *Scotland Street School: Second-Floor Plan*, 1904
Ink and watercolour on linen, 17¹/₁₆ x 24 in. (43.5 x 61.0 cm)
Dated
Office drawing
Strathclyde Regional Archives, Glasgow

165. *Scotland Street School: Model of the School, Janitor's House, and Section of the Playground as Completed in 1904*
Painted bextrine on a PVC core with painted photo-etched brass, acrylic, and resin; scale 1:60; 17³/₄ x 59¹/₁₆ x 37³/₈ in. (45.0 x 150.0 x 95.0 cm)
Made by Brian Gallagher, B. G. Models Ltd, Glasgow, 1995–96
Glasgow Museums

166. *All Saints Church, Merriott, Somerset, England*, 1895
Pencil, 7¹/₈ x 10 in. (18.1 x 25.4 cm)
Hunterian Art Gallery, University of Glasgow

■■ 167. *Capital, St. Wite's Church, Whitechurch Canonicorum, Dorset, England*, 1895
Pencil, 10¹/₄ x 8¹/₁₆ in. (26.0 x 20.5 cm)
Hunterian Art Gallery, University of Glasgow

■■ 168. *Details of Panels, St. Wite's Church, Whitechurch Canonicorum, Dorset*, 1895
Pencil, 10¹/₈ x 8¹/₁₆ in. (25.7 x 20.4 cm)
Hunterian Art Gallery, University of Glasgow

169. *The Chantry, Bridport, Dorset*, 1895
Pencil, 10¹/₄ x 8¹/₁₆ in. (26.0 x 20.5 cm)
Hunterian Art Gallery, University of Glasgow

■■ 170. *Falkland Palace, Scotland*, late 1890s
Pencil, 10¹/₄ x 8 in. (26.0 x 20.3 cm)
Hunterian Art Gallery, University of Glasgow

171. *The Castle, Holy Island, Northumberland, England*, 1901
Pencil, 8 x 10¹/₄ in. (20.3 x 26.0 cm)
Dated
Hunterian Art Gallery, University of Glasgow
See plate 202

172. *The Castle, Holy Island, Northumberland*, c. 1901
Pencil, 8 x 10¹/₄ in. (20.3 x 26.0 cm)
Hunterian Art Gallery, University of Glasgow

❖ 173. *Outhouse, Saxlingham, Norfolk, England*, 1905
Pencil, 10¹/₄ x 8 in. (26.0 x 20.3 cm)
Signed and dated
Hunterian Art Gallery, University of Glasgow

■■ 174. Maurice Grieffenhagen (English, 1862–1931)
Francis H. Newbery, 1913
Oil on canvas, 52 x 40¹/₄ in. (132.1 x 102.2 cm)
Signed and dated
Glasgow Museums

175. Francis Newbery (English, 1853–1946)
Charles Rennie Mackintosh, 1914
Oil on canvas, 43¹/₂ x 24³/₁₆ in. (110.5 x 61.4 cm)
Signed
National Galleries of Scotland, Edinburgh
See plate 13

THE CONTINENT

■■ 176. Charles Rennie Mackintosh and Margaret Macdonald (English, 1864–1933)
High-Backed Armchair, 1899
Oak, stained dark, with modern upholstery; lead panel by Margaret Macdonald, 54¹/₈ x 20⁹/₁₆ x 19¹/₁₆ in. (137.5 x 52.2 x 48.4 cm)
The Danish Museum of Decorative Art, Copenhagen

177. *Design for a Smoker's Cabinet*, 1899
Pencil and watercolour, 12¹¹/₁₆ x 14 in. (32.2 x 35.6 cm)
Signed
Hunterian Art Gallery, University of Glasgow

■■ 178. Charles Rennie Mackintosh and Margaret Macdonald Mackintosh (English, 1864–1933)
Smoker's Cabinet, 1903
Oak, stained dark; silvered-copper panels by Margaret Macdonald Mackintosh, 76¹¹/₁₆ x 41³/₄ x 15¹/₄ in. (194.8 x 106.0 x 38.8 cm)
Glasgow School of Art

❖ 179. *Stencil Designs*, 1900
Lithograph, 10 x 18³/₄ in. (25.3 x 47.5 cm)
From *Ver Sacrum*, no. 23, 1901
Hunterian Art Gallery, University of Glasgow

❖ 180. *Postcard of the Eighth Secession Exhibition, Vienna, Sent by Lili Wärndorfer to Charles Rennie Mackintosh and Margaret Macdonald Mackintosh*, c. 1900
Lithograph, inscribed by Lili Wärndorfer, 5¹/₂ x 3¹/₂ in. (13.9 x 8.9 cm)
Hunterian Art Gallery, University of Glasgow

181. Attributed to Charles Rennie Mackintosh
Design for a Four-Poster Bed, 1900
Pencil, ink, and watercolour, 7³/₈ x 8¹⁵/₁₆ in. (18.7 x 22.7 cm)
Signed and dated
Hunterian Art Gallery, University of Glasgow

182. *Cover for A House for an Art Lover Competition Portfolio*, 1902
Lithograph, 20¹³/₁₆ x 15¹/₂ in. (52.9 x 39.4 cm)
Signed on plate
From *Meister der Innenkunst: Charles Rennie Mackintosh, Glasgow: Haus eines Kunstfreundes* (Darmstadt, Germany: Alexander Koch, 1902)
Hunterian Art Gallery, University of Glasgow

183. *A House for an Art Lover Competition Entry: Perspective from the Northwest*, 1901
Lithograph, 15¹/₂ x 20¹³/₁₆ in. (39.4 x 52.9 cm)
Signed and dated on plate
Plate 6 from *Meister der Innenkunst: Charles Rennie Mackintosh, Glasgow: Haus eines Kunstfreundes* (Darmstadt, Germany: Alexander Koch, 1902)
Hunterian Art Gallery, University of Glasgow

184. *A House for an Art Lover Competition Entry: Ground and First-Floor Plans*, 1901
Lithograph, 15¹/₂ x 20¹³/₁₆ in. (39.4 x 52.9 cm)
Signed and dated on plate
Plate 1 from *Meister der Innenkunst: Charles Rennie Mackintosh, Glasgow: Haus eines Kunstfreundes* (Darmstadt, Germany: Alexander Koch, 1902)
Hunterian Art Gallery, University of Glasgow

185. *A House for an Art Lover Competition Entry: Perspective of the Reception and Music Room*, 1901
Lithograph, 15¹/₂ x 20¹³/₁₆ in. (39.4 x 52.9 cm)
Signed and dated on plate
Plate 7 from *Meister der Innenkunst: Charles Rennie Mackintosh, Glasgow: Haus eines Kunstfreundes* (Darmstadt, Germany: Alexander Koch, 1902)

Hunterian Art Gallery, University of Glasgow
See plate 162

186. *A House for an Art Lover Competition Entry: Perspective of the Dining Room,* 1901
Lithograph, 15¹/₂ x 20¹³/₁₆ in. (39.4 x 52.9 cm)
Signed and dated on plate
Plate 14 from *Meister der Innenkunst: Charles Rennie Mackintosh, Glasgow: Haus eines Kunstfreundes* (Darmstadt, Germany: Alexander Koch, 1902)
Hunterian Art Gallery, University of Glasgow

187. *There Is Hope in Honest Error,* 1901
Line block, 8⁷/₈ x 10¹³/₁₆ in. (22.6 x 27.8 cm)
Signed and dated on block
Hunterian Art Gallery, University of Glasgow
See plate 245

188. Margaret Macdonald Mackintosh (English, 1864–1933)
Cover for "Deutsche Kunst und Dekoration," 1902
Halftone colour reproduction, 11⁷/₁₆ x 8³/₈ in. (29.0 x 21.3 cm)
Signed and dated on plate
Hunterian Art Gallery, University of Glasgow

189. *Banner,* 1902
For the Scottish section, *International Exhibition of Modern Decorative Art,* Turin
Stencilled linen, 151³/₁₆ x 21¹/₄ in. (384.0 x 55.3 cm)
Signed
Hunterian Art Gallery, University of Glasgow

▦ 190. *High-Backed Chair,* 1902
For the Rose Boudoir, *International Exhibition of Modern Decorative Art,* Turin
Oak, painted white, with glass insets, stencilled linen back, reupholstered with silk, 60¹/₁₆ x 26³/₄ x 25¹¹/₁₆ in. (152.5 x 68.0 x 65.2 cm)
Hunterian Art Gallery, University of Glasgow
See plates 31 and 166

▦ 191. Margaret Macdonald Mackintosh (English, 1864–1933)
The White Rose and the Red Rose, 1902
For the Rose Boudoir, *International Exhibition of Modern Decorative Art,* Turin
Painted gesso on hessian, set with string, glass beads, and shell, 39 x 39¹⁵/₁₆ in. (99.0 x 101.5 cm)
Signed
Hunterian Art Gallery, University of Glasgow
See plate 64

❖ 192. Margaret Macdonald Mackintosh (English, 1864–1933)

245. Charles Rennie Mackintosh. *There Is Hope in Honest Error,* 1901.

The White Rose and the Red Rose, 1902
For the Rose Boudoir, *International Exhibition of Modern Decorative Art,* Turin
Painted gesso on hessian, set with glass beads, 39³/₄ x 40¹/₄ in. (101.0 x 103.5 cm)
Donald and Eleanor Taffner

▦ 193. *Panel,* 1902
For the Rose Boudoir, *International Exhibition of Modern Decorative Art,* Turin
Leaded glass, 27 x 13⁹/₁₆ in. (68.5 x 34.5 cm)
Museum für Kunst und Gewerbe, Hamburg

194. *Panel,* 1902
For the Rose Boudoir, *International Exhibition of Modern Decorative Art,* Turin
Leaded glass and metal, 15¹/₄ x 4¹/₈ in. (40.0 x 10.5 cm)
Glasgow School of Art

195. *Panel,* 1902
For the Rose Boudoir, *International Exhibition of Modern Decorative Art,* Turin

Leaded glass and metal, 15³/₄ x 4¹/₈ in. (40.0 x 10.5 cm)
Glasgow School of Art

▦ 196. Charles Rennie Mackintosh and Margaret Macdonald Mackintosh (English, 1864–1933)
Writing Cabinet, 1902
For the Rose Boudoir, *International Exhibition of Modern Decorative Art,* Turin
Ebonised wood, with glass insets; painted gesso-and-metal panels by Margaret Macdonald Mackintosh, 58¹/₄ x 48¹³/₁₆ x 11¹³/₁₆ in. (148.0 x 124.0 x 30.0 cm)
MAK-Austrian Museum for Applied Arts, Vienna
See plate 51

▦ 197. *Design for a Gesso Panel,* c. 1902
For Fritz Wärndorfer
Pencil and watercolour on brown tracing paper, 11³/₈ x 32⁷/₈ in. (28.8 x 83.5 cm)
Hunterian Art Gallery, University of Glasgow

■ 198 i. Margaret Macdonald Mackintosh (English, 1864–1933)
The Opera of the Winds, 1903
For Fritz Wärndorfer
Painted gesso on panel, set with string and glass beads, 7⁷/₈ x 7⁷/₈ in. (20.0 x 20.0 cm)
Signed and dated
Private collection; courtesy The Fine Art Society plc, London

■ 198 ii. Margaret Macdonald Mackintosh (English, 1864–1933)
The Opera of the Sea, 1903
For Fritz Wärndorfer
Painted gesso on panel, set with string and glass beads, 7⁷/₈ x 7⁷/₈ in. (20.0 x 20.0 cm)
Signed
Private collection; courtesy The Fine Art Society plc, London

199. *A Bedroom: Entrance Wall Elevation*, c. 1903
For a Dresdener Werkstätten für Handwerkskunst exhibition
Pencil and watercolour, 13¹/₈ x 20¹/₁₆ in. (33.2 x 51.0 cm)
Signed
Hunterian Art Gallery, University of Glasgow

200. *A Bedroom: Bed Wall Elevation*, c. 1903
For a Dresdener Werkstätten für Handwerkskunst exhibition
Pencil and watercolour, 12¹⁵/₁₆ x 16¹/₁₆ in. (32.8 x 40.8 cm)
Signed
Hunterian Art Gallery, University of Glasgow

201. *A Bedroom: Window Wall Elevation*, c. 1903
For a Dresdener Werkstätten für Handwerkskunst exhibition
Pencil and watercolour, 13¹⁵/₁₆ x 19⁵/₈ in. (35.4 x 49.8 cm)
Signed
Hunterian Art Gallery, University of Glasgow

202. *A Bedroom: Fireplace Wall Elevation*, c. 1903
For a Dresdener Werkstätten für Handwerkskunst exhibition
Pencil and watercolour, 13³/₁₆ x 20¹/₄ in. (33.4 x 51.3 cm)
Signed
Hunterian Art Gallery, University of Glasgow
See plate 178

203. *A Bedroom: Plan*, c. 1903
For a Dresdener Werkstätten für Handwerkskunst exhibition

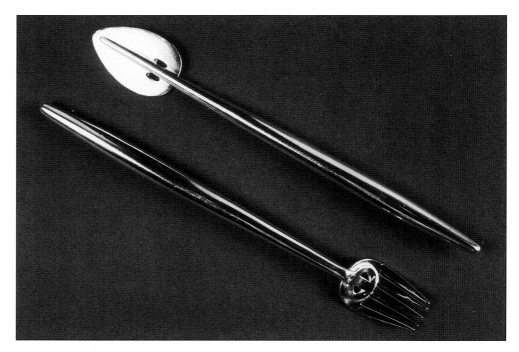

246. Charles Rennie Mackintosh. *Fish Knife and Fork*, c. 1903.

Pencil and watercolour, 13¹/₈ x 15¹/₂ in. (33.3 x 39.3 cm)
Hunterian Art Gallery, University of Glasgow

204. *Design for Cutlery*, 1901–2
For Francis and Jessie Newbery
Pencil, 10 x 27¹/₈ in. (25.3 x 69.0 cm)
Signed
Hunterian Art Gallery, University of Glasgow

205. *Soup Spoon, Meat Fork, Dessert Spoon, and Fork*, 1902
For Francis and Jessie Newbery
Silver, soup spoon, length: 10¹/₂ in. (26.7 cm); meat fork, length: 10¹/₄ in. (26.0 cm); dessert spoon, length: 9¹/₈ in. (23.2 cm); dessert fork, length: 9¹/₁₆ in. (23.0 cm)
Made by David W. Hislop
Private collection; courtesy The Fine Art Society plc, London

206. *Fish Knife and Fork*, c. 1903
Silver-plated nickel, knife, length: 9¹/₁₆ in. (23.0 cm); fork, length: 9¹/₁₆ in. (23.0 cm)
Hunterian Art Gallery, University of Glasgow
See plate 246

■ 207. *Fork and Spoon in Presentation Case*, 1904
For Eckart Muthesius

Cutlery in silver, fork, length: 6¹/₈ in. (15.4 cm); spoon, length: 6¹/₈ in. (15.4 cm); case in wood, lined with velvet: ³/₄ x 7 x 2¹/₂ in. (2.1 x 17.7 x 6.5 cm)
Fork, German hallmark; spoon made by David W. Hislop
Museum für Kunst und Gewerbe, Hamburg, Germany

■ 208. Josef Hoffmann (Austrian, 1870–1956)
Design for Three Chairs, 1904
Pencil, ink, and crayon on graph paper, 10⁵/₈ x 13⁵/₈ in. (20.7 x 33.8 cm)
MAK-Austrian Museum for Applied Arts, Vienna

■ 209. Josef Hoffmann (Austrian, 1870–1956)
Chair, 1904
For the Sanatorium Purkersdorf, Vienna
Oak, reupholstered with replica fabric, 35¹/₄ x 19¹¹/₁₆ x 19¹¹/₁₆ in. (89.5 x 50.0 x 50.0 cm)
Made by J. J. Kohn, Vienna
Ernst Ploil, Vienna

■ 210. Josef Hoffmann (Austrian, 1870–1956)
Egg Cup and Spoon, 1904
Silver, cup: 2⁹/₁₆ x 4¹/₂ x 4¹/₂ in. (6.5 x 11.5 x 11.5 cm); spoon, length: 3³/₈ in. (8.5 cm)
Made by the Wiener Werkstätte
MAK-Austrian Museum for Applied Arts, Vienna

211. Josef Hoffmann (Austrian, 1870–1956)
Two-Handled Basket, 1904
Silver, 8⁵/₁₆ x 2¹³/₁₆ x 1¾ in. (21.1 x 7.1 x 4.4 cm)
Made by the Wiener Werkstätte
Asenbaum Collection

212. Josef Hoffmann (Austrian, 1870–1956)
Sugar Tongs, 1904–8
Silver, length: 4 in. (10.2 cm)
MAK-Austrian Museum for Applied Arts, Vienna

213. Josef Hoffmann (Austrian, 1870–1956)
Design for Three Spoons, 1905
Pencil and ink on graph paper, 10¼ x 13⁵/₁₆ in. (20.6 x 33.8 cm)
Signed
MAK-Austrian Museum for Applied Arts, Vienna

214. Josef Hoffmann (Austrian, 1870–1956)
Salad Fork and Spoon, 1907–12
Silver, fork, length: 11³/₁₆ in. (28.3 cm); spoon, length: 11¼ in. (28.6 cm)
Made by the Wiener Werkstätte
MAK-Austrian Museum for Applied Arts, Vienna

215. Johanna Marie Hollmann (Austrian, 1883–1960)
Cabinet, 1904
Macassar ebony veneer with maple inlay, ivory handles, and enamel panels, 16⁵/₁₆ x 18¹/₈ x 8½ in. (41.5 x 46.0 x 21.5 cm)
MAK-Austrian Museum for Applied Arts, Vienna

216 i. Gustav Klimt (Austrian, 1862–1918)
Design for the Dining-Room Frieze, c. 1908
For the Palais Stoclet, Brussels
Pencil, watercolour, poster colour, and gilt bronze on tracing paper, 8¹¹/₁₆ x 29 in. (22.0 x 75.3 cm)
MAK-Austrian Museum for Applied Arts, Vienna

216 ii. *Design for the Dining-Room Frieze: "The Kiss,"* 1905–9
For the Palais Stoclet, Brussels
Pencil, watercolour, poster colour, and gilt bronze on tracing paper, 8¹¹/₁₆ x 29 in. (22.0 x 75.3 cm)
MAK-Austrian Museum for Applied Arts, Vienna

216 iii. *Design for the Dining-Room Frieze: "Dancer,"* 1905–9

For the Palais Stoclet, Brussels
Pencil, watercolour, poster colour, and gilt bronze on tracing paper, 8¹¹/₁₆ x 29 in. (22.0 x 75.3 cm)
MAK-Austrian Museum for Applied Arts, Vienna

❖ 217. Koloman Moser (Austrian, 1868–1918)
Bookplate, 1903
For Fritz Wärndorfer
Lithograph, 6 x 6¼ in. (15.5 x 16.0 cm)
Signed
Hunterian Art Gallery, University of Glasgow

218. Koloman Moser (Austrian, 1868–1918)
Chair, 1904
For the Sanatorium Purkersdorf, Vienna
Beech, painted white, with painted cane seat, 28³/₈ x 26³/₁₆ x 26 in. (72.0 x 66.5 x 66.0 cm)
Art et Curiosité Inc. (Christopher Payne)

219. Josef Maria Olbrich (German, 1867–1908)
Poster for the Second Secession Exhibition, Vienna, 1898

247. Otto Prutscher (1880–1949). *Plant Stand*, 1903.

Lithograph, 34¹/₁₆ x 20¼ in. (86.5 x 51.5 cm)
MAK-Austrian Museum for Applied Arts, Vienna

220. Otto Prutscher (Austrian, 1880–1949)
Plant Stand, 1903
Wood, painted white and black, with painted metal trays, 36½ x 15¾ x 15¾ in. (92.7 x 40.0 x 40.0 cm)
The Metropolitan Museum of Art, New York; Purchase, Lila Acheson Wallace Gift, 1993
See plate 247

❖ 221. Fritz Wärndorfer (Austrian, 1867–1939)
A Tragedy Play, 1909
Ink manuscript, 8¹¹/₁₆ x 5½ in. (22.1 x 14.0 cm), single leaf
Dated
Hunterian Art Gallery, University of Glasgow

BOTANICAL PAINTING

222. *Stork's-bill, Holy Island*, 1901
Pencil and watercolour, 10¹/₈ x 8 in. (25.8 x 20.2 cm)
Signed and dated
Hunterian Art Gallery, University of Glasgow

223. *"Cuckoo Flower, Chiddingstone,"* 1910
Pencil and watercolour, 10¹/₈ x 8 in. (25.8 x 20.3 cm)
Signed and dated
Hunterian Art Gallery, University of Glasgow

❖ 224. *"Japonica, Chiddingstone,"* 1910
Pencil and watercolour, 10³/₁₆ x 7⁷/₈ in. (25.8 x 20.0 cm)
Signed and dated
Hunterian Art Gallery, University of Glasgow

225. *"The Venetian Palace,"* 1914
Watercolour, 16¹/₈ x 22³/₁₆ in. (41.0 x 56.4 cm)
Signed and dated
George Smith

226. *Walberswick*, 1914
Pencil and watercolour, 10¹³/₁₆ x 8 in. (27.5 x 38.0 cm)
Signed and dated
Private collection

227. *"Anemone and Pasque, Walberswick,"* 1915
Pencil and watercolour, 10³/₈ x 8³/₁₆ in. (26.3 x 20.8 cm)
Signed and dated
Trustees of The British Museum, London

228. *"Bean, Walberswick,"* 1915
Pencil, watercolour, and gouache, 10¹/₈ x 8 in.
(25.7 x 20.3 cm)
Signed and dated
The Metropolitan Museum of Art, New York;
Purchase, Lila Acheson Wallace Gift, 1993

■ 229. *"Berberis, Walberswick,"* 1915
Pencil and watercolour, 9¹⁵/₁₆ x 7¹³/₁₆ in.
(25.2 x 19.8 cm)
Signed and dated
City of Aberdeen Art Gallery and Museums
Collections, Aberdeen, Scotland

230. *"Cactus, Walberswick,"* 1915
Pencil and watercolour, 10¹/₈ x 8 in. (25.8 x
20.2 cm)
Signed and dated
Sheffield City Art Galleries, Sheffield, England

■ 231. *"Fritillaria, Walberswick,"* 1915
Pencil and watercolour, 10 x 8 in. (25.3 x
20.2 cm)
Signed and dated
Hunterian Art Gallery, University of Glasgow

■ 232. *"Gorse, Walberswick,"* 1915
Pencil and watercolour, 10¹¹/₁₆ x 8¹/₄ in.
(27.2 x 21.0 cm)
Signed and dated
Trustees of The British Museum, London
See plate 71

233. *"Hazel Tree, Lambs Tails, Walberswick,"*
1915
Pencil and watercolour, 10¹⁵/₁₆ x 8¹/₈ in. (27.8
x 20.7 cm)
Signed and dated
Hunterian Art Gallery, University of Glasgow

234. *"Japanese Witch Hazel, Walberswick,"*
1915
Pencil and watercolour, 10³/₈ x 8⁵/₁₆ in.
(26.3 x 21.1 cm)
Signed and dated
Hunterian Art Gallery, University of Glasgow
See plate 211

❖ 235. *"Jasmine, Walberswick,"* 1915
Pencil and watercolour, 10⁷/₈ x 8¹/₄ in. (27.6 x
20.9 cm)
Signed and dated
Hunterian Art Gallery, University of Glasgow

■ 236. *"Petunia, Walberswick,"* 1915
Pencil and watercolour, 10¹/₈ x 8 in. (25.8 x
20.3 cm)
Signed and dated
Hunterian Art Gallery, University of Glasgow

❖ 237. *"Rosemary, Walberswick,"* 1915
Pencil and watercolour, 10⁵/₈ x 8¹/₄ in. (26.9 x
21.0 cm)
Signed and dated
Hunterian Art Gallery, University of Glasgow

238. *"Veronica, Walberswick,"* 1915
Pencil and watercolour, 10⁷/₈ x 8¹/₄ in. (27.6 x
20.9 cm)
Signed and dated
Hunterian Art Gallery, University of Glasgow

239. *"Willow Herb, Buxstead,"* 1919
Pencil and watercolour, 10¹/₈ x 7⁷/₈ in. (25.8 x
20.0 cm)
Signed and dated
Hunterian Art Gallery, University of Glasgow

LONDON

■ 240. *Shop and Office Block in an Arcaded
Street: Front Elevation*, c. 1915
Pencil, ink, and watercolour, 11³/₈ x 31⁷/₁₆ in.
(28.9 x 79.8 cm)
Signed
Hunterian Art Gallery, University of Glasgow
See plate 140

■ 241 i. *A Theatre: Front Elevation and
Sections*, 1920
For Margaret Morris, Chelsea, London
Pencil, ink, and watercolour, 17⁵/₁₆ x 28³/₈ in.
(44.0 x 72.0 cm)
Signed
Hunterian Art Gallery, University of Glasgow
See plate 155

■ 241 ii. *A Theatre: Plans*, 1920
For Margaret Morris, Chelsea, London
Pencil, ink, and watercolour, 17⁵/₁₆ x 28³/₈ in.
(44.5 x 72.0 cm)
Signed
Hunterian Art Gallery, University of Glasgow

❖ 242. *Studio-house, 49 Glebe Place,
Chelsea, London: Front Elevation*, 1920
Pencil, 11¹/₁₆ x 7¹¹/₁₆ in. (28.1 x 19.5 cm)
Hunterian Art Gallery, University of Glasgow

❖ 243. *Studios, 50 Glebe Place, Chelsea,
London: Plans and Rear Elevation*, 1920
Pencil, ink, and watercolour on tracing paper,
12¹/₂ x 19⁹/₁₆ in. (31.8 x 49.6 cm)
Hunterian Art Gallery, University of Glasgow

❖ 244. *Studios for the Arts League of Service
and 50 Glebe Place, Chelsea, London: Rear
Elevations*, 1920
Pencil, watercolour, and gouache, 15¹/₈ x 13³/₈

in. (38.4 x 34.0 cm)
Private collection; courtesy The Fine Art
Society plc, London

■ 245. *Three Studios in Chelsea, London:
North Elevation*, c. 1920
Pencil and watercolour, 10³/₈ x 14⁵/₈ in.
(27.6 x 37.2 cm)
Trustees of The British Museum, London
See plate 137

■ 246. *Design for the Front Door*, 1916
For 78 Derngate, Northampton
Pencil and watercolour on tracing paper,
12³/₁₆ x 8³/₄ in. (32.5 x 22.2 cm)
Hunterian Art Gallery, University of Glasgow

■ 247. *Panel*, 1916
For 78 Derngate, Northampton
Leaded glass, 8¹/₁₆ x 8¹/₈ in. (20.4 x 20.6 cm)
Hunterian Art Gallery, University of Glasgow

248. *Design for Furniture and Staircase
Screen*, 1916
For the lounge hall, 78 Derngate,
Northampton
Pencil and watercolour, 13¹/₂ x 20⁵/₁₆ in.
(34.3 x 51.6 cm)
Hunterian Art Gallery, University of Glasgow

249. *Design for Stencilled Mural Decoration*,
1916
For the lounge hall, 78 Derngate, Northampton
Pencil and watercolour, 31¹/₂ x 22¹/₄ in. (80.0 x
56.5 cm)
Hunterian Art Gallery, University of Glasgow
See plate 179

250. *Smoker's Cabinet*, 1916
For the lounge hall, 78 Derngate, Northampton
Wood, painted black, with plastic inlay,
23¹/₄ x 13 x 23 in. (59.0 x 33.0 x 58.4 cm)
The Board of Trustees of the Victoria and
Albert Museum, London

251. *Hall Chair*, 1916
For 78 Derngate, Northampton
Ebonised wood, with wicker seat, 43¹/₂ x 18 x
18 in. (110.5 x 45.7 x 45.7 cm)
The Board of Trustees of the Victoria and
Albert Museum, London

252. *Design for Furniture for the Guest
Bedroom*, 1917
For 78 Derngate, Northampton
Pencil and watercolour, 11¹³/₁₆ x 29¹⁵/₁₆ in.
(30.0 x 76.0 cm)
Dated
Hunterian Art Gallery, University of Glasgow

253. *Ladderback Armchair,* 1917
For the guest bedroom, 78 Derngate, Northampton
Mahogany, with modern upholstery, $40\frac{3}{4}$ x $19\frac{1}{8}$ x $16\frac{1}{4}$ in. (103.5 x 48.6 x 41.3 cm)
The Board of Trustees of the Victoria and Albert Museum, London

∷ 254. *Dressing Table,* 1917
For the guest bedroom, 78 Derngate, Northampton
Mahogany, with mother-of-pearl inlay and aluminium, 68 x $42\frac{1}{16}$ x 20 in. (172.8 x 106.8 x 50.8 cm)
The Board of Trustees of the Victoria and Albert Museum, London

255. *Towel Rail,* 1917
For the guest bedroom, 78 Derngate, Northampton
Mahogany, $28\frac{1}{8}$ x 24 x $7\frac{1}{4}$ in. (71.5 x 61.0 x 18.5 cm)
The Board of Trustees of the Victoria and Albert Museum, London

❖ 256. *Design for Dining-Room Furniture,* 1918
For W. J. Bassett-Lowke
Pencil and watercolour, $14\frac{1}{8}$ x $18\frac{7}{16}$ in. (35.9 x 47.1 cm)
Signed
Hunterian Art Gallery, University of Glasgow

❖ 257. *Sideboard,* 1918
For W. J. Bassett-Lowke
Waxed oak, stained dark, with plastic inlay, $41\frac{3}{4}$ x 90 x 23 in. (106.0 x 228.6 x 58.4 cm)
Donald and Eleanor Taffner

∷ 258. *Design for a Clock,* 1917
For W. J. Bassett-Lowke
Pencil and watercolour, $10\frac{5}{16}$ x 8 in. (26.2 x 20.4 cm)
Hunterian Art Gallery, University of Glasgow

259. *Design for a Clock,* 1917
For W. J. Bassett-Lowke
Pencil and watercolour, $10\frac{1}{4}$ x $8\frac{1}{8}$ in. (26.1 x 20.6 cm)
Hunterian Art Gallery, University of Glasgow

∷ 260. *Design for a Clock,* 1917
For W. J. Bassett-Lowke
Pencil and watercolour, $10\frac{1}{4}$ x $8\frac{1}{16}$ in. (26.1 x 20.5 cm)
Hunterian Art Gallery, University of Glasgow

261. *Clock,* 1917
Ebonised wood, with ivory and plastic inlay, $12\frac{3}{4}$ x $5\frac{3}{4}$ x $5\frac{3}{4}$ in. (32.4 x 14.6 x 14.6 cm)
Private collection; courtesy The Fine Art Society plc, London

262. *Clock,* 1917
Ebonised wood, with ivory and plastic inlay, $10\frac{1}{16}$ x $5\frac{1}{8}$ x $5\frac{1}{16}$ in. (25.5 x 13.0 x 12.8 cm)
Glasgow Museums
See plate 248

∷ 263. *Clock,* 1919
For the guest bedroom, 78 Derngate, Northampton
Oak, with stencilled decoration, mirror glass, and mother-of-pearl face with ivory inlay and painted hands, $14\frac{9}{16}$ x $9\frac{15}{16}$ x $5\frac{7}{8}$ in. (37.0 x 25.2 x 13.8 cm)
Trustees of The British Museum, London

∷ 264. *Candlestick,* c. 1917
Plastic, $16\frac{1}{8}$ x 6 x 6 in. (41.0 x 15.2 x 15.2 cm)
Trustees of The British Museum, London

265 i. *Design for an Advertising Label,* c. 1919
For Bassett-Lowke Ltd.
Pencil and watercolour, $10\frac{1}{4}$ x $8\frac{1}{8}$ in. (26.1 x 20.6 cm)
Hunterian Art Gallery, University of Glasgow

265 ii. *Design for an Advertising Label,* c. 1919
For Bassett-Lowke Ltd.
Pencil and watercolour, $9\frac{5}{8}$ x $8\frac{1}{8}$ in. (24.5 x 20.6 cm)
Hunterian Art Gallery, University of Glasgow

265 iii. *Advertising Label,* c. 1919
For Bassett-Lowke Ltd.
Lithograph on adhesive paper, $2\frac{1}{2}$ x $1\frac{13}{16}$ in. (6.4 x 4.6 cm)
Hunterian Art Gallery, University of Glasgow

266 i. *Design for an Advertising Label,* c. 1919
For Bassett-Lowke Ltd.
Pencil and watercolour, 9 x $8\frac{1}{16}$ in. (22.9 x 20.5 cm)
Hunterian Art Gallery, University of Glasgow
See plate 141

266 ii. *Design for an Advertising Label,* c. 1919
For Bassett-Lowke Ltd.
Pencil and watercolour, $10\frac{1}{4}$ x $8\frac{1}{16}$ in. (26.1 x 20.5 cm)
Hunterian Art Gallery, University of Glasgow

266 iii. *Advertising Label,* c. 1919
For Bassett-Lowke Ltd.
Lithograph on adhesive paper, $2\frac{1}{2}$ x $1\frac{13}{16}$ in. (6.4 x 4.6 cm)
Hunterian Art Gallery, University of Glasgow

❖ 267 i. *Design for an Advertising Label,* c. 1919
For Bassett-Lowke Ltd.
Pencil and watercolour, $8\frac{1}{8}$ x $10\frac{5}{16}$ in. (20.7 x 26.2 cm)
Hunterian Art Gallery, University of Glasgow

❖ 267 ii. *Greetings Card,* 1922
For Mr. and Mrs. W. J. Bassett-Lowke
Lithograph on card, $3\frac{5}{8}$ x $5\frac{1}{2}$ in. (9.2 x 13.9 cm)
Signed and dated on plate
Hunterian Art Gallery, University of Glasgow

268. *Textile Design: Basket of Flowers,* c. 1915–23
Pencil and watercolour on paper mounted on board, $12\frac{1}{16}$ x $12\frac{1}{2}$ in. (30.6 x 31.7 cm)
Signed
Hunterian Art Gallery, University of Glasgow

269. *Textile Design: Chequered Waves,* c. 1915–23
Pencil and watercolour on tracing paper, $10\frac{3}{16}$ x $5\frac{3}{8}$ in. (25.8 x 13.7 cm)
Hunterian Art Gallery, University of Glasgow

∷ 270. *Textile Design: Chevrons and Diamonds,* c. 1915–23
Pencil and watercolour, $21\frac{7}{8}$ x $19\frac{13}{16}$ in. (55.5 x 50.3 cm)
Hunterian Art Gallery, University of Glasgow

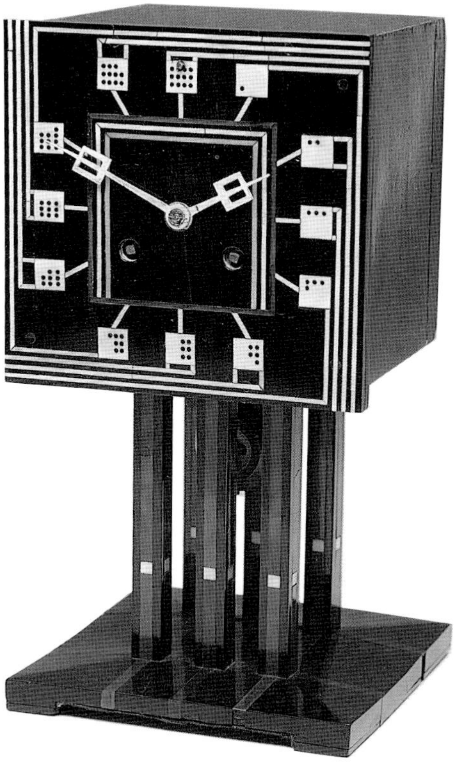

248. Charles Rennie Mackintosh. *Clock,* 1917.

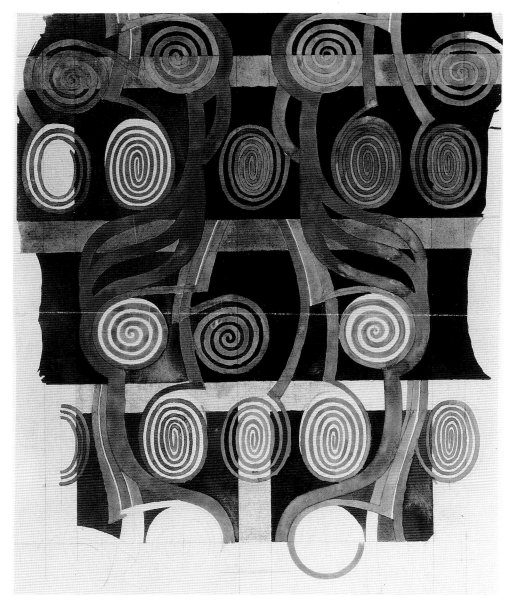

249. Charles Rennie Mackintosh. *Textile Design: Spirals*, c. 1915–23

271. *Textile Design: Roses and Teardrops*, c. 1915–23
Pencil, watercolour, and gouache, 10¹/₁₆ x 10¹/₁₆ in. (25.5 x 25.5 cm)
Hunterian Art Gallery, University of Glasgow

272. *Textile Design: Spirals*, c. 1915–23
Pencil and watercolour, 19¹/₈ x 15¹/₈ in. (48.5 x 38.5 cm)
Hunterian Art Gallery, University of Glasgow
See plate 249

273. *Textile Design: Stylised Daisies*, c. 1915–23
Pencil and watercolour, 14⁷/₁₆ x 11¹/₈ in. (36.6 x 28.2 cm)
Signed
Hunterian Art Gallery, University of Glasgow

❖ 274. *Textile Design: Stylised Flower*, c. 1915–23
Pencil and watercolour, 8 x 4¹⁵/₁₆ in. (20.3 x 12.5 cm)
Hunterian Art Gallery, University of Glasgow

275. *Textile Design: Stylised Flower*, c. 1915–23
Watercolour, 10¹/₈ x 9¹/₄ in. (25.7 x 23.5 cm)
Hunterian Art Gallery, University of Glasgow

❖ 276. *Textile Design: Stylised Flowers and Buds*, c. 1915–23
Pencil and watercolour, 18⁷/₈ x 21⁵/₈ in. (48.0 x 55.0 cm)
Hunterian Art Gallery, University of Glasgow
See plate 214

▪ 277. *Textile Design: Stylised Petunias*, c. 1915–23
Pencil, ink, and watercolour on paper hinged to paper, 14¹/₈ x 10¹⁵/₁₆ in. (35.8 x 27.8 cm)
Signed
George Smith

278. *Textile Design: Stylised Plant and Lattice*, c. 1915–23
Pencil and watercolour, 15⁵/₈ x 11⁵/₈ in. (39.7 x 28.8 cm)
Signed
Hunterian Art Gallery, University of Glasgow

▪ 279. *Textile Design: Stylised Tulips*, c. 1915–23
Pencil and watercolour on tracing paper, 15¹/₂ x 11³/₈ in. (39.4 x 28.4 cm)
Hunterian Art Gallery, University of Glasgow

280. *Design for a Memorial Fireplace*, 1917
For the Dug-Out, Willow Tea Rooms, Glasgow
Pencil and watercolour, 19⁵/₁₆ x 15⁹/₁₆ in. (49.1 x 39.6 cm)
Glasgow School of Art

▪ 281. *"Begonias,"* 1916
Pencil and watercolour, 16³/₄ x 14¹¹/₁₆ in. (42.5 x 37.3 cm)
Signed and dated
Private collection

▪ 282. *"Petunias,"* 1916
Pencil and watercolour, 20³/₄ x 21¹/₂ in. (52.7 x 54.0 cm)
Signed and dated
The Detroit Institute of Arts; City of Detroit Purchase

▪ 283. *The Downs, Worth Matravers, Dorset*, 1920
Pencil and watercolour, 17¹³/₁₆ x 21¹/₈ in. (45.2 x 53.7 cm)
Signed
Glasgow School of Art

❖ 284. *Peonies*, c. 1920
Pencil, watercolour, and gouache, 17 x 17 in.
(43.2 x 43.2 cm)
Signed
The Metropolitan Museum of Art, New
York; Purchase, Lila Acheson Wallace Gift,
1993

❖ 285. *Yellow Tulips*, 1923
Pencil and watercolour, 19¹⁄₂ x 19¹⁄₂ in. (49.5 x
49.5 cm)
Donald and Eleanor Taffner

286. *"The Grey Iris,"* c. 1923
Pencil and watercolour, 17 x 14³⁄₄ in. (43.1 x
37.4 cm)
Signed
Glasgow Museums
See plate 235

FRANCE

∷ 287. *"Mimosa, Amélie-les-Bains,"* 1924
Pencil and watercolour, 10¹⁄₈ x 8¹⁄₄ in. (25.7 x
21.0 cm)
Signed and dated
Hunterian Art Gallery, University of
Glasgow

∷ 288. *"Dianthus, Mont Louis,"* 1925
Pencil, watercolour, and gouache, 10 x
7¹³⁄₁₆ in. (25.3 x 19.9 cm)
Signed and dated
National Gallery of Canada, Ottawa

∷ 289. *Mixed Flowers, Mont Louis*, 1925
Pencil and watercolour, 10⁵⁄₁₆ x 8¹⁄₁₆ in.
(26.2 x 20.5 cm)
Signed and dated
Trustees of The British Museum, London
See plate 215

∷ 290. *Pine Cones, Mont Louis*, 1925
Pencil and watercolour, 10⁵⁄₁₆ x 8¹⁄₈ in. (26.2 x
20.6 cm)
Dated
Hunterian Art Gallery, University of Glasgow

∷ 291. *Héré-de-Mallet, Ille-sur-Têt*, c. 1925
Pencil and watercolour, 18¹⁄₈ x 18¹⁄₈ in. (46.0 x
46.0 cm)
Private collection

❖ 292. *"Bouleternère,"* c. 1925–26
Pencil and watercolour, 17⁵⁄₈ x 17⁵⁄₈ in. (44.7 x
44.7 cm)
Signed
Donald and Eleanor Taffner

∷ 293. *Fetges*, c. 1925–26
Pencil and watercolour, 18¹⁄₄ x 18 in. (46.4 x
45.7 cm)
Signed
Tate Gallery, London; Presented by Walter W.
Blackie, 1929
See plate 218

∷ 294. *The Fort*, c. 1925–26
Pencil and watercolour, 17¹¹⁄₁₆ x 17¹³⁄₁₆ in.
(45.0 x 45.2 cm)
Signed
Hunterian Art Gallery, University of Glasgow

∷ 295. *Palalda*, c. 1925–26
Pencil and watercolour, 21¹⁄₄ x 21¹⁄₄ in. (51.5 x
51.5 cm)
Signed
Private collection

❖ 296. *Port Vendres*, c. 1924–26
Pencil and watercolour, 11³⁄₈ x 15⁵⁄₈ in. (28.8 x
39.6 cm)
Signed

Private collection; courtesy The Fine Art
Society plc, London

∷ 297. *Port Vendres*, c. 1925–26
Pencil and watercolour, 10⁷⁄₈ x 14⁷⁄₈ in. (27.6 x
37.8 cm)
Trustees of The British Museum, London

298. *Port Vendres, La Ville*, c. 1925–26
Pencil and watercolour, 17¹¹⁄₁₆ x 17¹¹⁄₁₆ in.
(45.0 x 45.0 cm)
Signed
Glasgow Museums
See plate 200

299. *The Village of La Llagonne*,
c. 1925–26
Pencil and watercolour, 18 x 18 in. (45.7 x
45.7 cm)
Signed
Glasgow Museums

❖ 300. *La Rue du Soleil, Port Vendres*,
1926
Pencil and watercolour, 15¹⁵⁄₁₆ x 15³⁄₈ in.
(40.5 x 39.0 cm)
Signed and dated
Hunterian Art Gallery, University of Glasgow

❖ 301. *Fort Mailly, Port Vendres*, 1927
Pencil and watercolour, 14¹⁄₈ x 11¹⁄₄ in.
(35.8 x 28.5 cm)
Signed and dated
Glasgow School of Art

∷ 302. *"The Rock,"* 1927
Pencil and watercolour, 12 x 14¹⁄₂ in. (30.5 x
36.8 cm)
Signed and dated
Private collection
See plate 216

Contributors

ALAN CRAWFORD is a freelance architectural historian living in London. His publications include *Charles Rennie Mackintosh* (for the World of Art series), *Charles Robert Ashbee: Architect, Designer and Romantic Socialist,* and *By Hammer and Hand: The Arts and Crafts Movement in Birmingham.*

MARK GIROUARD was Slade Professor of Fine Art at the University of Oxford, 1975–76, and is now a freelance historian living in London. His many books include *Sweetness and Light: The "Queen Anne" Movement, 1860–1900, Life in the English Country House,* and *The Victorian Country House.*

JANICE HELLAND is an associate professor in the Art History Department, Concordia University, Montreal. Author of *The Studios of Frances and Margaret Macdonald,* she is currently researching another book on women artists, *Collaboration and Friendship: Women Artists in Nineteenth-Century Scotland.*

WENDY KAPLAN is curator of the Wolfsonian, Miami Beach, Florida, and of its inaugural exhibition, *The Arts of Reform and Persuasion, 1885–1945.* At the Museum of Fine Arts, Boston, she organised the exhibition *"The Art that is Life": The Arts and Crafts Movement in America* and was principal author of its catalogue. She is coauthor of *The Arts and Crafts Movement* and has contributed chapters to many other books on late-nineteenth- and early-twentieth-century design.

JULIET KINCHIN is currently a lecturer in Historical and Critical Studies at Glasgow School of Art, having previously established the Christie's Decorative Arts Programme at University of Glasgow in the 1980s. She has published extensively on decorative arts of the nineteenth and early twentieth centuries, particularly in the area of furniture and interiors, and is coauthor of *Glasgow's Great Exhibitions: 1888, 1901, 1911, 1938, 1988.*

PAT KIRKHAM is professor of Design History and Cultural Studies at De Montfort University, Leicester, England, and a member of the editorial board of *The Journal of Design History.* She has written widely on design, film, and gender issues. Her most recent publications include *Charles and Ray Eames: Designers of the Twentieth Century* and *The Gendered Object* (editor).

JOHN MCKEAN is course director of Interior Architecture at the University of Brighton in England. An architect, critic, and teacher, he has recently published four books, including *Crystal Palace,* and contributed to two anthologies about architecture in Glasgow, *Glasgow: Forma e progetto della città* and *Alexander "Greek" Thomson.*

PAMELA ROBERTSON is curator of the Mackintosh Collection at the Hunterian Art Gallery, University of Glasgow, and cocurator of the exhibition that accompanies this volume. Her publications include *Charles Rennie Mackintosh: The Architectural Papers* and *Charles*

Rennie Mackintosh: Art Is the Flower, as well as many exhibition catalogues and articles on Mackintosh and his contemporaries.

DANIEL ROBBINS is curator of British Art and Design, 1837–1950, at Glasgow Museums. In 1993 he organised an exhibition on the work of the Glasgow designer and architect George Walton, and he is the project coordinator for the Mackintosh exhibition. He contributed to *Glasgow 1900,* the catalogue produced for an exhibition at the Van Gogh Museum, Amsterdam, in 1992.

GAVIN STAMP is a lecturer at the Mackintosh School of Architecture at Glasgow School of Art and is the founder and chairman of the Alexander Thomson Society. His publications include *The English House, 1860–1914, The Changing Metropolis,* and *Robert Weir Schultz and His Work for the Marquesses of Bute.*

DAVID WALKER is associate professor of Art History at the University of St. Andrews and was formerly the Scottish Office's Chief Inspector of Historic Buildings. He is coauthor of *The Architecture of Glasgow* and *The Buildings of Scotland: Edinburgh* and has contributed chapters to many other books and journals on late-nineteenth- and early-twentieth-century architecture.

Index

Photography Credits

The photographers and the sources of photographic material other than those indicated in the captions are as follows (numerals refer to plate numbers, unless otherwise indicated):

T. & R. Annan & Sons Ltd.; Glasgow: 1, 5, 6, 30, 45, 69, 114, 117, 173, 186, 195, 221; Archives Départementales des Pyrénées-Orientales, Perpignan, France: 12; Austrian Museum of Applied Arts, Vienna: 51; Birmingham Library Services, England: 77, 81; The British Architectural Library, RIBA, London: 79; The Trustees of The British Museum, London: 71, 137, 148, 149, 215; Ralph G. Burnett, Glasgow: 88; Alan Crawford: 10, 217; Courtesy Christie's, London: 205; Jeremy Cockayne, Arcaide: 228; Crown Copyright: Royal Commission on the Ancient and Historical Monuments of Scotland: 73, 74, 99, 111, 139; M. Anne Dick: 227; Kate Fusin: 123, 124, 132; Glasgow City Council: 103; Glasgow Museums: 3, 16, 17, 18, 22, 23, 24, 25, 26, 27, 35, 38, 39, 40, 41, 43, 47, 48, 49, 50, 53, 58, 59, 61, 70, 95, 106, 109, 138, 143, 154, 159, 161, 182, 183, 194, 200, 210, 233, 235, 242, 243, 248; Glasgow School of Art: 36, 42, 54, 55, 57, 102, 104, 107, 119, 160, 168, 180, 199, 203, 206, 207, 219, 236, 241; Greater Glasgow Tourist Board: 100; William Hardie Ltd.: 84; Hessisches Landesmuseum, Darmstadt, Germany: 212; Hunterian Art Gallery, University of Glasgow: page 6, 7, 8, 11, 14, 15, 29, 31, 34, 44, 46, 52, 56, 60, 62, 63, 64, 65, 66, 67, 68, 78, 85, 92, 93, 96, 97, 108, 128, 140, 141, 144, 145, 147, 150, 151, 153, 155, 157, 162, 163, 164, 165, 166, 167, 170, 171, 174, 178, 179, 181, 187, 188, 192, 193, 197, 201, 202, 204, 208, 209, 211, 214, 222, 237, 238, 239, 240, 245, 246, 249; Norman M. Johnson, Lochmaddy, N. Uist, Scotland: 32; Anthony Kersting: 152; Juliet Kinchin: 19, 20; Copyright © 1994 The Metropolitan Museum of Art, New York: 156, 247; Courtesy The Mitchell Library, Glasgow City Libraries: 21, 37, 76, 80, 82, 83, 86, 90, 98, 146, 196; Courtesy Yoshinori Mori & CORE Architectural Association: 229; Copyright © 1996 The Museum of Modern Art, New York: 223; National Library of Ireland, Dublin: 4; Copyright © 1996 The Trustees of The National Museums of Scotland: 158; Courtesy the artist; photograph by Carl Okazaki Studio: 231; Mr. Iain Paterson; photograph by Derek Maxwell from the original in the Strathclyde Police Museum: 2; Private collection, courtesy Roger Billcliffe fine art: 213; Private collection, courtesy The Fine Art Society, plc, London: 175, 216; RCHME copyright © Crown Copyright: 184, 185; Scottish National Portrait Gallery, Edinburgh: 13; Scottish Record Office, Edinburgh: 105; The Royal Borough of Kensington & Chelsea Libraries and Arts Service, London: 87; Courtesy Royal Ontario Museum, Toronto: 169; Courtesy Scottish Television: 220; Olive Smith: 33; Liam Southwood and Bronwen Thomas: 189, 191; Gavin Stamp: 142; Suffolk Record Office (Ipswich Branch); reproduced courtesy The Frith Collection, Shaftesbury, Dorset, England: 9; Tate Gallery, London: 218; Courtesy the artist; photographed by Tendo Co., Ltd.: 230; Eric Thorburn: page 2, 28, 72, 75, 89, 94, 101, 110, 112, 113, 115, 116, 118, 120, 121, 122, 125, 126, 127, 129, 130, 131, 133, 134, 135, 136, 172, 176, 177, 190, 198, 225, 226, 232, 244; Virginia Museum of Fine Arts, Richmond: 224; David Walker: 91.